Sir James Abbott

Narrative of a Journey from Heraut to Khiva, Moscow, and St. Petersburgh

Sir James Abbott

Narrative of a Journey from Heraut to Khiva, Moscow, and St. Petersburgh

ISBN/EAN: 9783744754156

Printed in Europe, USA, Canada, Australia, Japan

Cover: Foto ©Andreas Hilbeck / pixelio.de

More available books at **www.hansebooks.com**

NARRATIVE OF A JOURNEY

FROM

HERAUT TO KHIVA, MOSCOW,

AND

ST. PETERSBURGH,

DURING THE

LATE RUSSIAN INVASION OF KHIVA;

WITH

SOME ACCOUNT OF THE COURT OF KHIVA AND
THE KINGDOM OF KHAURISM.

By CAPTAIN JAMES ABBOTT,

BENGAL ARTILLERY, AND LATELY ON A POLITICAL MISSION.

IN TWO VOLUMES.

VOL. I.

Second Edition,

WITH CONSIDERABLE ADDITIONS, AND A MAP.

LONDON:
SMITH, ELDER & CO., 65, CORNHILL.

1867.

PREFACE

TO REMNANT OF SECOND EDITION.

Since the publication in 1856 of the second edition of this work, Russia has made rapid strides into Central Asia. The arrest of her advance to India by the route of Khiva, in 1839, has preserved for 25 years an interval of 1,500 miles between her southern frontier and the tribes and states conterminous with our Indian frontier. But when Russia perceived that this direct advance of her army was calculated to weaken the good understanding between herself and her neighbour, far from relinquishing her ultimate purpose, she directed all her energies to an advance by a more circuitous route, viz., by the basin of the River Sirr, or Jaxartes, and through the Khanauts of Kokaun, and Khiva.

A fortified enclosure was established at the distance of one march from the Russian frontier. Wells were dug there, supplies were collected, and a garrison was inducted. The first fort being in a condition to hold its own, another and another were established, each one march in advance of the other, until a complete chain was formed between the Russian frontier and the cultivated land watered by the Sirr, or Jaxartes. Khiva could not afford to go to war with so powerful a State for the sake of a distant strip of unproductive steppe. And thus Russia has, without risk, advanced upon Kokaun by regular approaches, as if for the siege of a fortress, and with the same certain results.

News from the region of Russia's advance is so uncertain that the extent of her conquest or encroachment cannot be confidently stated. It is certain, however, that the Tartar state of Kokaun has been absorbed by Russia, and it is probable that she has possession of both Summarkund and Bokhára. If she be not at Bokhára to-day she will be to-morrow.

Three views may be taken of the advance of the Russian frontier towards India.

1. As likely to throw us immediately into hostile collision with her in Asia.

2. As a matter wholly indifferent to us, as regards our Indian Empire, and of extensive benefit to Central Asia.

3. Or as a matter beneficial to Central Asia, but tending no good to our dominion in the Eastern world.

At the present day, the second of these theories is in favour with the public. The author of this journal, however, cannot subscribe to it. Remembering the past history, and the past and present policy of Russia, he conceives that no sound mind can look with indifference upon the rapid and near approach of that State to our Indian possessions. Not that he considers Russia unwise enough to invade those possessions immediately, but because it is certain that her main object in the advance is to have the means of threatening Great Britain in Asia whenever any difference shall arise between the two States in Europe.

In the will which Peter the Great left to his successors, and which has dictated the policy of Russia ever since, it is provided in the 9th clause—

"We must progress as much as possible in the direction of *Constantinople* and *India*. He who can once get possession of those places *is the real ruler of the world*. With this view we must provoke constant quarrels, at one time with Turkey, at another with Persia; we must establish wharves and docks in the Euxine, and by degrees make ourselves masters of that sea, as well as of the Baltic, which is a doubly-important element in the success of our plan. We must hasten the downfall of Persia, push on into the Persian Gulf; if possible re-establish the ancient commercial intercourse with the Levant through Syria, and *force our way into the Indies*, which are the storehouses of the world. Once there we can dispense with English gold."

Accordingly in 1827, but for British interposition, Persia would have been annexed to Russia, and the Persian Gulf would have become a Russian bay. And again in 1854, Turkey must have been swallowed up, but for the armed interference of the Western Powers.

Were India peopled by Englishmen, Russia could not too soon approach her Northern boundary. But India being inhabited by peoples of race, religion and habits different from those of her Rulers; and the authority of Great Britain being maintained by means of troops composed chiefly of those alien races; the close proximity of a State, whose policy has ever been to sow discord in the States around her, is much to be regretted.

Had Russia been in possession of Kokaun and Bokhára in 1854, does any one believe that the Sipahi mutiny would have been deferred until 1857?

It is certain that the advance of Russia southward bodes to British India no more good than it has wrought to every State, whom her frontier has approached. Her very existence is one of extension. And her means of extension are by intrigues with the subjects of neighbouring States, for the propagation of which she maintains a vast organised staff, whose operations baffle all vigilance.

The vast tract of country annexed by Russia within the last three or four years, which may be roughly computed at an area of 690,000 square miles,*—viz., of Khaurism 150,000 square miles, of Kokaun 360,000, of Bokhára 180,000, consisting for the most part of deserts enclosing three rich and fertile valleys—

---

* Having a population of not more than 8 to the square mile, Europe possessing 65 per square mile. The great proportion are of warlike and independent spirit, dwelling in difficult deserts, and strongly bigotted Muhummedans.

cannot pay one-half of the expence of its governance. It is useful to her, chiefly, as the means of dictating to Great Britain in Europe, by threatening her in Asia.

There may be no possibility of preventing such encroachments; but let us not slumber under them in order to wake suddenly in one of those panics to which our scorn of all precaution renders us so liable. Let us consider what steps we have taken in the course of nine years, to replace the Sipahi army which we then destroyed. Have we made any attempt to strengthen our position by the introduction into our Indian army of foreign elements from Africa and Arabia? Have we absolute need for the enormous band of armed police with which India is overrun; or should we not be safer both in peace and in war with one-fourth of its present strength? It behoves us to give prompt consideration to these questions. Too much time has already been lost, and it is impossible to say how much more leisure may be allowed us.

Before concluding this preface, I would wish to advert to the effect of this journal during the Crimean war. I had received much kind hospitality from the Russians during my passage through their country. It gave me, therefore, much gratification to find my experience of the Russian people quoted against the rabid attempts of some journals of that day to sow hatred between two nations that had so long been allies, by imputing to the Russians the most barbarous cruelty to the wounded of the French and English armies. Assuredly if the mission to which this journal relates had produced no other benefit than to check such unfounded and mischievous prejudice, it would not have been in vain

December, 1867.

ADVERTISEMENT.

Owing chiefly to the absence from England of the Author, when the Second Edition of this work was printed by Messrs. Madden & Co., the typographical errors were so numerous, that it has been deemed advisable to reprint the 48th Chapter.

The Map also, from the same cause, was omitted from the Second Edition, a deficiency now remedied.

WRITTEN ON THE SHORE OF THE CASPIAN, KHAURISM.

April, 1840.

Victoria!—From thy thousand isles,
    Thy realms beyond the sea,
Old ocean wreathes his brow in smiles,
    To bless, to welcome thee.—
Throughout each palace crystalline,
    Each far-resounding dome,
With ocean-pearls the Naiads twine
    Their sea-green locks—they come;
They come, light dancing o'er the Deep,
    As motes in sunny beam;
In music o'er the waves they sweep,
    Victoria still their theme.
        Queen of the Isles,
        Queen of the Deep,
Of Freedom, Valour, Beauty, Queen.

Note.—Only two of the stanzas were written as dated, the attack recorded in the Journal having immediately followed.

No sceptre needs that lily hand,
  Bend but thy beauteous brow,
Old Ocean's thunders shake the strand,
  They quell each haughty Foe.
Forth the white-pinioned squadrons fly,
  Those eagles of the wave;
The red-cross Banner streams on high
  Its beacon to the Brave.

The war-blades bright and keen:
Red roll the Floods, wild, curl, and sweep,
  Hoarse voices chime between—
    " Queen of the Isles!
    " Queen of the Deep!
    " Of Freedom, Valour, Beauty, Queen."

Blessings on Her, whose very name
  Breathed in the Scythian Wild,
The Scythian's stony heart could tame,
  And free* sad Slavery's child!
Britannia's name, till then unheard,
  With thine sweet union found:
Old Oxus own'd the blest accord,
  And trembled at a sound.

* See page 158, Vol. I. Journal.

Then clank'd the riven chain: the Deep
    Gave up its dead:—and keen
Leapt forth the prison'd fires.—They weep,
    They bless a power unseen,
        Queen of the Isles,
        Queen of the Deep,
    Of Freedom, Valour, Beauty, Queen.

Victoria; bid thy standard wave,
    Fling far each giant fold,
Dropp'd with the pearls of ocean's cave,
    With India's gems and gold!
On that red cross the circling sun
    Ne'er sets:—and winds that blow,
Shake from each fold a blessing down
    On some sad child of woe.
O'er earth and wave, where'er its deep
    Dread shade of peace is seen,
A Heaven on earth the Ransom'd keep,
    Starr'd in thy ray serene,
        Queen of the Isles,
        Queen of the Deep,
    Of Freedom, Valour, Beauty, Queen.

But, when its thund'rous folds are freed,
    When the fork'd fire-bolts glance,
'Mid warrior shouts and tramp of steeds,
    And gleam of serried lance:

When earth and sky its gloom deplore,
   And Ocean's terrors rise,
And, hurl'd upon a hostile shore,
   Th' Armada shatter'd lies
Whilst surges roar and tempests sweep,
   — Each fearful crash between,
Justice, dread voice accord shall keep,
   And Mercy hymn serene,
      Queen of the Isles,
      Queen of the Deep,
Of Freedom, Valour, Beauty, Queen.

PREFACE TO THE SECOND EDITION.

ONE of the reviewers of the first edition of this work seems to have supposed that the author kept no journal of his wanderings. This is a mistake which reference to p. 225, vol. i., first edition, would have prevented. From the hour of his departure from Heraut to that of his arrival at Khiva, and again from his departure from Khiva to the hour of his captivity, a regular journal was kept, which was restored to him on his release. The exceeding jealousy of the government of Khaurism rendered it imprudent for him to record daily occurrences during his residence at Khiva; and after his escape from captivity, and until his arrival in England, his wound rendered it impossible to journalise.

In the conversations which took place at Khiva and elsewhere, he has avoided as much as possible the repetition of the words, "I said," "he said," and has recorded, to the best of his memory, the conversations as he should have written them at the moment. He is far from meaning to assert, that he has recorded the exact phraseology of either party, nor has he always given either the conversations or the events in their exact sequence; but he has faithfully exhibited the substance of both. The conversations were of such peculiar interest that they were repeatedly referred to; and, indeed, in several cases the subject was studied previous to his audience, that his imperfect Persian might not fail him.

But in searching back for thoughts and feelings which occurred to him during his captivity, which appeared to him curious, but which could be rendered interesting only by minuteness of detail, he fears he may have sometimes become tedious, and sometimes chargeable with egotism; for the original journal was written for the eyes of relations, and, in abridging it, great difficulty was found in the selection of passages to be retained. In the present edition, it is to be hoped many of these blemishes have been corrected.

In the second volume, towards the close, some chapters will be found upon Russian politics. These (with the exception of Chapter XLVIII.) are reprinted as they were published in 1842. The present war may render them interesting.

The reader is begged to remember that the author did not start upon this tour primed and prefaced, and provided with books relating to the countries he was to visit, and with instruments for scientific research. He was taken from the army, which had reached Candahar by a march of 1,300 miles, to ride 350 miles more to Heraut; and thence, with a few days' notice, to ride 600 miles across the desert to Khiva. The results of his own observation he has given; but he had not the advantage of comparing them when made, or previous to publication, with those of predecessors in travel.

CONTENTS.

	PAGE
Preliminary Remark	xxi

CHAPTER I.

Departure for Heraut—Anecdote of the Poet Jaumie—Arrival and Reception at Purwana—Peer Muhummud Khaun, commander of my Escort—Parting Benediction—Kytoo Ridge—Cross country Path to Khooshk—Valley of the Khooshk—Arrival and Reception at Khooshk, the Jumsheedee Capital—Departure—Peril from Petticoats—Reception at a Jumsheedee Khail—Translation of 40 Virgins—Kara Tuppah—Singular Sagacity of the Scorpion of Peshawur—Freemason's Hall—Anecdotes—Chummunie Bhyad—Slave Dealing at Heraut—Cause of the Vuzeer suffering it—Sabres of Khorussaun—District of Baudkhiss—Kullah-i-Mowr, Toorkish frontier—Reception by the Yahmoots of Punjdeeh—Inconveniences of Guestship—Dismissal of Peer Muhummud Khaun 1

CHAPTER II.

The Tent of Plenty of the Yahmoot—Gift Horses—A Toorcumun Breakfast—The Sawney Old Khetkhoda—Peer Muhummud Khaun's Farewell—Extraordinary Power of Yar Muhummud Khaun over his Agents—Valley of the Moorghaub—Junction of the Khooshk Rivulet with that River—Visit from a Panther—Approach to Yoollataun—Reception there by the Governor—

Distrust of the relations between England and Russia—Presents—Muhummud Aumeen Beeg—The Zunouk—Departure—The Old Cauzie of Yoollataun—Probable Origin of Colonel Stoddart's Imprisonments at Bokhara—Hopes of the Slaves at Yoollataun—Approach to Merv—Want of Courtesy of the Governor in my Reception—The Jews of Merv and Meshed—Insulting Conduct of a Servant of the Governor—My first Turban—Visit to the Governor—Insulting Reception, its Origin, and Motive—Preparations for the Passage of the Desert—Jew Merchants—Suspicious Circumstances—Conversation . 20

CHAPTER III.

Jew Merchants—Their Estimation at Merv—Visit to the Khaloofauh—Atmosphere of Merv—The Son of the Soofie Ool Islaum—Dinner—Ignorance of the State of Europe—Gifts—The Gift Horse—Visit from the Governor Nyaz Muhummud Bac—Nature and Properties of a Gift in Eastern Lands—Saleh Muhummud—My Prepossession in his Favour—Persian Ambassador to Khiva—Merv—Departure from its miserable and inhospitable Plain—Aspect of the ancient Site—Slave Caravans—Condition of the Victims—Toorcumun and Oozbeg Women—Economy of a Toorcumun Tent—Objection to too much Bosom—Preference for broken-in Partners of the Yoke—Other Toorcumun habits—A Day's March in the Wilderness of Kara Koom—Landmarks—Sagacity of Camels—Instance of the excessive Cold at Cabul—Toorcumun Notions of the Glory of the Heels—Aspect of this Wilderness . . . . . , . . . 43

CHAPTER IV.

Reception at the House of an Oozbeg Gentleman—Message to the Khaun Huzurut—Ram Fight—The Light of Mutton Tails—Birdler Beeg's Return—Reception of my Message by the Khaun Huzurut—Escort sent to conduct me to my Lodging—Aspect of Khiva and its Suburbs—Dress of Oozbeg Women—My Quarters—Extreme Jealousy of this Government—Arrangements for my Accommodation—Indelicacy of the Mehtur or Minister—Ruminations—Anecdote of Hajji Feroozooddeen—Summary of Difficulties—Difference between Fate and a Razor . . . 61

CHAPTER V.

Glistering Atmosphere and Excessive Chill of the Air at Khiva—Vivers—First Audience at the Court of Khiva—Town—Artillery—Palace—Minister's Levee—The Mehtur—Khojeh Mhirahm—Interpreter—Nobles of Khiva—Access to the Royal Presence—Black Tent—Audience—Ullah Kooli Khan, King of Khaurism—Dismissal—Suspicions of the Khaun Huzurut—Restrictions upon Ambassadors at Khiva . . . , . . . 72

CHAPTER VI.

Second Audience—The Russians—Persians—Bokharians—Colonel Stoddart—Treachery of the Cauzie Moolla Hussun—Message from the Minister—Visit to him—Reception—Bokhara—Colonel Stoddart—Plan for his Rescue—Particulars of the late Skirmish with the Russian Force N. West of the Sea of Aral—Ignorance and Timidity of the Minister—Extreme Difficulty of Negociation with such an one—Messenger from the Khaun Huzurut to the Umuneer of Bokhara, for the Release of Colonel Stoddart 81

CHAPTER VII.

Third Audience of the Khaun Huzurut—Exemplification of British Policy in Afghaunistaun—The Great Mogul—Expertness of Russian Artillerymen—Dismissal—Proposal that my Letters should be read by the Khaun Huzurut—Difficulties of Correspondence—Rapacity of the Minister—Fourth Audience, promise to restore the Russian Captives—My Objection to urge their unconditional Release, whilst a Russian Army was advancing upon the Capital—Nature and Origin of the Misunderstanding between Russia and Khiva—Russia the Aggressor—Estimated Strength of the Army of Invasion—Its Arrest by the Snow—Skirmish—Terrors of a 6lb. Shot—Ruminations . . . 96

CHAPTER VIII.

Discussion of Routes—An Oozbeg Chart of World—Relative Extent of the British and Russian Dominions—English Habits

—The Khook and its Varieties—My Unhappy Ignorance—Appology to the Tuscans—Necessity for foregoing all Geographical Research, imposed by the extreme Importance of my Mission, and the extreme Suspicion with which I was regarded—Another Audience—Meyendorf's Travels—The Air-gun—Discussion of Routes—Impractibility of that by the Balkaun—Difficulties of the Orenburgh Route—Recommendation by the Khaun Huzurut of that by Mungh Kishlauk and Astrakan—Questions relative to Europe, Dress, Dwellings, Climate—Telescopes, Astrology, Female Kings—Number of Cities, Russia, China 107

CHAPTER IX.

Delay in my Mission, and my Impatience under it—Cross Examination upon Articles of Faith—Kawff—Baub Ool Mandeb—People and Customs of Hindostaun—Mungh Kishlauk Guide—His Testimony—Another Audience—Inhabitants of the Ocean—Fish—Serpents—Submarine Sailing—Gun Vessels—Sea Fights—Towns in the Sea—Magic—Contrivances as wonderful in common Use by the British—Steam Looms—Mints—Telegraphs—Steam Vessels and Steam Carriages—Our Well of Alchemy—Origin of the Ducat—Private Intelligence—Extreme Anxiety of the Khaun Huzurut to effect Colonel Stoddart's Release, and bring him to Khiva 119

CHAPTER X.

Interview with the Mehtur—The Book-insolence of the Minister—My Resentment of it—Audience—Account of the Murdered Strangers—Purchase of Ummeer Beeg's Freedom—Minister's Love of Watches and of Calomel—The Air-gun—Paper Kite of Khaurism—Its Musical Properties—Its Mechanism . . 129

CHAPTER XI.

Visit of an Afghaun Priest—Reports relative to Bokhara—Feast given by the Khaun Huzurut—Arrangement of Guests—

Purgatory of Knees and Ankles—Persian Ambassador—Punishment of Dinnerodoxy—Inauk of Huzarusp—The Bee—An Oozbeg Dinner—Holy Ardour of the Priests—Accounted for upon Muhummedun Principles—Virtue of the Narr of Soups—Mutton, Spartan, Maigre, Chicken-broth, Ox-tail Mock-turtle—Turtle 136

CHAPTER XII.

Report of the Advance of the British Arms to Bulkh, and toward Tehraun—Prospect of my speedy Departure—Extreme Difficulty of procuring Money—Promises of Shroffs and of the Minister equally false—Delay in transmitting my Despatches—Private Channel established—Liberation of Ummeer Beeg—Narrative of his Capture and attempted Escape—Mutilation of his Ears by Yakoob Mehtur—His Disposition to revenge the Injury—Release of Twenty-two of the Daughters of the Afghauns in honour of H. M. the Queen of Great Britain—Captain Pottinger's Rescue from Captivity of some Forty or Fifty Children . . 145

CHAPTER XIII.

The Ummeer of Bokhara's Refusal to release Colonel Stoddart—Endeavour to make me solicit the Company, on my Mission, of an Oozbeg Ambassador—And to persuade me to prefer the Orenburgh Route—Private Intelligence—Presents for the Emperor of Russia—Arrangements for the Exchange of Captives—Reasonableness of the Khaun's Propositions—His extreme Anxiety, and evident Sincerity on this Point—His Amusement at the Motion of my Pen—And Curiosity respecting my Epaulettes—His Majesty's Tribulation at my Want of a Cocked Hat and Plume—Muhummud Shauh—Dismissal—Reveillée of Nizaum, the Sleeper of Sleepers—Visit from a Relation of Birdler Beeg—His Account of the Skirmish with Russia—Difficulty of raising Funds—Fresh Attempts to make me apply for an Oozbeg Ambassador, and for Permission to proceed viâ Orenburgh—Disconcerted by a Discovery—Visit from the Minister—Renewal of those Efforts—His happy Confidence in Destiny—Heroic Spirit . 160

CHAPTER XIV.

Departure of the Persian Ambassador—Difficulty of procuring correct Intelligence—Inefficiency of my Establishment—Presence of the Persian Ambassador, how far useful to me—Alarm occasioned by the Reports of the British Advance—Resolution of the Khaun to put down Slave-dealing—Final Audience—Subject of Change of Route renewed—The Guide Hussun Mhatoor, chief of the Chowdhoors—The Khaun's Charge to him—To me—His Message to Her British Majesty—Importance to Europe at this Moment of the Kingdom of Khaurism—Parting Charge and Farewell—Fruitless Endeavours to cash my Bills—Deceit and Treachery of the Mehtur—Inhospitality, Meanness, and Cruelty of the Court—Quit Khiva in the almost certain Prospect of perishing
... ...
meer Beeg—Departure from Khiva 171

CHAPTER XV.

Departure from Khiva—Palace of the Toorruh—Priggery of the Toorcumuns—Umbarr, an ancient Site—Report of gigantic Human Bones—Dahsh Howz—House of the Guide—His Obstinacy Message from the Mehtur—The great Mare's Nest—Its Origin—Journey resumed—Inhospitality of the Guide—Capture of a Russian Interpreter—My Objection to see him—Journey resumed—Reception at the Den of Thieves 185

CHAPTER XVI.

Visits from Toorcumuns—Khail of Yahmoots—Dress of Toorcumun Women—Fierceness of the Watch-dogs—Visit to the Ruins of Old Oorgunj and to a Toorcumun Fair—Entertainment at a Khail—Cure of Jaundice—Toorcumun Dinner—Economy of a Toorcumun Tent—Dress of Children—Ruined Fort Shoomanki—Deserted Bed of Oxus—Distant View of Oxus and the Lake Loudahn—Slaves—Cliffs of Chalk and Marl—Ruined Castle of Kohna Wuzeer—Of Burrasun Gelmus—Another Enchanted Castle—Ibrahim Aat'h—Entrance to Kuzzauk Land—Distant View of the Channel occupied by the Oxus when it fell into the Gulf of Balkaun—Anecdotes of the Bahrukzye Chiefs . . 201

CHAPTER XVII.

Chase of the wild Ass—Miry State of the Steppe—Intense Cold on on the higher Land—Antelope of the Steppe—Dry Basin of a Lake—Particulars of the Murder at Khiva of the two European Travellers and their five Servants—Manners of the Kara Kulpauks and other Oozbegs—Character of the Country—Chalk, Cliffs, etc. 216

CHAPTER XVIII.

Rapacity of the Guide—Physiognomy of the Kuzzauks—Nizaum's extreme Amusement at the Sight of beardless Men—The Dragon of Heraut—The Petrified Dragon of Cundahar—Existence of a Species of Boa amongst the Mountains of Afghaunistaun—Anecdote of Shauh Kaumraun—Singular Fate of a Tent Mallet—Chalk Cliffs—Kuzzauks 227

CHAPTER XIX.

Story of Hautim, the Arab—Face of the Country—Melancholy Prospects—Anecdote of the Ex-Ummeer Doost Muhummud Khaun—Some Account of the Descendants of Cyrus the Great—Herds of Galloways—Kuzzauks—The Snake—Ali's Dream—Origin of Tobacco—Lawfulness of Pig-tail—Goat's Milk—Liberty of the Fair Sex *sometimes* abused 242

CHAPTER XX.

Ferocity of Toorcumun Horses—Cliffs of Crystallized Lime—Account of the Death of Futteh Khaun—Vuzeer of Heraut—Resistless Power of Destiny—The Falcon and the Crow—Perverseness of Guide—Tent of Dana Bae, the Kuzzauk—The Napkin of Khaurism—The Desert Bird 253

CHPATER XXI.

Cliffs of Shell Sandstone—Burial-ground—First Glimpse of the Caspian—Difficulties suggested by the Guide—Entire Absence of Boats—Desperate Posture of my Affairs—Expedient suggested by the Guide—His Refusal to accompany me farther—Prospect of utter Ruin—Alternatives—Basin and Cliffs of the Caspian—False Report of Sails in Sight—Signals—Resolution to proceed to Dahsh Gullah—Repetition of Signals—Their Fruitlessness—Appearance of Dana Bae, the Kuzzauk—His Agreement to conduct me—Announcement and Departure—Letter to the Khaun Huzurut—Suspicious Circumstances—Ruinous Habits of my Interpreter 264

CHAPTER XXII.

The Treacherous Messenger—Perplexities—Resolution to Return—How altered—Farther Symptoms of Treachery—Appearance of a Clump of Toorcumun Horse—Bivouac in the Rain—Symptoms of Treachery in the Guide—Fresh Perplexities and Difficulties—Reach a Kuzzauk Tent—The Kuzzauk Bride—The Hyæna—Reach Dana Bae's Tent—Interchange of Spoons—Arrangements for the Journey—Greed of Dana Bae—His formidable Oath—Dismissal of the Hyæna—Night in a Kuzzauk Tent—Journey resumed—Incessant Anxiety and Watchfulness—Arrive at a Chain of Mountains—The Black Russian Ambassador—Singular Weather-worn Rocks—Fresh Causes of Suspicion—Reach the Caspian 280

CHAPTER XXIII.

A Rencontre—Its Result—Hasten our March—Toilsome Ascent of the Cliffs of the Caspian—Suspicious Conduct of the Younger Guide—Bivouac at the Summit—Absence of the Younger Guide—Meditations—Carelessness of my People threatening us with Ruin—Lighten the Camel Loads—Farther Preparations—Resumption of Journey—Ahris Mhatoor—Descent—Treacherous Conduct of the Younger Guide—Attempt to secure the Elder in my Interests—The Monk—Bivouac—Suspicious Action of Dana Bae—The Alarm—The Night Attack—Result—Reflections—The Interposition—Fate of Three of my Suite . . . 298

CHAPTER XXIV.

Hilarity of the Young Guide—The Letter—Scene—Consultations and Reports of the Kuzzauk Assailants—Night on the Field of Strife—Meditations—Desperate Posture of my Affairs—Triumph of the Coward Yar Muhummud—State of my Party—Symptoms of a Move—Ahris, the Hero—Retrograde Movement—Helpless Condition of my Meerza—Our shattered and melancholy Cavalcade—Halt at Soosun Uttah—Summud Khaun's Sagacious Arrangement for our Safety—Spite of the Younger Guide—The Curse of the Koraun—Arrival of Tents—Arrangements for our Disposal—Yar Muhummud and the Tempter—First Repast as Captives—Soft Flattery in an unknown Tongue—Character of Ahris Mhatoor—The Covenant—Night Alarms—Varieties of Death—Second Night of our Captivity 316

CHAPTER XXV.

Capture of Maimood and Ali Muhummud—Consultations of our Captors—Third Night of Captivity—Further Consultation—Harassing Demands—Division of Booty—The Blandishments of Beauty out of her Teens—Sentiment of Sheep's Tails—Delicacy and Sympathy of Kuzzauk Women—Misery of our Position this Day—The poor Meerza's View of the Case—Further Partition of Spoils—Recovery of the Royal Presents—Rape of the Cloak and the Kerchief—Three of my Suite taken off as Slaves—Rescue of Nizaum—Survey of Summud Khaun—State of my Wounds—New Guide to Mecca—Lamentable Want of Religious Fury amongst the Kuzzauks 329

CHAPTER XXVI.

Embarrassment of Ahris Mhatoor—Considerations—The scotched Snakes—Fidelity of Cherkush—The Bond—The Negotiator—The Shippish—Sensation he produces in London—Whether he acknowledges the Emperor of all the Russias—Liking of a Kuzzauk for Nizaum—Messenger from Hussun Mhatoor—News from Dahsh Gullah—Valuation of plundered Property—The Golden Banquet—Shift Camp—Virtue of Patience—Golden Colic . 339

CHAPTER XXVII.

Hopelessness of our Predicament—Ali Muhummud's Project—The Afghaun Horsemen—Congratulations of a Bear—Apparition of Saleh Muhummud—Greetings—Recapitulation—The Search—Confabulations—Happy Disposition and bright Mind of Saleh Muhummud—Consultations—Joy of my Party—Confusion of Enemies—Ummeer Beeg—Delicacies unknown to Heliogabalus—The Tit-bit 368

PRELIMINARY REMARKS.

WHEN Major Todd, in June, 1839, arrived as Envoy at Heraut, he selected Moolla Hussun, a Mahomedan priest of great respectability, as bearer of a letter of friendship to the Khaun Huzurut (Supreme Lord) of Khiva, called also Khaurism Shauh, or King of Khaurism. Moolla Hussun arriving at Khiva when the state was threatened with a Russian invasion, was well received, and on his return was accompanied by an Oozbeg lord, Shookkuroolla Bae by name, as ambassador from the Khaun Huzurut to the Indian government. The letter borne by this ambassador accepted of the tender of British friendship, and made several demands which could not be complied with upon the responsibility of Major Todd. It was in answer to this mission that the envoy deputed me to visit the court of Khiva.

The news brought by the Khiva ambassador rated the Russian force at 100,000 fighting men, who were said to be still in the Kuzzauk country, north-west of the sea of Aral. In return for the envoy's present of a very handsome rifle, he sent a very sorry specimen of the boast of Khaurism, in shape of a broken-down nag. This, however, had probably been substituted by the minister for the horse originally sent. The presents entrusted to my care were a Persian sabre and a Heraut rifle for the Khaun himself; a rifle for his brother, the Inauk of Huzarusp; and a matchlock rifle for the Governor of Yoollataun. The royal presents were very unworthy of the occasion; but the British Toshchkhanch* had been exhausted, and as I was to ride *chuppah* (post), my haste to present myself before his Majesty was to serve as an excuse for their poverty. Such trifling particulars throw light upon the manners and customs of a country: it is also but justice to myself to state (so far as political considerations will allow) the very trifling means I had of conciliating favour.

The kingdom of Khaurism is separated from the Russian district of Orenburgh by a considerable belt of steppe, held by Kuzzauks, whose chief, or Sooltaun, is nominally tributary to Russia. The Russians call this people Kirgheez,† to distinguish them from their own Kuzzauks, or Cossaqs, who are Christians, but the name is unknown to the people themselves. Khaurism is bounded on the west by the Caspian, on the south-west by Persia and Heraut, on the south-east by Bokhara, on the north-east by Kokaun.

The present capital of Khaurism is Khiva, lying in N. lat. 41° 20′, and E. long. about 60°, and about

* With each British mission in Central Asia is a magazine of rare articles and dresses of honour, intended as presents to sovereigns and nobles, or rewards for the services of others.

† Kirgheez signifies those who dwell in Khurgah, or tents of felt derived, say the Russians, from Khur, an ass, and Gah, a place—the place of the ass, or ass' stable. It is probable that this is the real origin of the Persian word, given in derision by the Persians to their foes the Tartars.

forty miles west of the Oxus. It therefore bears from Heraut about north-north-west, and is distant from it, by the road, something less than 600 miles, of which, after passing the mountain barrier of Heraut, nearly the whole is a barren steppe, where even a tent is rarely discovered.

The former capital was Oorgunj, and two towns of this name have successively enjoyed the dignity. A country so cut off from the rest of the world by wide steppes, whose rare inhabitants are plunderers and slave-dealers by profession, was too little known to be correctly designated; accordingly, Khaurism is a title with which few are familiar, whilst the capitals Oorgunj and Khiva have in turn given their names to a kingdom which, whatever its wealth and political importance, is at least sufficiently extensive. Khaurism is about 800 miles in length, north and south, by nearly 600 east and west, comprising an area of nearly 480,000 square miles. It is of much importance to bear in mind, that Bokhara is entirely severed from Russia by Khaurism. The latter kingdom joining Kokaun in the desert, about 360 miles east of Khiva.

The greater part of Khaurism (as its Persian name implies), viz., all that is west of the Oxus, belonged to ancient Persia. The descendants of the Persians are still existing under the name of Sart. They are known by their beards, a distinction for the sake of which the Oozbegs, the present lords of the empire, frequently condescend to intermarry with them. The Tooreumuns who inhabit the steppe between Khiva and the Caspian are more particular; and accordingly beards are rarely seen amongst them. The Kuzzauks, whose country extends from the northernmost limit of Khaurism to an irregular line from the south of the Sea of Aral, drawn west-south-west to the Caspian, would in turn be despised by the more polished Sart. The presence therefore of a beard in a Toorcumun or Kuzzauk khail (camp) may generally be traced to some Persian slave of the family. And if we consider the extreme value and importance to the nations of Asia of an appendage by which they swear, and upon which they pray, we may appreciate the strength of the temptation under which it has been introduced into any household.

Messrs. Smith, Elder & Co. *are in no way responsible for the errors corrected as below.*

ERRATA, VOL. I. ABBOTT'S KHIVA.

Page x., line 18, *for* " prefaced," *read* " prepared."
,, 2 ,, 17, *for* " of Purwana," *read* " to Purwana."
,, 5 ,, 21, *for* " wiling," *read* " whiling."
,, 16 ,, *note, for* " Koophun," *read* " Koopheen."
,, 16 ,, *note, for* " Soondi," *read* " Loondi R."
,, 24 ,, 4 *from foot, for* " the Yar," *read* " Yar."
,, 28 ,, 9 *from foot, for* " Bumeen," *read* " Aumeen."
,, 37 ,, 2, *for* " with," *read* " within."
,, 78 ,, 12 *from foot, for* " Nuggeeb," *read* " Nuqqueeb."
,, 91 ,, *note, for* " Grouir," *read* " Groom."
,, 99 ,, 13, *for* " Mehtur," *read* " the Mehtur."
,, 104 ,, 11, *for* " have," *read* " had."
,, 107 ,, 10, *for* " my," *read* " by."
,, 109 ,, 11 *from foot, for* " Now it," *read* " Now as it."
,, 113 ,, 18, *for* " A airgun," *read* " An airgun."
,, 119 ,, 2 *from foot, for* " Noguy," *read* " Nuqqueeb."
,, 120 ,, 5, *for* " or West," *read* " and West."
,, 145 ,, 3, *for* " I heard," *read* " I had heard."
,, 199 ,, 12 *from foot, omit* " to."
,, 227 ,, 11, *for* " woman," *read* " camel."
,, 230 ,, 16, *for* " moulds," *read* " moulds itself."
,, 230 ,, 15 *from foot, for* " cord," *read* " chord."
,, 249 ,, 5, *omit* " Heraut."
,, 249 ,, 3 *from foot, for* " enquiries," *read* " auguries."
,, 287 ,, 12 *from foot, for* " girl perhaps," *read* " girl of perhaps."
,, 304 ,, 4, *for* " depended," *read* " depending."
,, 311 ,, 18, *for* " rise," *read* " raise."
,, 328 ,, 10 *from foot, for* " insolence," *read* " violence."
,, 331 ,, 13, *for* " horses," *read* " horse-furniture."
,, 335 ,, 10, *for* " draw the," *read* " draw."
,, 340 ,, 12 *from foot, for* " In his," *read* " his."
,, 342 ,, 12 *from foot, for* " was," *read* " were."
,, 350 ,, 19, *for* " months," *read* " mouths."
,, 354 ,, 9, *for* " pain," *read* " pang."
,, 358 ,, 11 *from foot, for* " the Ulla," *read* " Ulai."
,, 360 ,, 5, *omit the first* " had."
,, 361 ,, 8, *for* " had," *read* " had had."
,, 364 ,, 4 *from foot, for* " long life," *read* " life long."
,, 379 ,, 1 *do., for* " be to trod," *read* " be trod."

NARRATIVE OF A JOURNEY,
ETC.

CHAPTER I.

Departure from Heraut—Anecdote of the Poet Jaumie—Arrival and Reception at Purwana—Peer Muhummud Khaun, Commander of my Escort—Parting Benediction—Kytoo Ridge—Cross-country Path to Khooshk—Valley of the Khooshk—Arrival and Reception at Khooshk, the Jumsheedee Capital—Departure—Peril from Petticoats—Reception at a Jumsheedee Khail—Translation of Forty Virgins—Kara Tuppah—Singular Sagacity of the Scorpion of Peshawur—Freemason's Hall—Anecdotes—Churumnie Bhayd—Slave-dealing at Heraut—Cause of the Vuzeer suffering it—Sabres of Khorussaun—District of Baudkhiss—Kullah-i-Mowr, Toorkish frontier—Reception by the Yahmoots of Punjdeeh—Inconveniences of Guestship—Dismissal of Peer Muhummud Khaun.

ON 24th December, 1839, I quitted Heraut in progress to Khiva, and several trifling arrangements being found incomplete, halted at a village near the Eed-gauh, where I was hospitably entertained by a descendant of the poet Jaumie, whose tomb is at the Eed-gauh. This poet, by birth a Herautie, has a name only less esteemed than those of Haufiz and Saadi. It was related to me by a native of Heraut, that a poet who in his day had some celebrity, came to visit Jaumie, and challenged him to a trial of poetic skill. They sat on the banks of the Jooe Unjeer (fig canal), a running and pure stream from the Hurrie rood, and for several days they continued the combat, answering one another in the most beautiful verse; all who loved poetry collected to hear them; but, said the narrator, Jaumie was a *Bul-bul*, and the third evening, when the visitor was in mid discourse with Jaumie, and the verse of the latter continued to improve in power and sweetness beyond the measure of human song, the stranger was observed to betray unwonted languor; his head gradually sunk upon his breast; when his answer was expected, he continued silent, and when a friend strove to arouse him, he was found to be—dead. Traditions of this nature are implicitly believed by Asiatics, who would deem the doubt of them akin to infidelity. The belief upon which this tale is founded is universal, viz., that the Bul-bul, when out-done in melody, droops its head upon the breast and expires.

I quitted this village the next morning, and after much delay, occasioned by the falling of the baggage from the pony's back, reached Purwana, in a high valley about eleven miles distant from Heraut. The road lies between close hills, of no considerable height, and ascends the entire distance of Purwana. As it is not my purpose to publish any particulars relative to the practicability or otherwise of this mountain chain, I shall content myself with describing the general aspect of the country. This village is depopulated by forays of the Jumsheedees, a people of Toorkish origin, but tributary to Heraut. These men, encouraged by the connivance of the Vuzeer Yar Muhummud Khaun, are ever on the watch to seize, for sale to the Toorcumuns, the miserable subjects of Heraut. Here are profuse Kaureeze,* and a little cultivation. The people, who are Taujiks, received and entertained me very hospitably. Around this village are hills and high plains producing wormwood, which is browsed by the wild antelope. The tombs of the five saints who founded the village, are seen in the neighbourhood.

* Kaureeze are chains of wells, the first dug down upon the stream at the foot of the mountain in a water-course, where the verdure denotes water. On reaching the spring, its course is ascertained, and another well is dug down upon it to make sure of it. The intermediate channel is then cleared, and the direction of the stream further being taken, another and another well is dug, until the number sometimes amounts to hundreds. As opportunity offers, the water is led through an artificial tunnel to the surface of the valley.

Unless I could deem myself the most interesting personage of the group now proceeding to Khiva, it were unpardonable to omit mention of those who formed my retinue. This I shall from time to time take occasion to do, as any incident happens to bring them prominently forward.

The most important person was the Afghaun Peer Muhummud Khaun, a relation of the Vuzeer of Heraut. He was given me by the Vuzeer as commander of an escort of five horsemen, to be increased to fifteen on approaching Punj Deeh. The instant I saw him I perceived that he was far too respectable for the petty office assigned, and this threw me on my guard. Peer Muhummud Khaun is a very handsome man, and his beauty is of a striking character. His features are nobly formed, his eye is large, dark, and expressive. His teeth are of dazzling whiteness. When first he waited upon me at Heraut, I was very busy, the twilight was settling into darkness, and I did not observe his approach. When I looked up, I saw before me a figure which almost startled me by its resemblance to our best portraits of Edward the Third. The effect was increased by the shadow of a large dark blue turban and a cloak still darker. Presenting himself to me as sent by one whose cunning is only to be surpassed by his villany, whom I believed by a similar messenger to have contrived the imprisonment of the gallant, but unfortunate Colonel Stoddart, he was regarded by me with singular interest, and that of no pleasing character. He has naturally become the chief object of my attention, and as I can understand his Persian, and he by dint of excessive intelligence contrives to make out a good deal of mine, I am in deep conversation with him whenever the road permits it. He has orders to escort me to Merv, to Khiva if I think fit; and as for very important reasons he is extremely anxious to attend me to the latter place, I have an advantage which I shall not for a moment suffer him to forget.

Here I received a letter from Major Todd. We separated under circumstances sufficiently gloomy. I leave him in the very stronghold of robbers. I go myself, as agent of the British Government, to a Court of the language and manners of which I am utterly ignorant, and to accomplish that of which the most sanguine have no hope. It is simply a matter of duty, and as such entered upon cheerfully, and with full determination to carry my efforts to the uttermost.

The man who brought me this note had formerly been in my service whilst marching to Herant. He

riding whip to him; remembering, however, my political office, I did not strike him, but I perceived that he was highly offended. On reaching our camp in the evening, and retiring to bed, I observed that he had not brought me my gun, which he always carried, and which he had orders to place in my bed at night. I also observed that his right hand was bandaged, and that he was very reluctant to let me look at it. I called for the gun; he made a hundred excuses for not bringing it. I went to his bedding, where I found it. I drew it out of the oilskin case, and found the right cock down on the nipple and the left on full cock. I conceived immediately, what his countenance expressed, that he had cocked it with the intention of shooting me; but relenting perhaps, or deferring his intention, had endeavoured to let down the cocks, and had caught his thumb under one of them. I now insisted upon examining the wound, and found it just as I suspected. I took no notice of this little demonstration, nor ever condescended to use precaution against a creature so contemptible. Under the influence of a present, he now took leave of me, on the high plain above Purwana, and holding his turban in his hand before his eyes, uttered a thousand benedictions upon me.

Avoiding now the more direct and difficult passes of the mountain ridge of Kytoo, we crossed that chain without accident, meeting neither dwelling nor tent, excepting two ruined Rabaht (hospitia) in the valley, and descending some grassy heights, pitched at evening in a hollow, where we found a little water. We were now on the road to Khooshk, the capital of the Jumsheedees, as recommended by Yar Muhummud Khaun, on the plea of my being provided by their chieftain with a further escort of ten horsemen.

These grassy heights are in spring infested by small green snakes, not generally deemed venomous. They have a sufficiently desolate aspect: but their grass in some measure relieves this—one solitary flock of sheep in the distance, and the wild antelopes of the wilderness, were the sole living things we saw. Kytoo, covered at the summit with snow, holds awful pre-eminence over the solitude.

27th December. The clouds collected during the night, and a drizzling shower added nothing to the comfort of my followers, who having no tent, covered themselves with felts as best they could. I heard them, however, making light of it, and wiling the night with laughter and fun. The horses piquetted to short iron pegs driven into the earth, which offered no resistance whatever to any efforts to get free, and unaccustomed to pass the night in the open air, were constantly breaking loose, and I was rather surprised to find the number complete at break of day. It was then, that looking in the direction of Kytoo we saw that mountain chain covered from summit to base with snow, and congratulated ourselves with no little thankfulness on having already passed this barrier, where travellers every year are lost in the snow. A very distressing cross-country path, over steep hills covered with grass, brought us to the rivulet Khooshk, which we ascended to the capital of that name. The valley here is picturesque and interesting. The low hills which form it, are quite naked, or produce only grass. Not a leaf is to be seen. Yet being fringed with the black tents of the Jumsheedees, and peopled with living things, men, women, horses, and sheep, the contrast to the country just passed was strong and welcome. The women in groups were engaged in working upon the banks of the stream. Their dress is either a petticoat or very loose drawers, over which the shift falls. On the head is an ugly white cloth wound round the head, under the chin, and falling upon the shoulders. Their faces, therefore, are exposed, being in fact not worth the cost of concealment, but the dress were sufficient to smother the charms of a Venus. The black tents which form the capital of the Jumsheedees are of thick felts, supported by a light and moveable framework of wood. Their shape is circular, and their dark hue is received from the smoke of firs lighted within: but sometimes from the colour of the wool. Khooshk, however, has a few mud huts and a fort (so called), resembling a dilapidated farm-yard. The Jumsheedees reckon their own number at 15,000 families, or 75,000 souls; but this is probably an exaggeration; for having now passed through about fifty miles of their country, I have scarcely seen a human being.

I had been throughout this march in conversation with Peer Muhummud Khaun, hoping to gain some hint of the Vuzeer's object in sending me hither, Khooshk being two marches off the road. I found, by cross-examination, that he had a letter from the Vuzeer to the Jumsheedee chief, but he believed, he said, that it was merely an order for my escort. I sent him on to announce my approach, and he returned with a single horseman to conduct me to the place prepared for my reception. This was extremely discourteous, for the chief should himself have come to meet me, or at any rate have received me at the threshold. I had, however, no means of enforcing respect, being for the moment in his power, so I alighted at the steps leading to my apartment, which was probably the best he had to offer, and made myself as comfortable as circumstances would allow. Here I found an unusual thing in the shape of a tolerably wide chimney. Upon applying fire, however, I soon found that it was a luxury only in appearance, as none of the smoke would pass up it. After several hours, Mahomed Zemaun Khaun, the Jumsheedee chief, made his appearance, attended by Peer Muhummud Khaun. He is a man who affects great frankness, and his manners are lively and rather agreeable, although unpolished. He welcomed me to Khooshk; said that he heard I had expressed some distrust of the Vuzeer's motives for sending me thither, and laid his note open before me. This note was certainly all I could desire, but it was probably not the only one. After a very short visit he jumped up, and saying, "Farewell," left the room as briskly as he had entered. To judge by this man's countenance, a physiognomist would give him credit for courage, conduct, decision, and generosity; yet in the late siege of Heraut he betrayed a lamentable want of all those qualities.

During that unfortunate and disastrous investment, the Herauties in vain expected succour from this wild tribe, who, by seconding the efforts of the besieged might have done infinite mischief to the Persians. Whilst the Jumsheedees seemed to be hesitating, a Persian force was sent to Khooshk to beat up their quarters. Instead of taking advantage of their strong country to harass or destroy the Persians, they fled without resistance to Meroo Chauk, leaving their country and a good deal of grain buried in the earth to the mercy of the Persians. The Jumsheedees are of Toorkish descent, as their habits and physiognomy imply. They are short, stout, very dark, with decidedly Tartar features. Wherever water and soil are found, a little cultivation is maintained by them, but their wealth consists in flocks of sheep and herds of horses of Toorcumun breed, generally received by them in exchange for slaves whom they capture in the Heraut district. They are arrant cowards, and, like all Tartars, superstitiously fearful of artillery

The marked coldness of my reception here, by a chief who had been most handsomely treated by the British Envoy, would have sufficed to prevent any prolongation of my visit, had such consisted with my haste to reach my destination. This coldness I well knew to be the suggestion of the Vuzeer of Heraut, who was concerned by all means in his power to frustrate my mission.

Whilst I was girding up my loins, the Khaun was announced, and came running into the room with his usual liveliness, saluting me with an air of frank cordiality. After having exchanged with me a few words, he suddenly rose, and proposed that I should resume my journey. I was too ignorant of the usages of the Tartar tribes to resent what appeared so boorish. My host saw me to the door of my little cell, where he stopped, whilst I stumbled down the broken steps. A large crowd of idlers stood around the gate to see the Englishman depart. I was dressed in the Afghaun attire, consisting of a double set of stiff petticoats. Two or three officious fellows were at my elbow to shove me up into the saddle. The horse was very large, and had no mane, and my petticoats hung around me like so many shirts of mail. A miscarriage I perceived was inevitable. I determined however to do my best. With infinite difficulty, I thrust my left foot into the stirrup, and flinging aside my petticoats made a desperate spring for the saddle. I might perhaps have reached it in peace, and not without glory, but one fellow thrust with a jerk at my elbow, and another gave me a forward impulse from the back, so that my petticoats became entangled with my right knee, and afterwards with the high cantle of my hussar saddle, and I was fairly caught, like a bird upon a limed twig; moreover, my predicament struck me in so absurd a light, that I was guilty of a fit of laughter, to the infinite dismay of all my suite.

"Ullah Kurreem!" (God is merciful), shouted my old Meerza, when he perceived I was actually in the saddle, stroking his beard with the right hand. "Shookkur!" (Thanksgiving), replied old Summud Khaun, the Steward, imitating the action. "Bismillah!" (in the name of God), I said, turning my horse's head, and gladly quitting the den of inhospitality. My people begged me to make a short march, as the cattle had been starved. The old Meerza remarked Khooshk (dry) is its name, and dry we have found it. I had not suspected the old fellow of mettle sufficient for so bad a pun.

We passed down the valley of the Khooshk rivulet, averaging about half a mile in width, and bounded on either side by sloping grassy downs, sprinkled with flocks of sheep and goats. Under the low sunny cliffs and hills the Jumsheedees had pitched their black tents in considerable numbers; and in the fields of the valley, hundreds of mares and colts were grazing. The scene was extremely pleasing. The valley is highly susceptible of culture, and has once been well tilled. Toward evening we halted at a Khail (camp), and sent for the Khetkhoda. He came, and took my hand between both his own, in the usual fashion, but was evidently reluctant that we should tarry and put his hospitality to charges. "Am I welcome?" I inquired. "You are welcome." "You did not say so at first." "What does it signify?" said a servant of Muhummud Zemaun Khaun, "if he wont make you welcome, I will." "On no account," I replied, "I will have no forced hospitality. Since I am welcome, I will dismount; otherwise I would have gone elsewhere." It must be observed, once for all, that I always made a handsome present, three or four times exceeding the expence incurred, to any person who lodged or entertained me. I was therefore the less scrupulous about their first inclination, knowing that they would afterwards be very well contented. I wished to have put up in the camp itself to observe the manners of the people; but, out of respect for me, they brought a tent bodily to the spot where I was seated. The women were the chief locomotives; and, being inside, the tent appeared to have found legs of its own. One of these women was pretty, and the fair sex here seem to have the advantage of the men in features and complexion. However, there are many slave girls of other nations present, and the females whom I meet are probably of this class.

In the morning resuming my course down the river valley I passed a scene resembling that of the previous day. A couple of mud huts near the left border of the valley were shewn me as the residence of forty the hills, as the place of worship to which they had resorted, when surprised by a force of some neighbouring tribes. In this extremity, the virgins prayed for death, and were instantly translated; but whether by men or spirits does not appear. The translation of forty fat virgins is nothing to a Moosulmaun's faith! The Toorcumun horses would have found it practically no joke. The place is called Chhehl Dochtur, or "the forty virgins." The tradition, as well as name, is evidently Persian.

Kara Tuppah, the black mound, was now in sight, being an artificial hill about 150 feet in height, crowned by a ruined circle of defences. It stands in the elbow of the valley, overlooked by lofty hills on the west. The bend of the valley is very wide, and Kara Tuppah was not only girdled by black tents, but crowded by caravans from Merv proceeding with grain for Khooshk. Here Muhummud Zemaun Khaun's servant was to leave me, after furnishing the escort of ten Jumsheedee horsemen. But I had been pondering the necessity of employing these men. It struck me, that as they would hold themselves in authority to Peer Muhummud Khaun, I should literally become his prisoner, and he might dispute my orders when directed to return. Some excuse for dispensing with their services was necessary. I first objected to the number on the score of provision. A smaller number, they said, could not venture to return by that route, owing to a death feud between Muhummud Zemaun Khaun and the children of Derveish Khaun, late chief of the Jumsheedees, and slain by the present chief. "But I have no death feud with the children of Derveish Khaun, and if ten Jumsheedee horsemen who *have*, and who are the most arrant cowards in the world, can return alone, surely we, who can muster four good sabres, can have nothing to apprehend." It must be observed that Peer Muhummud Khaun, after receiving from the British Treasury allowance for himself and five troopers, had brought not one fighting man with him. I called the chief's servant, gave him a handsome present, and a note to his master, saying, that I did not require the escort; and having dismissed him passed on.

Beyond Kara Tuppah there are few black tents: but large flocks of sheep are still met with. The shepherds come even from Merv to this pleasant valley, bringing water and all other necessaries on asses. The men of Kara Tuppah hate the authority of the present chief; and beyond this limit no Jumsheedee of his following presumes to dwell.

It was my object to keep Peer Muhummud Khaun constantly engaged in discourse, for various reasons. It gave him an idea of my favour and confidence; it improved my miserable Persian; and, as I generally turned the conversation upon the persons composing the Court at Heraut, it served to disclose to me his own character, even when it failed to reveal to me theirs. There was not a person, however insignificant, nor act however trivial, that was not made subject of discussion, and, by returning again and again to the charge, and placing each point in a novel light, I made it extremely difficult for him to prevaricate without detection. I knew that all his future prospects depended upon his accompanying me to Khiva, and that I might depend upon any trifling sacrifice that should give him hope of this; and as it was his own, as well as the Vuzeer's wish that I should suppose him a personal enemy of the latter, he was not scrupulous in revealing his iniquities. At the same time, as he could not tell how much was known to me, he dared not very grossly violate the truth. But sometimes the conversation took a lighter turn, and to-day we had a variety of anecdotes as credible as the relations of the great liar Josephus.

The scorpion of Peshawur, he said, is of great size, and its wit is equal to its bulk. A gentleman of that city lying one morning upon his bed, with his hand hanging down, saw a portly fellow approach the hand, squint up at it, and then standing a tip-toe, endeavour to sting it. Failing in his attempt, the scorpion went away, but soon after returned with another, whom the gentleman supposed, from a certain "Je ne sais quoi," might be his wife. Mounting upon her back he made several fresh efforts to reach the hand, but in vain. Far from being disconcerted, off he trudged again, returning now with his wife and wife's mother. He placed the latter below, the wife on her back, and standing upon wife's shoulders would inevitably have stung the gentleman, had he not in good time withdrawn his hand.

Peer Muhummud Khaun had heard, he said, of a house in England opened once a year for the reception of letters, and where they who were so fortunate as to gain admittance, were bound by the most solemn oaths to reveal nothing they should see or hear. That the knowledge there revealed to them in a single hour, surpassed the joint knowledge and experience acquired by fifty sages in the course of a long life.

This evidently is Freemason's Hall.

The old Meerza striking in, related, that a poor man having nothing to present to Timoor Lungh,* brought him the thigh of a grasshopper, saying, "Behold thine

---

* Better known in Europe as Tamerlane. Lungh signifies lame, and Timoor alone is the proper name of this king. In Asia he is generally called the Ummir Timoor.

ant, O Timoor, hath brought thee according to the measure of his capacity." This anecdote has for foundation the tradition that King Solomon having been placed by the Almighty in sovereignty of men, demons, and the brute creation, was receiving their voluntary tribute, when the Court was a good deal amused at seeing an ant enter, dragging along the thigh of a grasshopper, which it deposited at the monarch's feet with evident complacency. The elephant turned up his nose, and the hyæna laughed outright at this mighty addition to the royal treasure; for the one had brought him on its back a budding aloe tree, and the other a rich necklace, rent from the throat of a young maiden, whom he had surprised and slaughtered at her mother's tomb. But Solomon sternly rebuked either, declaring that none that day had honoured him, as he felt honoured by the little ant.

"A particular friend of mine," said Peer Muhummud Khaun, "was one day chasing a fox upon the hill side, when suddenly a snake struck his dog, which instantly swelled to an immense size and began to shake violently. What was the amazement of my friend to see the flesh and skin fall to tatters, and scatter by the shaking on every side, leaving a very perfect skeleton of the dog, which my friend preserved, and still shews as a great curiosity." "The venom of some snakes," I replied, "is very virulent."

Toward evening, we reached a spot fitted for encampment, about two miles short of Kullah Chummunie Bhayd. The jungle grass was here on fire, and a large flock of perhaps 1000 sheep, guarded by three shepherds, stood near. We asked them to sell us a young sheep. They bargained to exchange it for a little tobacco, which one of my servants produced. They long refused, but at length accepted the money I forced upon them. The proper price was five tungas, or about one and nine pence, but an Englishman is never satisfied until he has paid double.

Leaving this spot at daybreak, we again followed the Khooshk rivulet. The scene continued unchanged, excepting perhaps that not a human dwelling was visible. Large flocks of white sheep still sprinkled the hills on either side, but those hills were growing more arid and sandy as we advanced. The castle of Chummunie Bhayd is ruined and deserted. It presented a fine effect in the haze of the morning, guarding with its ragged ramparts the passage of the valley. A few miles further, are the ruins of another castle called Howzi Khaun, or "the cistern of the chief." In a plain near this ruin was fought, a few years since, the battle between Derveish Khaun, late chief of the Jumsheedees, and the Huzaruhs assisted by Mahomed Zemaun Khaun; Derveish Khaun was slain, and Mahomed Zemaun Khaun instated in his authority. Hence the death feud between the latter and the children of the former. The Meerzah assured me that at Khooshk he had seen within the Khaun's enclosure no less than twenty Toorcumuns waiting to purchase the slaves of Heraut as the Jumsheedees bring them in. One of these Toorcumuns was returning in disgust, and had joined my party. He had been offered only two slaves for his horse, a very fine one, which I have since purchased for 30 ducats, or 15*l.* Slaves, therefore, are tolerably cheap. The valley of Heraut, already nearly depopulated by the late Persian invasion, is thus daily deprived of the slender means possessed of recruiting its exhausted numbers. It is natural to inquire what can induce the Vuzeer to a measure of such insane folly. The question has long puzzled me. My late conversations with Peer Muhummud Khaun have, I believe, furnished a solution. The Vuzeer, previous to the Persian invasion, had possessed himself of all but the shadow of the supreme authority. In another month or two he would certainly have deposed Shauh Kaumraun, and have usurped his place. Such views, however suspended by circumstances, are never wholly relinquished; and Yar Muhummud Khaun, having his relations in every important post in the kingdom, is apprehensive only of the opposition of the tented tribes. These he conciliates at every risk of present damage to the state, as well as by profuse liberality. Every rare sword or other costly article that falls in his way he sends to these chiefs, and great part of their wealth being amassed in kidnapping, he winks at the practice, though sensible of its pernicious consequences.

Peer Muhummud Khaun was shewing me his sword yesterday. It is an Isfahaunie sabre, of rather coarse workmanship. I asked him what was the highest price he had ever known to be given for a blade. He said that the Vuzeer had possessed one purchased for 9,000 Heraut rupees, or about 300*l.*, and that he had given it to the Beegler Beeg of the Huzaruhs. That good blades are now very rare in Heraut, and perhaps confined to the royal treasury.

"What constitutes the goodness and value of a blade in your eyes?"

"It must be finely shaped, finely watered, and handsomely mounted."

"But do you subject it to no test?"

"None at all."

"And if it break in battle?"

"It is our destiny."

I explained to him the proofs to which we subject our blades in Europe, and also those employed in Hindoostan, and shewed him my own sword, making him observe its elasticity.

"But," said he, "it has no water?"

"No! It was made for use, and not for display; your weapons are toys, ours are instruments. We go to battle to fight, not to play; and would give nothing for a blade, however handsome, that would expose us to the mercy of an antagonist. I once proved one of your finely watered blades upon a steel helmet. It shivered at the first blow. Your own blade, you perceive, has no elasticity. It is bent, and at present useless. In battle, should it meet another sword, it would either turn in your hand like a piece of lead, or snap in halves."

In fact, I have given much attention to the subject, and am convinced that in this country nothing is known of the real excellence of a sabre. The grain of the Isfahannie blade is infinitely coarser than that of the Damascus blade. The former is very inferior in finish, has a dull, round edge, intended to resist the shock with armour, and has no elasticity. It is too

We now quitted the district called Baukiss, which may be Baudkhiss the Windy, or Baughiss, the Eastern name of Bacchus. The name of the succeeding district is Mowree,* and here we found the ruined castle, Kullah-i-Mowr, having still one wretched cell capable of sheltering a traveller. An extensive Kawreeze in the middle of the valley remains to attest its former high state of culture, and suggests the notion, that in other days the waters of the rivulet were expended in irrigation, ere they could reach Kullah-i-Mowr; at present this valley harbours not a living soul. We met not less than six or seven caravans of grain from Merv. At this castle commences the kingdom of Khaurism.

I was weak enough to yield to the entreaties of my people, and put up for the night in a reed jungle. We were scarcely settled, when one of them came to report having seen two horsemen mount the high ground above us, and after a careful scrutiny of our camp, retire. I sent a couple of my horsemen to reconnoitre, and prepared for the worst. They soon returned with news that the horsemen belonged

---

* It is curious to meet together the names of Bacchus and of his birth-place, Meroo or Meros. It is certain that this tract was overrun by Alexander and his armies; but Arrian and others place Mount Meros and Nusa between the Indus and Koophun or Soondi.—R.

to a caravan, and they brought one of them before me.

The night passed without accident, and starting with daylight, we tracked the Khooshk until its valley is lost in that of the Moorghaub, or Awb-i-Mowr. We then ascended the latter river to the largest Khail, or camp of Punj Deeh; passing the ruined vineyard and deserted fields of a once populous and cultivated district. My guide, the Birdler Beeg, who was once petty governor here, was now quite in his element. He sent a man ahead to apprize the Khetkhoda that a guest had arrived; and a horseman, well mounted, soon approached, quitted his saddle, and took my right hand in both his own, saying, "You are welcome; you are very welcome." We followed him to the Khail, where about three hundred black tents of the Yahmoot Toorcumuns were pitched, in the form of two hollow squares; and I soon perceived one of these tents walking bodily towards me. The Khetkhoda, a tall, sawny, miserably-looking fellow, here made me welcome with a second edition of hand-joining; and, spreading a handsome carpet on the earth, begged me to be seated, until my habitation should be ready. I did so, and soon perceived that we were surrounded by a crowd of curious faces, all decidedly Tartar, yet not generally uncomely. The softness of the eyes, opening with lids equally arched, gives a feminine, and therefore not unpleasing, expression to the countenances of the children, who are sometimes fair as Europeans.

Two or three little girls wore a red cap tricked with gold and silver ornaments, fantastic, but exceedingly becoming; but no adults of the fairer sex appeared. As the old Khetkhoda and several others understood Persian, we got on tolerably well together, and in about half an hour, the tent was ready for my reception, and I was escorted to it in due form.

I found the floor spread with fine carpets, the manu-

VOL. I.

facture of the Khail. One of these had almost the softness of velvet, and would have sold elsewhere for a high price. These Toorcumun tents are the most comfortable of dwellings in this serene climate. A house cannot be adapted to the vicissitudes of heat and cold which mark the year. Whereas by removing a portion of the felt covering, this tent is open to the air in summer; and in winter a fire lighted in the centre makes it the warmest of retreats, all the smoke rising through the skylight in the roof. Not to mention the great advantage of being able to migrate, dwelling and all, to a sunny or a sheltered spot.

An unforeseen difficulty now occurred. I required four days' supply of provisions for my people and cattle. Being a guest, I was forbidden to purchase these, and could not possibly accept them! I made my Meerza represent to the Khetkhoda that unless he would consent to regard me as a neighbour, and not a guest, I must quit his Khail and pitch elsewhere. After some demur, my request was complied with; and Summud Khaun, my steward, came to report his success in bargaining. I desired him not to bargain with men who were treating us so liberally, but to give them whatever they might demand. Presently afterwards in came Summud Khaun, and with a wink of the eye, asked whether it were my pleasure to give the price of a camel for a sheep?

"Certainly not," I replied.

"Then," said he, "you must allow me to bargain."

In fact, the scruple as to guestship once removed, each vied with the other to overreach me. Evening was now closing in; my host had left me, but Peer Muhummud Khaun still lingered. I had now satisfied myself, beyond any reasonable doubt, that he was sent to countermine me at Khiva, and that he had despatches from the Vuzeer to both the governor of Merv and the minister at Khiva. I therefore no longer hesitated to blight his hopes, or to deprive myself of the most agreeable of companions. I had allowed him to fancy himself a great and growing favourite, as by that means I was enabled to pump him the deeper; for I knew that it was worth his while to tell me all he knew, if he could by this means persuade me to take him on to Khiva. I now suddenly addressed him—

"Peer Muhummud Khaun, this is the Khiva territory,—I require your escort no farther. You will return to-morrow morning to Heraut."

He was thunderstruck; and it was long before he could utter a word. When he recovered, he pleaded hard, but to no purpose; excepting that I gave him a note for the British Envoy, begging that all his expenses might be made good to him, provided all should go right with my mission at Khiva; for I was still apprehensive that he would find means to send on his despatches.

CHAPTER II.

The Tent of Plenty of the Yahmoot—Gift-Horses—A Toorcumun Breakfast—The Sawny Old Khetkhoda—Peer Muhummud Khaun's Farewell—Extraordinary Power of Yar Muhummud Khaun over his Agents—Valley of the Moorghaub—Junction of the Khooshk Rivulet with that River—Visit from a Panther—Approach to Yoollataun—Reception there by the Governor—Distrust of the Relations between England and Russia—Presents—Muhummud Aumeen Beg—The Zunnuk—Departure—The old Cauzie of Yoollataun—Probable Origin of Col. Stoddart's Imprisonment at Bokhara—Hopes of the Slaves at Yoollataun—Approach to Merv—Want of Courtesy of the Governor in my Reception—The Jews of Merv and Meshed—Insulting Conduct of a Servant of the Governor—My first Turban—Visit to the Governor—Insulting Reception, its Origin and Motive—Preparations for the Passage of the Desert—Jew Merchants—Suspicious Circumstances—Conversation.

JANUARY 1st, 1840.—It was scarcely light, when I observed the curtain of my door moved from time to time, to admit a pair of curious eyes. I therefore threw it up, and soon had a full assembly of rustic figures, in lamb-skin caps, coarse woollen cloaks, and half boots of clumsy shape, secured with thongs of leather. Among the rest came two servants of the Merv governor, plain quiet-looking fellows, whose huge cylindric caps of black lamb-skin denoted their pretensions to rank. After due salutation the company was seated in a circle around the tent, and I observed that Birdler Beeg took a seat above the governor's people. He was here quite in his element; and his extreme good nature showed to advantage. He chattered alternately in Toorkish and in Persian. He grinned, he laughed, he asked whether the tents of plenty of the Yahmoot were not better than the house of famine of the Jumsheedee. The two cylindric-hatted gentlemen sate in profound silence, looking their dullest. I called for tea, and having but a single goblet, sent it in turn to the several guests as they were ranged. Presently, in came a Fuqueer, and with a merry countenance, and an abundance of compliment, asked for alms. I gave him a few tungahs, or silver coins, upon which he stood up and formally prayed for my prosperity, in which all present made the usual signal of joining, by presenting the spread hands in front of them, and then collecting from their beards the drops of grace supposed to fall in answer. " It is as the precious ointment which flowed down upon the beard, even Aaron's beard, and went unto the skirts of his raiment."

The Fuqueer then departed in great glee. Just as he reached the door, the clown sitting near it gave him a tremendous thump on the back, and a thunder-peal of laughter. This, in an English cottage, would have been sufficiently characteristic.

A tall fellow now insisted upon my acceptance of a horse; his neighbour pressed upon me another, and all begged I would step out and examine the offerings. After a thousand excuses, I was obliged to comply, and found no less than three fine horses waiting my acceptance. The owners mounting them, displayed their paces, and then again pressed them upon me. I replied that it was not the custom of my country to accept presents without making some return, and that I was a traveller, and unprovided with means. " Never mind," said the tall fellow, " you shall have my horse, and I will take nothing in return." " But," I said, " what am I to do with so many horses on a journey; horses are an encumbrance to a stranger?"

" But you are not a stranger. This is your home, and your country;" replied the sawny old Khet-khoda.

" How would it answer," insinuated Peer Muhummud Khaun, " to give me one of the horses?"

I replied that he must wait the result of my mission.

Finding it impossible to escape, I accepted one horse, and gave the owner a note to the Envoy at Heraut, begging him to give the Toorcumun an equivalent. The hospitality of Toorcumuns is a sacred form, in which the heart has no concern. They were well pleased with my arrangement; neither am I certain that but for some expectation of the kind, they would ever have been so free with their gifts. The Birdler Beeg was one of this tribe, and extremely anxious that I should form a favourable opinion of his people, as well as of his influence amongst them; and I have no doubt that he incited them to present their horses by his tales of British liberality. The horses presented were a huge chestnut of clumsy figure, which all my servants fell in love with, size being every thing in their eyes; a strong, well-compacted white horse, with dark points; and a delicately formed grey, about 15½ hands high, having an exquisite head and neck, and showy paces. The back sinews of this horse were so distant from the bone, that at first sight I pronounced them to be strained, and it was only after minutest scrutiny that I believed the Birdler Beeg's assurance, that this is a peculiarity of the breed, and a supposed excellence in the eyes of Toorcumuns. I selected this horse. We adjourned to my tent, and sate a while in discourse. The Toorcumun whose horse I had not taken was a little vexed. "I offered you," he said, "a much finer horse than the grey; but you refused him." "I am a traveller," I replied, "what could I do with so many horses?" He took up one of my pistols. "I have got a pair of flint and steel pistols, would you like to see them?" I assented, and he produced a miserable little pair of pocket pistols, which I well remembered to have been presented to Ubdoolla Sooltaun, one of the Jumsheedee chiefs. "Here," he said, slapping them down upon the carpet, with an assumption of frank generosity that was very amusing, "you shall accept these,—you shall." I declined, however, most decidedly, and just then breakfast was announced. It consisted of macaroni made in the Khail, not fluted, but rolled into broad thin cakes, and cut into thongs by the women, with their husbands' swords. It was stewed with kooroot and milk, and some of the sweet syrup of grapes. It was by no means unpalatable, but a huge wooden ladle, the sole article of the kind procurable, disconcerted all attempts on the part of Peer Muhummud Khaun, to eat it without treason to his magnificent beard. As I had a tea-spoon of my own, I contrived matters pretty well. After this, some stews of mutton and bread were produced. I then rose to take leave. A little boy was hanging about the Khetkhoda: "Is that," I inquired, "your young thing (Buchehha)?" "He is my son (pisr)," replied old Sawny. The distinction is very important in these countries. Another child was mounted upon the Khetkhoda's horse. Thinking this must also be his son, I was about to slip two ducats into the boy's hand, but asked first, "Is that also your son?" "Naugh!" grunted old Sawny, in evident perturbation. We proceeded. The Khetkhoda kept close to my side, and, watching his opportunity, brought his knee close to mine, and asked in a whisper, "What have you told to be given for the horse?" "What is he worth?" I inquired in return. "Hah!" said the fellow with an abrupt shy, "What is he worth: what is he worth?"

The Birdler Beeg coming up, whispered mysteriously that the agents of the Governor of Merv expected a present of at least a cloak. I excused myself as being a traveller, and at that moment utterly unprovided. I now begged the Toorcumuns not to accompany me farther, and took leave in due form, at a small stream. However, whilst our horses were drinking, I observed that the Khetkhoda was still present, and mysteriously whispering the Birdler

Beeg. The latter coming up, announced the purport to be a reminiscence of my intended gift to his child. "I do not perceive the child here," I replied, looking round. "No!" said the Khetkhoda, "but I can give him the money." I took out the two brightest ducats and presented them, saying they might serve as ornaments to his child's head. He perused them long, and with evident satisfaction. Something, distantly related to a grin, drew up the right corner of his mouth, contrasting oddly with his habitual sawny sneer. I saw that our friendship was nothing the less; but it was a strange commentary upon the supposed disinterestedness of these wild tribes.

Peer Muhummud Khaun rode very disconsolately at my side. "You have at length thrown off," he said, "your evil genius. You are as a man who has been haunted by an unclean spirit through the wilderness, and who, reaching at length to a place of fountains, by prayer and lustration, rids himself of the fiend." The simile was singularly apposite; Yar Muhummud Khaun had sent this man to be my evil spirit at Merv and Khiva. Had I not suspected his views, my ruin had been certain. A man of this kind, a creature of the Vuzeer, is believed to have contrived the plot to which Colonel Stoddart is still a victim. Peer Muhummud Khaun was eminently qualified for his part. Of the most gentlemanly address, the most pleasing and insinuating manners, he never for an instant forgot his place, but was always watchful and attentive. Then his intelligence supplied half the words my vocabulary wanted, and he seemed the very person requisite upon my forlorn expedition, to give me hints of the customs of the people with whom I was to dwell, and maintain decorum amongst the rest of the establishment. But there was one fatal drawback to all this,—he was the tool of the Yar Muhummud Khaun, Vuzeer of Heraut.

The fellow had contrived to gain such a share of my interest, that I found myself devising a thousand little schemes for retaining him, could I but purchase his allegiance, and make him my own by present liberality and future prospects. I remembered, however, too many instances of such attempts proving dead failures.* Whatever the means employed by the Vuzeer for securing his instruments, it had hitherto proved most effectual. They often hated him, they were assailed by hopes and prospects on the other side; yet they faithfully served him. Not an instance to the contrary had occurred, although very many such were pretended. In nothing did the genius of the man stand more pre-eminent than in this—that hated and regarded by his countrymen as a monster of iniquity, none dared to betray him; and whilst our Envoy could offer the most unlimited prospects of advancement for faithful service, and no promise of the Vuzeer, even when made, could be relied on, every attempt to win over to our side the instruments of the Vuzeer had been a failure. I had questioned Peer Muhummud Khaun upon this secret power of the Vuzeer. He said that ere he entrusted any agent, he got him over to his quarters, and made him swear solemnly upon the Koraun to be faithful to him; but I could not learn what particular solemnity rendered this oath upon the Koraun more binding than others, which the natives of the country are constantly breaking, nor was the explanation otherwise sufficient. It seemed, however, sufficiently certain, that Peer Muhummud Khaun would not have been entrusted with his present mission, were there any

* This subject has occupied much of my attention; and I am inclined to think that the extraordinary ascendance of the Vuzeer was maintained by the conviction he contrived by his agents to impress upon all classes, and which certainly was in operation from the hour of our arrival at Heraut, that the instant our treasure was expended he would exclude the mission from his walls; whilst this feeling prevailed, none would unreservedly embrace British interests. This note and its text were printed in 1841, published in 1843. I need not say that the tragedy has since been acted out, that as soon as Yar Muhummud Khaun had strengthened himself with British gold, he ejected the British mission from Heraut, and one time after murdered his master, Shauh Kamran, and seized the throne.

chance of his betraying trust. He had probably been chosen, because the Vuzeer had formerly injured him, the words of defiance had passed between them; so that it was easy for him to pass himself as a personal enemy of the Vuzeer.

As I bade Peer Muhummud Khaun farewell, I did not attempt to hide the regret it cost me. I told him that if inclined to serve the English faithfully and sincerely, the note I had given him to the Envoy would open to him the fairest prospects. But that we wanted acts, and not professions; that the latter could be purchased anywhere. I told him that his prospects would greatly depend upon my reception at Khiva. Should it prove unfavourable, I should be assured he had sent on the despatches, with which the Vuzeer had entrusted him.

My route lay along the left bank of the Moorghaub, and I crossed by a bridge the dry channel of the Khooshk, at its junction with the former river. The cause of this failure of its waters I do not know. The Moorghaub is here a deep stream of very pure water, about sixty feet in breadth, and flowing in a channel, mined to the depth of thirty feet in the clay soil of the valley. The banks are very precipitous, and fringed with tamarisk and a few reeds. The valley itself is, at Punj Deeh, about nine miles in breadth, but narrows as we advance. Here it is about three-fourths of a mile in breadth. On the east bank are sloping sandy hills, about 600 feet higher than the valley. On the west is the desert, a high sandy plain, overrun with low bushes and camel thorn, and extending to the mountain barrier of Persia. The valley of the Moorghaub has once been well cultivated, but is now from Punj Deeh to Yool-lataun utterly deserted, owing to the late distractions of the country. It abounds in pheasants, chuccores, and rock-pigeons. The panther and bear are also to be found. At long intervals are seen the ruins of buildings; but I observed not a black tent in the solitude. Towards evening I chose a spot for my camp amongst the brushwood, bordering the river, and excepting that the horses were occasionally frightened from their picquets by the sudden whirr of a pheasant, the night passed without accident.

Resuming my course with day-light, I passed by a good and much beaten road down the river valley. Scene as before. All the party are rejoicing to be rid of Peer Muhummud Khaun, who, whilst he made himself so especially agreeable to me, contrived to be hated by every individual of my suite. Instances of his meanness were now related, which to any one unacquainted with Asiatics, might well seem incredible. At evening I found a well-sheltered spot amongst the tamarisk trees, and settled there for the night. Two large fires were lighted, but darkness had scarcely fallen, when I heard a panther prowling close round the camp, with that mewling cry which I have so often heard from the tigress. It approached so near, that my people fled from it, and came to apprize me. I caught up my gun and a pistol, and went in search of the animal; but the darkness of the night, and density of the jungle baffled me. I therefore made my people light a third large fire, and keep up the blaze throughout the night. But notwithstanding all these precautions, I was prepared for some mischief to the cattle. My people lying close to the blaze of their fires were more secure. Until midnight the cries of this unwelcome visitor continued, and once during the night he again appeared, but morning broke without accident.

At sun-rise we pursued the course of the Moorghaub as before. My horse, generally remarkable for his steadiness, was starting at every leaf; it was evident that he had had a visit from the panther. In fact the creature approached him during the night so close, that he broke from his picquets, and I sprang out of my tent to his assistance. My new Yahmoot horse was led by the groom, riding a Yaboo, or baggage galloway: but although the path would admit of but one horse abreast, nothing can persuade this proud creature to follow in the steps of the Yaboo. We met a caravan at every third mile, laden with wheat and barley from Merv. They take back in exchange slaves of both sexes, chiefly from Heraut.

As I approached Yoollataun, the desert aspect of the country was a little broken by symptoms of recent culture. Three women, one of them mounted on horseback, and all unveiled, met me. No male was at hand to protect them. They have a singular complexion, ruddy, but not fair. Their features are far from agreeable, more particularly their eyes. But the specimens I have seen are not sufficient. After some farther advance, a few mud walls became visible, and amongst them here and there a black Tartar tent. The road was now every where entangled amongst sluices and canals of running water. The Khails, or moveable villages of black tents increased, and the valley opened widely on either side, being in fact a large plain bounded by the desert. I sent forward my Toorcumun to acquaint the governor of the district, Muhummud Aumeen Beeg, of my approach: and on drawing nearer, five or six horsemen, sent by the Beeg, met and saluted me. We passed large Khails of black tents, whose male inhabitants lined the road to stare upon us. One of these, approaching, kissed my hand, and informed me that he had been a servant to Colonel Stoddart. His name I regret I did not commit to paper.

I was now close to Muhummud Bumeen's place. A few low walls, two or three Toorcumun tents, and a routie of blue cotton cloth, formed the palace of the rustic worthy. Outside I observed a party of horse awaiting my arrival. They advanced as I drew near, and I learned on enquiry that the governor was amongst them. The Birdler Beeg informed me, that it is the fashion here to shake hands without dismounting; but observing that the governor had his hand upon the pommel, as if expecting from me a similar movement, I drew up my horse and alighted. The Khethoda of the Khail was there, a venerable man. The Beeg always gave him precedence. We embraced very lovingly, touching alternately the right and left breasts,—a species of exercise infinitely absurd to the beholder, when there are twenty or thirty persons to be embraced in succession. I got off for the present with two. We remounted, and rode together to the mansion. Muhummud Aumeen Beeg was mounted upon a very beautiful bay Yahmootie horse, powerful, active, and full of fire. The path being narrow he abandoned it to me, and spurred over the uneven ground, proud of showing his horsemanship. One of his servants was almost equally well mounted upon a grey. I afterwards ascertained that he had purchased the two horses for 70 and 60 Tilla's, 560 and 480 Co.'s Rupees, or 56*l*. and 48*l*. They were horses of considerable size, and are the finest I have ever seen in eastern lands

I dismounted at the door of a black tent prepared for my reception, and was ushered in by the Beeg and Khetkhoda. A comfortable fire of wood embers burned in the centre. My host insisted upon occupying the lowest seat, and said, "Khoosh aumudeed," (you are welcome,) several times, and then added in Toorkish, "It is all the Persian I know." I replied, that it was a very pleasant sentence in the mouth of a friend. Bread, raisins, and sugar were now brought, and succeeded by some enormous melons, for which Merv is celebrated, and which I found very refreshing. One or two of the party spoke Persian, so that I got on pretty well. I explained, that the object of my mission was the establishment of friendship between the English and Khivan governments; described to them the state of Europe, and the nature of our jealousy of the aggressions of Russia. An old man present asked, "Have you ever been at war with Russia?" When I replied in the negative, he shook his head. This suspicion of our jealousy being a pretence, originates with the Vuzeer Yar Muhummud Khaun, who, anxious to prevent an alliance between the British and Khiva, has taken this method of disconcerting it.

Previous to my arrival here, I had been in some perplexity about the presents I had in charge, viz. three rifles and a sabre. I thought one of these must needs be intended for the governor of Merv; and if so, none was left for Muhummud Aumeen Beeg, for whom, nevertheless I had a strong notion that something had been sent. Having no means of solving my perplexity, I determined to let the notes explain themselves, and accordingly gave the Beeg his letter from Major Todd, and another sent him by the prince Muhummud Yoosuph. Both were carried off to be read and translated to the Beeg, whilst I continued to chat with those left in the tent. Presently the Beeg returned, bringing with him an old gentleman, the Cauzie or Judge of Yoollataun. The excessive politeness of this worthy, assured me that he had some mischief in view. The Beeg's face also was full of busy importance, and a kind of dogged resolution that boded me no good. The Cauzie produced the letters I had just delivered. The Beeg desired him to read them aloud. He did so, and I was pleased and relieved to find that one of the rifles was intended for Muhummud Aumeen Beeg. "Now," said the Cauzie after a deep pause, "the Envoy says he has sent the Beeg a rifle. Where is the rifle? Let us see the rifle." It was evident that all present thought I had intended to defraud the Beeg. I could scarcely forbear laughing, but calmly ordered the gun to be produced. The Beeg seized it as if in terror that it might yet escape him. He tore off the cloth case, and examined it with intense scrutiny. When he came to the lock and found a matchlock, he muttered, as if he thought I had palmed off upon him some inferior article.

On my first arrival at the tent, whilst sitting in a circle with my entertainers, a servant had brought in my holster pistols, and some other articles, which I had hastily made him carry away, lest he should disturb the company. This had evidently excited the suspicion of the Beeg; for he now said, "the prince Muhummud Yoosuph informs me that Major Todd has sent me a brace of pistols; but I do not see them." "His information was not good," I replied; "the Envoy had intended to send you a brace of pistols instead of a matchlock, but Cauzie Moollah Hussun assured him that they would not be valued, as they were destitute of ornament." "The Cauzie said very wrong: there is nothing we value more." I replied that I would write for a brace for him, and that if there were any other respect in which my government could oblige him, I trusted he would let me know.

Muhummud Aumeen Beeg is a short, stout, round-faced Oozbeg, of the family of the reigning Khaun Huzurut. He is said to be a worthy man, and well inclined toward the English. He is very hospitable, but full of peculiarities characteristic of country life, and is in fact an Oozbeg squire. He gave me the option of having my provisions sent me raw, or dressed in his kitchen. To save him trouble, I preferred the former arrangement. I slept comfortably in the Oozbeg tent. In the morning some of the wretched loops and buttons of my Afghaun attire having given way, I sent Nizaum to get them mended, and this being accomplished, desired him to call the tailor to be rewarded. He was horrified at the idea. "It's a woman," said he. "Well then let her send some one for the present." Off went Nizaum, but soon returned with the lady herself, who came smirking and half covering a face, which, sooth to say, was not worthy of the pains. I gave her a ducat, which quite reconciled her to having borne the glance of an unbelieving eye. She had scarcely gone when Birdler

Beeg came breathless with haste to ask what in the world I had been at with the Zunnuk. Zunnuk is the contemptuous epithet for woman, the feminine of mannikin.

Breakfast was brought, and having discussed it, I prepared to depart. I repeated my proffer of writing to Heraut for any thing that would please the Beeg. He replied, I require nothing but a brace of flint and steel pistols, rather short in the barrels. This was the exact description of my own weapons, which he had been overhauling, and which he still persisted in thinking intended for himself. I would have taken leave of him at the door; but he insisted upon escorting me a fursuk, and off we started.

Perceiving that the old Cauzie was a man of consequence in the household, I had been paying his child great attention; and now took the opportunity of slipping five gold pieces into his hand. The old gentleman was delighted, and as I have since heard, proclaimed my praises at the top of his gamut.

Colonel Stoddart's old servant also accompanied us, following me to some distance after I had taken leave of the Beeg. I fell into conversation with him, and found it to be his firm conviction that the imprisonment of Colonel Stoddart, was owing to a letter written by the Vuzeer Yar Muhummud, to the Ummeer of Bokhara. This man has since visited Bokhara with the view of effecting Colonel Stoddart's release. His opinion jumps with a conviction I have long felt. It is well known that terms of defiance had passed between Colonel Stoddart and the Vuzeer, which the latter was the last man in the world to forget or forgive. An outward reconciliation had taken place, but such could but serve to inflame, by suppressing the resentment of such a fiend as Yar Muhummud. It would appear also that the Vuzeer, in addition to his letter to the Ummeer, sent a man of his own in company with Colonel Stoddart; and to this man's advice is attributed all the evil consequences that fell upon Colonel Stoddart, whom he had persuaded to believe him an attached follower.

In pursuing this conversation the man winked at me, and said in a low voice that he could not speak his sentiments before the Birdler Beeg. I made the Birdler Beeg ride on, and asked why? He replied, "He is a bad man. I have had much dealing with him." I demanded facts: but he would say no more. There seems to be amongst Asiatics a natural hatred and jealousy of one another, which will not suffer them to rest so long as by any means they can injure one another's reputation or interests. The Birdler Beeg I knew to be a rogue of the first water in money matters; but although I have by cross-examination made him confess that he has a letter from the Vuzeer to the Mehtur, and that the former gave him twenty ducats, which assuredly he would not have bestowed without hope of profit, yet, as the Birdler Beeg has received already six times as much from us, and has hope and promise of more in case of proving useful, the motive to treachery is not easily conceived, excepting indeed that there is a natural bias that way in all Asiatic minds.

I find that my arrival caused many delusive hopes amongst the slaves of my host's household. The notion that I was on a mission for the freedom of all the captives at Khiva had got abroad, and fearing that the slaves should seek my protection, their masters had them chained until my departure. Summud Khaun, amongst others, saw a poor fellow of his own tribe, whom some time ago I had unwittingly affronted, and who now implored me to release him. The case was as follows. We were spending the day at Capt. Pottinger's tent in the valley of Herant. A young man of very ridiculous appearance attracted notice by some very clumsy action in removing plates, &c. I asked who he was, and Summud Khaun replied, a S'hugzye, i.e. Ishaukzye, or son of Isaac; but the word in his mouth sounded so like Sugzye, or

Dog's son, that I repeated it with a shout of laughter. I soon found I had done wrong. Summud Khaun, who is also an Ishaukzye, was seriously hurt and offended; and I determined never again to joke upon patronymics so long as I should remain in this country. I now assured Summud Khaun that I would not forget the poor fellow at a more seasonable moment; but that at present to release captives would seriously prejudice my mission; as, should an idea that such was the object of my mission reach Khiva, the whole population would be in alarm, their wealth consisting chiefly of slaves. I desired him and my other servants, therefore, to discountenance this notion to the utmost of their power.

Continuing to pass over the sandy plain, I arrived shortly after noon, near the castle of Merv, where resides the governor. I had the night before sent to warn him of my approach. I now despatched a man to certify him of my arrival. Yet he suffered me to approach the castle without any symptom of a greeting. I therefore determined upon shaming him by pitching outside, and chose a spot for the purpose. In the course of half an hour, a party of horsemen approached, headed by three confidential servants, whom the governor has the impudence to call his Vuzeers. They saluted me, apologised for delay, saying that their master was abroad when my messenger arrived, and begged permission to escort me to a Seraie prepared for my reception. I replied that they found me pitching my tent, under the idea that I was not welcome to the Bae. That I could still make myself very comfortable here, if the governor were less than friendly in his feeling. That I had sent a messenger the night before, and another this morning, so that the Bae could not fail of being apprized of my arrival, and any tardiness of hospitality must therefore be imputed to his disposition.

The messengers in reply, entreated me not to disgrace their master by pitching outside; assured me no messenger had arrived the night before;

and that the messenger of this morning had found the governor superintending the work of a canal. It was not my object to drive matters to extremities; I therefore mounted and accompanied the messengers. A large crowd of people had collected to gaze. The horsemen of the escort, to the number of thirty, galloped to and fro, flourishing and firing their arms. A black tent was hastily erected within an enclosure for my accommodation. In the mean while I sate in a routie of canvass. The governor did not make his appearance; otherwise, there was much shew of respect and attention.

The usual repast was set before me—bread, raisins, melons, and apples. Evening closed, the governor had not appeared, and I felt that I was slighted. Birdler Beeg now entered, saying that one thing would be expected of me. That as the Bae had lately lost his brother, the late minister of Khiva, it would be proper for me to pay the first visit, and say the fat'h or blessing. I objected that this custom could not apply to guests, far less to strangers, since the one *had* actually called, and the other could not be supposed to know any thing of the family afflictions of his entertainer. That, nevertheless, as I would not on any account seem to fail in any token of attention or good will, I would humour the fancy of the Bae.

I had sent for Moolla Haroon, a Jew merchant, who was to cash my bills on Merv. He now came, and I had some chat with him. He had entertained the Missionary Joseph Wolff, in his passage through Merv, and spoke of the kindness he had heard designed for his nation by British benevolence. The subject is always a touching one. The condition and history of this people have deep claims upon public sympathy; and just now they have been subjected at Meshed to a fresh and fearful persecution. A rumour during the Mohurrum was spread, that the Jews had killed a dog in ridicule of Hussun and Hosein, nephews of the Prophet, whose death is at that time celebrated.

The consequence was a massacre, and the complete spoliation of the Jews, their wives and daughters being sold as slaves. It appears that Muhummud Shauh has sent a nobleman to Meshed to order restitution of the plunder. Alas! who shall restore their insulted honour to the wives and daughters of Israel, or their blood, spilt in the streets of Meshed! Several of the Jews of Meshed had fled hither and found protection. Haroon described the governor of Merv as a just man, but admitted that he was no friend to the English. Whilst he was yet engaged in conversation with me, some person came to the door and called him, and almost instantly after, entering, struck him on the head and carried him out. I was extremely angry, but had sufficient reflection to refrain from using my sword. I called my people, and ordered them to ascertain from whence this outrage came, that I might quit so inhospitable a roof if necessary. They brought the Jew back, and with him an officer of the governor, who assured me, the offender had acted without orders, and that he, the officer, had instantly rebuked him. I was far from satisfied with such an excuse, but, sending for Birdler Beeg, bade him inform the governor of the outrage committed upon his guest, and insist that the offender should be punished. He replied, that he was ready to obey, but knew that the governor, on getting my message, would decapitate the offender. That he was quite certain the outrage did not proceed from the Bae himself. This assurance, ill-founded as I have now cause to believe it, calmed me for the time. I know the horrible barbarity of native punishment, and could not risk the life of a fellow creature upon such a quarrel; so I consented to drop the matter, until some fresh shew of discourtesy should render it incumbent upon me to seek redress.

Next morning, after having wound on, with aid of my Meerza, my first turban, being about twenty mortal yards of white muslin, to which I verily thought there was no end, I mounted my horse to call upon the Bae.* I entered the mud castle of Merv, and found a black tent pitched with the enclosure. In this were seated three Oozbeg gentlemen; but, as I had never seen the Governor, I was at first at some loss to distinguish him. He sat lowest. They saluted me by taking my hands between their own, and then motioned me to the highest seat. Bread and a mixture of syrup and ghee were brought, and I ate a few morsels. My next neighbour, a greybeard, acted interpreter, and commenced in a strange way, by asking my age. I stared. He repeated the question. Not understanding enough of the manners of this barbarous country to be prepared to take offence slightly, I informed him. He next asked my name. I again stared, but answered the question. I did not perceive, until afterwards, that these queries had been put designedly, under the impression that I was hotheaded, like my countrymen, and would commit myself by some act of resentment, that should place me in the power of my enemies;—a little piece of service, for which I feel gratefully indebted to Yar Muhummud Khaun. It was thus that he contrived Colonel Stoddart's captivity.

They then inquired the purport of my mission, which I explained; and afterwards whether the English and Russians had ever been at war. I replied in the negative. Whether we spoke the same language. No! the languages were entirely dissimilar. "Pray," inquired the Bae, "what is the English for Doost?" "Friend." Upon this the Bae spoke in Toorkish, and as it seemed to me, was calling in question the accuracy of my reply "What," I demanded, "is the Russian for Doost?" He answered "Braat'h." I therefore easily saw through the snare laid for me. The governor had expected me to translate Doost by our word "brother." Had I done so, I should have been proclaimed a spy, for no assurances would after-

* Pronounced always "Boy."

wards have sufficed to persuade my enemies that the languages of England and Russia differ. Several incidents that had occurred at Heraut previous to my departure, enabled me to trace this little stratagem to Yar Muhummud Khaun.* I did not until evening know, that his despatches had arrived at Merv before me, carried by a Toorcumun, who passed me in the night.

The party repeated several times the Khoosh Aumudeed, but accustomed to the long formal visits of the Herauties, I did not take the hint to move. I observed the governor whisper Birdler Beeg, who rose and looked at me. I looked inquiringly at my next neighbour, who had the insolence to say " Rooksut," a form of dismissal applied only to inferiors. I walked out of the tent in no good humour, but knew not how to resent the affront, from ignorance of the habits of the country. I therefore deemed it wiser not to appear sensible of it, than to make myself ridiculous by any impotent ebullition of indignation.

I sent my Meerza to the Khaloofauh, a priest of great reputation, with a polite message, saying, that I had brought him, from the British Envoy at Heraut, a beautiful Book of Prayers, in Arabic, which I begged him to send a trustworthy person to receive. He sent accordingly his eldest son, a fine youth of about twenty-two years, to whom I delivered the exquisite little volume. In return he invited me to dine with him the following day.

I was now busied with preparations for crossing the desert. As water must be carried sometimes six marches, or even ten, when the wells happen to be dry, camels are requisite for any number of persons exceeding four. I hired accordingly six fine camels, at two Tillas (about fourteen shillings) each, pur-

---

* I had heard Major Todd, at Heraut, mention to Yar Muhummud this word Braat'h as one of the few Russian words having an almost parallel meaning in England. I cannot answer for the correctness of the assertion.

chased ten skins of water, and laid in a store of Jowarr for twelve days, at the rate of 12lb. for each horse daily, there being no grass in the desert. I took bread ready made, and plenty of tea, sugar, and raisins for my servants. I here exchanged my Jumsheedee cap for a cylindric hat of black lambskin, such as is worn by the Oozbeg.

Determining that no personal pique should prevent me from conciliating, as far as possible, the governor of Merv, whose good offices it was of importance to secure, I purchased here a handsome Persian sabre and Toorkish firelock, which I sent as presents to him. My Meerza came back most gaudily attired in a robe of honour, formed of sarsnet, covered with broad flowers of gold and silver thread. The material resembles kinkaub, but is said to be made in Russia, and is brought from Bokhara. It is often very handsome.

Finding, here, that there is not the slightest prospect of negotiating bills at Khiva, I have been endeavouring to raise a little money here. But the Jew, Moolla Haroon, who was to have assisted me, dares not, without the governor's permission, and the governor will not grant it, upon the plea that Haroon is dishonest and a beggar; I am therefore obliged to use the services of an old rogue whom he employs and favours, Ibraheem or Ismael by name. He commenced by making difficulties; but at length promised me 200 ducats. I conversed with him whilst the money was coming. He said he had lost all his property in the last massacre at Meshed. He then prayed for the success of the British arms. I told him we had no longer any enemies; that all was now as we could desire. He laughed, and immediately added, "May your sabre be prosperous." Knowing that he would not dare use this language in an open tent, unless assured of the support of the governor, I began to feel seriously uneasy. He now complained of his condition, to which I replied by the reports I had

had of the justice of the governor. " Very true," he said, " but these people account us infidels. They regard you in the same light. Don't you wish *this name* were for ever extinct?" " What name?" I inquired in surprise. " The name of Muhummud," he replied in a low cautious voice, fixing his eyes upon mine. I saw the extreme peril of my position, and that this old fellow had been sent to pump some mischief out of me, or to entangle me in my talk. " That is a bad speech of yours." I replied, and immediately changed the conversation. But I confess I have not so easily got rid of my uneasiness, to find myself so surrounded with spies and other miscreants of the governor.

A young Jew now entered, of the most prepossessing countenance, features beautifully regular, and an eye corresponding in beauty of form and in lustre, the most clear and guileless that could be conceived. I looked upon him with much interest. This was a son of Israel. How lovely must not her daughters be! This was one of that scattered and persecuted race, erst the chosen of Heaven, and now the scorn of the World. The young man, as he seated himself, said, pointing to the old man, "This is my father;" and the old man replied, " This is my son." I believed neither; and my suspicions were at once awakened towards the youth, in whom I was disposed to feel so lively an interest, yet it was impossible to meet his eye with distrust. A mystery there was, unexplained; but its nature I could not conjecture. When I asked on what terms I was to have the gold, the young man refused to make any; saying, that it was quite sufficient to have done me a service. " But what," I inquired, " do you know of me?" " We know that the English are everywhere kind to the Jews, and we have heard that your people are striving to collect together our scattered race, to restore them to their kingdom."

I have met with deceit in so many forms, that I am not easily duped. I was on this occasion particularly jealous of any emotion, because I believed the old Jew to be acting a dishonest, if not a treacherous part towards me; and the young man had voluntarily identified himself with the senior, by calling him his father, when I felt certain no such relationship subsisted. Yet I could not see here the object of deceit, where I was the person to be obliged, and had no prospect of serving either of the Jews. If they hoped to win my confidence to the betrayal of any secret, their labour was lost, as I had no secret to betray. I replied, that the English did indeed feel a strong interest in all relating to the Jews. That many of our people devoted their lives to the good of this persecuted race. That in England we granted them all the rights of free citizens, including a share in offices of state and legislation.* That there, they form a most respectable and powerful body, and are amongst the richest of mankind. That we believe the Jewish Scriptures, and that Jesus Christ was of the house of David, and of the family of Israel. I assured him, that his brethren should never repent any service rendered to the English. That our views in these countries were quite free from guile. That we desired neither territory nor to promulgate our opinions by the sword. That we wished to see good faith and justice prevail, and security of life and property, and should use to this end the utmost influence of our example; but that we had no views of conquest or self-aggrandisement. That these countries were not worth our acceptance, and that our empire was already too extensive. That our views being such as I declared, it was the interest of every creature, whether Jew, Muhummudan, or Hindoo, to aid us and make much of us.

* I reprint this, as it appeared in the first edition. The reader will remember that I left England a boy of sixteen years, and had been living mostly in the Jungles since.

CHAPTER III.

Jew Merchants—Their estimation at Merv—Visit to the Khaloofauh—Atmosphere of Merv—The Son of the Soofie Ool Islaum—Dinner—Ignorance of the state of Europe—Gifts—The Gift Horse—Visit from the Governor, Nyaz Muhummud Bae—Nature and Properties of a Gift in Eastern Lands—Saleh Muhummud—My Prepossession in his Favour—Persian Ambassador to Khiva—Merv—Departure from its miserable and inhospitable Plain—Aspect of the ancient Site—Slave Caravans—Condition of the Victims—Tooreumun and Oozbeg Women—Economy of a Tooreumun Tent—Objection to too much Bosom—Preference for broken-in Partners of the Yoke—Other Tooreumun Habits—A Day's March in the Wilderness of Kara Kootu—Landmarks—Sagacity of Camels—Instance of the Excessive Cold at Cabul—Tooreumun Notions of the Glory of the Heels—Aspect of this Wilderness.

NEXT morning (for this conversation passed in the evening) the Jews brought me a shawl and several cloaks, etc. The price demanded was absurdly small, not above a third of that charged at Heraut. I remarked this to the Jews. The reply was, "We have told you, according to promise, exactly how much these articles cost us, and we never lie." It is indeed a singular fact, that the Jews in these parts have a character for truth, which gives their word more weight than the oath of a Moosulmaun. "At Heraut," I said, "this shawl, for which you ask eight Tillas, would cost thirty." "Yes!" replied the old Jew, "and we were about to send it to Heraut." "No! no such thing," interrupted the youth, "the gentleman has heard the price. He shall have it for that, or if he likes to make us some trifling per centage for profit, well and good." It was a singular and novel position in which I found myself. The absurdly small price asked was sufficient assurance of the sincerity of the Jews. It is true, they had nothing to apprehend in trusting an Englishman's honour; but they might have asked double the sums they placed upon their goods, and still have got the credit of dealing honestly by me. When I had selected such articles as were requisite for the Tosheh Kaneh, I placed a handsome per centage on the amount, that they might not be losers.

At noon I mounted my horse and rode over to the Khaloofauh's abode. I had a rare specimen of this abominable plain, passing through an atmosphere of dust that almost stifled me. My road lay through the Bazaar of low huts, which constitutes the present city of Merv. I issued from thence into the plain of deep fine sand, shewing not in the whole of its wide extent of some three thousand square miles a blade of any herb, far less the leaf of any tree, but raked up by the lightest wind, until the sky is blotted out by the dust. I found the Khaloofauh's black tent pitched on the banks of a sluice from the main canal. On entering, the inmates rose to receive me I was greeted first by the son of the Soofie ool Islaum, and afterwards by the Khaloofauh. The former is a guest of the latter. The Soofie ool Islaum, a man of very extensive power in the spiritual world, had conferred the title of Khaloofauh upon the father of the present incumbent. The son of the Soofie, persecuted by Muhummud Zemaun Khaun, and forced to fly from Khooshk, has found refuge here, and is treated with the highest consideration.

After some discourse, water and a basin were brought round, and we washed our hands, drying them, as usual, on our handkerchiefs. Then a filthy cloth of chintz, greased to the consistence of leather, was spread on the ground before us. It is considered thankless to wash from a table cloth the stains of former banquets, or to suffer a crumb to be lost.

Upon the table cloth metallic trays were set, containing pilaus, hot and very greasy. Tucking up my right sleeve, I set to work, spilling half the rice into my lap, and making little way against the practised fists and elbows of the priests. As for the Khaloofauh, he shewed himself a man of might in the mysteries of the table, tearing large handfuls of mutton from the bone, as a bear might claw the scalp from a human victim, and plunging elbow-deep into the hot and greasy rice. Seeing how little progress I made, he said, laughing, we have a proverb, " that you should never spare the cates of the Derveish. They come from heaven, you know, and cost nothing."

The two sons of the Khaloofauh were the only attendants. This, I find, was ordered as a compliment. It recalled sundry remembrances of the patriarchal histories. At length even the Khaloofauh's arm waxed faint, and his jaw wagged more slowly; and then, with fists greased above the wrists, we sat waiting for the water which was to laugh at the slush upon our fingers, and eventually be absorbed, with a large mass of highly-scented mutton fat and gravy, by our handkerchiefs, haunting us for the rest of the day, with the stale smell of pilaus. And then we all joined in the fat'h, or grace, and swept the descending benediction off our beards.

Conversation ensued; questions regarding Europe were asked and answered. The existence of more than one European nation was a novel idea. When I assured the company that there were some thirteen, the least far more powerful than the king of Persia, I was heard with civility, but probably with very little credence. As the British had entered Candahar from the South, it was scarcely possible to persuade them that London, as they term England, lies not in that direction, but North North West.

The son of the Soofie is a handsome and gentlemanly man, and far better informed than the generality of his countrymen. I explained to him the system of British policy in Asia, and the objects of my present mission. These are quite incomprehensible to most of those in whose society I am thrown. They cannot understand two nations, both called Christian, both Feringees, who have never been at war, becoming in Asia, the one invader, the other benefactor of a Mahomedan power.

In this country of Tartar caps, the turban is confined to the priests, and is small and ungraceful, being a tight thong of muslin, wound upon a cap fringed with black lambskin, which gives it a singular appearance.

After dinner, a chogah, or cloak of camel's hair, was placed before me on a charger by one of the Khaloofauh's sons, being designed as an offering of hospitality; and the Khaloofauh informed me, that the son of the Soofie had a horse for my acceptance outside. This was a hint to take leave. The Soofie's son was too holy a man to move from his place, but the Khaloofauh saw me to the door, and followed me outside, where a fine-looking grey horse was held by a groom, awaiting my acceptance. This was led before me to my abode. I fancied it had rather a lame gait, but it was in high spirits, and extremely frisky. I had been previously informed of the intended gift, and it was hinted to me, that as it might prove an encumbrance to my march, the Khaloofauh would send it for me to Herant; where it would a second time serve as a gift, and greatly multiply the Soofie's credit for liberality. As, however, Major Todd had already too many of these wretched gift-horses, and Birdler Beeg's tit had broken down, I disappointed the holy man by taking on the horse.

The governor, Nyaz Muhummud Bae, had expressed his intention to return my call, and was now announced. Impoliteness is difficult to an Englishman; and I several times detected myself offering the surly old bear more attention than he deserved. We sat together at the upper end of the tent in profound silence, which I broke by some indirect remarks and questions. The Bae did not, I think, utter above two words during the interview. I had called for tea, and there being some delay in serving it, and the fellow becoming fidgetty, he was so impolite as to issue orders himself for it. He then rose without any salutation, and marched to the door. I, of course, condescended him none.

My Meerza now received a message from the Khaloofauh requesting his attendance, and on his return asked mysteriously whether I had written to the British Envoy to inform him of the Soofie's gift. Finding that I had done so, he begged, in the name of the Khaloofauh, that I would not entrust the note to his particular friend and guest, Saleh Muhummud, but send it to him. I gave the note accordingly. Then the Meerza whispered, "What have you valued the horse at?" "Why do you ask?" "The Khaloofauh is anxious to know." "What do you think it worth?" I said. "Forty ducats." "Very well, I have said forty ducats." Off the old Meerza trudged to deliver the note and the information. Such is the nature of a gift amongst this people. It is as the meat we generously fling to the ocean with a large barbed hook in the centre. Such, too, is the friendship and good faith between them. Saleh Muhummud, son of the principal Cauzie at Heraut, a particular gentlemanly young man, had extolled to the skies the Khaloofauh and Soofie's son. But they could not trust him to deliver a note, from which they expected profit. They were right, too; for his father, the old Cauzie, would certainly have taken his per-centage. This youth, Saleh Muhummud, so pleased me by his intelligence and alacrity, that I have begged Major Todd to send him to me at Khiva, if he thinks Government will sanction to him a suitable salary. It seems to me that I could make important use of him in sounding others, and gathering the information requisite to enable me to steer with security.

I learned at Merv two facts of importance. First, that the Persian ambassador has just passed through Merv in great state, charged with costly presents for the Khaun Huzurut. Secondly, that Peer Muhummud Khaun, whom I dismissed at Punj Deeh, has actually sent on to the governor of Merv, by the hand of a Toorcumun, the despatches he received from Yar Muhummud Khaun. All this bodes me no good.

Merv was one of the most ancient cities of Asia. It was situated in the plain, about twelve miles east of the little Bazaar which at present bears its name, and was watered by a canal from the Moorghaub, or Awb-i-Mowr. It was founded by fire-worshippers, of whose fort, called Kullah Ghubbah, there are yet remains. And it long formed a portion of the Persian empire, whose boundary on the east was the river Oxus. Its vicinity to this boundary, and its disjunction from the inhabited parts of Persia by wide deserts, must have early rendered it obnoxious to molestation from the Toorkish and other tribes, and Merv has probably changed masters as often as any city in the world. Latterly, as the Persian dominions have shrunk upon their heart, Merv has always belonged either to the Toorks or to some of the petty principalities of the neighbouring mountains. It has within a few years been wrested from Bokhara by the Khaun of Khiva, and forms one of the most important districts of Khaurism. During the misrule and anarchy of the last sixty years, the ancient dam of the Moorghaub was neglected and carried away. The city, in consequence, became uninhabitable, and was utterly abandoned. The dam is again set up, and the lands are brought under culture, but the ancient site continues a deserted ruin. The present Merv is an assemblage, upon the Moorghaub, of about one hundred mud huts, where a considerable Bazaar is held. The entire waters of the Moorghaub are dispersed over the sandy plain for the purposes of irrigation. This profusion of water renders the soil productive; but it has not strength to bear any but the poorer kinds of grain. The plain is perhaps an area of sixty miles by forty, or 2400 square miles, running on every side into the desert. About 60,000 Tooreumuns are said to live upon this plain, chiefly as cultivators. And the revenue in land and other taxes amounts to about 300,000 Tillas, or 210,000 Co.'s Rupees, or about 21,000*l*.

The trade passing through Merv is very considerable; Merv connecting Bokhara and Persia, Khiva and Afghanistaun. Indeed the position of Merv is so important, that it never will be long abandoned, and might, with judicious care, rapidly rise from its dust into wealth and consequence.

My arrangements completed, I bade farewell to Merv with no wish ever again to behold it. I had not proceeded a mile, ere I discovered that the gift-horse of the holy man was dead lame, of an old and incurable strain. We crossed the dry channel of the Moorghaub, and proceeded by a well-beaten road in direction East North East. I soon perceived, upon the Eastern horizon, the ruins of the ancient Merv, of which a mosque and several forts form the principal features. The city is said to have been smaller than Heraut, i. e. less than four miles in circuit. From this distance I might have estimated it at eight times the dimensions. The fact seems to be, that several sites have in turn been occupied and abandoned, retaining each some vestige of its former fortifications; and these lying, in a continuous line, give an impression of vastness to the deserted site. I regarded it with much interest, and regretted the haste which prevented me from visiting it. On the horizon around us were many tuppahs, or artificial mounds, of considerable elevation. These are supposed to have been forts.

I was glad to quit this wretched, though much vaunted plain, and enter the desert, which is a paradise in comparison. To the north of the ancient city is said to exist the tomb of the hero Ulp Urslaun,* one of the most remarkable characters in Asiatic history. I could, however, learn no particulars relative to it. At our halting ground, I discovered that we have two caravans in company. They had brought grain from Khiva, and are returning thither laden with slaves, many of whom are natives of Heraut. The whole number, men, women, and children may be about twenty-five. Some of the women are very decently clad, and seemed to have been in good circumstances until seized for this inhuman traffic. One poor female was mounted astraddle upon a camel behind her master. Her child, an infant, was lodged in a grain bag hanging from the saddle. This poor wretch has an inhuman master, and is the picture of misery. Her master has lost two children to the Persians, and is trying by this horrible trade to raise money for the purchase of their freedom. The other women put the best face upon their condition. Their masters have no object in treating them harshly. At night they share with them their blankets and cloaks, and in the day-time I often observe the women laughing with their captors. The children also, having plenty to eat and nothing to do, probably rather enjoy themselves. But the men are chained together by the throats at night, so that rest is scarcely possible, whilst the contact of the frozen iron with their skin must be a torture. For them also no carriage is found, they walk the whole way, every step of which renders their captivity more hopeless. These poor fellows look very wretched, and unfortunately, any attempt to render their lot less terrible, would expose them to suspicion and to fresh hardships. My heart is full of heaviness, when I think of all the heart-rending misery of which this system is the cause.

* I write this name (generally spelt Alp Arslan) as it is pronounced, the rather, that, knowing only the incorrect spelling of the name, I could learn nothing about the Conqueror or his Tomb whilst in Toorkestan.

On the road I stopped at some black tents to make inquiries. I heard the inhabitants busy within, but all our calling was long in vain. At length Birdler Beeg entered one of the tents and brought out from it a man, who came and saluted me with much shew of cordiality, although he had been deaf enough, so long as there was any hope of escaping the hospitable claims of strangers. From him we inquired the road, and procured a draught of water. The women, so curious in cities, did not even peep. Birdler Beeg boasts the beauty of the Toorcumun women, but it probably consists of small, sparkling eyes and a rosy complexion. Their features can seldom be regular or very delicate. The women of the Oozbegs are said to be lovely, but neglected by their brutal lords. Peer Muhummud Khaun declares that they are not without their revenge, being allowed to drive where they like, in covered carts, with the male slaves of the family, and having entire charge of the purse. That a handsome male slave will, in consequence, often refuse his freedom when it is offered him. All this, however, Birdler Beeg, as in duty bound, strenuously denies.

The Toorcumun women are by all accounts modest, and not concealed. When a traveller enters a Yahmoot Khail, he is accommodated in the public guest tent, if there be one. If the camp is small, there is probably no guest tent, in which case he is admitted into the family tent of his host, where he finds the wife and children. At night, under veil of darkness, the several parties undress. The children are early married, the boys at the age of fourteen years, the girls at that of eleven or twelve years, and before the age of puberty. The marriage is immediately consummated, and a tent is provided for the young pair, which is pitched near that of the boy's parents. It is considered a reproach to have an unmarried daughter to the age of twenty years, and such ladies are little in request as wives; for, said Birdler Beeg, their bosoms become so large. I have in Hindoostan seen a girl of nine years, living as wife with a man of thirty; but the practice is uncommon in that country, where marriages are seldom consummated until both parties have attained puberty.

The daughters of Toorcumuns are always purchased. If respectable, at not less than 100 Tillas, about 700 Co's Rupees, or 70*l*. If the first wife die, the widower must pay double for a second, although the husband should be still a child. In return for the price bestowed, the bride is generally provided by her parents with furniture of proportionate value. A widow, if young, fetches a higher price, as being broken into the manège. Strange as it may appear, men and women never eat together. I asked Birdler Beeg the reason. "Is woman an unclean animal?" "No!" he said, "but a man would be laughed at who should eat with a woman, he would be called 'a pretty Miss.'" He was much astonished at learning that we suffer our women to eat from the same dish with ourselves. He asserted that some liberty of choice is allowed the young people; but I have heard this denied, and believe, that as a general rule, it may be said to be quite unknown.

I was describing England one day to Birdler Beeg, if indeed a process, in which every idea is to be created ere it can be applied, can be termed description. He asked, "And what could induce you to quit such a paradise?"

"The hope of making myself a name."

"What! your King I suppose will make much of you?"

"No! without being known to my King, I may win myself a name!"

"Oh! yes! yes! your King being a woman, cannot of course confer honour, but her Vuzeer will."

When I informed him, that beside the honour which the Queen and her Ministers confer, there was a society, a public, whose opinion was of the utmost consequence to an Englishman, the idea was incomprehensible. There being in Toorkestaun neither aristocracy nor people, nor any right nor honour but the King's pleasure.

Our camp was at Kara Tuppah, where was a small Khail (or camp) and a sluice of pure water from one of the canals. Early next morning I resumed my march over a plain, encumbered by sand-hills, and sprinkled with low jungle. The lower lands are occasionally cultivated, and have old water-courses and remains of habitations, speaking of a more prosperous period. The country is rather a wilderness than a desert, produces an abundance of dry fire-wood, and plenty of camel thorn, but no grass whatever. I met an old Tooreumun gentleman riding a fine horse, and followed by a young girl of about sixteen years, riding astraddle, fair, with feminine features, but insipid. Her head-dress was remarkable, being adorned with silver ornaments, fantastic and pretty; but I was too much occupied with the face, to retain any distinct impression of the shape. The sight of the most ordinary female countenance is a rarity not to be neglected. We had filled the water-bags at Kara Tuppah, so were independent, when at noon we sat down in the wilderness and awaited the arrival of the camels.

It is needless to detail each several stage, where all were precisely alike; but it may be interesting to sketch a single day's trip, with all its pleasures and inconveniences. I rise then at midnight, and sit at a blazing fire, sipping tea without milk, until the camels are laden and have started. I then mount and follow them, and as camels walk something less than three miles an hour, soon overtake them. As the cold is intense, and our feet are by this time fully numbed, I alight and spread my carpet, and a large fire is soon made, around which we all sit half an hour. Wood is very abundant, and so dry that when the hoar frost or snow is shaken from it, it kindles instantly. It is likewise so deficient in solidity, that a stem, the thickness of a man's body, is torn up by the roots without difficulty.

We now mount again, and proceed in silence, for the path admits not of two abreast; and the freezing of the vapour of the breath, upon one's beard and mustachios, renders the motion of the jaw singularly unpleasant. Indeed, in raising the handkerchief to one's face, it is tangled in a disagreeable manner with the crystals, and the chin has become so brittle, that a very slight tittilation is painful. Jupiter is now far above the horizon, and Venus is shining gloriously upon the desolate wild. And by degrees, we perceive the day itself slightly winking in the east, and again we pull up, to light a fire, and to thaw our frozen extremities. We sit until day is fully confirmed, when the Birdler Beeg and my Meerza, and sometimes Summud Khaun spread their cloaks, ascertain the true position of Mecca, and duly say their prayers. The other servants do not seem to think the ceremony expected from them, as they have less title to consequence. One day, when Birdler Beeg and the Meerza had both risen from their knees and were approaching the fire, the Meerza said to the Toorcumun, "Salaam alikoom," which was as much as to say, I hail you a brother. The other, however, did not condescend to answer the salutation, thinking himself far too orthodox to own such fraternity. I have witnessed the same scene acted over a purer faith, and in a better land. The High Churchman speaks with infinite scorn of the humble Methodist, the zealous puritan. The very enthusiast, upright of heart and gentle of spirit, whose words are sincerity, whose soul glows with the least earthly love; yet deems himself entitled to speak of " poor dear such an one," and to mourn the condition of many a perverse brother and sister, over whom, perchance, the angels are rejoicing.

When shall we behold the bequest of Jesus pervading the hearts, and directing the conduct of all? When shall we see the will to do good, divested of the proneness to think evil of our neighbours? If, indeed, so great a blessing is yet in reserve for man's perverted race, the prayer which those pure lips have taught us, will be robbed of its foremost petition. The kingdom of Heaven will be amongst us, and the hope of it shall be swallowed up in sight.

Ere the sun breaks from the horizon, we are once more mounted and away. The profusion of hoar frost upon the leafless jungle sheds a glory over the desolate scene. It is a sight unwitnessed by me for seventeen years, and brings back many pleasant remembrances tinged with sadness. Now we are close upon the traces of the camels. The slave caravans keep them company. The hardy Toorcumuns, as they trudge along in their clouted, laced boots, and legs wound around with woollen cloths, and their white sheepskin caps, heavy with hoar frost, have no cause to envy us, whose knees are cramped with the saddle, and whose feet are again freezing in the morning air. How frosty their cheeks and sharp noses appear, peeping above the cataract of ice which clings to their scanty beards, and below the snowy mass which overhangs their brows. The captive ladies are wisely invisible. They have tucked themselves below the felts of their Kujawurs, and yet I fear, in spite of all their management, have but a chilly berth. But there is one poor wretch, who has no such defence against the weather. Whose knees, like ours, are cramped with the saddle of her camel; but who has not, like us, a sufficiency of clothing, nor the option of alighting to renew life at the fire. What is her condition, and what the hope which supports her under her misery? Is it hope of escape? Alas! he who once enters Khiva abandons all such hope, as surely as he who enters hell. His prison-house is girdled with trackless deserts, whose sole inhabitants are the sellers of human flesh; escape is as impossible from Khiva, as to the wretch thrice-girdled in the black folds of Styx. If she has still a hope left to support her spirit, it is the chance, faint and dim, of falling into hands less cruel, than those which now oppress her. Her home, her country, her husband, her friends, are lost, and for ever; and the child which hangs like some worthless article of merchandise from the camel's side, shall, if it continue to live, know neither home, nor country, nor one right that should be common to the human race.

The magnificent camels, in their long shaggy fur, little heed the weather. The icicles hang from their beards, and hoar frost garnishes their heads. Their large, full, lustrous eyes, seem acquainted with hardship, but not with trouble. They are the very philosophers of patience, who conquer all things by tranquillity of spirit. Many a " Salaam alikoom" is wished me as I pass, and Birdler Beeg has just stopped to take a puff of the kullyaun, and exchange a light-hearted laugh with his countrymen. On we march with lengthened pace, and at ten o'clock strike off the road to seek a hollow, convenient for a halt. We choose that which is sheltered from the wind and exposed to the sun, and has, besides, an abundance of firewood; as for camel-thorn, there is never lack of that. My carpet is spread, and Shakespeare is open, and this is real enjoyment; for the cramped limbs may now extend themselves, and the warmth of the sun and of the fire are equally agreeable. But this is not all, for the camels have now arrived, and I see Nizaum, my Nazir, under way to my carpet, bearing hot bread and the concreted juice of grapes; and having been nine hours in the frosty air, the appetite is something whetted. My people also have made themselves tea, and a stew swimming in the fat of ram's tails; and leaving Byron to sing, "The *Isles* of grease, the *Isles* of grease," they swallow whole *continents* at a gulp. By degrees the warmth and ease of my position " steal my senses, shut my sight," and I am not sensible of external objects, until the loud " Bismillah" awakens me to see the caufila depart.

Then it is once more " Mount and go," nor do we draw rein until four o'clock, when we again choose a position of bivouac and collect fire-wood for the night. Again come the camels, and now my funny little tent is pitched, and I instal myself within it; in due time devour the fat stew they have made me, and sleep until midnight; when I rise, and call the people who have crept under their thick felt coverings, and are well wrapped in furs.

Such is a life in the wilderness, sufficiently tedious and irksome at first, and painful until habit has accustomed the limbs to the constraint of the saddle, for so many hours daily. This constrained posture, aided by the excessive cold, so paralysed the nerves of the legs, that for twenty days after my arrival at Khiva I had scarcely the use of my right foot, and all my servants complained of constant pain in the extremities. Unfortunately my old Meerza having lost just forty of the two-and-thirty teeth he once boasted, and having moreover an all-of-a-heap manner of speaking, so that the first word of his sentence runs down the heels of the last, all conversation with him is out of the question; and Birdler Beeg understands just enough of Persian to misinterpret mine. I therefore feel doubly the loss of Peer Muhummud Khaun, who spoke the language well, and caught my meaning readily.

After the second march, the path became both vague and difficult as the sand hills increased, and the track was often quite effaced by the wind. In this difficulty we looked for ocks, or landmarks, generally the skeleton of a camel hung upon a bush, but often, masses of dark wood, piled upon some conspicuous point. At night, it need scarcely be observed, these are utterly invisible. They are also few and far between, but whenever a camel's bone is to be found in the sand, you may be sure you are not far from the true route.

One night, when I rose as usual for the march, I

found the earth a foot deep in new-fallen snow. I confess I thought it madness to proceed until daylight; but Birdler Beeg assured me there was nothing to apprehend. "But," I said, "you lost your way, just now, in broad day-light, and but for my compass, would never have recovered it." This was fact. The air was foggy; we wandered off the road, made a fire, sat down, forgot our bearings, and sent men due North, instead of South, to look for the camels. Their errand failing, I had recourse to my compass, and recovered the path by it. The features of this irregular plain are everywhere precisely similar, and nothing is easier than to go astray. "What are we to do?" I inquired of Birdler Beeg.

"We must follow the camels!"

"The camels! and who are they to follow?" there is not a star visible, and the night is pitchy dark."

"Oh!" said Birdler Beeg, "the camels never go astray."

I was far from satisfied, but had no alternative, so followed the track of the camels, which, without turning head to the right hand or left, followed all the windings of the invisible path through the deep snow, as confidently as in day-light. This faculty is very wonderful, and utterly unaccountable by any knowledge we possess, of animal sensation.

One night, when I had dismounted to thaw my feet, my Meerza asked me how I found them. I replied, that if he asked after my knees or my calves, I could give him some information, but that beyond them I could not speak, not being very certain that I possessed feet.

"That," said the Meerza, "reminds me of a tale relating to Cabul, which, as every one knows, is excessively cold in winter. Two men were sleeping there, wrapped in the same cloak. In the morning, one of them awaking, commenced as usual to scratch his head. Finding very little benefit from the operation, he dug his nails in pretty deep, and was ploughing away in great contentment, when his friend, starting, asked him, what the deuce he was at?

"Scratching my head to be sure."

"*Your* head. What, do you mean to say this is your head that you are tearing to pieces, like a great tom cat, with your infernal claws?"

"Of course I do," replied his friend, continuing the operation with a yawn.

"The devil it is!" replied the other, seizing the scratching fingers between his teeth, and speaking through his nose. "If this is your head, these are your teeth."

And he bit him until he roared a confession of his error.

The hoar frost upon the bushes greatly delighted me. I had not seen it since leaving England. I robbed the bushes of their crystals as I passed them, to quench my thirst. When the wind, which is generally N.N.East, changed to West, it brought clouds from the Caspian, which always fell in snow. The air at other times was excessively cold; we preserved our noses, only by constant manipulation. A case of felt on the outside of the boot is the only thing that will effectually protect the feet. No provision, inside the boot, will avail, if the leather be exposed to the air; for its pores become saturated with vapour, and in this state it is instantly converted into a mass of ice.

The greater part of this tract is safe to travellers, provided with passes; but, at about the fourth march, we approached a well, where, Birdler Beeg informed me, caution was requisite, as the Persian, or rather Tartar horsemen, subjects of Persia, make occasional forays hither from Dèrèguz. We therefore remained at this well only long enough to procure a supply of water. Several marches here are considered perilous from the above cause.

The next morning, taking precedence of the camels, we pushed on for a couple of hours in silence, when it appeared that Birdler Beeg had lost his road. This was awkward, and every attempt to recover the track involved us in hollows, which were as lakes of dense camel-thorn, extremely annoying to the horses, whose legs they lacerated. Moreover, every now and then, I found myself on the brink of a deserted well, so walled in with thorns, that I was saved only by the sagacity of my horse, from falling into it. It was very dark, and I knew not what means Birdler Beeg might have of finding the path, in a country so destitute of features. He went on, however, confidently, through jungles of camel-thorn and thickets of tamarisk. At length we heard voices a-head; and loosened our sabres. Birdler Beeg coming up, asked in a whisper what I should do, if they should prove to be Koozulbaush. I replied, that an Englishman had but one way of proceeding in all cases,—and that was to advance. But he replied "they may be ten to one. In such cases it is the Toorcumun fashion to run; no shame attaches to it; I myself have often run."

I perceived that he was not to be depended upon at a pinch. We, however, approached the voices with some caution, but soon recognised our own people, whom we were right glad to find.

Another night when we had as usual dismounted, and Ali Muhummud, my interpreter, had made a fire of brushwood, three horsemen, whose hoof-sounds had been lost in the deep sand, suddenly stood at my elbow. I seized my weapons, but Birdler Beeg found that they were friends; Toorcumuns travelling from Khiva, with despatches for the governor of Merv. This was a warning of the ease, with which even horsemen may at night, in this desert, surprize an unwary foe. These men had no camels, but carried water for themselves and cattle, their own and their horses' food and clothing on the crupper of their saddles, making the whole distance of about 360 miles in six days. If it is considered that the horses' barley alone for this journey, weighs 60lb. and the horse clothing at least 20lb. more, this will not appear a very light feat. It is constantly performed, however, by the Toorcumuns.

The aspect of the desert, or rather wilderness from Merv to Khiva, is that of a sandy plain, broken into the most irregular surface by deep pits and high mounds, the whole thinly sprinkled with bushes of three several kinds, between which grow wormwood and the camel-thorn. On approaching Khiva, the surface is often ploughed into ravines and ridges, whose course is north and south, giving some idea of abandoned water courses, and traditionally reported to be old channels of the Oxus. It is more possible, that they may have served such purpose to the Moorghaub, when, previous to the monopoly of its waters at Merv, it flowed into the Oxus: but my observation was too limited to enable me to decide the question. The ridges are gravelly, but there is no want of sand. Wells on this route are found at long intervals, in one case of 160 miles. The water is generally brackish, but there are exceptions; on approaching Khiva, there appeared a very thin sprinkling of grass, which our horses eagerly devoured. But no dependence is to be placed upon the pasture of this wilderness, and the traveller must provide barley or jowarree, sufficient to supply the place of fodder. The latter is preferable when the horses have been trained to eat it, 10lbs. of jowarree being, in respect of nourishment, equal to 12lbs. of barley.

CHAPTER IV.

Reception at the House of an Oozbeg Gentleman—Message to the Khaun Huzurut—Ram Fight—The Light of Mutton Tails—Birdler Beeg's Return—Reception of my Message by the Khaun Huzurut—Escort sent to conduct me to my Lodging—Aspect of Khiva and its Surburbs—Dress of Oozbeg Woman—My Quarters—Extreme Jealousy of this Government—Arrangements for my Accommodation—Indelicacy of the Mehtur or Minister—Ruminations—Anecdote of Hajji Feroozooddeen—Summary of Difficulties—Difference between Fate and a Razor.

THE plain of Khiva is visible from some distance, lying much lower than the surface of the wilderness. It has no beauty, and yet the sight of trees, in which it is wealthy, is ever pleasing to the wanderer of the desert. At about 2 o'clock P. M. we had reached a large pool in the cultivated plain. It was so hard frozen, that attempts to get at the water failed, although we assailed it with our battle-axes. Birdler Beeg recommended me to halt here whilst he rode on to announce my arrival at Khiva. He accordingly solicited a night's lodging at a respectable dwelling in the neighbourhood. The reply was as kind as could be desired. The father and five or six grown up sons came forth, saluted, and conducted me to the guest chamber, receiving and disposing of my servants and cattle with much attention. The guest chamber was the first apartment, on the right hand side as I entered the rude portico. It had neither window nor chimney, things unknown in Khaurism. The place of both was supplied, by tearing a small hole in one corner of the roof; a hearth near the centre of the room was speedily supplied with a large heap of live charcoal. A heavy door of coarse wood, turned upon wooden pivots, let into the masonry above and below. It was such a place as an English farmer would use as a wood or coal house. But it sheltered me from the wind, and was not unwelcome.

Bread, raisins, melons, and grapes were instantly set before me, after an invariable custom of the Oozbegs. I found the melons delicious. My people were cheered at the sight of these dainties, of the value of which, only the traveller of the desert can form a proper notion. I now sent on Birdler Beeg, desiring him to see the Khaun Huzurut himself, if possible, and as it was important at the outset to secure for the mission a footing suitable to the power and character of the British Indian Government; I desired him to dwell upon the vast superiority of Great Britain over Persia (the ambassador of the latter having been received with distinction) and to procure for me as handsome a reception as possible. It may appear strange that such a suit was to be made to the throne direct, but at this primitive court the king is the only real man of business, settling with his own fiat the ceremonies that at other courts devolve upon ministers or officers of state.

Toward evening, my host came to beg me to come outside, to witness the combat of rams trained for the purpose. This is a common pastime in some parts of India, but I had never witnessed it. I was rather disappointed in the force put forth by the animals, and in their power to resist the concussion of meeting heads. After several severe shocks, one of them was evidently the worse for it. He appeared stupified, sneezed very often, and shewed no desire to renew the fight, which the other pressed upon him. It is a spectacle not worth seeing, but it is always something, to have proved by personal experience so much, of any exhibition.

As the evening closed, large lumps of fat from the tail of the sheep were brought by my host to supply the iron pan, which propped upon a greasy and very filthy pedestal of wood, served as a lamp to the apartment; and soon afterwards a pilau of mutton was served up.

In the morning, Birdler Beeg returned, saying that he had seen the Khaun Huzurut himself the evening before. Being anxious to gain as much knowledge as possible of the forms of this Court, I desired him to relate exactly what had happened. The Khaun Huzurut, he said, was seated in his black tent, transacting business. Birdler Beeg informed the Mehtur of his arrival as my guide, and found that intelligence of my approach had already reached Khiva. The Mehtur waited upon the Khaun Huzurut with the information, and Birdler Beeg was almost immediately summoned to attend the Khaun. "When I approached the tent," he said, "I trembled."

"Why? have you not often appeared before the Khaun Huzurut?"

"Yes; but a king's a king. He is not like other mortals. He has the power of life and death, and a single word or nod of his suffices for either. I left my shoes at the door, lifted the curtain, entered, and joining my hands in front bowed my body, and said, 'Salaam alikoom;' but my agitation was so great, that I could scarcely muster breath for the words. The Khaun Huzurut received me very graciously, and I delivered your message. He smiled, questioned me about the journey, but more particularly of the doings of the English at Heraut. I said that the English had done every thing for the Herauties. That an alliance had taken place between them and Shauh Kaumraun, but that the Vuzeer still sells the people into slavery. After many inquiries I was dismissed, and learned from the Mehtur, that orders had been issued to receive you with distinction. Accordingly, a guard of horsemen has been sent in front, and the master of ceremonies follows with about a hundred more;* quarters are assigned you in one of the Vuzeer's palaces beyond the town."

I dressed accordingly, and was scarcely ready when the master of ceremonies arrived, with his Oozbeg and Toorcumun horse. He was a fine man, tall and stout, with squarish face, a ruddy complexion, long half-closed eyes, good features, and, merit of merits, a decent beard. He is an Oozbeg, and a good specimen of his race. After an interchange of civilities, we mounted and proceeded toward the city. I had exchanged my Afghaun dress for my only full dress suit,—an embroidered surtout with golden epaulettes. The master of ceremonies rode beside me, and the horsemen followed in close column, some of them from time to time dashing from the ranks, discharging their fire-arms, and wheeling their horses at speed; my impression of their horsemanship was not favourable. Many of the bridles were richly decorated with gold, silver, and precious stones, which gave them a splendid effect; there were, also, some very handsome matchlock and firelock rifles, the fabric of Heraut and Persia. The horses greatly exceed in size those of Hindoostaun. But some were disproportionately small, and I observed none that I should have valued very highly. The Oozbegs and a few of the Toorcumuns wore the high cylindric Oozbeg cap of black lambskin. I call it cylindric, but it is generally rather larger above than below, so as to be the frustrum of a cone inverted. The larger the cap, the more dignified is it considered. The Toorcumuns, however, generally wear their own black, lambskin cap, which is smaller, sits close to the head, and ends above, not like the Persian in a point, but slightly rounded. It is a far more convenient head-dress than the Oozbeg, but is not so graceful as the Persian cap. The horsemen rode in a dense mass, which would

* At my Audience, the Khaun assured me that he had sent 100 more horsemen to meet and join me on the way, but that taking the wrong road, they had missed me.

have had a more military effect, had there been any uniformity in their arms. But some bore spears, others sabres alone, and a few carried rifles.

After riding a couple of miles, the town of Khiva appeared on our right, and we entered a country, laid out in gardens and dwellings of the gentry. The houses have all one character, being an enclosure of very lofty clay walls, flanked by ornamental towers at the angles, which give them the appearance of castles. This name (Gullah) they bear at Khiva. The exterior has but one visible opening, which is the entrance, lying generally between two towers, and being a spacious gateway, flat above, and roofed throughout, to its termination in the court behind the house, or rather within the enclosure. On one side of this, a door admits to the men's apartments, and on the other side, the women's quarters are constructed. The walls, built with great regularity of rammed clay, are generally fluted, an effect given them perhaps by the hurdles of straight branches, between which the clay is supported whilst soft, and during the process of ramming. The gardens are surrounded by very low walls of similar construction, allowing the eye to command many estates from a single point of view. The trees* are apparently a species of elm, wide, and very shadowy; the poplar, and the plane tree. The appearance of the country is pleasing, but it is too flat for beauty, and I observed that neither grass, weed, nor wild flower will grow upon the banks, although canals from the river plentifully irrigate the whole valley.

The population of the neighbourhood turned out to stare at the Feringee Eelchie. The men wore the Oozbeg attire. The women's dress differed from that of the men, in the substitution of a species of cylindric turban for the cap; and a cloth, which after passing over this turban, was gathered under the chin.

---

* The trees being out of leaf, I could only guess of their nature, from the figure of their stems and branches.

In other respects, there seemed a strange confusion of attire, the women wearing a chogah, or cloak, of quilted chintz, precisely similar to that of the men, with Wellington boots and very loose drawers. The complexion of the women was very ruddy, shewing more red than white. Their countenance too round or square for beauty, and their shapes (unless indeed they owe the effect to their apparel) clumsy in the extreme. Their eyes are dark, long, and ill opened. The brow delicately pencilled. They are accounted beauties, in a region where fair complexions are at a premium; many of them showed their faces boldly, others muffled the lower part of the visage, in the white cloth which passes under the chin.

I was not long in reaching the house, or as they were pleased to term it—palace, prepared for my reception. It was a large building, having several miserable rooms, ill-shaped, ill-proportioned, unfloored, unplastered, and having neither window nor chimney. The smallest of these had been spread with felt. It was about twelve feet square; had a heavy rough-hewn door turning on pivots; and a hearth in the centre for charcoal: a small hole had been broken in the roof to let in light and let out smoke. I received here the master of ceremonies, made him partake with me of the refreshments provided, and then explored the premises. I explained to Birdler Beeg, that I must have one of the largest apartments for the reception of the nobles and chiefs, when they visited or dined with me. He opened wide his eyes. "Therefore," I continued, "pray look out for carpets and felts, and other suitable furniture without delay, for I suppose the Mehtur (Premier) will call immediately." He answered me with another broad stare, and when the master of ceremonies had left me, explained that it was quite unusual for Eelchies to hold intercourse with the inhabitants of Khiva. Whether or not the Mehtur would call, he could not say; but had never heard of such a ceremony, and was sure that the Mehtur would not dare to do so, without orders from the sovereign. I asked, whether the nobles and gentry held no social intercourse, entertaining one another at their several abodes. He said, "No;" that Government, i. e. the Khaun, was jealous of any such meetings.

I soon found that I was not alone in the house, but that the distant apartments were occupied by an officer of the Mehtur's household, placed there, avowedly, to attend upon me and supply my wants, but really, as a spy upon my actions. He came to ask me, on the part of the Mehtur, how I would like to arrange my table. Whether he should send me the money allowed by the Khaun Huzurut for my expenses, about 2 Tillas, or 28 shillings daily; or whether he should send me the provisions undressed, or whether they should be sent ready cooked. I replied, that being the Khaun Huzurut's guest, I could not refuse any food His Majesty might be pleased to send me. At the same time I could not presume to arrange the mode of furnishing it. Only I begged to be excused from receiving gold for the purpose, the very spirit of the relation between host and guest seeming to be violated by such an arrangement. That if the provisions were to be purchased by me, I had brought with me the requisite funds. If the Khaun Huzurut should be pleased to send me provisions, I should receive them as a compliment from His Majesty.

The Mehtur was well contented with an arrangement, by which he gained about 14 shillings daily. Such are Premiers at Asiatic Courts. The day had not passed ere Birdler Beeg came to say, that the Mehtur was impatient to see the shawls, which he had heard I had brought for him. This was the more indelicate, that the shawls were not sent him from Herant, but purchased by me at Merv, and therefore he could only guess that they might be intended for him. I replied, that I expected the usual

F 2

compliment of a visit from him, after which, I should think of sending him any present I might think fit to offer him. He replied, that the Mehtur dared not call upon me, unless expressly sent by the Khaun Huzurut; that if, therefore, I should wait for a visit, I should, in all probability, have no opportunity of presenting the gifts. All this was excessively indelicate, but it may once for all be observed, that the delicacy which is occasionally affected in other countries of Asia, is here never dreamed of. Perceiving this, and not feeling at liberty to make an enemy of the Prime Minister, I sent him the pair of shawls by the hand of Birdler Beeg. The latter worthy, in answer to my queries, said he did not think I should be summoned to an audience until the day ensuing, the interval being allowed me to recruit my strength, after the passage of the desert.

In the evening, Nizaun cooked for me a pilau of pheasant with rice and raisins. This bird is killed in large numbers during winter, when the snow exposes it to view. For dessert I had good grapes, some indifferent apples, and delicious melons. After dinner, I went out into the court. I gazed upon the stars, my companions in so many wanderings. Clime, people, manners, language, laws, how often had they changed: but this page of heaven, those bright and glorious intelligences, remained as before, unimpaired and unchanged; excepting that the planets in their courses moved from house to house, presaging happiness or woe to the sons of men. Was I really at Khiva, that capital so famous, yet so little known, of which half the existing accounts are fabulous? Travellers, presuming upon its separation from the civilised world, to hang upon it their wildest marvels. And in what did this city differ from others, familiar to the traveller and the merchant?

The sky was remarkably pure and brilliant; the air piercingly cold. I drew closer my posteen, or cloak of fur. I thought of the fanciful story which

Summud Khaun had related, when I purchased that cloak.

"Feeroozooddeen* was one night seated in durbar. The night was excessively cold, the teeth of his people chattered, in spite of themselves. He looked round upon them with a smile, and said—We will soon teach you to bid defiance to the cold. He signed to his steward, and bade him bring from the store-room a number of posteens, corresponding to the number of his attendants. When these were distributed, and each had wrapped himself up, he said to one of these, now Daood Khaun, take a light, give my compliments to the cold, and beg him to enter. The servant obeyed, but returned immediately with the candle extinguished. The cold, he said, in answer to your hospitable invitation, has rudely blown out the light. Indeed, said Feeroozooddeen, then give the light a posteen (fur cloak), and now go and usher in the cold." These posteens are generally of doombha's skins; the fur inside, the leather tanned to the consistence of wash leather, stained a buff colour, and beautifully embroidered with floss silk. The price at Heraut was about eight ducats, or 4*l*. each. The more wealthy, however, wear cloth cloaks, lined throughout with furs from Siberia.

I have said that the sky was brilliant. It was now the hour of repose, and the busy murmurs of the neighbouring city had ceased. The light breeze of night, blowing from the frozen wastes of Siberia, cut like the keenest sabre, whenever it found contact with the skin. Yet I lingered long in the open air, to listen to a singular species of melody with which the air was filled; and which resembled the distant music of a hundred Eolian harps. It was singularly pleasing. To my ear, separated as I was from home, friends, country, the conveniences, comforts, endearments, and security of civilised lands, the pleasure

* I insert this anecdote from memory, and am not quite certain I have attributed it to the proper person.

was intimately tangled with pain. I could not conjecture its origin: but I was not in a mood to ask questions of my people, and postponed the elucidation to a more prosaic hour. My present position was one of interest and deep anxiety. I had been sent to execute, what might well appear an impossibility, and my fame, as well as life, was staked upon the venture. When I considered my imperfect knowledge of even the Persian tongue; my utter ignorance of that of the Court and people, as well as of their manners and temper; my entire want of instruments suited to my need: that my sole instrument of intercourse with the natives was Ali Muhummud, a ransomed slave, new to my service, and of whose capacity or fidelity I knew nothing; when I considered the lightness of my purse; the impossibility of recruiting it at Khiva; the poverty of the presents to be offered the Khaun Huzurut, contrasted with the lavish gifts, which, it was well known, had been bestowed upon the Government of Heraut; my want of suite to give dignity to my mission; that the Vuzeer Yar Muhummud Khaun had agents at Khiva, secretly engaged in thwarting my endeavours, and throwing the most dangerous suspicions upon my motives; that the Persian ambassador had just preceded me, at the head of a hundred horse, and laden with handsome presents; that it must be his object to hinder the meditated alliance; that Doost Muhummud Khaun, the Ex-Ummeer of Cabul had also agents at Khiva, who would, naturally, if possible, poison the Khaun's mind against the English—a nation whose very existence was a recent discovery at Khiva. When I considered, that in demanding the confidence of the Khaun, I was empowered to promise him nothing, but rather to make excuses for non-compliance with every request he had made,—I confess, the case appeared to me as desperate as possible. Yet I had undertaken the mission, with hopes equally overcast, and I was determined that it should not fail for want of zeal and devotion. Such reflections occupied me until midnight. Yet, strange to say, the sense of difficulty rather inspired than discouraged me. I have felt the same through life—a deadness and want of enthusiasm for tasks of easy accomplishment: a self-confidence and energy awakened by the presence of difficulty. I stripped off my heavier garments, and lay down upon my carpet, commending myself and my concerns to the care of HIM who had been from childhood my never-failing refuge, and slept in peace, until day dawned through the miserable aperture in the roof of my apartment.

Nizaum, the toughest and slowest of sleepers, was stirred, after a quarter of an hour's bellowing in his ear, and sundry punches in the ribs, from the chief of the foot-fingers. He sleeps like one under the influence of opium. I have seen nothing so helpless. He and the rest of my little suite occupied one of the largest rooms, if room it could be called, that had floor, walls, and roof of mud, unwhitewashed; and rafters unhewn. The Old Meerza, it appeared, had been in much apprehension of his throat; which Summud Khaun endeavoured to assuage, by reminding him that whatever is to be, *will* be. That if his throat is to be found some morning disunited, disunited it will be found. This argument, an unfailing sedative to Summud Khaun's own mind, was not always so effectual in the case of the Old Meerza, who could not perceive the especial advantage enjoyed by him whose throat is cut by destiny, over him whose throat is cut only by a razor. He was, however, ashamed to yield in piety to a man who received forty rupees a month less than himself, so put the best possible face upon the matter.

CHAPTER V.

Glistering Atmosphere and excessive Chill of the Air at Khiva—First Audience at the Court of Khiva—Town—Artillery—Palace—Minister's Levee—The Mehtar—Khojeh Mhirahm—Interpreter—Nobles of Khiva—Access to the Royal Presence—Black Tent—Audience—Ullah Kooli Khaun, King of Khaurism—Dismissal—Suspicions of the Khaun Huzurut—Restrictions upon Ambassadors at Khiva.

HAVING dressed, and being restricted to a single apartment (the others being too cold and comfortless to be inhabited), I took a walk in what was ingeniously styled—the *Garden*, being a high walled enclosure, stuck here and there with a leafless shrub. The walls would not admit of my seeing anything beyond the area, and indeed there was no outlook afforded from my miserable palace, so that I soon learned to sigh over the memory of many a cheerful dog-kennel of my happier land. The air was searchingly cold. In England, nothing is known approaching to the chill of the Khiva winter. My towel, hung up to dry in the small room warmed with a large fire of charcoal, instantly became a mass of ice. If the door was left open, the passage of the wind was detected, as it blew over any liquid, by its sudden conversion to a solid form, and there was no thaw excepting in spots where the sun-beams accumulated. In the shade, the snow always lay feathery and granulated, incompressible into masses, so that snow-balls could not be formed.

But the sun now shone cheerily through the cutting air, lighting in its passage myriads of minute particles of mist (small as the motes of the sun-beam, and invisible, like them, excepting in the brightest light): which the intense chill of the air was continually freezing, and which, falling in an unceasing shower of light, gave a sparkle to the atmosphere, that savoured of enchantment. This effect I have observed only at Khiva. Mixed as it was with the sounds of aërial music, of the origin of which I was long ignorant, it lent an air of poetry to the spot, which was welcome to an existence so dull and prosaic.

Nizaum now summoned me to breakfast, formed of the flat Afghaun bread, and the concreted juice of grapes, of the consistence of treacle; and being now in the land of cows and goats, I had bargained for a daily supply of milk for my tea, which was accordingly brought me in form of a thick mass of ice, solid throughout. Half-dried grapes and melons were produced in abundance. Both these fruits are hung up by the stalk, and thus preserved throughout the winter. The melon is long in form, very large, and of the deep green of the water melon. It is a delicious fruit. The grape is probably inferior to that of Heraut, Furrah, and Candahar. The bread of Khiva is unpalatable, and it was long ere I discovered, that butter is made and preserved fresh throughout the winter. It is abundant, and of excellent quality. The secret of its preservation is to melt it over a very low fire, and constantly to skim the surface. The particles more subject to decay are thus separated from the butter, which instantly recovers its firmness, and does not at all resemble the ghee of India. It is poured whilst melted into large jars, which are then closed. In this state it remains fresh and sweet almost any number of months, often retaining its golden hue to the last.

After breakfast, Birdler Beeg called to say, he thought I should be summoned to an audience that evening. I spent the day in arranging my thoughts, and endeavouring to mould into Persian such phrases as I thought I might have occasion for. It was not until evening had well set in, that the arrival of the master of ceremonies summoned me to attend the Khaun Huzurut. I exchanged my Afghaun attire for my only suit of uniform. Unfortunately, the cocked hat and plume, the most indispensable portion of an Eelchie's attire in Eastern lands, were absent without leave. Instead of a sash I tied a shawl round my waist; and learning that it was unusual to brace on a sabre at audience, carried, instead, a handsome Persian dagger.

I ordered all my available servants to attend, bearing the sabre and rifle to be presented to the Khaun, and preceded by the master of ceremonies, rode slowly toward the palace. A large number of natives, despite the lateness of the hour, had collected on either side the road, to gaze at me. I afterwards learned that death had been publicly denounced upon any who should molest me by word or deed, and was assured that nothing less would have secured me from insult. I know nothing of the people of Khaurism that can warrant such an assertion. On approaching the town we entered a considerable suburb, and afterwards passed through a miserable bazaar to the gateway; for Khiva is fortified. The house-tops were covered with women, collected to stare at a figure sufficiently monstrous in their eyes. It was not long before we reached, through some very poor streets, the citadel, within which resides the "Father of Victories," the king of Khaurism.

It is a poor brick building, forming an angle of the city defences. Near the gate stood the artillery of Khaurism, consisting of about 22 brass field-pieces, of from 6 to 12 pound calibre, very indifferently mounted upon carriages having wooden axles. One or two tumbrils were also to be seen. These guns are objects of extreme veneration to the people of Khiva. At the gate the master of ceremonies dismounted, and begged me to do the same. I then marched through the dense crowd collected to see me, and ascended, through the gateway, the pavement leading to the Vuzeer's Hall. Not being advertised of the locality, and having no one near me from whom to inquire, the master of ceremonies being ignorant of Persian, I naturally concluded that this was the royal apartment; so leaving my shoes at the door, I entered, and looked around me to discover which of the assembly was entitled to homage. A row of common-looking figures, in the Oozbeg dress, were seated opposite. The chief of these might be old King Cole himself, for aught I knew; however, there was no time for inquiry, so I bowed to the chief person, and said "Salaam alikoom," peace be upon you. There was a smile, for they all conjectured the fact, that I had mistaken the Prime Minister for the King; however, no harm was done, and I seated myself at the minister's side.

I sat kneeling, to my infinite discomfort; good manners prescribe this posture, and to sit cross-legged (which to an European is comparatively easy) is regarded as boorish, unless permission of the company be first asked. The Mehtur, or Premier, a little, dark, high-featured, long-bearded man (who always reminded me afterwards of the knave of clubs), dressed in a huge Oozbeg cap and cloak of quilted chintz, said, "You are very welcome," and instantly a piece of greasy chintz was spread before me as a table cloth, and bread, raisins, loaf sugar, and fruit were placed before me. Not yet habituated to this custom, I asked the Mehtur to partake; but he excused himself, it being unusual for the host to eat with his guest the first meal. I therefore broke off, and ate a small piece of bread, and the cloth and refreshments were removed. This hospitable ceremony is invariable amongst the Oozbegs, from whom, I believe, it is derived, even where practised by the Toorcumuns. The Mehtur now addressed several compliments to me, and was evidently nettled at my slowness of reply. The fact is, that his pronunciation of Persian is barely intelligible, and my own ignorance of Eastern idiom, makes me unready in any exchange of compliments. A messenger from the Khaun Huzurut now summoned the Mehtur. He rose, beckoned me to remain seated, and left the hall. I had leisure whilst he was absent to look around me. Next and above me sat the Khojeh Mhirahm, a handsome old man, who, having been an instrument of the last Khaun's degraded pleasures, retains considerable influence at Court, and is accounted a man of talent. Parallel with him, but upon the left of the Mehtur's seat, was a young priest, who, owing to his knowledge of Persian, acted as interpreter, and was also one of the Mehtur's secretaries. On my right, at some distance, sat about twenty loutish-looking fellows, in the usual Oozbeg attire. These were the nobles of Khiva. They took no share in the conversation, either then or on about a dozen other occasions, when I met them at the Mehtur's palace. At the door sat my own and some of the Mehtur's suite.

In about half an hour, during which I found my posture, dressed as I was in the tight attire of Europe, scarcely supportable, the Mehtur returned, and begged me to follow him to the royal presence. We proceeded through some dark and uneven passages crowded with guards, until we reached a small court in which a black tent was pitched. The Mehtur entered, and I followed, leaving my slippers as I lifted the curtain. I bowed, and said "Salaam Alikoom," and then stood in the prescribed form, which resembles the military position of ease. The Khaun returned the greeting, "Alikoom Salaam," then assured me I was welcome to his Court, and asked the nature of my mission. I replied, that I had been sent by the British Envoy at Herant, in answer to His Majesty's mission thither. That I bore credentials from the British Envoy, and also some very unworthy presents, my haste to present myself at the Court of Khiva not permitting me to bear anything more bulky. That I had instructions to promote, to the utmost of my power, the friendship that had so happily sprung up between the British and His Majesty's government, and to place at His Majesty's disposal whatever knowledge I possessed. I made a lame business of it; but the Khaun, an amiable and good-tempered man, smiled at my mistakes, and listened patiently to my explanations. It is to be observed, that as the Khaun understands very little Persian, I communicated by means of the young priest before mentioned, who understands about as much Persian as myself, but speaks with an entirely different accent, so that the difficulties were manifold.

It is not my purpose to touch upon political matters at the present moment. This will, I fear, abate considerably from the little interest connected with my narrative, as the crisis was one of the utmost importance, not only to the Khaun himself, and to England in an especial manner, but to the universal world. For had Russia succeeded in creeping to Khiva, the affairs of Asia must have undergone a revulsion, the consequences of which would not have closed, perhaps, with the present or coming century; and would, probably, have embroiled all the principal nations of Europe in tumult and war. The reasons which tie my tongue as to the political details of my mission, must prevent me likewise from exposing, for the benefit of Russia, all the immediate and eventual consequences, which would have attended the extension of her empire to the banks of the Oxus; suffice it, that my country is well aware of the extreme importance of the step, and will, if she be wise and true to herself, regard as a breach of mutual confidence any future encroachment of Russia upon the territories of Khaurism.

The letter from the British Envoy was received by the Mehtur, and read aloud to the Khaun Huzurut, who again assuring me I was welcome, dismissed me.

Ullah Koolie Khaun, the present king of Khaurism, is about 45 years of age, and so far as I can judge, rather under the middle height. His face is round. The features are high and regular; the expression is the most amiable possible; but there is an absence of vigour, for which, at the present crisis, nothing can atone, unless it be the powerful interposition of some foreign power. His eyes are long, and not well opened. His beard is decent; his family having some mixture of Sart blood. He is inclined to be stout. He was seated upon a carpet, and supported by cushions. Before him a wood fire blazed up, sending its smoke and sparks through the skylight of the tent. He shifted his posture from time to time. It was always ungraceful and unkingly. Sometimes cross-legged, sometimes kneeling, sometimes half reclining. His dress was a green cloak, fringed and lined with dark sables, and shewing at the waist a gold chain, the exact use of which I know not. On his head was the Oozbeg cylindric cap of black lambskin. He wore no ornament, and his sole insignium of office was a large dagger in a sheath of gold, which lay before him. No guards were visible about the tent; but the doors of the court were guarded. The black tent of felt which he occupied was of the usual dimensions, i. e., about 24 feet in diameter, and quite unadorned, its sole furniture being the carpet and cushions, on which he reclined. His attendants were the Mehtur, the young priest who interpreted, the Khojeh Mhirahm, the Sheikh ool Islaum, and the Nuggeeb (I think he is called). The two latter are the heads of the priesthood in Khaurism. None of these men are of distinguished appearance, nor is their dress many degrees finer than that of the yeomanry of the country. The Mehtur brought the Khaun his kuliaun (or pipe) whenever it was called for. This, say the strict Mahommedans, is Ullah Koolie Khaun's only vice; for he neither snuffs nor drinks, and has no more than four wives at a time.

I mounted my horse at the gate and rode quietly home, musing upon my interview. The night was excessively cold, and my clothes were scarcely sufficient protection against the chill of the air.

In the morning Birdler Beeg came to me, and was very anxious to know how I liked my reception. As I conjectured, that whatever I might say to him would be borne straight to Court, I was guarded, and asked how the Persian ambassador had been received. He assured me that the Persian was not admitted into the royal tent, and that my admission was a mark of particular favour. I remarked, that at other Courts British Eelchies were allowed a seat. That at Tehraun a chair is set for the Eelchie. He protested that such was never the case here, and I believe he is right, and that only the Khaun's brother and certain priests are ever allowed a seat in the royal presence. He said that the Khaun was disappointed that I had said so little. I replied, that with us it was considered disrespectful to speak much, without special injunction, in the presence of a monarch.

The Khaun Huzurut, he said, had desired him to ask me for a letter and the rifle, which he heard I had brought for his brother, the Inauk of Huzarusp. I learned, upon questioning the Birdler Beeg, that the Khaun had some suspicion that the contents of the letter might not be agreeable to himself. I was therefore happy that he had taken this unkingly precaution, and delivered the letter and gun, begging that His Majesty would cause both to be delivered to the noble hands for which they were destined.

When next I saw Birdler Beeg, I told him that I wished to look about me, and desired him to order my horse, and be himself in readiness to attend me in my ride. He appeared perplexed, and at length said, I had better first ask the Khaun Huzurut's permission, as ambassadors at Khiva are expected to confine themselves to their own abodes. I argued the point, but he brought instance upon instance, and assured me that the Persian ambassador was under the same restraint. Soon after, my servants came to report, that, wishing to visit the Bazaar, they had been checked by Yakoob Bae, the officer living on the premises. I summoned this worthy. He said, that it was usual to restrict the servants of Eelchies to their quarters for the first two or three days, and until permission for them to go abroad had been asked and granted. I therefore desired Birdler Beeg to step over, and present my compliments to the Mehtur, and say that I felt very unlike a British functionary, and much more like a state prisoner, under such restrictions; and begged him to use his influence with the Khaun Huzurut for their removal. That the Khaun Huzurut's ambassador at Herant was free from the moment of his arrival, to go and to send whithersoever he pleased, and that I claimed a like freedom. The Mehtur replied, that I must address myself personally to the sovereign. Birdler Beeg was, however, in the course of the day, summoned to attend the Khaun, and being asked how I was satisfied with my reception, replied bluntly, that I complained that I had got into a prison instead of a guest chamber. The Khaun laughed, and sent me word, that I was at liberty to send my people abroad, and myself to ride out.

CHAPTER VI.

Second Audience — The Russians — Persians — Bokharians — Colonel Stoddart — Treachery of the Cauzie Moolla Hussun — Message from the Minister — Visit to him — Reception — Bokhara — Colonel Stoddart — Plan for his Rescue — Particulars of the late Skirmish with the Russian Force N. West of the Sea of Aral — Ignorance and Timidity of the Minister — Extreme Difficulty of Negotiation with such a One — Messenger from the Khaun Huzurut to the Ummeer of Bokhara, for the Release of Colonel Stoddart.

THAT night, I was again summoned to attend the Khaun Huzurut. He received me as before. Asked me, whether I was very indignant at being a prisoner, and whether there were any objects in the neighbourhood that I wished to examine. It never enters the head of an Asiatic, that a man may go abroad for the sake merely of air and exercise. I replied that I was the first British Eelchie, that had ever been thus restricted. That if the usage of the country demanded it, I would comply without a murmur. I named his garden palace as an object of curiosity, and he gave orders that it should be opened for my inspection. He then pressed me very hard upon the subject of his requests of the British Government. I answered, that the points in question involved considerations too important to be decided upon by Major Todd. That even Sir W. M'Naghten would probably not act without reference to the Governor General. That I could not be certain that the Governor General himself would decide, without consulting Her British

Majesty. That they were questions that could not be anticipated, and had therefore not been provided for in the instructions issued to our ambassadors.

His Majesty was not satisfied. "You call yourselves my allies," he said, "yet you refuse every one of my requests, at the moment of my utmost need."

He then discussed the subject of my journey to Russia, and afterwards asked whether the Russians are idolaters. This was an awkward question: for a Mahomedan cannot understand the exact difference between bowing the knee to images and pictures of the Deity, and the breach of that second commandment which says, "Thou shalt *not* bow to the image of any thing in the heavens above, or the earth beneath, or the waters under the earth." Poor ignorant creatures! I therefore answered with some caution. "They do not consider themselves such."

"But they worship pictures and images?"

"They do."

"Are they Christians?"

"They so term themselves; but are of a different faith from the English, who use no images nor pictures in their worship, accounting the practice sinful."

"Is their language the same as yours?

"No! entirely different. We cannot understand one another in our several tongues."

"Then how are you to speak to them?

"In French, another language of Europe."

"Is there another European language?"

"There are upwards of thirteen, belonging to separate kingdoms."

"Is Russia the most powerful of these kingdoms?"

"By no means. England is first in extent of dominions, number of population, and in wealth. If your Majesty will permit me, I will prepare in Persian a brief account of the political divisions of Europe, and of British policy in *these* countries. As I *speak* Persian so imperfectly, this may be more intelligible to your Majesty, than any attempt to give these particulars verbally."

The Khaun Huzurut nodded, and smiled his consent. He then inquired,

"Are you the enemies of Persia?"

"Far from it. We are the natural allies of all Moohummedan states, because they intervene between Europe* and India. It is therefore our object to preserve their independence. Your Majesty must have heard all we have done for Persia, and that we once interposed to save her from imminent destruction." I here gave the particulars of Sir J. M'Neil's interposition. It was very evident, that this was the first the Khaun Huzurut had ever heard of the threatened destruction, and unexpected rescue of the adjoining kingdom. I continued—"We have at present some differences with Persia; Muhummud Shauh opened our ambassador's despatches, an insult of which we insist upon redress." This I particularised, as a hint to the Khaun himself, that he might not do the same lightly or unwarily. "When our demands are complied with, I have no doubt the Queen of England will again admit the king of Persia to her alliance."

"My ambassador at Heraut tells me, you understand by looking at a hill, whether or not it contains gold."

"I know a little of the science to which your Majesty alludes; but could not say certainly, that such and such a hill does or does not contain gold. I could only, by examining the rocks, pronounce whether gold is ever or often found in rocks of that character."

"I have some hills that formerly produced gold; can you tell me anything regarding them?"

"If your Majesty will allow me to see them, I will do my best."

---

* I must observe, once for all, that I do not feel authorised to publish the explicit terms, by which I found it necessary to make my meaning understood at this simple court.

"Can you cure diseases? My ambassador says you can?"

"I have very little skill; and being a stranger here, should be reluctant to exert it."

"I have deafness, and a running at the ear. Can you cure that?"

"The person of a monarch is sacred; life and death, disease and cure, are at the disposal of God. Should your Majesty get worse, you might attribute the circumstance to my agency; and the friendship, so happily commencing between the two Governments, might thereby be interrupted."

"Do not fear. Whatever happens, no evil shall befall you."

"I fear nothing for myself; and were I not here as an Eelchie, would gladly risk my life, for the hope of curing the Khaun Huzurut. But my Government sent me hither as an Eelchie, and not as a doctor."

He continued to urge me warmly, and feeling almost certain that I could cure his ear; and ashamed that my reluctance should be attributed to motives of personal fear, I was sore tempted to comply; but I remembered the arguments I had just offered, and persisted in my determination. I, however, recommended him to wash the ear frequently with soap and water, and to sit always *facing* the wind; precautions from which I myself, in a similar case, had derived benefit.

"Are you friends or enemies of Bokhara?" was his next query.

"We sent an ambassador to Bokhara, to offer the Ummeer friendship. He was afterwards to have proceeded, I believe, to Khiva, with similar offers to your Majesty; but the Ummeer, violating the laws of nations and the rites of hospitality, seized and imprisoned him. Such an act, unless speedily redressed, may bring the vengeance of my Government upon Bokhara. Your Majesty must have influence with the Ummeer, and would do an important benefit to the

Moosulmaun world, in exerting it for the liberation of Colonel Stoddart; for the British are extremely reluctant to enter into war with any of the Moslem States, their natural allies."

"I am on terms of defiance with the Ummeer; he will not listen to me."

"But his ambassador was lately at Khiva?"

"He departed without obtaining his object. The Ummeer is mad."

"Your Majesty is a friend and ally of the king of Kokaun. If both yourself and that monarch should urge the release of Colonel Stoddart, the Ummeer would not dare to refuse."

"The Ummeer thinks, from the pains you take for Colonel Stoddart's release, that he is some very great man; and as he fears you will some day molest *him*, detains him to exchange for some city, or some high ransom. Would your Government give any high sum for his release?"

"My Queen has thousands of subjects, the equals in birth and rank to Colonel Stoddart. Had Colonel Stoddart been taken in war, a ransom might probably be thought of. But he was the Ummeer's guest, and the representative of my King at the time of his seizure. The insult, if not redressed, may be avenged. So far from the Ummeer gaining a city in exchange for Colonel Stoddart, were he to ask only a single rupee, the British Government would refuse the demand with scorn. The pains we have taken for Colonel Stoddart's release proceed from our reluctance to war with any of the states of Islaum. But for this reluctance, we had long ago sent a couple of thousand soldiers, to drive the Ummeer out of his kingdom."

After some time the Khaun asked, "Do you know Cauzie Moolla Hussun?"

"Yes! well!"

"Do you consider him your friend?" with a slight smile.

"He has always so professed himself, and has received many benefits from the English."

The Khaun laughed. The cause I did not comprehend until the day following. I was now dismissed, and returned to my miserable quarters. The next day Birdler Beeg called. "I have just seen," he said, "a letter from Cauzie Moolla Hussun to the Khaun Huzurut; that is, I have heard the Mehtur read it aloud." He says, 'Your Majesty desired, that if any one was sent as Eelchie to Khiva, I might be selected. I told this to Major Todd; but he has disregarded your Majesty's request, and sent Abbott Sahib. I therefore recommend your Majesty to be on your guard; for had the purpose of the mission been honest, why was not I selected as Eelchie?'"

I now comprehended the Khaun Huzurut's smile, when asking of the Cauzie's friendship. I remembered, also, that the day I was selected for the mission, the Cauzie had said in my presence to Major Todd, "The Khaun Huzurut requested, that if any one was sent back to Khiva, I might be the person." Major Todd did not remark the tone in which this was said. But when the Cauzie departed, I pointed it out to him, saying, "That is a disappointed man, and will do all in his power to thwart my mission." Afterwards, the Cauzie entered with such apparent heartiness into every arrangement for my comfort, and gave me such solid and valuable advice respecting the people of Toorkestaun, that I accused myself of having harshly misjudged him, and felt double gratitude for his supposed good offices. My first judgment, it will be found, was correct; and to all persons dealing with Asiatics, and especially with natives of Afghaunistan, I would recommend, as the only safeguard to the duties entrusted to them, the harshest possible construction of motives. Such will be found, in the end, harsh only as applied to the nations of Europe; but just, and therefore charitable, in their present application.

This Cauzie Moolla Hussun is the father of Saleh Muhummud, the youth to whom I took such a liking at Merv, and whom I had begged Major Todd to send me to Khiva, if he could be spared. Saleh Muhummud was destined to play a conspicuous part in the sequel. I now added to the letter I was writing Major Todd, a request, that whomsoever he might send with the cash necessary for my expenses, it might *not* be Saleh Muhummud, nor any other member of the Cauzie's family, detailing my reason for this wish. This letter was not received (it will afterwards appear) until, providentially, Saleh Muhummud had been despatched to me.

Knowing that the discovery by the Khaun of any secret correspondence with Heraut, would awaken his distrust, to the injury of my mission, I had, at the last audience, begged his Majesty to allow me the means of sending letters to Major Todd, and he readily promised me a Toorcumun horseman for that purpose.

The Birdler Beeg now came to inform me, that the Mehtur wished to see me at his palace. This was something quite new to me. "Surely," I said, "the Mehtur knows where to find me. I am an Eelchie, and a stranger, the guest of the Khaun Huzurut; the representative of the greatest Government on earth; at all other eastern Courts, the Vuzeer calls upon the Eelchie, if he has any thing to say; or if he cannot do that, sends him, at least, a more ceremonious message."

"At Khiva," replied Birdler Beeg, "the Mehtur dares not call upon any Eelchie, without special orders from the Khaun. It is the custom here, when there is any business to be transacted, for the Eelchie to call upon the Mehtur."

It was sometime before I could reconcile myself to compliance with so barbarous an usage. But I reflected, that the Mehtur having so little freedom of action, must be considered as speaking always the words of his master. That a summons from him, therefore, was, bonâ fide, a summons from the Khaun, which must be obeyed in the first instance, even should it be necessary to remonstrate upon its incivility. That if this were an immemorial custom, I could scarcely expect it to be suddenly altered on my account, and that in yielding compliance with such a custom, I in no wise compromised the dignity of my Government. Above all, I remembered that the present was no season for the settlement of punctilios, for which there would be ample leisure hereafter, when Khiva should be relieved from the presence of a Russian army of invasion. That it was my most important duty, at present, to gain confidence, and conciliate favour with all classes. I accordingly told Birdler Beeg to reply to the Mehtur, that supposing the message I had just received to emanate from the Khaun Huzurut, I should comply with it. I then dressed, and rode over to the Mehtur's palace.

A large number of Oozbegs and Tooreumuns were seated at the entrance of the Mehtur's palace. They rose as I approached, and helped me to alight. Birdler Beeg ushered me through the house, to the apartment occupied by the Mehtur. I entered and saluted him. He did not rise, but returned my salutations with a clumsy nod: for his manners (if indeed they deserve such a title) are the most bearish possible; an endeavour being ever apparent to conceal his want of dignity of mind and bearing, under a tone intended to be haughty, but which, from natural deficiency of proper pride, is only ungentlemanly. I sat at his side by his invitation. He then said, " Khoosh Ammudeed" (you are welcome); the usual bread and fruits were set before me, and a basin of horrible tea, being a strong decoction made over the fire without milk, and with little sugar. Some nobles of the Court, who were seated at a distance, were signalled to withdraw. I am recording, after a considerable lapse of time, conversations and events well remembered, but not in the exact order in which they occurred. Nevertheless, I conceive it better to endeavour to arrange them, because, in so doing, many particulars are brought to remembrance, which might otherwise escape me, or find no convenient place of insertion.

The Mehtur inquired through his interpreter, what were our dispositions towards the Umuneer of Bokhara.

I replied, that they had been friendly until he seized our ambassador. The natives of these countries, be it observed, have but one name for all Government Emissaries, viz. Eelchie, which we may interpret as we please, ambassador, envoy, or agent. They themselves do not understand the difference of grades. The messenger of a sovereign is, according to their notions, an Eelchie or ambassador, however high or low his rank otherwise, and to attempt to make distinctions, would only subject our agents to be treated with neglect, as less than the ambassadors of all the petty states around. A British agent is therefore obliged to assume both the title and the consequence of an ambassador, and to insist upon all the rights accorded to such functionaries. But to continue. I added, " How would the Khaun Huzurut like to see a British army at Bokhara?"

" Not at all. Is the seizure of an Eelchie a sufficient cause of war?"

" Ample! Have you not heard that we are on terms of defiance with Persia, because Muhummud Shauh presumed to open a letter, addressed to our ambassador at Tehraun? Now, as the Khaun Huzurut would ill like to see our troops at Bokhara, and we are reluctant to war with the kingdoms of Islaum, I trust he will prevent the necessity, by inducing the Umneer to release Colonel Stoddart."

" Has any army advanced towards Bokhara?"

" That I cannot say; but it is a thing that may happen any day, unless Colonel Stoddart be released.

It is a thing which would long since have happened, but for the reluctance above mentioned: for we are the natural allies of the Muhummedan states."

He replied, "The Ummeer will not listen to the Khaun Huzurut. But the Khaun proposes the following plan for Colonel Stoddart's rescue. The Colonel is allowed to ride about Bokhara" (of this I had some doubt.) "The Khaun will send thither a small party of Tooreumuns, provided with a note from you to Colonel Stoddart. These men will meet him on any day he may appoint, carry him by force, on a swift horse, through the gates of the city, and not pause until they are beyond pursuit; a stronger party will meet and protect them, and they will bring the Colonel to Khiva. What say you to this proposal?"

The proposal was so far tempting, that I knew no other possible method of effecting Colonel Stoddart's release. But when I considered that the execution was to be entrusted to men, of whose sagacity, courage and fidelity, I knew nothing; that Colonel Stoddart might be so closely guarded, as to render the scheme impracticable; and that a hint of such a design being on foot, might cause the Ummeer to take the Colonel's life, or at any rate to subject him to fresh hardships and indignities; moreover, that it was highly probable this high-spirited officer might refuse to make his escape; I rejected the proposal with grateful thanks to the Khaun, upon the plea of the peril in which it might involve that gallant, but ill-fated officer.

The Khaun Huzurut had instructed the Mehtur to give me all possible information respecting affairs upon the frontier. I now proceeded to inquire more minutely into particulars, of which I had already gathered the substance from Birdler Beeg and the Tooreumuns we met in journeying to Khiva. The Mehtur's statement was elicited at the expense of much cross-questioning; I shall therefore couch it in my own words. The Khaun Huzurut had despatched an army of 40,000 horse, under command of the Ghoosh

Beegie,* the second officer of the state, to repel the Russian invasion. The invaders, the Mehtur persisted in estimating at four or five hundred infantry and a few guns. This absurd estimate had undoubtedly in view, to make British aid seem matter of little consequence. It had, however, a grotesque effect, when the result was understood. The Ghoosh Beegie advanced with the utmost resolution as far as the N. Western angle of the sea of Aral. It then suddenly occurred to him, that five or six hundred Koozulbaush and Toorcumun horse would answer the purpose of sweeping the idolaters from the face of the earth, fully as well as 40,000. So halting in his position, about 120 miles short of the small advanced post of the Russians, he despatched a party, with orders to seize the Russian cattle, and do any other mischief in their power. This party, finding the snow five feet in depth, were obliged to drive before them unladen Kuzzauk galloways, to beat a path or channel through it. Through this track they advanced, the snow standing high on either side. They fell valiantly upon the cattle of the Russians, and were carrying them off in triumph, when the Russians perceiving them, sent in pursuit a party of about one hundred fusileers, who coming up with the frozen horsemen, and warmed with their own exertions, shot them like sheep. The Toorcumuns fled, leaving some thirty or forty of their party on the field, and bearing with them the consoling hope, that one Russian had been hurt. The Russian field-pieces opened upon the fugitives, who never drew rein until they reached the main army.

The Ghoosh Beegie, from this little affair, conceived so supreme a contempt for the enemy, that he immediately wrote the Khaun Huzurut, saying, that he and his horsemen found the weather very cold; that the Russians were a miserable set of wretches, in all

---

* Lord falconer, literally lord of the winged things. He is second in dignity of state attain... the Mehtur, or Groom, is first. So simple ... the construction of a Tooc... sh Court.

not exceeding three or four hundred half-starved, pig-eating, idol-worshipping sons of burnt fathers; and that, as the Khaun Huzurut could, at any leisure moment, give them a brush with the besom of destruction, he humbly opined that it was quite needless to expose 40,000 men and horses to the rigour of the season, and that he should be very much obliged to His Majesty for permission to return. The Khaun Huzurut, on hearing this, very good-naturedly recalled the force to winter quarters at Ghoonguraut, near the southern border of the sea of Aral. They had returned in a miserable condition: many of them mutilated by the frost; some had lost one, some both hands; others the feet, the nose, the ears, the lips, the whole cheek, in some cases even the tongue; for the intense chill so paralyses the nerves, that those subjected to it are unconscious of the state of the members of their body; the tongue at night finds its way out of the mouth, and is instantly frozen and destroyed. The troops, however, had not yet returned to Khiva; they came in previous to my departure from that city.

Such, amid a thousand hesitations and contradictions, I learned to be the state of things on the frontier. The Russians had advanced from Orenburgh, and occupied a fort, or, as I conjectured, an entrenched camp upon the Yem (called by the Kuzzauks Djem, and by the Russians, Embah), a small brackish stream, forming, with the Irghiz, the northern limit of Khaurism. They had also pushed on a detachment, which was entrenched half way between the Yem and the sea of Aral, and it appeared to be with this detachment that the skirmish had taken place. The Mehtur believed that there were about 12,000 troops at Orenburgh, as a corps of reserve. He had heard of no advance from Astrakhan.

I then questioned him as to the limits of the frontier of Khaurism.

"You must ask the Khaun Huzurut," was the reply. It would, of course, be impossible for the Mehtur to conjecture where it might seem good or convenient to the Khaun to fix the boundary of his kingdom. All other geographical queries were equally unsatisfactory. It was evident that the Mehtur knew next to nothing of the features of his country, and that he was in terror of disclosing even that nothing, lest it should in any way clash with the Khaun's will and pleasure. To transact business with such a man was next to impossible. This he didn't know; that he would not answer; and the other I must ask the Khaun at my next audience. Great part of what he told me I knew to be false, and being restricted from all intercourse with other natives, it was extremely difficult for me to form a satisfactory judgment of the real aspect of affairs. Two Kuzzauks had, I was secretly informed, estimated the Russian force at 100,000 men, which was the estimate brought by the Khivan ambassador. The Ghoosh Beegie had killed another Kuzzauk who had just reconnoitred the Russian camp, because he had openly declared their numbers 10,000 just as the Ghoosh Beegie had written the Khaun, rating them at 3 or 400. The Khaun himself called them between 4 and 5,000, and my best intelligence estimated them at 7,500 fighting men. Yet the Mehtur insisted that they were no more than 4 or 500. I was afterwards told by a soldier who affected to have been upon the expedition, and who had either contrived to enter my room at Ooralsk, or been sent purposely, that, including the reserve, they did not exceed 7,500; a force too small for the purpose, yet which I was inclined to believe to be all employed until General Perroffski, their commander, a man of the strictest honour, asserted, as a reason that Great Britain should take no umbrage at such an expedition, that his entire force did not exceed 10,000 fighting men.

I asked the Mehtur whether the Russians had issued any proclamation previous to the invasion, informing him that such was an invariable custom amongst the nations of Europe.

He replied in the negative. This however was not true; for Russia printed and issued a statement of her grievances, declaring that she made war, not with the people of Khaurism, but with Ullah Kooli Khaun, and inviting his subjects to rise against their lord, a proclamation, be it observed, which entitled the Khaun to treat every Russian captive as a common robber, and hang him without trial. I am not sure, however, that the Mehtur was aware of this proclamation. I was not, until I reached Nuov Alexandrof (Dahsh Gullah).

I asked what the Mehtur believed to be the plea of Russia for this invasion; but he referred me to the Khaun.

"When was the invasion first reported?"

"The Russians have been always encroaching, and building forts on our frontier. This year they have come in greater force and a little farther than usual."

I told the Mehtur that I must urge, in the strongest terms, the speedy delivery to Russia of all her subjects enslaved in Khaurism; that, without this act of justice, they could expect no assistance from us in the adjustment of their quarrel; that justice was a sacred law, which we could not infringe for any consideration; that the reason we were the greatest nation on earth was, that we were the most just, and had therefore the confidence of all other nations.

He assured me that the Khaun would release all the captives.

Afterwards, our discourse took a turn which need not be detailed. Suffice it that, when I had been obliged to excuse myself from directly answering any one of the demands of the Khaun, the Vuzeer bluntly asked me, "What then *have* you come hither for? If you will grant none of our demands, of what use is it to call yourselves our allies?"

I replied that, if I had come in vain, the loss was

my own, and not his, nor his master's; and that I was quite ready to return. But that I offered them, what none had ever repented of accepting,—the friendship and good offices of the greatest nation on earth. It was for the Khaun to judge whether he should accept or reject them, or whether, without them, he could secure his kingdom against a Russian invasion; or whether the deeds of arms lately exhibited gave him any confidence of success in a struggle with Russia. I begged him to remember that the late result was from the opposition of 40,000 troops of Khiva to 400 Russians,* and asked what he purposed doing, if Russia should appear 40,000 strong, as she easily might, and *would*, if necessary. This lowered his assumed tone. I enquired whether the Khaun purposed using my services. He replied, "Yes! yes!" and was evidently alarmed at the picture I had drawn.

The result I derived from this interview was simply that the Vuzeer was bent upon deceiving me, with a view to hold cheap the assistance of England. Information I had gained none; all that was true I had previously heard, and the greater part I knew to be false.

That night I was awakened by a messenger from the Khaun Huzurut, who informed me that he was to proceed in the course of an hour towards Bokhara, with a letter for the Ummeer, urging the release of Colonel Stoddart. It was hinted to me that the Khaun had written in terms which the Ummeer would not dare to disregard. I gave this messenger a handsome present, and I believe he was sent me for the purpose of receiving it, as much as with the view of satisfying me of the Khaun's solicitude for the release of Colonel Stoddart.

* I here used the Mehtur's own estimate against him; the numbers of the Khivan army were much smaller.

CHAPTER VII.

Third Audience of the Khaun Huzurut—Explication of British Policy in Afghaunistan—The Great Mogul—Expertness of Russian Artillerymen—Dismissal—Proposal that my Letters should be read by the Khaun Huzurut—Difficulties of Correspondence—Rapacity of the Minister—Fourth Audience—Promise to restore the Russian Captives—My Objection to their unconditional Release whilst a Russian Army was advancing upon the Capital—Nature and Origin of the Misunderstanding between Russia and Khiva—Russia the Aggressor—Estimated Strength of the Army of Invasion—Its Arrest by the Snow—Skirmish—Terrors of a 6-lb. Shot—Ruminations.

AT my next audience, I read, at the Khaun's desire, the sketch I had drawn up of the political divisions of Europe, with which I deemed it important he should be acquainted—shewed him how a nation, politically allied to us in Europe, had, in Asia, interests separate from ours. I presented the Khaun with a map of the world, wherein I had inserted, in Persian characters, the names of the principal states and cities—shewed him how important to the interests of our Indian empire was the integrity of Khaurism and Persia, yet how useless to us would be the lands of those states, too poor to pay the expense of occupation, and a stronger barrier to India in their independence than they could be in our hands. I painted to him, in strong colours, the horrors of war between the higher powers of Europe, costing the lives of millions, the trampling to dust of lesser states, the expenditure of endless treasure. I shewed that true policy consisted in avoiding such wars, by timely measures in preventing the approach of a mighty nation, whom, nevertheless, we did not fear.

I then gave a brief narrative of the late campaign in Afghaunistan. His Majesty Shah Shoojah-ool-Moolk had been our guest the last twenty years. We protected and supported him; but to his entreaties for an army to recover his possessions, we had replied, that we had no quarrel with Doost Muhummud Khaun, and the chiefs of Candahar. That we could not constitute ourselves judges of the affairs of neighbouring states, so long as they did not molest us. But that when we discovered that the Ummeer and the chiefs had entered into a compact with our enemies, to admit through their territories an army for the invasion of India, the aspect of the case was changed, and giving His Majesty Shah Shoojah an army of 20,000 men, we reseated him upon the throne of his ancestors. That it was our system never to break a treaty, nor to be the aggressors in a war. That in the heart of our Indian possessions existed several Muhummedan and other states, having rich lands and revenue, and no armies for their protection; that, nevertheless, we never had molested nor ever should molest them, unless they should become the aggressors. That our empire was built on justice and good faith, and the confidence which those principles begot for their possessors.

When I had concluded a paper, of which the above contains but the heads of matter, and which was therefore somewhat lengthy, His Majesty inquired, "Of whom did you conquer Delhi?"

"Of the Mahrattas, a race of Hindoos who had wrested it from the Moguls."

"Does not a Mogul king still reign there?"

"Yes! on taking Delhi we guaranteed to the Emperor, whom we found beleaguered there, all the territory left him by the Mahrattas. He enjoys it still. The revenue is twelve lacs."

After some inquiries as to the military force of Russia, the Khaun inquired, "How many guns has Russia?"

"I cannot form an idea, but the number is great."

"I," said the Khaun, "have twenty, how many has the Queen of England?"

"The number is too great to be reckoned, and therefore no account is kept of them. The seas are covered with the ships of England, each bearing from twenty to one hundred and twenty guns of the largest size. Her forts are full of cannon, and thousands lie in every magazine. The very posts in our streets are often made of guns, which, in Persia and Afghaunistaun would be considered excellent. We have more guns than any nation in the world."

"And how often can your artillerymen fire?"

"Our field artillery can fire about seven times in a minute; but such firing would produce little effect."

"The Russians fire their guns twelve times in a minute."

"Your Majesty has been misinformed; I myself belong to the artillery, and know such firing to be impossible."

"The Persian ambassador asserts it."

"He is misinformed. No artillery on earth are more expert than the British, yet we never by choice fire more than four rounds in a minute, because we would not throw away our fire, as must happen when the gun is not pointed each time of firing. We count not the number of shots fired, but the number that take effect."

I was now dismissed, but not until I had again urged the necessity of conveying my letters to Heraut, and had again been promised an immediate opportunity. When I afterwards urged this subject upon the Mehtur, he said, "Cannot you write your letters in Persian, and submit them, in the first place, for the perusal of the Khaun Huzurut?" I replied that such an indignity would not, I was assured, be put upon an agent of the British Government. That my services were not forced upon the Khaun, who was at liberty to trust or distrust me, as he thought fit. That if he trusted me, he would not distrust my letters. If he distrusted me, the sooner he dismissed me on my return to Heraut, the better.

The Mehtur said, "Very well, prepare your letters as you please, they shall be sent forthwith." Nevertheless, no orders were issued for their conveyance, and I was still reluctant to engage in secret correspondence with Heraut (a matter of the utmost difficulty from a position so isolated by deserts), because, the discovery of such a system would increase tenfold the suspicions, already haunting the Khaun's mind.

I once more urged Mehtur to remember his promise of giving freedom to Ummeer Beeg, a Goolaum, or Government officer attached to the Persian mission, who had been taken prisoner and made a slave by Toorcumuns, whilst carrying despatches from Colonel Stoddart, at Heraut, to Sir John M'Neil. He promised that the man should be speedily released.

Birdler Beeg, a few mornings after my arrival, came to me with a message from the Mehtur, asking whether I had not got some little presents for him, such as a brace of pistols, penknives that cut steel, telescopes, and watches?

"You, of course, assured him that I had not. That I travelled Chuppah (post), and could with difficulty carry the few presents destined for the Khaun Huzurut."

It was sufficiently manifest, from Birdler Beeg's manner, that he had told a very different tale: a piece of treachery, which the favours he had received rendered doubly base.

"Your watch," the Mehtur says, "will do very well."

"Tell him he cannot have it. It was the gift of a brother no longer living. And besides, I cannot march in any comfort without it." The fact is, that all my distances were estimated by the watch, and when, afterwards, I was deprived of it, had the utmost difficulty in calculating them.

"The Mehtur," replied Birdler Beeg, "has set his heart upon it."

"He cannot have it. I will procure him one from Heraut or Cabul."

"Then your pistols."

The pistols also were a gift. They had their history. With one I had killed a tiger, as he was preparing to spring upon my elephant, and another had been my forlorn hope when I was charged in a bear's den. I was most reluctant, of course, to part with them. Fortunately, their extreme simplicity rendered them valueless in the eyes of men with whom decoration is everything. Even my telescope was an old and tried companion: but it was necessary to produce something, so I gave it and my thermometer, and several other trifling articles. The Mehtur, I found, dared not to keep to himself the telescope and thermometer. They became the property of the "Father of the conqueror of Heroes, the Father of Victory, the King of Khaurism."

At my next audience, I commenced by a serious remonstrance upon the delay attending the transmission of my letters. "It is now," I said, "several weeks since my arrival at your Majesty's capital, and my Government knows not whether I am alive or dead. Whether I have been received hospitably, or as Colonel Stoddart was received by the Umineer of Bokhara."

"What," said the Khaun with a smile, passing the edge of his right hand across the top of the middle finger of the left, "does Major Todd think I would treat you so?"

He then desired me to be seated. I obeyed, but almost immediately rose, saying that I thanked His Majesty for this attention to my Government, but that, as his prime minister and all the nobles were standing, with his permission I would do the same.

Some very important arrangements, respecting my farther proceedings, were then made and discussed. During which I urged, as a *sine qua non*, the surrender of all Russian slaves.

The Khaun said that he was ready to restore them, and asked, whether I thought they should be sent with me to meet the General commanding the Russian expedition. In that case, he said, what security have I that he will not keep the prisoners, and continue to advance upon my capital.

I could offer him none, I have no power that could have sufficed to arrest the progress of a Russian invasion. I had been sent on the spur of the moment without even credentials from the head of the Indian Government. I saw the full delicacy of the case. That it was almost a certainty, that this tardy surrender of captives would only hasten the march of the Russian army upon Khiva, and that my share in the release of the captives would then naturally be regarded by the Khaun and all the Tartar states, as a connivance with Russia, a notion that would blast all our influence in these countries. I was even now labouring under some lingering suspicion of being a Russian spy, a character which Yar Muhummud Khaun had prepared for me at Khiva, before my arrival, and which several persons had attested on oath before the Khaun; and there was a panic in these countries, waiting only some similar plea for gaining full activity, founded upon the belief, that Russia from the north, and England from the south, both nations of Christendom, and Feringees, were advancing in concert, to sweep the religion of Muhummud from the face of the earth. It was for this cause that, in speaking of our alliance, I was careful to make it embrace all the Muhummedan states, lest we might be thought to be playing one against the other, and weakening all. I need not say, that I most strictly adhered to fact in this representation, for the grasping policy of our neighbours has rendered all these kingdoms the barriers of our security. Bearing these reasons in view, I declined urging the immediate and unconditional surrender of the captives, although I insisted, in the strongest terms, upon the necessity of their ultimate and unreserved restoration; for which the Khaun gave his ready promise. I also shewed the necessity of furnishing me with every minute particular, relative to the misunderstanding with Russia, from its earliest origin to the present moment. The Khaun assured me I should know all, offering himself to supply the greater number of particulars, and referring me for the rest to the Mehtur. He desired me to question him freely, and I took advantage of the permission, of the result of which the following is an abstract.

"In the days of my father, Madreheem Khaun, there was friendship between Russia and Khiva, a free interchange of commerce and civilities. Khiva was at war with Bokhara, and, you are aware that my territories separate Bokhara from Russia, so that caravans, passing between those countries, are obliged to pass through Khaurism. About twenty years ago, during the war of Khiva and Bokhara, Russia sent a rich caravan to Bokhara, escorted by two hundred regular infantry and two guns. Should this force have joined the Bokhara army, the reinforcement, owing to the discipline of the Russians, had been formidable to Khiva. Madreheem Khaun therefore sent the commander a polite message, saying, that he could not suffer any troops or reinforcements to pass through his territories to his enemies, but that the road to Khiva, his own capital, was free to the Russians, who should receive protection and hospitality. The Russian commander refused the invitation, and endeavoured to force a passage through the Khaun, my father's, territory, thus flagrantly violating the subsisting peace. Madreheem Khaun, of course, ordered that he should be opposed by the Toorcumun and Kuzzauk horse, just after his passage of the Sirr, or Jaxartes. But the Russians, drawing up in a compact body, and stockading themselves, made a most desperate resistance, so that after much loss, the Toorcumuns and Kuzzauks contented themselves with plundering the caravan. The Russians, however, retreated, losing many of their men, to their own frontier. Thus originated the first breach between the states, which has widened, gradually, by petty aggressions on both sides; the Russians enticing over to their country my subjects, who are the wealth of my land, and my Kuzzauks and Toorcumuns, on the frontier, occasionally capturing Russians. About five years ago, the Russians built Dahsh Ghullah (literally the stone fort, which I afterwards found to be Nuov Alexandrofski, on an inlet of the Caspian), within my territories; and three years after they seized my caravans, trading in their country, and five hundred and fifty of my merchants, whom they retain prisoners in Russia."

" And what steps has your Majesty taken for their release?"

" I sent, three years ago, an ambassador with letters for the Emperor, begging him to exchange captives. The governor of Orenburgh (not the Emperor) wrote me in reply, that I must first release every Russian in slavery, and that then he would release my merchants. I sent again an ambassador, and with him, in earnest of my intention to release the captives, six of the Russian prisoners, begging that an equal number of my own people might be returned, in proof of the Emperor's willingness to exchange, and promising, in that case, to surrender all the Russians. The Russians kept the captives, imprisoned the brother of my ambassador, and sent the ambassador back with a verbal message to my letter, to the same effect as the former. The relations of my merchants assailed me with petitions, and yielding to them, I condescended to send a third ambassador with 110 captives, and a letter as before. The

Russians retained these, but rendered no return. Another verbal message from the governor of Orenburgh was the sole answer to my letter to the Emperor. I therefore perceived that Russia was only playing upon my credulity. It is six months since the return of my last ambassador."

"And how long has your Majesty known of preparations for the invasion?"

"It has sometime been reported to me, that the governor of Orenburgh had promised the Emperor of Russia possession of Khiva in the space of seven years, of which the present is the fifth year. About six or eight months ago, the Russian governor sent agents into the northern part of my territories, to purchase camels, upon some feigned pretext. Guessing for what they were designed, I forbade the sale, upon pain of death to the seller. Nevertheless, some of my Kuzzauks, on the northern frontier, supplied a considerable number to Russia."

"And what is the strength of the invading force?"

"From four to five thousand fighting men, and some guns."

"But other troops must be following this small force."

"At Orenburgh are 12,000 more."

"Is there any Russian fort or town south of Orenburgh?"

"Yes! I have heard that the Russians constructed a fort or entrenchment (Sungur) called Auk Gullah, half way between Orenburgh and *the lake of Khaurism (sea of Aral). They have also an entrenched camp upon the Yem (Embah), and an advanced post, between that and the lake of Khaurism, upon one of the springs of the Yem."

"And what are they doing?"

"They are arrested by the snow, which lies there to the depth of five feet. They await a thaw, to advance."

* Duugiz i Khaurism.

"What are your Majesty's news from the seat of war?"

"My horsemen had a skirmish with the Russians, whom they would have swept from the face of the earth, but for the severity of the cold, which froze them in their saddles. The Russians, sitting over fires, aimed with deadly certainty, and killed many of my horsemen. As the latter retreated, the enemy's guns opened upon them. "See," he added, producing from the corner or rather side of the tent, by a nod to the Mehtur, a six-pound ball, highly polished, as if it had been used for the game of bowls; "that is one of the deadly missiles, with which my subjects were assailed in their retreat."

I could scarcely restrain a smile, as I looked at my old playfellow, the six-pound shot, and then glanced at the lengthened physiognomy of "the Father[*] of the conqueror of Heroes, the Father of Victory, the King of Khaurism." I perceived pretty plainly, that so long as the six-pound shot remained in the royal pavilion, it would keep ajar the door of reconciliation.

I returned to my house in a state of mind not easily described. I examined and re-examined my position, but reason assured me there was nothing to amend. The most extensive benefit to my country might be the result; evil, should it ensue, would be confined to my own head. I only hoped the Khaun would use despatch in my mission, as every hour increased the peril of Khiva, and placed the means of averting it, farther out of reach. My position was novel and romantic. I was already the representative of two states, Great Britain and Herant, at the Court of Khiva. I was now to become in fact, though not in name, the ambassador of a Khaun of Tartary to the Court of the Muscovite. There were, heaven

---

[*] One of the letters with which I was entrusted by the Khaun Huzurut commences thus—"The words of the Father of the conqueror of Heroes, the Father of Victory, the King of Khaurism."

knew, sufficient difficulties and dangers in my path; but it was the path of duty.

I could not sleep that night, but went often into the snow-covered Court, to gaze upon the stars, and think of the possibility, how faint, yet how precious that amid my many adventures, some happier wave of destiny might cast me upon my native shore. The nine hundred miles of snowy desert disappeared before my excited fancy. The difficulties at posts and out-posts were all as nothing. I had, in the determination to succeed, a talisman, which nothing could impair or confound.

CHAPTER VIII.

Discussion of Routes—An Oozbeg Chart of the World—Relative Extent of the British and Russian Dominions—English Habits—The Khook and its Varieties—My unhappy Ignorance—Apology to the Tuscans—Necessity of foregoing all Geographical Research, imposed by the extreme Importance of my Mission, and the extreme Suspicion with which I was regarded—Another Audience—Meyendorf's Travels—The Air-gun—Discussion of Routes—Impracticability of that by the Balkaun—Difficulties of the Orenburgh Route—Recommendation by the Khaun Huzurut of that by Mungh Kishlauk and Astrakhan—Questions relative to Europe, Dress, Dwellings, Climate—Telescopes, Astrology, Female Kings—Number of Cities, Russia, China.

THE next day I had an interview with the Mehtur at his palace. He commenced, by doubts of my finding a free passage by the Orenburgh route, where so many of the Khaun's ambassadors had been arrested. I could but repeat arguments already adduced. I allowed that, by the Orenburgh route, I might more probably be detained, upon plausible pretexts, than on any other, because the invasion was by that route, and the Commander might find it convenient to delay my progress, whilst pushing on my forced marches to Khiva. But I saw no necessity for taking that route. I observed, on Burnes's map, that the Russian, Moravief, had arrived at Khiva, viâ the Balkaun. I knew not what should prevent my embarking at the Bay of Balkaun, and sailing to Astrakhan. This route must, even now, be open, I thought, or, at any rate, the Caspian would be free from its ice, by the time (twenty days hence) I was likely to reach it. The Mehtur, who knew not, I believe, previously, of the existence of this route, promised to consult the Khaun Huzurut about it.

He asked what escort I required. I replied, whatever the Khaun Huzurut might deem sufficient for my protection, through his own territories. That I did not wish to travel in state, and thought that a large number of horsemen, besides being difficult to feed in the desert, might increase my embarrassment, by occasioning alarm and suspicion at outposts. He observed, that this escort might be detained by the Russians. I replied, that they need not proceed the entire distance, but might halt some miles short of the frontier, giving me a guide to pilot me the rest of the journey, and accompany me back in case of a repulse. He asked me, whether I thought the Khaun should send an Eelchie of his own with me. I said, that the Khaun would of course do as he pleased. If the Eelchie were sent, I would accompany him: but, if he wished for my opinion, I could not recommend such a measure. Three Khiva ambassadors had, already, been arrested, and insulted. My chance of a free passage lay in my present disconnection with Khiva. The company of a Khiva envoy would, probably, form an excuse for repulsing me.

A map of the world, the production of a profound Oozbeg philosopher, was then produced; I begged a clue to this singular chart, and was rather surprised to find that Italy lay north of England; and Russia south of China. My poor English map of the world would, I foresaw, fall into great discredit, in presence of so well authenticated a chart. As to pleading the cause of Italy or China, I was not fond enough to attempt anything so hopeless. But after turning up the whites of my eyes, in compliment to the profound science of the Oozbegs, returned the map, considerably enlightened upon the subject of Eastern geography.

My own map, or rather the map I had given the Khaun, was called for, and the Mehtur begged me to point out the British and the Russian dominions. "Ah," he said, "Russia is larger than England."

"You are mistaken. This very question was the subject of a bet between the English and the Russian missions at Tehraun, which, after the most careful investigation, was decided in favour of the English. England has absolutely more territory, about five times the number of subjects, and several times more revenue than Russia. But this is not all; for a glance at the map will shew you, that the water of the world exceeds, about three times, the dry land, and, wherever the ocean rolls, there my Queen has no rival."

We then fell into conversation upon the habits of Europe.

"Are you fond of hawking?" he enquired: "does your Queen hawk?"

"My Queen is an accomplished rider, but hawking, although much practised in former days, is at present almost impossible in England, owing to the high state of cultivation."

"But in the wilderness?"

"We have no wilderness; at least the few scraps left by the plough may be several days' journey (i. e. Eastern days of journey) distant. The whole country is like a garden."

"But you could ride over the fields?"

"The fields, in England, are each a separate garden, so to speak, enclosed with ditches and a wall of thorny trees; the entrance being a high gate on hinges. Now, it is necessary, in following the falcon, to keep the eye ever fixed on the heavens, it is impossible to hawk over enclosed fields; but we follow the stag, the fox, and hare."

"But how, over these walls?"

"We teach our horses to leap them."

"That must be dangerous. Our horses cannot leap."

"We account this the most exciting circumstance of the chase, because it tries the mettle of the horse, the courage and skill of the rider."

"Do the English eat Khook (pig)?"

"Eat what?" I inquired, very innocently.

"Khook" (pig).

"What is Khook?"

Now, neither the Mehtur nor the interpreter having ever seen a pig, in all their lives, it was no easy matter for them to describe the unclean beast. The interpreter commenced a clumsy attempt; I heard him out patiently, and then said—

"You mean that animal with long ears and a sweet voice. The Khur (ass). No! we never eat anything so unclean."

This was a back stroke at the Oozbegs, which I thought might be useful. They devour the wild ass.

"I don't mean the Khur," persisted the interpreter, "I mean Khook, Khook," looking me in the eyes. "Don't you know what Khook is?"

I hadn't the slightest intention of knowing. "Khook," I repeated dreamily with a most lamb-like stare of innocence; "Khook. Oh! you mean that big bird with red cheeks, that flaps his wings and wakes us in the morning; yes, we eat him."

"No! I don't mean the cock; but Khook, Khook."

"Well then," I said, if it is neither beast nor fowl, perhaps it is a fish."

The interpreter could not, in politeness, press the matter farther. The question, I well understood to proceed from any thing but idle curiosity. The knowledge, that the English are a pig-eating generation, would have been, at that moment, an effectual barrier to all alliance between the states; for a hearty detestation of pork may be said to be the only vital spark surviving, in the religion of him of Mecca. My own servants had not a suspicion of our monster-eating propensities. For they had seen me slay several plump wild hogs, and leave the carcases in the field—a necessary precaution, which every member of the mission equally observed.

Ah! ye luscious, cosy ones of the earth! ye savory haunched Tuscans! Beloved of Achilles and Theseus! Not abhorred of the all-beauteous Helen! How often hath my heart bled, my mouth watered in vain, as I left you to the foul jaws of the grave-digging Hyæna, the fouler beak of the loathsome vulture! Visit not, with lean haunches, my involuntary crime! Think of the glorious amends I made you in London, when out of eye-shot of the faithful Summud Khaun! Think, ye jolly ones, of the thin red slices, deep set in consolidated marrow, edged with melting amber, stuck with cloves from the Indian Isles! Say, did I not make amends in those few days, by the keenness of my gusto, for seventeen years of lean abstinence from your classic bounties, eaten to the tune of "fresh rolls and golden butter," digested (O! forgive me) beneath the inspiring influence of my native skies!

My time passed heavily enough at Khiva. I had once gone forth to see the King's garden and palace, but I was attended by the Major Domo, and received a hint, that it might be as well not to speak to, nor even to look, attentively, at any one I might happen to meet. On visiting the Mehtur afterwards, he inquired what I had made the dimensions of the garden, and seemed incredulous, when I assured him I had made no measurements. This little incident was a lesson to me, to prefer complete seclusion, to the humiliation of being dogged by spies, and of being myself suspected of spying out the nakedness of the land. I had early perceived, that the main difficulty at Khiva, and my most important duty, would be, to win confidence, in spite of all the engines set on foot, to render me suspected. I was not without my share of curiosity, and knew of how much consequence to the learned world are all particulars, relative to the Oxus and the Sea of Aral, which I had long thirsted to visit. But I remembered, that in a few months, could I only win the confidence of the Khaun, all these objects would be open to our investigation, and that my own political duties could not, for an instant, be weighed against those relating only to science. I therefore resigned with a sigh, but without jealousy, to some more fortunate successor, discoveries quite within my reach, but which prudence forbad me to stretch my hand to grasp.

I had brought with me a few oft-perused books, which were some relief to the tedium of my imprisonment; but my furniture was so miserable, that I had little temptation to use the pen; an exercise, during which I was obliged to bolt my door; and, indeed, I dared not make any memoranda, which sent to Herant, and opened on the road by the Khaun, might have seemed to him the production of a spy; or which, falling into the hands of Russia, would have been useful hints to her, in her designs upon Khiva. Certain very important particulars, of which a copy had been sent to Cabul, and which I wished to bear to the British ambassador at St. Petersburg, lest the said copy should be lost, I travestied, threw into verse, and committed to memory, destroying the paper. They are curious, but cannot just now see the light.

When next I was summoned to attend the Khaun Huzurut, and ushered, as usual, in the first place, into the Mehtur's durbar, a French book was placed before me, and I was asked whether I could read it. I opened, and found it to be the travels of Meyendorf to Bokhara, from Orenburgh. I informed the Mehtur of the nature of its contents. He opened it occasionally, and begged me to read a passage into Persian, a task, at that time, by no means easy to me. I felt the whole time a little uneasy, because the traps already laid for me, made me apprehensive of a snare, and I thought it probable this book had been taken from the Russians, and would pass as a Russian book; in which case, my affirmation of ignorance of the Russian tongue would appear a falsehood. I was careful, therefore, to explain, that this language was generally used in Europe, as a medium of intercourse between states, whose language differed; even as Persian is employed throughout the East. I offered to translate into Persian any part, or parts of this work, for the information of the Khaun.

I was soon summoned to attend the Khaun in his black tent. He asked some further particulars of the book, which I rendered him. He then told me, it had been seized in a caravan, proceeding from the Russian frontier to Bokhara. Many seals and letters were also exhibited, but the latter being in the Russian character, were to me illegible.

The Khaun enquired of the manufacture of guns, and whether, in this art, the English did not excel all other nations. I assured him he was rightly informed. He ordered several guns to be produced, and I told him the names of the cities in which they had been made. A air-gun was then placed in my hand, and I was asked whether I could tell, what it was? I, of course, explained, and asked for the air-pump, which was produced. The gun, however, was out of order, and the key was lost; I offered to repair it, and it was sent to my quarters for the purpose: but owing to my being obliged to make up every instrument I required, and a wooden model for the key, it was many days before I could repair the damage. This gun had no maker's name, nor could I ever learn its history; but I guessed, from the mystery attending it, that it had either been taken in the plunder of a caravan, or from the travellers, murdered about two years previously at Khiva.

I explained to the Khaun the nature and power of the steam gun, which discharges sixty balls in a minute, thus rendering utterly impracticable any breach defended by it.

Speaking of Colonel Stoddart, the Khaun said, "I hear, that the Russian ambassador at Bokhara applied to the Ummeer, for Colonel Stoddart's freedom, and that he should be delivered, for the purpose, to the

Russian government. That, upon this, the Ummeer summoned Colonel Stoddart, and asked him whether the Russians were likely to treat him well, and what he thought of the proposal; and that Colonel Stoddart replied, 'The Russians would undoubtedly treat me well; but when my own Government demands me, what will your highness answer?' That the Ummeer was much struck with the nobleness of such an answer, from one who was in prison, and in hourly danger of death; and taking off his own rich cloak of sables, made them clothe Colonel Stoddart in it, and lead him, on horseback, through Bokhara." This anecdote, which the Khaun fully credited, I have not, to this day, means of confirming or contradicting. It accords so well, however, with the spirit of this high-minded officer, whose sufferings were paralleled only by his fortitude, that I had no difficulty in believing it. General Perroffski afterwards confirmed the fact of his attempt to release Colonel Stoddart.

My approaching journey was discussed. "What retinue did I require?"

The Khaun Huzrut knew best what was necessary to guard me through his territory; but I thought that three or four Russian slaves, placed at my disposal, might facilitate matters, serving as an earnest of the Khaun's intention to free the remainder, and acting as guides and interpreters to me upon the Russian frontier. The Khaun readily promised I should have them, and gave orders to that effect to the Mehtur, who, by a manœuvre, eventually deprived me of them. I referred to my late discussions with the Mehtur, and enquired the route viâ the Balkaun. He replied, that the people of those parts, Yahmoot Toorcumuns, were in open rebellion to his authority, and were plunderers by profession. He could not, therefore, secure my safety by that route. But that, farther north, was the port of Mungh Kishlauk, whence the Bokhara caravans embark for Astrakhan, and vice versâ. That the distance was about 16 days' journey from Khiva, i.e. 480 miles. That the Caspian was at present frozen, but that inquiries should be set on foot respecting this route, and the Toorcumun chief of those parts be called to consult with me. I urged strongly the vital necessity of despatch; but the Khaun answered, that the roads at present were closed by the snow, and the Caspian by the ice. That were I now to start, I should, in all probability, be brought back a cripple, like his Toorcumun horsemen. I replied, that I would run any risk to myself, rather than incur the detention, which would be certain ruin to my project. But that I would clothe myself and servants in furs, and had no apprehension. He asked, whether I did not find my scanty European dress much too light for the climate. I explained, that it had been made in Hindoostaun, of which the climate is very warm. That in England, we wore a dress of similar fashion, but admitting of several under-garments.

"England, then, is cold. Is it as cold as Khiva?"

"The cold there is of a different character; here it is excessively dry, with little wind and a clear sky; in England the sky is generally overcast, there is much wind, and too much rain."

"How then can the people exist, with such a dress?"

"Our houses in England are better adapted to exclude the weather; they have a chimney in each room, glass windows, and floors of plank."

"Yes, your rich men's houses. But what do the poor do?"

"The poor have glass windows, chimneys, and floors of plank. The house of a labourer in England is far more comfortable than the palace of a nobleman in Persia or Herant."

"But your poor cannot be always at home."

"When abroad they are either walking or labouring, either of which occupations keeps them warm; and besides, their dress is of thicker materials than mine, and its closeness to the body excludes the wind better than does the loose dress of Khiva."

"When you come to see me, put on your warm Asiatic dress. You look cold in that which you wear."

I bowed.

"Have you any telescopes with which you can see the interior of a fort or house? I have heard of an Englishman who had one."

"No; we have telescopes that turn people head downwards,* which, perhaps, has given rise to your Majesty's idea, and we have instruments for measuring from a distance the height of the walls; but we have none that would shew us the interior from without." I then described Herschel's grand telescope. He asked the use of it. I replied that each planet had its own peculiar form, which could be ascertained by means of a telescope; that the moon, in particular, appeared drawn so near that we could make maps of her surface; that by means of telescopes we had discovered planets that were not previously known to exist, and fixed stars where, to the naked eye, there appeared but a void in the heavens.

"Do you practise astrology?"

"No; we make many calculations by the position of stars, of the sun, and of the moon, but we do not believe that the destiny of man can be discovered thereby."

"Is your king really a woman?"

"She is."

The Khaun smiled, and all his satellites, as in duty bound, giggled.

"How," he inquired, "can she rule, being roo-posh (concealed)?"

"Our females, like those of the Toorcumuns, are

---

* When surveying in Rohilkund, I once occupied the castle of a village in the Shahjehanpoor district, and exhibited to the principal Zumeendar the effects of my night telescope, which inverts objects. A report got abroad that I had a telescope which sets people, at any distance, on their heads, and all the women of the village were instantly shut up, lest I should take this liberty with them.

not concealed. The Queen of England has ministers, who transact business for her."

"Are they women?"

"No, they are men. They receive their general instructions from the Queen, and act accordingly."

"But how can your Queen administer justice?"

"Our kings do not, like your Majesty, administer justice in person; there are Cauzies appointed for the purpose. These commit the proceedings and the evidence to paper; and in cases of life and death the Queen reads the particulars, and confirms or annuls the sentence by a stroke of her pen."

"Do you always choose women as your kings?"

"No, we give preference to heirs male; but when there is a female and no male, rather than disturb the country by introducing a new family of claimants of the crown, we crown this female. One of the greatest of our kings was a woman."

"Is your king married?"

"No; she is very young."*

"But she will marry?"

"Inshallah."

"And if she marry, does her husband become king?"

"By no means; he has no authority in the state." Here there was some more smiling.

"How many cities has your king?"

"They are too numerous to be computed."

"Russia," said the Khaun, "has four hundred, Hindostaun two hundred, but China has the greatest number. Do you know anything of China?"

"We have merchants there."

"It is the most powerful of empires."

"We do not consider it such. About five and twenty years ago we sent thither an ambassador in a gun-ship; the Emperor insisted that he should knock his head on the ground seven times on entering the

* I did not hear of her Majesty's marriage until several months after this conversation.

presence; he refused, but consented to bow seven times, provided the prime minister of China would do the same before a picture of the king of England. The Emperor, in great wrath, ordered the guns of his fort to open upon the ambassador's ship. The ambassador's ship returned the salute with about forty heavy guns, and speedily destroyed the castle. The Chinese have neither army nor fleet, but their country is highly populous and productive."

I give the last anecdote as I related it, but although I believe the main facts are correct, I may very possibly have failed in the minutiæ, my remembrance of Lord Amherst's Embassy not being very distinct.

CHAPTER IX.

Delay in my Mission, and the impatience under it—Cross Examination upon Articles of Faith—Kawff—Baub-ool-Mandeb—People and Customs of Hindostaun—Mungh Kishlauk Guide—His Testimony—Another Audience—Inhabitants of the Ocean—Fish—Serpents—Sub-marine Sailing—Gun Vessels—Sea Fights—Towns in the Sea—Magic—Contrivances as Wonderful in Common Use by the British—Steam Looms—Mints—Telegraphs—Steam Vessels and Steam Carriages—Our Well of Alchemy—Origin of the Ducat—Private Intelligence—Extreme Anxiety of the Khaun Huzurut to effect Colonel Stoddart's Release, and bring him to Khiva.

SEVERAL days elapsed, since the Khaun had expressed his determination to use my services: but the day of departure seemed as distant as ever. I fretted with impatience at a delay, which threatened to render my agency vain. The Khaun Huzurut in reply said, that the roads were not yet open, that the direct route, viâ Orenburgh, was buried five feet beneath the snow, and that the Caspian was still frozen. I said, that I would run any risk, rather than the failure of my mission, which delay must occasion. That if it were necessary to await the breaking up of the ice from the Caspian, I had better do so on the shores of that sea, to be always watching my opportunity, lest the first boat should escape me. But I could, at any rate, even now try the Orenburgh route, which, by one properly clad and mounted, might be passed.

I was summoned to an audience of the Khaun Huzurut. In the Mehtur's palace I found an unusual assembly, of which the Khojeh Mhirahm, the Nogay, and several other priests formed the conspicuous group. After the withdrawal of the usual symbols of hospitality, the Mehtur commenced a cross examination relating to our religious tenets. The Khaun, it appears, was in dread, or some of his holy men were so for him, lest he should commit his affairs to an idolater or other unholy person.

"Are the Russians Christians?"

"They so profess themselves."

"Do they worship images?"

"They employ images and pictures in their worship."

"Do the English employ such?"

"By no means. It is now about three hundred years since England separated herself from those nations who use such symbols, believing it to be a forbidden custom."

"What do you think of God?"

"That he is a Spirit, without figure or material substance. That he is one, and has no partaker of his Deity. That he has existed from all eternity, and will exist for ever. That he is pure, holy, almighty, and omniscient."

"And which way do you turn when you address God in prayer?"

"We turn towards God."

"Where is he?"

"Everywhere, above, below, around; creation is filled with his presence."

"We turn towards Mecca."

"And *we*, toward God."

"What do you do with your dead?"

"We bury them in the earth."

"How do you turn the bodies?"

"We have no order on this head, but I believe they are generally laid east or west."

"Do you believe in the resurrection?"

"We do."

"What do you believe of it?"

"That at the appointed day, the dead shall arise.

They who have done good to life everlasting, and they who have done evil to the torments of hell."

"We believe the same. Do you believe that Christ shall come again?"

"It is so written in our books, that at the resurrection Christ shall appear, to judge the quick and the dead."

"But do your people expect him now immediately?"

"There have, ever since the death of Christ, been men so simple as to interpret the Gospel thus. But it is not the general belief of Christians, nor of any of the sober-minded amongst them." This was a ticklish subject, at the moment of a panic, caused by the Christian arms.

"Do you believe Christ to be the Son of God?"

"What do *you* call him?"

"He was the son of Huzurat Mariam."

"And his father?"

They could not answer this. "But what," I added, "do your own books call him?" Another pause. "Do they not call him Rooh-oollah. The Spirit of God? Will you explain this. The spirit of a spirit. I will then inform you, why *we* call him, as he called himself, the Son of God."

They had no answer. To my accomplished and ever-honoured friend Major Todd, Envoy at Heraut, I was indebted for this query, which is unanswerable by an orthodox Muhummedan.

"You don't use images or pictures in your worship."

"No; I have already assured you that we regard it as senseless and forbidden, because God is without form, and he alone is worshipped."

"But the Russians use them!"

"I have heard that they do."

"And what do you say of those who do so?"

"We say that they are unwise."

"Do you not call them Kawfurs?" Infidels.

"Kawfur is a term of reproach, and we are commanded to bestow no ill names upon fellow men, for we are all alike the work of God's hand. Idolatry is simply ignorance. No man, knowing that God is without form, would worship an idol."

"God's hand you say. Has God hands?"

"I spoke figuratively. God is a spirit, and has no members."

"But the Russians are Christians?"

"They so call themselves."

"And they worship images. The English are Christians, do they not the same?"

"Are you a Kawfur? I have twice told you, that the English do not worship idols, are not Kawfurs. How do you like being asked if you are a Kawfur? If you do not like it, why do you insult your guest by the question?"

This I said with much assumed warmth of manner, for I was anxious to close a discussion, that might be embarrassing if carried farther. The Mehtur apologised, and begged me not to be affronted. The interpreter, at a signal from him, discontinued the questions, which had all been concocted and written down for the occasion. What followed were matters of curiosity.

"Have you ever seen the mountains of Kawf?"

"Never; but many of our travellers have crossed them."

"Indeed; where are they?"

"They separate Persia from Roume."

"These are not the mountains I allude to. I mean those, in which Alexander the Great shut up Gog and Magog and the jins, in large caverns."

"These are the very same."

"No! No! The Kawf, I mean, has never been seen, and cannot be crossed. The first morning shews itself, through a chink in these mountains, which are far away to the east, but nobody knows where. You say that Colonel Stoddart has sailed round the world, did he never see them?"

"Not the Kawf you allude to, but he has probably seen the mountains which we, the Persians and Turks, call Kawf, although their present name is Elboorz, for he was long in Persia."

"Have you ever seen Baub-ool-Mandeb (I believed this was the name), where an angel stands whirling a fiery sword?"

"The entrance to the Arabian sea is so called, but I never heard of the angel."

"The next question related to some well in Hindoostaun, where some other angel dwelt, or was confined, but it has escaped my memory."

"How is Hindoostaun peopled?"

"Chiefly by two races, the Hindoos and the Moosulmauns: the first being the original inhabitants, the second descendants of the soldiers of Sooltaun Maimood of Ghuzni, who was a Toork, although his soldiers were generally Afghauns; and descendants of the soldiers of Timoor Lungh, who were Moguls. The number of my Queen's Muhummedan subjects exceeds the entire population of Khaurism and Bokhara. They are undisturbed in the exercise of their faith, and their rights and property are as secure as those of Englishmen. The bulk of our Indian cavalry, those employed at Cabul, are Moosulmauns, generally Soonnies. This will shew you how absurd are the reports made to the Khaun by our enemies, that we cast the Koraun into the ditches at Cabul. Such an act would lose us, in all probability, our empire in India."

"Are there any men in India who worship dogs?"

"I have heard of none; one of their idols has the shape of a monkey, another has an elephant's head. The cow is sacred, and they will not kill the wolf, nor the most deadly of their snakes, because they are sacred to the Goddess of Destruction. Their most extraordinary superstition is the tenderness some of them have for animal life. This is carried so far, that lands are left by the pious to feed men who are to feed upon their bodies the lice and descendants of the lice of the testator."

These topics were continued, to the extreme amusement of all the company, but the rest of the conversation has escaped me.

The Mehtar, who had been summoned by the Khaun, now returned and asked me whether I wished to go to St. Petersburg. I replied that I wished to do exactly as the Khaun Huzurut might command; that for myself the undertaking was fraught with peril, not only to my life, but to my fame; for, if it should not succeed, I should be in disgrace with both my own government and the Khaun Huzurut: that, nevertheless, I was quite ready to go, and saw the necessity of losing no time in doing whatever was to be done; for the snow was fast melting, and opening the road of the Russian advance. He assured me I should be speedily under way, and asked by what route I purposed travelling. I said that I had lately been given to understand, by messages, that the Khaun Huzurut had decided upon the Orenburgh route; that I left the choice to his Majesty. He replied that the Orenburgh route was not open; that the Khaun Huzurut thought *that* by Mungh Kishlauk preferable. I was surprised, but rather agreeably so, for I considered this route the least difficult. He added that the Khaun Huzurut wished me to consult a Mungh Kishlauk guide upon the subject. This guide, a Kuzzauk in a sheepskin cloak and wolf-skin bonnet, both with the fur inward, was accordingly introduced. In answer to my queries, he said that the Caspian, by the time I could reach it, would be free from ice; that at Mungh Kishlauk were always plenty of boats, belonging to the Russians and Nogyes, or Russian Tartars; that the Caspian had been frozen as far as to three miles from the shore, but was now nearly free from ice; that he was just arrived from thence, and had found snow upon the road: that Dash Ghullah was about three marches from Mungh

Kishlauk, was garrisoned by 500 Russian infantry and some artillery; that it lay north of Mungh Kishlauk; that Mungh Kishlauk was west of Khiva, and distant from it sixteen camel marches, or 480 miles; that the Bokhara caravans found boats there every year for Astrakhan; that there was no town there, but there were very extensive camps of Kuzzauks and Toorcumuns. This was all that I could learn of him through the interpreter, and the result was favourable to the Khaun's present intention. I expressed my readiness to follow this route.

I then attended the Khaun Huzurut. He was as usual very gracious; asked whether I had selected my route, whether I had consulted the guide, and when I should be ready to start. I replied that I was given to understand his Majesty preferred the Mungh Kishlauk route, a sentiment in which I heartily concurred; that I had consulted the guide, and would be ready to start in three days, provided that orders were given to allow me to make the requisite purchases. He then asked many questions relating to Europe. "Was it true that the ocean contained monstrous fish?"

"Quite true; I had seen many that were upwards of fifty feet in length, and had walked in the skeleton of another of ninety feet."

"Are there any sea-serpents?"

"There are undoubtedly in the sea serpents of ordinary size. I myself have seen many. But it is reported that the sea contains a serpent of enormous size, upwards of 100 feet in length and of great thickness, with head and long mane like those of the horse, which it elevates to a great height above the waters. This I had *not* seen, and its existence was doubtful."

"Is it true that your ships sail under water?"

"It is not true; we have machines by which we can descend safely and remain at the bottom of the sea. Indeed an American invented one, in which a man could travel about under water. Its object was, to convey and fix to the bottom of enemies' ships boxes filled with gunpowder, to be ignited by means of a lock connected with clock-work."

"I have heard that your ships carry guns."

"This is quite true; the largest vessels have 130 or 120 guns, the medium 74, carrying balls of 32 or 64lbs."

"What is the use of these guns? Do ships ever fight?"

"Ships of different nations have the most terrible engagements. It sometimes happens that the guns on either side amount to 1500. A ship of 120 guns fires sixty guns at once at the same enemy, and that when the ships are grappling. No battles on land can compare for terror with sea engagements: sometimes a shell or a red hot shot falls into the powder magazine of a vessel, and its crew of 1200 souls are blown to atoms. But ships are also employed to take towns and fortresses."

"What! are there towns in the sea?"

"Yes, there are towns on lands surrounded by the sea; there are many others by the sea-side. St. Petersburg is one of these. Such towns can be destroyed by ships of war. England is surrounded by the sea. Your Majesty has outposts of horsemen on your frontiers, who place a single sentinel on watch, to prevent intrusion: instead of that sentinel, *we* plant a ship of seventy-four guns, which flits to and fro, day and night, about the point it is to guard, and and suffers nothing hurtful to enter. Your Majesty's sentry carries, perhaps, a matchlock; my Queen's sentry carries seventy-four of the largest guns, and 700 armed men."

"Do the English practice magic?"

"No! but they have machines and inventions more wonderful. Looms with wheels innumerable, moved by steam, that weave cloth, almost without the direct agency of man. Mints worked by steam, which coin silver at the rate of 100,000 pieces a day;

and at which men are employed only to feed the machine. Telegraphs, by which we can send news, the distance of four hundred miles, in two hours. Steam vessels that move in the teeth of a gale; and steam carriages that travel at the rate of forty miles an hour; so that, were such introduced into the Khaun Huzurut's dominions, people might start this evening from Khiva and dine to-morrow at Herant, which, at present, is a journey of twenty-two days."

The Khaun Huzurut inquired the nature of our telegraphs.

At that time I had not heard of the application of galvanism to this purpose. I said, "they were of two kinds, one a series of towers, at long distances, upon which flags were displayed, as signals one to the other, these flags being moved by machinery into different figures, for each of which there is a corresponding word or sentence known to those stationed at the towers. The other process was effected by means of thin iron tubes, running under ground from station to station, and filled with water. This water, being struck at one end, rises instantly at the other and strikes a little drum or bell; the number of pulsations giving the word or sentence to be communicated." For want of terms common to the two languages, and, indeed, from my imperfect knowledge of Persian, I found it very difficult to explain these things. But the importance of the telegraph seemed to be felt by the Khaun. He inquired, if it would not be possible to introduce it into his dominions.

I replied, that it was not impossible, but would be a very difficult task, and the expense would be in proportion, as chains of towers must be erected at intervals of fifteen miles; each of these towers must have a telegraph, telescopes, and an establishment of intelligent men to make and receive signals.

"I have heard from good authority that you have wells of such wonderful property that lead or iron dipped into them becomes silver, and copper is changed into gold. Is this the case?"

"By no means."

"Whence, then, do you get the ducat, which, every one knows, is made thus?"

"The ducat is not an English coin, but the currency of several other states of Europe. It is made, like other gold coins, of gold found in mines. As for British gold, the commerce and credit of the entire world is our well of alchemy."

I was now dismissed, and returned full of hope of speedily departing on my mission. A mission, fraught with peril and perplexity, yet in which every hope and interest was embodied. My secret intelligence tallied very well with what I observed. The Khaun had been assailed by those who affirmed that they knew me for a Russian spy, and that the English were only a clan of Russians, but, by cross-examining the Persian ambassador, he had got the better of these suspicions. At the same time, it had been represented to him, that the English are a nation very jealous of insult, and very chary of the blood of their people; that, although they never break treaty, they never forgive the death of a fellow-subject; and that they might, should any evil befall me on the journey, attribute it to treachery, and make it subject of quarrel; hence all the expedients used to make me beg to be sent to St. Petersburg. This was a point I had been unwilling to concede at first, from fear that it might strengthen suspicion of some connivance with Russia, and, latterly, for the sake of consistency. One cause of delay, I was assured, was the desire of the Khaun to get Colonel Stoddart over to Khiva, either that he might send him, and reserve me as a hostage, or reverse that arrangement. Colonel Stoddart was represented to him as a very tall man, who wore a cocked hat and plume, and this, and the efforts made for his release, had given the Khaun a great idea of his rank and consequence.

CHAPTER X.

Interview with the Mehtur—The Book—Insolence of the Minister—My Resentment of it—Audience—Account of the murdered Strangers—Purchase of Ummeer Beeg's Freedom—Minister's Love of Watches and of Calomel—The Air-gun—Paper Kite of Khaurism—Its musical Properties—Its Mechanism.

WHEN next I saw the Mehtur at his palace, there lay before him a prayer-book, bound in coarse calf, with brass clasps. He put it into my hand, and asked if I could read it. I opened and found it to be in Russian character, and therefore replied in the negative. This book, from what followed, I have since fancied was part of the property of the European travellers murdered at Khiva: and that the object of showing it me was, to ascertain whether those travellers were or were not English, as they pretended. I was not then so familiar as I am now, with the Russian character, and may possibly have mistaken some other for it. The Russians disown the murdered travellers, in toto. The character of this book, supposing it to have been their property, would *prove* nothing. I asked the Mehtur whence he had procured this book, but he would give me no answer. He asked what documents would be requisite for my mission. I informed him. He sent for his interpreter, and for a book, handsomely bound and secured by a lock of gold set with turquoises. This he opened, and read aloud at several parts. It was in Toorkish, and seemed to be a register of letters, written by Kings of Khaurism to other potentates. He asked me several particulars, and seemed much at a loss how her Majesty of England was to be addressed, being a female. I explained to him the nature of the form, usual on such occasions. We then had some conversation upon the subject of my mission, and, upon recalling to the Mehtur an assurance he had once given me, but which he was now afraid to acknowledge (the Khaun Huzurut having altered his mind), he told me I lied.

I had borne with difficulty the insolence of his messages, when he wished to see me. I had that day received one, which was couched in the following words: "The Mehtur calls you," and I had felt myself obliged to inform him civilly, that more politeness was requisite. Now, to tell an Asiatic he lies, is no great thing in a land where everyone lies according to his rank, and the greatest man is the greatest liar; but, in order to avoid a species of insult, not over grateful to a British officer's feelings, I had particularly explained to him that we suffered no such freedom, and that, to give a gentleman the lie, was an insult to be washed out only with blood. I felt, therefore, that he was without excuse in the present insult, offered, in my person, to my Government, and rising, expressed, in the strongest terms, my sense of his incivility, and then walked out of the house, mounted my horse, and rode home.

In the evening I attended the Khaun Huzurut. The particulars of this audience are not all fresh in my remembrance. After some preamble, he observed, "Two travellers arrived at Khiva, some time ago, calling themselves Englishmen. They came from Meshed, and were attended by five Persian servants. It was told me that they were Russians, and I demanded their passports, or other testimonials. They had none, and had entered my territories and capital without permission or report. I ordered, that they should be searched and cross-examined. They proved to be Russians, and I gave orders for their execution."

He related all this with a pleasant countenance:

but, it may be believed, I heard it with feelings in which indignation mingled. The travellers, indeed, if Russians, were spies, and therefore justly treated; and, if of any other nation, had no business there without the testimonials necessary to identify them, or without compliance with the usages of the country. There was also no doubt, that they were supposed to be Russian spies when executed. But still, to the native of a free and civilized land, such murders (and death without open trial deserves no better name) appear both cowardly and horrible. I could not express indignation at an act, just, according to the notions of the country; but I expressed my deep regret that the Khaun Huzurut should so have acted, and my voice perhaps expressed something more. "If," I added, "your Majesty had imprisoned or otherwise secured them. But God alone can restore life."

"It certainly is a pity," said the Khaun, with a good-humoured smile, and in the tone in which mere mortals speak of the death of rats, "but they were Russians and spies, and arrived at a moment when I was incensed by the seizure of my ambassador. They called themselves English, but were proved to be Russian spies. At that time, I had never heard of such a nation as the English. Some days subsequently, the gallantry of an Englishman (Captain Pottinger, the hero of Heraut) was reported to me, and I inquired who the English were. No one could satisfy me, but the most learned were of opinion, that the English were a petty tribe (Taifah) of the Russians. Soon after this, news was brought me, that the English had conquered Hindostaun, and were invading Cabul."

The Khaun then inquired, what assurance I had that the Russians would not murder, or at any rate arrest me? I replied, that our Governments were at peace. That an English ambassador was at St. Petersburgh, a Russian ambassador at London. That amongst the nations of Europe free intercourse was maintained between the states until declaration of hostilities, and that Russia had too great respect for Great Britain to molest a British subject.

The Khaun remarked, that they had arrested all his ambassadors.

Such things, I said, might occur where retaliation was impossible; but that the capitals of Great Britain and Russia were only ten days' sail apart, and that the naval and military force of England were too formidable to be trifled with.

At my next interview with the Mehtur, certain letters were produced, and translated from Toorkish into Persian, for my information. I took copies, and corrected several capital errors; I discussed with him other public business, and then pressed upon him the release of the Goolaum, Ummeer Beeg, reminding him of his oft-repeated promise to release him.

"What," said he, "will you give me for him?" It is to be observed that he had promised to free him without price.

"Any fair price."

"You shall have him for a thousand ducats."

"Such a sum was never given for a slave, unless he were a chief. Forty ducats would be a large price, but, for the sake of friendship, I will give you a hundred."

"I won't take money for him; I will give him for your watch."

This was a hard bargain, but I could not for an instant hesitate to end, by any sacrifice of sentiment, the misery of poor Ummeer Beeg, so I drew out and gave him my faithful companion, and he promised that the Goulaum should be released, a promise of which the execution was long deferred. Ummeer Beeg, was a Government servant, and his release formed part of my instructions. I did not, therefore, scruple to charge Government the price of an ordinary silver watch; though, had it been necessary, I had willingly stripped myself of all my property to procure the freedom of this gallant fellow.

The Mehtur was as delighted with the watch as I have seen a child with his first rattle, before the poetry of the thing has given way to curiosity and the organ of destructiveness, and he has discovered the simple and prosaic process by which those glorious tooth-enlivening sounds are produced. But far from being contented with this addition to his stock of three or four, he begged me to write to the British envoy and minister at Cabul for another, adding, that no number of watches would satisfy him, and that he very much desired a night telescope. He again pressed me to doctor his sick servant, and, although the case was very simple, and I believed I had the means of curing it, I steadily declined, upon the oft-urged plea, that my mission was of too much importance to be risked for any consideration. Success in one instance would have rendered it impossible to refuse aid in others. Some of the patients might get worse under treatment, or die, or be executed, within twenty years of taking the Feringee medicine, and the British character would be lost. He also begged for some more calomel, but this I declined, regretting that I should already have suffered his solicitations to prevail. I was curious to know the purpose for which he required it. He had obtained the former supply upon pretence of some alchemical experiment. He now assured me that he took it daily. I remonstrated in the strongest terms against the folly of employing this medicine idly, telling him its horrible effects, but he only laughed. Mercury is a nostrum, to which Asiatics ascribe many miraculous properties, for instance, the determining of the sex of the child to be begotten. He afterwards pressed me for what he called warm medicines, to invigorate the constitution. I am very dull at such hints, being myself a water drinker; and he was at length obliged to state pretty broadly the nature of the medicine in request, to wit, brandy or other spirits. I assured him I had none, and never used such things. I could indeed have procured him a supply from the Jews and Hindoos, who, in spite of priestly and royal edicts, make this article for the nobles of Khiva, had I deemed it either a safe or respectable means of ingratiating myself with him.

As I had now completed the repairs of the Khaun's air-gun, I exhibited it, to his great astonishment and delight. I shewed him how to use the pump, to load and discharge the piece, and explained to him, by means of the former, the principle of the steam engine. I was not present when it was taken to the Khaun, but understand that he was equally delighted. The Mehtur pressed me hard to repair his watches, but having no instruments, I would not run the risk.

In riding home, poor Ummeer Beeg, whose release I had just purchased, came and kissed my hand. I begged him, for the present, to keep aloof, lest he should incense his master against him; telling him, I doubted not he would be set free in a few days.

Seeing some children on the road with their paper kites, I approached to examine the contrivance by which these toys emit a musical sound whilst floating in the air. The contrivance is very simple, and quite worthy of adoption into England. The kite is a square, formed upon two diagonals of light wood, whose extremities are connected by a tight string, forming the sides of the square. Over the whole paper is pasted. A loose string upon the upright diagonal receives the string by which the kite is to be held, and a tail is fastened to its lower extremity. The transverse diagonal, or cross-stick is then bent back like a strung bow, and fastened by a thread or cat-gut. Of course, every breeze that passes the kite vibrates this tight chord, and the vibrations are communicated to the highly sonorous frame of the kite. And, as numbers of these kites are left floating in the air all night, the effect is that of aerial music; monotonous, but full of melancholy interest. On my first arrival at Khiva, I was much struck with this novel, dreamy melody, which continued the livelong night. My servants had assured me it proceeded from the Jew's harps, which the women of Khiva are fond of playing, and that the Mehtur, whom I had once asked about it, turned pale with anger, thinking that, like the last ambassador from Heraut, I had been serenaded by the fair ones of Khiva. Alackaday! no such good fortune was mine.

CHAPTER XI.

Visit of an Afghaun Priest—Reports relative to Bokhara—Feast given by the Khaun Huzurut—Arrangement of Guests—Purgatory of Knees and Ancles—Persian Ambassador—Punishment of Dinner-odoxy—Inauk of Huzarusp—The Bee—An Oozbeg Dinner—Holy Ardour of the Priests—Accounted for upon Muhummedun Principles—Virtue of the Narr of Soups—Mutton, Spartan, Maigre, Chicken Broth, Ox Tail, Mock Turtle—Turtle!

ABOUT this time an old Afghaun priest was brought to see me. He was a tall, and had been a fine man, but was evidently labouring under some malady. His face was ridiculously like an old he-goat's and his cough, which was almost incessant, completed his resemblance to that quadruped. He commenced, with many gasps, to ask whether I had brought with me any strengthening medicines. I desired him to state his case, which he attempted, but I could make nothing out of it, excepting that fits of extreme debility assailed him, and that he had heard I had medicines for strengthening the heart. I told him, I dared not give medicine at Khiva, but recommended the use of cheretta, free air, simple food, and as much exercise as he could bear. On hearing this, he gasped twice as much, was sure I had medicine, warm medicine for strengthening the heart, and entreated me to bestow it upon him. I perceived now, what my water drinking habits always made me slow to understand — that he required wine or brandy, and again assured him that I had not the articles he desired, and that I never made use of them.

I then inquired the news from Bokhara. This, as he related it, was full of interest; he confirmed the

Khaun Huzurut's intelligence, and added, that the Ummeer had previously turned Doost Múhummud Khaun out of the city, on some suspicion, but allowed him a house in the suburbs, where he was much neglected. That the Ummeer one night sent for the Doost's youngest son, a youth of fifteen: a summons which, coming from such a monster as the Ummeer, was equivalent to the grossest insult. That the Doost's eldest son sent back an answer of defiance, and collecting his people about him, prepared to quit a country where guests were liable to such treatment. That the Bokhara forces were sent to attack him, and found him, and his little band of 400, encamped in a burying ground. That two thousand Oozbeg troops attacked the post, but after several hours fighting, were repulsed with great slaughter. Upon learning which, the Ummeer had desisted from hostilities.

This news, which I had no other reason to doubt than any other news, of which, in these countries, about ninety-nine particulars in every hundred are lies, delighted my servants, and were received by all the Afghauns at Khiva, with great exultation. The English bayonet, they said, and the Afghaun scimitar, will conquer the world. I have never been able to discover, whether there was any truth whatever in this ingenious tale.

When I had given this old priest a present, and dismissed him, I inquired of my servants, if they knew what ailed him. "O! yes," they replied, "his malady is a third wife, whom he has just married."

Notwithstanding that I had purchased Ummeer Beeg's freedom, days and weeks elapsed, and still he was not released. Every time I visited the Mehtur, I saw the poor fellow at a distance, eyeing me wistfully. He was easily distinguished by his tall, manly figure and handsome features, which no meanness of dress could disguise. Once he had called upon me: but I entreated him to forbear any such demonstration, lest he should rouse the jealousy of the Mehtur, his master, against him. I assured him, that if the Mehtur should neglect his promise, I would appeal to the Khaun Huzurut, who certainly would see justice done to him and me. Meanwhile, I was wearing out myself with impatience.

The festival of the Moohurrum arrived. I am perhaps noticing it in the wrong place. Khulluts, or dresses of honour, were sent for me and my suite, consisting of very indifferent cloaks for me and them, and an Oozbeg cap for myself. For these wretched articles, I was expected to pay about double their actual cost, as the fee of the Major Domo, who brought them. On this day the Khaun and all the nobles attended at the mosque, and some of my people went thither also. My religion kept me at home, and I was not sorry of any excuse for avoiding crowds, in which the boorishness of the Oozbeg and Tooreumun exposes a stranger to many petty provocations and annoyances.

The ceremony, as described by my servants, was not worthy to be witnessed or detailed. The principal Musjid (mosque) is not domed, but flat-roofed, propped upon pillars of wood.

A few days subsequent to this ceremony, the master of ceremonies waited upon me, and informed me that the Khaun Huzurut had prepared a feast, at which he requested my attendance. He added, that as I should have to sit a long space, I had better dress in my Asiatic attire; and it was suggested that I should wear the Oozbeg cap, sent me by the Khaun, instead of my turban of white muslin. This was probably to avoid scandal to the priesthood, who alone, in these countries, wear white turbans, and who were to be there in full divan.

I went accordingly at the hour appointed, and was ushered into a large hall of the palace, in which I found assembled some sixty or seventy persons, chiefly, priests. The principal of these, the Sheikh-ool-Islaum, was seated at the head of the room. On the right hand, an unbroken line of priests succeeded, seated on their knees, their backs against the wall. A member of the royal family divided the place allotted me, from the lowest of these priests. A space was left vacant on the left of the room, below the principal priests, but above the rest of that line. This was afterwards occupied by the Inauk of Huzarusp (brother to the king) and the Bee, I cannot give the sound by any other arrangement of letters,) son of the predecessor of Madreheen Khaun, the present Khaun's father. All sat in profound silence; I gave them "the Salaam alikoom" and took my seat, a little disgusted at finding it so low. The head Moolla assured me I was welcome, and asked several questions, some relating to the distance of places; whether Shauh Shoojah had not married a daughter of England, and whether the English were really masters of India, etc. etc. On all which points, I satisfied the curiosity of his holiness.

Meanwhile the priests sat, very much like a couple of rows of jackasses in the mood digestive; eyes earth-fastened in deep abstraction, and heads hanging, like gourds, at various angles with the body. None but the Sheikh-ool-Islaum ventured to utter a word, and the few, which I addressed to the sprig of royalty beside me, were answered with screwed up mouth and knitted brows alone. It was evidently not etiquette to converse at so solemn a banquet.

My knees and ancles now began to give me the most exquisite torture. None but a creature so stiff-jointed as myself, can imagine how much I suffered from this posture, in spite of considerable practice. Once, at an audience of Shauh Kaumraun, when attempting to rise from the torturous posture prescribed by etiquette, I fairly fell on my face, unable to support the weight of my body, upon my almost dislocated ancles. I now sounded the royal sprig, to know whether I could, without indecorum, shift my posture; but my sole answer was glum looks;

and the Sheikh-ool-Islamm was at so great a distance, that I hesitated to make the uproar, necessary to attract his attention. At length flesh and blood got the better of shame, and, in a voice of thunder, I roared, " I am in great pain, excuse my shifting my posture."

The effect was quite electric. All the hanging gourds of heads, all the half-closed mutton eyes, all the pendulous tympana that garnish those hanging excrescences, were suddenly upraised, awakened as from a trance, and fixed upon me in startled horror; whilst, with infinite pain and difficulty, I unbent my knees, and twisted them into the posture by tailors loved. The relief was so great, that I held at nought the general astonishment, which, however, excited me to a mirth I could scarcely control.

We had sat thus, I think, a full hour, when in marched my rival, the Persian ambassador, a handsome fellow, evidently of the Gujjur tribe.* He had all the ease of the higher orders of his countrymen; and he needed all, in an assembly of the most virulent enemies of his religious creed, who, moreover, could scarcely be supposed in the best of humours with one, who had kept dinner waiting a mortal hour; an offence not easily pardoned by churchmen, and equivalent in most countries to a charge of heresy. He took his seat on the side of the room opposite mine, i. e. the left side, and three grades lower. The Sheikh-ool-Islamm gave him welcome, and after a short pause, inquired, " Whether the three first Khálifs were usurpers?"

" By no means," replied the Sheah, with the most perfect indifference of manner.

" And what say you of those who deny their title?"

All eyes were turned upon him with glances of triumph. He attempted to parry the question, but it would not do. It was repeated clearly and dis-

---

* To which belongs the present King of Persia.

tinctly, and he was obliged to answer; for there is but one safe answer to such a question.

"They are Kawfurs."

A giggle ran through the assembly, for this is the grossest insult that can be offered a Sheah, and the office of ambassador is no guarantee against such insults. "You are perfectly right," replied the Sheikh, with a sneer: but nothing could shake the ease and self-possession of the Persian. It is impossible to say, what might not have been the consequence, had he openly denounced, as usurpers, the first Khálifs;—the entire failure of his mission had been certain, his murder probable. But Sheahs have no scruple in renouncing their faith, when it places them in jeopardy. They conceive, that they are under no obligation to answer questions, which the interrogators have no right to ask. We intend some day to write a chapter upon lies, black, white, and grey, and shall therefore at present make no remark. But it is just to mention, that the whole of this conversation was carried on in Toorkish, which the Persian spoke fluently, so that I could only guess by the Arabic words and names, by the countenances of the guests, and the after report of my people, the nature of the questions and answers.

This ambassador had been sent on a special mission of harmony, with the profession of belief of all Muhammedans as the message of his master to the Khaun, and had probably been instructed to make any religious concession, in order to gain his point, of which one item was the release of the 30,000 Persians, said to be slaves in Khaurism, which was equivalent to asking the Khaun to give him 900,000 ducats, or about 450,000*l*. a sum by no means exorbitant, as the price of the service to be rendered, viz. the rescue of Khaurism from the invasion of Russia.

After about half an hour more, the Inauk of Huzarusp, brother to the Khaun Huzurut, and his cousin the Bee entered, and took their seats at the head of the left row, below the principal Moollas. To enter late is an assumption of consequence, which the Persian had exercised pretty freely. The Inauk could not have made his appearance with propriety until some time after all were assembled. The Inauk is a tall, large-built man, with high features, and an air of sound sense and intelligence. He stoops in his gait, like all natives of the country, who, when not rolled up in the saddle like sacks, are rolled up like balls upon their nummuds.* He is considered to be a man of clear judgment and decisive character, and is, perhaps, the only real soldier in Khaurism. His stature and strength are much vaunted, and few horses, it is said, can carry him. He was dressed in a cloak of dark green, lined with fur, and, like that of the Khaun, secured or ornamented at the waist in front with a chain of gold. On his head was an Oozbeg cap, of black lambskin. The Bee, who, with exception of the gold chain, was similarly attired, is a fat, heavy-looking man, who appeared to me of rather low stature. His eyes are never lifted from the earth, probably from the sense of being an object of suspicion to the Khaun, as son of the first Oozbeg king of Khaurism. He is, nevertheless, treated by the Khaun with marked distinction. He is said to be amiable.

Symptoms of dinner now broke out; several long pieces of chintz were brought in, and spread around the room, opposite the company: on these were ranged flat cakes of bread; then basins of mutton broth, swimming in fat, and finally some wretched pilaus and cups of mingled butter and grape juice. For the soup, which was served in earthenware basins, clumsy wooden ladles were at hand, but none of those exquisitely carved spoons of wood used in Persia and Afghaunistaun. I, who abhor soups and broths of all kinds, played a miserable spoon on this occasion, in spite of all the exhortations and the excellent

---

* A carpet of felt.

example of him at my elbow. But I observed that the priests had entirely lost their supineness now that work was in hand. The hanging, pumpkin heads became firm set upon their stalks, the half-closed, greasy eyes shot scintillations of consuming fire upon the sacrifice; the jaws, that seemed so languid, 'twas doubtful if they could masticate anything so profane as a jelly, began their preliminary cross-cuts, and flourishes, like the shears of Gattie or of Ross, shears whose keen, vigorous slashes have many a time made us shudder for our ears.

Doubtless these holy men practise conviviality, as Queen Zenobia practised matrimony, or Miss Seward* fermentation, to wit, for the result—the sacred meditations, the sublime ecstatic visions, the quick coming fancies evolved from tough mutton and its decoction during the process of rumination. Alas! that fruits so spiritual should be culled from roots so material! That these sainted gentry should be compelled to nourish their gifts upon the self-same material as inspireth him who howleth at the moon! Rather let us believe that this son of defilement gathereth and deriveth whatever of poetry he offereth to the pale star of night from the kindred (be it spoken in all reverence) which this community of voracity gives him with holy, earth-despising men.

The cloth was removed; the cold water was poured over our greasy fingers. The fatness of the dinner was carefully wrapped in our handkerchiefs, and as carefully deposited in our pockets. We blessed God for the meal, and stroked our beards, as many, at least, as were so fortunate as to possess any. It must be confessed that the greater number of flourishes cut the impassive air, and might, to a fanciful view, have

---

* The anxiety of this fair amazon to render her sex for ever independent of the other is a recorded fact, and slow fermentation was the process. Single-handed, however, she could produce nothing higher in the scale of being than a maggot, and even in the production of this Dr. Darwin had a hand. It was not, perhaps, the first maggot that had called the learned Doctor "Father."

seemed as signals to Rowland and Son to hasten to the rescue. It is somewhat absurd, at first, to see a gentleman, with chin as smooth as a glass soda-water bottle, sweeping away at arm's length with all the grimace of a curly lion, as if the dew of benediction could settle for an instant on that barren excrescence, or require both arms to gather it in. We now rose and broke up, the Inauk leading. I need hardly say, it was a welcome relief. It may here be observed that, whilst the Afghauns cook the most savoury stews and kawaubs, or fries, the Tartars have no notion of any method of cooking meat, save that of boiling.

CHAPTER XII.

Report of the Advance of the British Arms to Bulkh, and toward Tehraun—Prospect of my speedy Departure—Extreme Difficulty of procuring Money—Promises of Shroffs and of the Minister equally false—Delay in transmitting my Despatches—Private Channel established—Liberation of Ummeer Beeg—Narrative of his Capture and attempted Escape—Mutilation of his Ears by Yakoob Mehtur—His Disposition to revenge the Injury—Release of Twenty-two of the Daughters of the Afghauns in honour of H.M. the Queen of Great Britain—Captain Pottinger's Rescue from Captivity of some Forty or Fifty Children.

AT the next audience, the Khaun asked me, whether it were true that our armies had advanced to Bulkh. I heard nothing of such an intention, but should not be astonished at the fact: as such a move were perfectly justified by the aggression of the Ummeer of Bokhara. He said, that a merchant had just arrived from Bulkh, who had seen our army encamped there. That no defence had been made, but that the force was peaceably purchasing supplies of the inhabitants, who flocked from all quarters to the camp.

"And what," I enquired, "is the Ummeer about?"

"He is in great trepidation; has released Colonel Stoddart, and is treating him with the highest distinction; saying, that he will make a shield of him. He has arrested all the merchants who were leaving Bokhara, shut up their goods in the town, and declared that they must fight for them."

Part of this information was, perhaps, communicated to me by others; but, as I am uncertain, it will save time to place it on the Khaun's lips with this explanation. The whole, on reaching St. Petersburg,

I found to have been a fabrication; no British force having advanced beyond Bamián. The Khaun added—

"Have you heard that 20,000 English troops are marching upon Tehraun?"

I had not:—"From whence are they?"

"They arrived by sea at Busheer; the sea is covered with their vessels. A man has just arrived from those parts, who saw both army and fleet. What think you of the news?"

"That it is utterly unfounded. We could have no possible object in such an invasion, at the present moment."

"Nevertheless, it is quite true. We have, as I said, an eye-witness."

"He is deceiving your Majesty. The news is quite incredible."

It is scarcely necessary to apprize the reader, that this intelligence, like the former, proved totally destitute of foundation. Should the reader never have visited central Asia, he may ask, To what purpose could such fabrications be got up? If he has been resident in that country, he will neither ask, nor attempt to answer, so idle a question; nine-tenths of the news he has there heard, being of precisely similar character: the most bare-faced and ingenious lies, uttered by those who have apparently no motive for the fabrication, and under circumstances, that admit of no possibility of their being themselves deceived: lies, invented and promulgated from the sheer love of deceiving.

I had now some prospect of speedy dismissal, on my journey. I was permitted to consult a few guides, supplied by the Mehtur, and also a very intelligent Hindoo merchant, named Diarâm, on the subject of my journey. This man readily promised to supply, upon my bills, any sum I might require: and having at heart the release from slavery of two young women of the royal family of Heraut, and to send in honour to that city, a blind prince of the family of Shah Shooja-ool-Moolk, as well as to make a few presents to influential people, to keep up a good feeling toward our Government, I desired him to have in readiness 800 ducats, which he promised to do. He, however, delayed the supply of this money, and eventually declared he could not procure me a farthing. He made a profound mystery of his reasons; but I have no doubt that the Mehtur interdicted his good offices, for I complained of the fraudulent conduct of Diarám to him, but he took no notice of it. This put me to the utmost inconvenience; for, depending upon this supply, and anxious to preserve in the breast of the Khaun Huzurut that good feeling which the capriciousness of despots renders obnoxious to the most trifling causes, I had, in reply to the Khaun's offer of procuring me all needful supplies, said, that I had come as the friend of the Government, and not to tax it in the hour of danger, when the Khaun would have need of all his funds and resources. In my present extremity, I was obliged to apply to the Mehtur, begging he would obtain me the means of cashing bills on Heraut, for which I would give a handsome premium. He promised to do so, and I thought the matter concluded.

The Mehtur taxed me with the supposed advance of the English arms to Bulkh. "You said, you did not desire war with Muhummedan powers, and now you are invading Toorkestaun."

"In saying so, I added, that the Umneer of Bokhara had given my government the grossest provocation, and that I could not say how much longer we might forbear."

"And Persia?"

"It is, in all probability, a false report, that we have entered that country. Were it true, it were perfectly just and proper."

"What, for opening your ambassador's letter?"

"Yes! for opening our ambassador's letter. A

British ambassador, at any foreign Court, is the image, at that Court, of the most powerful of earthly sovereigns. An insult to him is an affront to that sovereign, and none ever insulted my Government with impunity."

The Mehtur now consulted me upon the nature of the presents proper to be sent to the Emperor of Russia, and Her Majesty the Queen of England. For the Emperor, I recommended rare sabres and daggers, and the beautiful, jewelled harness of the country. For my Queen, I said, it would scarcely be appropriate to present arms; horses I could not convey with me, and the country produced nothing else. But, I added, that the Khaun Huzurut had it in his power to present to Her Majesty, the Queen of England, the richest, noblest, and most acceptable of offerings.

He asked what that might be.

"The freedom," I said, "of some of the daughters of the Afghauns, who are pining in slavery at Khiva. If the Khaun will send some of these, say twenty, in honour back to their homes, I will answer for it, my Queen will esteem it the most precious of gifts, and the highest of compliments."

When this was repeated to the Khaun Huzurut, he was much struck, and calling his favourite wife, asked her what she thought of the taste of English ladies, and a British Queen, who delighted not in rich jewels and ornaments, but in acts of mercy to the human race. He gave instant orders to carry the measure into effect. Owing, however, to the avarice of the Mehtur, who was charged with the execution, a great many old women, I was told, were of the number. I remonstrated, saying, that I had specified daughters, and not grandmothers; that some of these poor creatures had outgrown their desire to revisit Heraut. That many of them, probably, had no homes, nor any to look to, for support; and that to send the worst of any article, as a gift to a sovereign, was a species of affront. The Mehtur, however, had made his arrangements, and replied, that if my Queen desired others, the Khaun Huzurut would at any time release them, at her request. I was invited to inspect them, but from delicacy to Asiatic prejudice, would not go. The conversation in the King's haram I received from very good authority, but could not, with safety to the party, explain more.

About a week previous to this period, I had, by the most urgent remonstrances, persuaded the Khaun to place a courier at my disposal. This man had received my letters for Major Todd, Envoy at Heraut, and Sir W. M'Naghten, Envoy and Minister at Cabul, and with them a handsome present. But he evinced not the slightest symptom of moving, although the Mehtur had the effrontery to declare, that he was on his journey to Heraut. I remonstrated to no purpose; but a curious circumstance, or rather observation, was elicited. I came to Khiva very ill supplied with sealing-wax, and the Russian wax there is quite useless. Some odds and ends of Indian wax, black and dark green, were all left to me; and with these I had secured my packets. "Why," inquired the Mehtur, "do you use dark wax?"

"Because I have got no other."

"That is not the reason. It is for fear we should break your seal."

"You would not be so mad. See what Persia has suffered by such a breach of the faith and hospitality of nations. But why could you not break a black seal?"

"Because there is no black wax at Khiva."

"And is there red wax?"

"Abundance."

It seemed pretty evident, that the idea of breaking the seal had crossed the mind of the Mehtur. The worst of it was, that should they break the seal, in all probability they would destroy the packet, to prevent discovery. Or the interpreter might be an enemy, instructed to give a mischievous interpretation to the contents. I discovered also, that by a truly Asiatic spirit of economy, the messenger was destined to convoy to Heraut, when in due process of time they should be collected, the twenty-two women, whom the Khaun intended to liberate. I appealed to the Khaun himself; assured him that the most mischievous consequences might result to his own kingdom from the delay. That my Government, taking it for granted, from my silence, that I had been either murdered or imprisoned, would interest themselves no farther for the safety of His Majesty. He laughed, and said, that the courier should be instantly despatched; but the man did not really quit Khiva until twenty-one days after his receipt of my packet.

I had, however, previously despatched to Heraut packets by two separate messengers. The operation was a delicate one: for, after receiving the packet and gold, the messenger might have taken them to the Khaun, and have received my head in exchange; and the loss of his own would have been the certain consequence of any detection; but I trusted to the power of gold, and to the firm faith in the word and promise of an Englishman, which prevails throughout these countries. One of these messengers was the old Cauzie of Yoollataun, him whose claw I had anointed with the mammon of unrighteousness.

It seems, that from that moment I had become the subject of the honest gentleman's prayers and holy reveries. Never distilled the dulcet and emollient oil of palms upon skin more happy from the unction. Being a magistrate as well as priest, he was an excellent judge of the weight of a plump Bokhara* Tilla, and conceived that a tree producing such superlative fruit, was worthy to be cherished by all of orthodox principles. So, after vainly endeavouring, for weeks, to satisfy his craving for my presence by dreams and

---

* The Tilla of Bokhara is one of the purest of gold coins. Its value may be about thirteen shillings. The Tilla of Khiva is very inferior in purity and value.

reveries, he mounted his nag, and rode across the desert, 380 miles, or thereabouts, in quest of me, the scent of the golden fountain refreshing him as he proceeded. On reaching Khiva, he contrived, but in the most cautious manner, to intimate his presence to Summud Khaun; informing him, that he had come to purchase the freedom of a relative, but wanted five ducats to make up the sum demanded. I immediately sent him fifteen, and with them the tiniest little packet in the world, which, I assured him, was an order on Heraut for fifteen more. The ecstasies of the old gentleman are indescribable. Had I at that moment thrust out a cloven foot or a little curly pig's tail (much the more horrible of the two to a holy Moolla), I believe he would have knelt down to kiss either devoutly. In the conveyance of dispatches, liberality cannot be too strongly enjoined. The objects of a mission costing thousands, and involving interests more precious far than gold, may be defeated by grudging a few guineas for the conveyance of intelligence. But in Central Asia especially, letters are generally conveyed at risk of life, and a handsome reward is therefore just, as well as politic.

I feel myself here embarrassed by anachronisms, into which I have fallen. It was a day after the receipt of the false news of our capture of Bulkh, and about a week previous to my departure from Khiva, that poor Ummeer Beeg, the Goolaum whose liberty I had long since purchased of the Mehtur, was at length released and sent to me. My room was full when he arrived. He threw himself at my feet, and, seizing my hand, covered it with kisses, and bathed it in his tears. I was deeply affected. The full sense of liberty can perhaps be felt only by the spirit that has fought and struggled and suffered and pined and done all but crouch to win it. The sense of all his wrongs and torments, his years of bondage, oppression, and scorn, came over him in that moment of weakness, and those were probably the first tears that since his boyhood he had known. I raised him up with the greatest difficulty; I was not ashamed of the moisture in my own eyes, as I said to him, "You have suffered long and deeply for the British Government; but your sufferings are at an end, and your reward is come. You have been despised, for our sake, by the Toorcumun and Oozbeg. You shall now be honoured and cherished by the English. Your sufferings shall be forgotten by you, to be remembered by us; that is your place, Ummeer Beeg (pointing to the highest seat). None here has done and suffered for the Queen of England what you have; none, therefore, here is your equal in honour."

Nothing, however, could induce him to sit in my presence. He stood before me weeping like a child; every word of kindness but called forth fresh tears. It seemed that to such a spirit there was no medium between the entire mastery of his own emotions and prostration before them. I perceived, that so long as I spoke words of comfort to him, his sorrows must flow; and conjecturing all it must cost him to be seen in that unnerved condition, led the conversation to his immediate views and wishes.

"What were these? What did he desire?"

He would follow me over the world.

"It is not to me that you owe anything. I am but an agent of my Government. I should be delighted to have you with me; but I go on a most perilous and painful mission. The chances of death or captivity are greatly against me. You have suffered enough already, and shall not, with my will, suffer more. You shall return whither you please, to Heraut, or to your home in Persia."

"I *never* can return to Persia," he replied, with a gloomy look, pointing to his mutilated ears.

"You are wrong, Ummeer Beeg, they are your greatest glory:—they are testimonials of your fidelity to the British Government, and of your personal courage and gallantry. I will give you such a certificate as shall make every one envy you the loss, and Major Todd will give you another. He bade me greet you kindly, and say: 'The Toorcumuns have cut off Ummeer Beeg's ears, but I will re-make them of gold.' Tell me the particulars of your captivity."

"I was entrusted by Colonel Stoddart, then at Heraut, with despatches for the British Envoy and Minister at Tehraun. Colonel Stoddart, in giving them me, enjoined me, on no account to offer hopeless resistance to any very superior number of Toorcumuns, or other plunderers, 'For,' said the Sahib, 'should you become a slave, I may be able to redeem you; but death would place you beyond human aid, and would not save your despatches, nor in any way benefit your masters.' The road at that time was much infested, yet I had just conveyed by it, to Heraut,* a considerable sum of gold for Colonel Stoddart. When I approached Toorbut Sheik Jaumie (I think this was the place), I perceived hoof-prints on the road, and climbed a slight hill to look around me, lest I should be surprised. I could see nothing, so proceeded. A little farther on, as I approached some thickets, I found myself confronted by about forty Toorcumuns. I brought my carabine down to the ready, and cocked it. They drew back, and we parleyed.

"'Who are you?' they inquired.

"A servant of the English ambassador.

"'You are a Gujjur,' i. e. Persian.

"No! I am in the service of the English, the allies and friends of Heraut.

"'Lay down your arms.'

"I won't. I will shoot the first man that approaches nearer.

"'What good will that do you? You'll be a dead man the next instant.'

---

* This I know to have been the case, having heard it from the Secretary of Legation, Major Todd.

"Not till I've despatched five or six of *you*, you may then do as you please. I carry pistols.

"They tried to put me off my guard; but I stood firm, asking them what good it would do them to stop the servant of the English Government. They continued to close round upon me; and knowing that, if the strife commenced, I was lost, and remembering Colonel Stoddart's injunction, and that my life would not, indeed, save the despatches, I at length surrendered. They stripped me, and made me over to five of the party, to be carried to Khiva. My arms were bound fast to my sides, and I was set upon a horse, in the midst of my conductors. We proceeded several days, and, as I was perfectly quiet, they became less vigilant; until, one day, as they had halted to refresh themselves, whilst some were smoking and others lying at full length, I contrived to get near the horse that seemed to me the fleetest, and suddenly springing upon its back, put it to its speed. I was of course instantly discovered and pursued, yet, being well mounted, might have escaped, had my arms been at liberty; but they were fast bound to my sides, so that I could neither urge on the horse to his utmost, nor hold the reins, nor attempt, when overtaken, to defend myself. My pursuers speedily came up with me. One thrust at me with a spear, which grazed upon my ribs, the other made several cuts at me with his sabre, one of which wounded me severely in the left arm. The sabre happily was blunt, so that the other blows barely penetrated my thick cloak. They then seized the rein and stopped the horse.

"They carried me to Khiva in this wounded condition, cruelly ill-treating me on the road, and at Khiva they gave me to the Khaun Huzurut, who, after a while, bestowed me upon the late Aga Mehtur, Yoosuph. He was a kind master, and a good man, but his people were like all Oozbegs. The overseer was very cruel. We were made to work like horses, dragging carts and lifting burthens. One day, when

I was ill, and unequal to this drudgery, the overseer threatened to strike me unless I worked harder. I recommended him not, complaining that I was sick, and unequal to the task. He struck me. I sprang upon and felled him to the earth, and would have despatched him on the spot, had not the other servants pulled me off. He complained to the Minister, who, having heard both sides of the question, commended my spirit, and commanded that I should never again be struck. I was afterwards better treated; but the love of liberty was too powerful to be resisted. You know, Sir, how surrounded is Khiva by deserts, inhabited only by men-eaters (Audum Khor). The nearest point of safety is about 350 miles distant, and the whole space is a desert, without food for man or beast, and almost without water. Nevertheless, without arms, and without provisions, I twice fled by night to this desert, preferring death to bondage. I was pursued by the Toorcumun horse, and retaken. They carried me back to my master. He kindly pardoned me; but, henceforth, I was watched with greater vigilance. At length he died, and his son, the present minister, succeeded him. I determined upon another effort for my freedom; and, seeing the necessity of being better provided than before, contrived one night to seize a sword and some provisions, and again made for the desert. Three horsemen found my track, and followed close upon my heels, riding, at long intervals apart, not dreaming that they had anything to apprehend from a slave, who was on foot. I watched my opportunity, and, as the first approached me, sprung upon and disarmed him, granting him his life, only upon his most solemn promise no farther to molest me. The second approached, and then the third; each in turn shared the same fate, and was spared upon the same terms. They left me. I wandered over the desert in search of water, but could find none. That day passed, and the sun of the next day found me parched with thirst, and almost exhausted. I struggled on till noon was passed, then threw me down in the sand to die, and was quite insensible, when a Toorcumun stumbled upon me. He poured water, from his leathern bottle, down my throat, placed me behind him on his horse, and carried me, scarcely alive, back to Khiva. My master, the present Minister, immediately ordered his servants to cut off my ears, for which I should have supped upon his blood before this, but that a ray of hope of my release reached me, through Moolla Hussun."

Such was the narrative of Ummeer Beeg. I cannot, of course, vouch for the accuracy of every particular, and never understood how he contrived to disarm, without killing, three Toorcumuns, or how it was that they kept the promise they had sworn to him. My dislike to seem, at such a moment, incredulous, prevented me from cross-questioning him. Birdler Beeg had informed me, as an excuse for the mutilation of Ummeer Beeg's ears, that he had cut down two Toorcumuns of a party sent to take him; so that I have no doubt of the correctness of the main facts, and that, whatever of the marvellous may appear in it, to those who read this page, is attributable to my imperfect narration.

As soon as the room was clear, I called back Ummeer Beeg, and, making him close the door (a precaution I would recommend to all in these countries when cash is to be discussed), drew out my purse, which was full of gold, and poured it into his hands, promising him a farther supply, should I be able to cash my bills.

"Now," I said, "Ummeer Beeg, I have heard you express the most virulent hatred toward the Mehtur."

"He is the son of a dog, and I will yet know the taste of his heart's blood!"

"You have just grounds for your anger, Ummeer Beeg, but you know that at present you are my servant, under my protection, released by my means, and armed by my hand. If you slay the Mehtur, I shall bear the blame, and my government will be the sufferer. If, therefore, you have the slightest regard for either, you will forego your just revenge."

"You have purchased my blood, you can do what you please with me; order me to stab myself, and I will do it. If you command it, the Mehtur shall live; but my palate is parched with a thirst, which only his blood can alleviate. The taste of his heart's blood," lifting his hands to his lips and throwing back his head like one quaffing delicious wine, "until I know that, I shall not know peace."

Ummeer Beeg stood before me a genuine child of nature, with all the stormy power belonging to such a character, and all its tendency to that which in civilized lands is crime, but which, where laws protect not the innocent, may be justly regarded as virtue. Faithful as steel to his trust, affectionately attaching himself to those who treat him kindly, grateful for benefits, proud of that degree of liberty to which he was born, his very sense of justice, his very pride in the uprightness of his own purpose, became a volcano of vengeance when inflamed by wrong. Nevertheless, his word being passed to me, not to injure the Mehtur, would, I knew, be religiously observed, and I gave myself no further uneasiness on that score. I felt how invaluable would be such a follower in the perilous and difficult enterprize before me; yet I would not for worlds have suffered him to endanger his liberty and life any farther. Had he accompanied me, I believe I could have baffled all the artifices of those bent upon my destruction: but who shall say I should have been the gainer?

I sent for a dress of honour for Ummeer Beeg. No cloak in the house was long enough by many inches, so I was obliged to purchase one expressly for him. He soon cut a very different figure in a handsome Oozbeg cap and cloak, and I desired him to look out for a good horse and handsome sabre. I was, however, unable in the end to raise money for the purchase of these articles. His release cast a gleam of sunshine upon the troublous prospect around me.

I had previously enjoyed a ray even more consolatory. The night succeeding that on which I had requested the release of the daughters of the Afghauns, a deputation came from the Khaun himself, saying that the order was issued for the release of these miserable captives; that the instant they could be collected together, they should be sent whithersoever I chose to name, and that the Khaun wished to know whether that should be Calcutta or London. I was infinitely amused by this simple query, and, with my most grateful and heartfelt acknowledgments, begged to represent to his Majesty that to the sovereign of about 250 millions of subjects, the persons of twenty-two females were no great boon; whereas the happiness of a single individual of the number would be accepted as such by my Queen; that, to effect such an object, it was necessary only to restore them in honour to their own homes at Heraut; that Shauh Kamrann would participate in the satisfaction their release would give, as they were his Majesty's subjects; and that my Queen, being a woman, would feel the compliment of selecting individuals of her Majesty's sex for release. He departed with this message, after I had refreshed his fingers with gold, for a royal message is supposed to be always entitled to such recompense. Unfortunately, my pretty speeches having to undergo, in the first place, the purgatory of my own imperfect Persian, afterwards the rack of my interpreter's dulness, and then the wheel of the Oozbeg's asininity (if there be such a word, and if not, it is high time there be) reach the Khaun Huzurut, I suppose, very much as a fine lady would reach her ball-room chased and torn by fox-hounds—a thing of rags and tatters.

As soon as the messenger had departed, various remarks were made by my people. Old Summud

Khaun said, "Your journey, Sir, has not been in vain."

"No," I replied, "whatever now befalls me, death, captivity, or success, I shall bless God that I have visited Khiva. Never did sleep steal over me more sweetly than that night; never was my heart more replete with gratitude.

On reaching Heraut, we had found a large number of children, who had been rescued from slavery by the exertions of Major Pottinger, and were now brought up, under proper instructions, at the expense of our Government. I confess I envied Major Pottinger more the glory of this deed, unknown and unnoticed as it was, than that which he had spread through the world as the defender of Heraut. He however had, by great exertion, by manly and determined interference, and sometimes by force of arms, effected the enfranchisement of these children. I had but to use the name of the Queen of England, and the fetters fell, as by magic, from the neck of the slave. It was a triumph to my Queen and to my country; but my own share in it, though gratifying, deserved no praise. "Now," I said, as I settled my head upon the bundle of clothes which served me as a pillow, "if I can but effect the exchange of the Russian and Oozbeg captives, I will leave, without an envious sigh, the glory of slaughtering their fellow men to conquerors and kings." The prospect had in it more of difficulty than of hope, yet my labours, aided by the able and zealous exertions of Captain Shakespear, were, after many sufferings, eventually crowned with success: all the sufferings fell to my lot, all the laurels to his; the former could not, perhaps, have fallen upon a spirit calmer under the burthen, nor could laurels flourish over a more deserving brow.

CHAPTER XIII.

The Ummeer of Bokhara's Refusal to release Colonel Stoddart—Endeavour to make me solicit the Company, on my Mission, of an Oozbeg Ambassador—And to persuade me to prefer the Orenburgh Route—Private Intelligence—Presents for the Emperor of Russia—Arrangements for the Exchange of Captives—Reasonableness of the Khaun's Propositions—His extreme Anxiety, and evident Sincerity on this Point—His Amusement at the Motion of my Pen—And Curiosity respecting my Epaulettes—His Majesty's Tribulation at my Want of a Cocked Hat and Plume—Muhummud Shauh—Dismissal—Reveillee of Nizaum, the Sleeper of Sleepers—Visit from a Relation of Bârdêr Beeg—His Account of the Skirmish with the Russians—Difficulty of raising Funds—Fresh Attempts to make me apply for an Oozbeg Ambassador, and for Permission to proceed viâ Orenburgh—Disconcerted by a Discovery—Visit from the Minister—Renewal of those Efforts—His happy Confidence in Destiny—Heroic Spirit.

AT my next audience, the Khaun Huzurut informed me, that the Ummeer of Bokhara had sent a decided negative, to his (the Khaun's) two several remonstrances, for the release of Colonel Stoddart. The reply of the Ummeer was "You have one English Eelchie, what would you do with another. Do you grudge my having *one*?"

I replied, that I deeply regretted the Ummeer's insanity; but that the Khaun Huzurut's friendly attention to the request of my Government, could not be impaired by the conduct of the Ummeer, but was as precious as if crowned with the desired success. I begged, in the name of my Government, to offer His Majesty the warmest thanks.

"And when will you start for St. Petersburg?"

"Whenever the Khaun Huzurut commands me. I

require only three days for preparation, provided that I have full permission to purchase and hire, and that the people of Khiva are allowed to supply my wants."

"Which route will you follow?"

"Your Majesty has already decided upon the Mungh Kishlauk route, and I heartily concur in the selection."

"Were it not as well, that my own ambassador accompanied you?"

"The Khaun Huzurut knows best, what probability exists that any one in company with your Majesty's ambassador, will be allowed to proceed to the Russian capital, or even just now, to cross the frontier."

The Khaun used many endeavours to make me solicit the company of this functionary, which he evidently had much at heart. This, I learned from my private intelligence, was a lingering remnant of distrust. I parried all his arguments by unanswerable reasons; but added, that if the Khaun Huzurut really believed the presence of an Oozbeg ambassador would facilitate matters, I would take him with me. So long as my *opinion* was demanded, I could state, only, what I had repeatedly urged.

"Do you not think," he said, "the Mungh Kishlauk route will delay you longer than that by Orenburgh?"

"Your Majesty has already decided for me that point. I will follow whatever route the Khaun Huzurut may be pleased to select; but, unless some additional reason be assigned for a change, I should prefer the route already selected. The Orenburgh route is still buried deep in snow. At this season it will occupy, at least, two months, being a distance of 900 miles. Owing to the snow there is no pasture there for camels. I must, therefore, in addition to the food, clothing, &c. of my servants and horses, carry food and forage for the camels themselves. Now a slight calculation will shew, that no camel can carry its own forage for two months, even supposing it has no other burden. Again, the Kuzzauks on the frontier are in rebellion against the Khaun Huzurut, as your Majesty lately informed me. How can I pass through them to the Russian camp? Your Majesty's passport were a passport to the land of death."

"But by the other route, the ice of the Caspian will detain you."

"All your Majesty's guides assure me not."

The point was, for the moment abandoned; but I saw that the Khaun had it much at heart, and I cudgelled my brains for a sufficient motive. The other route had been deliberately selected by the Khaun himself, as the result of many inquiries; and whatever the cause of this sudden alteration of choice, the motives assigned were evidently not genuine. My suspicions were aroused, and I stood upon my guard. My private intelligence stated, that this extreme anxiety to change the route, proceeded from a wish that some of the Khaun Huzurut's people should be present, when I met the Russians, to judge by my reception, whether I was a spy or a true man, and also what degree of influence I possessed with that nation, in my capacity of British agent. This was probable enough; and the desire to send with me an Oozbeg ambassador, robbed the scheme of all appearance of a wish to destroy me.

The presents for the Emperor of Russia were then produced. They consisted of a double-edged dagger, the handle of which was a mass of jewels elegantly set in ivory. A small head stall studded with pure gold, in which were set rough rubies and emeralds, and an Isfahaunee sabre. The Khaun asked me what I thought of the latter. I could not judge from the scabbard.

"Draw it," he said.

"Not in the presence of a king."

He laughed. "You have my permission."

I drew it accordingly, and examined the blade.

"That's a better blade than you brought me," observed the Khaun.

"The shape is not so perfect; but the water is finer. Your Majesty remembers that Heraut is a ruin, and that I rode post, at a few day's notice, to place my services at the Khaun Huzurut's disposal. Our Tosheh Khaneh (magazine of rarities) had been quite emptied, by our liberality to the king and nobles of Heraut."

My despatches, enclosed as usual in bags of sarcenet flowered with gold, were delivered to me. They were written in Toorkish, the Court language, but a Persian translation had been given me. They are curious, but I have not permission to publish them. The Khaun Huzurut bade me read aloud to him my Persian translation, whilst his Meerza followed me, word by word, on the originals.

I then inquired, "What shall I say if the Russians object to the exchange of captives, upon the plea of distrust? The Russian slaves are much scattered in your kingdom; how are they to feel sure, that all have been restored?"

"In that case, say that a Russian agent may come here, and shall have full power and opportunity to search for and release every Russian captive, and to carry him to Russia, provided, of course, that he wishes to return. Some have lucrative employment at Khiva, as artificers. Write this down in my presence, that you may not forget it; and add, that if the Emperor pleases to send me a responsible person as security, he shall receive the whole of his subjects without further demur, upon condition that mine be released when those reach Russia. Or, if the Emperor prefers to reverse the arrangement, I will send him a responsible person as a hostage, whilst he releases my subjects."

I sent for my pen and ink, and stepping down into the dry cistern of masonry sunk in the tent, placed my paper upon the ground, and wrote as the Khaun

Huzurut dictated. He made me repeat what I had written, to make sure of its accuracy, and was evidently in earnest. His astonishment at the rapid motion of the pen was great, and that it should traverse from left to right. He sent for the pen (which was of steel in a travelling case of ivory), and examined it attentively. When all was complete, he inquired—

"Who gave you those golden things (my epaulettes) on your shoulders?"

"I purchased them."

"Did not your queen give them you?"

I was the more amused at this question, because ignorant at the time that military rank at Khiva is conferred by the Khaun himself, by the present of a dagger in a golden or silver sheath, according to circumstances. The golden scabbard entitles to the command of a thousand horse; the silver, of one hundred. The Father of Victory was evidently fishing to find out the consequence of the person whom he was entrusting with such high offices and authority. How he would have been horrified, could he have conjectured that the person who was giving himself such airs at his Court, demanding a degree of deference never before accorded to a mortal, and setting deliberately at defiance, in the question of his route, the opinion of the Father of the Conqueror of Heroes and his Prime Minister, was still but a subaltern in his own corps, and a Captain only by brevet. It also so happened, that the epaulettes on my shoulder were those of an Ensign's rank: for, my own having been worn to pieces in hard service, I had purchased those of an Ensign whom we lost in the Bolaun Pass. These epaulettes underwent some strange vicissitudes. They were taken from me by the Kuzzauks, but afterwards surrendered; and being similar, or nearly so, to those of a Colonel in Russia, received much homage from guards and sentinels, not to mention postmasters and inn-keepers. I replied to his Majesty—

"That the queen had given me the rank which entitled me to wear them."

"But Colonel Stoddart has a large cocked hat and plume."

"I have just come from the wars, and a march of some 2000 miles, and have lost all my finery."

I had secret intelligence, that the Father of Victory was in much tribulation, at my want of a cocked hat and plume. He could not be satisfied that I was quite the right thing, or that Russia would pay any respect to a little man in a forage cap. Colonel Stoddart had been described to him as a tall, stern man, with the hat and cock's feathers aforesaid, who would frighten the Russian Generals out of their shoes; and I believe that, could Colonel Stoddart's release have been effected, he would have entrusted him, in preference, with the negotiation.

The Khaun then cross-examined me, with reference to some false impressions of our military consequence, which he affected to have received from the Persian ambassador, who, he said, had also accused me of false statement. It was evidently his wish to provoke me to retaliate; but this was a littleness I was not prepared to exhibit. I contented myself with disproving the Persian's statements, and asking His Majesty whether he would for an instant weigh the word of a Gujjur (Persian) against that of an Englishman. He laughed, and asked what sort of person was Muhummud Shauh, the present king of Persia.

"I have heard that he is naturally amiable, well-informed, and free from vice; but he is too much under the influence of his Vuzeer, which, in spite of his predilection for the English, inclines him to Russian counsels."

I was now dismissed, but not until the Khaun Huzurut had repeated his instructions to me, respecting the release of the Russian captives. He was evidently in earnest on the subject. His manner to me was kinder than ever.

I rode home in silence, wrapped in many thoughts. How despairing had been my first visit to the palace; how triumphant my last. A Hand of Might had prepared and smoothed the way. I had not vainly trusted my cares and perplexities to Him. I remembered that this day, the 1st of March, had given me the joy and pride of my being, the spirit of my better star. The auspices were happy.

After thundering at the gate of my dwelling for upwards of half an hour, Nizaum, by the greatest good fortune in the world, happened to awake, and hearing certain dim sounds, which were terrifying the neighbourhood for a mile around, began to suspect there might possibly be some one at the door, and came accordingly. This man's talent for slumber amounts to genius, and commands respect accordingly.

I have nearly forgotten to mention the particulars of a visit from one of Birdler Beeg's relations, who happened to have belonged to the detachment sent by the heroic Ghoosh Beegie to sweep the Russians out of the land. I inquired how it had come to pass, that 40,000 invincibles of Khiva had received such a reverse from 400 half-starved Russians. Birdler Beeg had, I said, all the way from Heraut, vaunted to me the prowess of his brethren, and given me an impression that they were very Roostums.

"Why," he said, "we fought at great disadvantage. The snow was five feet deep, our path a deep ditch, so to speak, trampled through it, where we could make no front. The cold was so intense, that if we let our hands down from the ample sleeves of our cloaks, to grasp a sabre or a spear, they withered in a moment. None of us wore less than four or five thick cloaks, and as many nether garments as he could beg, borrow, or steal. Of course, our arms were huge bundles of woollen cloth stiff with ice; and were as useless to us as if they had been made without joints. Those amongst us who had sense, and the slightest regard for their ears and noses, had drawn over their heads the nose-bags of the horses, in which they had perforated two holes, as means of reconnoitring the enemy. We were, in fact, large heavy sacks of frozen cloth. The Russians, meanwhile, were sitting over fires in their trenches, amusing themselves at our expense. Now they rubbed their hands over the fire, and now they up with their muskets and shot us, and again they warmed their hands, loaded, and fired. It was fine fun for them, I dare say; but we thought it no joke. And when they started in pursuit of us, the exercise kept their blood warm, and we sat on horseback wholly at their mercy, or dropped off, slaughtered like muttons, until we had the sense to take to our heels."

I had, for some time past, been most anxious about the funds necessary for my journey. As this journey had for its object the salvation of the Khaun Huzurut's kingdom, it seemed impossible that he should place in my way any insuperable difficulty; and yet the merchants of Khiva had either been instructed not to cash my bills, or else the report which began now to prevail, that the Khaun meditated my destruction, deterred them. The Mehtur, to whom I had repeatedly applied, always promised that every thing should be arranged as I desired. Once I had hopes that he would be tempted by the handsome premium I offered, to cash them from his own funds; but this hope at length failed me. I told him, that although the journey I had in view was for the Khaun Huzurut's own interest, and my life and fame were to be perilled in his cause, yet that I did not wish to draw upon the resources of His Majesty at a moment of emergency; but, as I could not possibly stir without money, begged he would either procure it from the bankers, or grant me a loan, upon my bills, from the royal treasury. He was profuse of promises, and it was a subject with which, as a British agent, I could not decently trouble the king himself.

The scheme of sending with me an Oozbeg ambassador, was again and again urged upon me. I had but one answer. He should accompany me, if the Khaun Huzurut desired it; but I could not recommend it. Many words were wasted upon the subject; for all their arguments, when examined, fell to the ground. At length, it was urged that I should be safer with an ambassador. Undoubtedly, I should: the treachery, practised upon me, would never have been ventured upon. But the Khaun had a thousand other means of securing my safety; and the personal safety of an individual was not, for a moment, to be thought of, when the fate of empires was in the balance. I stood firm, therefore, upon the old ground; had given my opinion, but was ready to execute the Khaun's pleasure, however contrary to my own views. That an Englishman's word being sincere, could not be altered, to meet even the pleasure of a king. That I could not say, I thought *that* wise or advisable, which I believed was injudicious and mischievous. That the real motives for sending with me an ambassador could not have been offered me. That to conceal them from me, was neither friendly nor just. That, if distrust was the motive, it was far wiser for the Khaun to send his own ambassador alone, and let me return to Heraut. It was a duty he owed himself and empire, not to confide his safety to any, in whose truth and fidelity he had not the firmest confidence. This was all that could be elicited from me, coaxing was fruitless, and bullying always recoiled on the Mehtur's own head.

The Orenburgh route was another point strongly urged upon me. Against the difficulty of feeding my suite, it was proposed that I should ride Chuppah (post) with a Kuzzauk guide and one servant. I agreed, and the guide was sent me, accompanied by an Oozbeg, who partly acted as interpreter; the Kuzzauk dialect and pronunciation being difficult to those acquainted only with the Toorkish of Khiva.

Ummeer Beeg, however, assisted, being perfectly acquainted with the Toorkish tongue. This guide, whose manner betrayed his eager desire that I should follow his route, assured me, that the snow on the Orenburgh route was nearly melted, and would be entirely gone in a week; an assertion, which I knew to be utterly false, as six weeks would not suffice to dissolve it. He stated, that there was not the slightest difficulty in passing the 900 miles of desert, to Orenburgh.

I enquired, whether he could himself guide me the entire distance to the Russian camp. The Oozbeg explained the question to him, and a sharp controversy immediately ensued between them, in the heat of which they forgot that Ummeer Beeg was present, and understood all they said. At the conclusion of the controversy, the Oozbeg gave, as the Kuzzauk's answer, that he could and would conduct me the entire journey. Ummeer Beeg immediately desired to speak to me in private; I cleared the room, and he said—

"For heaven's sake, Sir, do not go with that guide, for the Oozbeg did not give you his real answer, which was, that he could only guide you through his own tribe, where he must make you over to another tribe, which would deliver you to a third, and so on. If you go with that man you are lost. The Khaun Huzurut's protection will avail you nothing, unless the man to whom he delivers you here is held responsible for your safety to your journey's end."

Upon this subject there could not be two opinions. Moreover, several of those Kuzzauk tribes were in open rebellion against Khiva; all were expecting daily a change of masters, and, of course, the Khaun Huzurut's authority, in such a country, must be held extremely cheap, and might be of little avail, even should the first guide accompany me throughout. This, however, was a risk previously foreseen, and which I was willing to incur. The other was not to thought of; it was death, without a reasonable chance of success. When, therefore, I saw the Mehtur, I frankly told him what the guide had said, and that I could not, of my free choice, be bandied from guide to guide, and from tribe to tribe. He strove hard to shake my purpose, but in vain.

He had volunteered to pay me a visit before my departure, and arrived, one morning, at an early hour, when my only room was being swept, and I was walking in the space called a garden. My servants were out of the way, and the servants of the house neglected to summon me, so that when, by accident, I passed into the court, I found him sitting there, on his haunches, against the wall, without even a carpet or a nummud, and looking much more like a large watch-dog, than the Prime Minister of the Father of the Conqueror of Heroes. It was, although most unintentionally, an acquittance in full of all his incivility to myself; yet my worst enemy would never have been thus treated, under my own roof; and I am sure I never condescended to admit *him* to such a distinction. I hastened to him, and made a thousand apologies, and endeavoured, by the most assiduous attention, to make amends for the apparent slight. I suppose he received my apologies at the usual valuation of such ware. He, however, affected to be satisfied; and sundry huge loaves of sugar, some fruit, bread, raisins, and tea, being set before him, our conference commenced by his trying to force me to ask the favour of an Oozbeg ambassador, as my companion, and permission to travel the direct route to Orenburgh. The reasons he urged were frivolous, and easily refuted. They were not, I knew, genuine. My private intelligence, moreover, assured me, that the Khaun Huzurut had been recommended to send me with a confidential person of his own, by the route proposed, in order that this person, on approaching the camp, might precede me, and ascertain from the Russians, what degree of influence my journey might produce upon the affairs of Khiva. If they found the Russians sufficiently simple to allow of its importance, I was to be permitted to pass on. If they should disallow it, I was to be brought back, by force, if necessary; and if the Russians should be so wise as to proclaim me a spy, I know not how I was to be provided for; but there could be no difficulty in disposing of me quietly. This determined me, more strongly than ever, against both propositions. It appeared to me, that since the receipt of my despatches, I had lost, at Court, some of the Khaun's confidence. I was not aware, until some days after, that this was owing to the testimony of several fresh witnesses, who had identified me, on oath, as a Russian.

The Mehtur had come quite determined to carry his point. Of course, quite ignorant of the English character, he warmed as he proceeded, until he began to lose sight of the respect due to me, and obliged me to assume the tone which, from past experience, I knew would overawe him. He complained of the warmth he had provoked, and was evidently nervous under it. I replied, that I could be temperate in tone and language, when treated as a British agent was entitled to be treated. But that, when respect for my office was forgotten, he had no right to suppose I should burthen myself with the remembrance of what was due to his. That I never was the first to depart from the calm, dispassionate tone, proper to all political discussions; but, on the contrary, I perceived that my extreme politeness and mildness were occasionally mistaken for want of spirit, and that attempts were then made to pass affronts upon me. I was obliged to shew that I perceived these, and that they were resented, as slights offered to my Government.

I begged once more to recommend precautions indispensable to the safety of the kingdom, and without which my mission must be unavailing.

"Oh!" he replied, "God will never give us into

the hands of Kawfurs; yet, if our destiny be thus written, no effort of ours can alter or prevent it."

"Believing all this, I wonder you take the trouble to eat and drink. Your destiny being predetermined, you would not die an hour the sooner, should you starve, nor be a whit the worse than is written."

"Yes: but it is my destiny to eat."

"Then pray let it be your destiny to defend the point of approach, which I have pointed out, or, the next page in the volume of your destiny, will be the loss of Khiva."

"Oh," said the Mehtur, fiercely, "if we fall fighting the Kawfurs, we pass straight to paradise."

"And your women? What kind of paradise will your wives and daughters find in the arms of Russian soldiers?"

He was silent.

"You have seen," I continued, "the result of a skirmish with 400 Russians. Are you prepared to meet, face to face, 7,000 with their artillery? If you had rather starve them, than be beaten by them, take the advice of a soldier in this matter."

I perceived, however, that my words were thrown away upon this incapable minister. It was one of the most serious impediments I had to encounter, that my business was to be transacted with one who could neither think himself, nor adopt the ideas of others. Had his noble father, the late minister, been alive, my difficulties had been greatly diminished, and my influence at this Court complete.

Seeing that he could not shake my determination, he left me. It had been my intention to treat him with precisely the degree of civility he had shewn me, that is, not to rise when he entered or departed, and to give him a seat below mine, but the unfortunate blunder, already mentioned, made it incumbent upon me to atone, as far as possible, by extreme civility, so I led him to the door, and bade him farewell.

CHAPTER XIV.

Departure of the Persian Ambassador—Difficulty of procuring correct Intelligence—Inefficiency of my Establishment—Presence of the Persian Ambassador, how far useful to me—Alarm occasioned by the Reports of the British Advance—Resolution of the Khaun to put down Slave-dealing—Final Audience—Subject of change of Route renewed—The Guide, Hussun Mhatoor, Chief of the Chowdhoors—The Khaun's Charge to him—To me—His Message to Her British Majesty—Importance to Europe at this moment of the Kingdom of Khaurism—Parting Charge and Farewell—Fruitless Endeavours to cash my Bills—Deceit and Treachery of the Mehtur—Inhospitality, Meanness, and Cruelty of the Court—Quit Khiva in the almost certain Prospect of perishing in the Wilderness—Parting Instructions, and Farewell to Uummeer Beeg—Departure from Khiva.

THE Persian ambassador had, some days since, departed from Khiva. The Khaun Huzurut had sent him, for his travelling expenses, 900 Tillas of gold (about 540*l.*), and, I believe, presents for his master. My information respecting his mission was always imperfect. I was utterly destitute of proper instruments of intrigue. My Secretary, to whom I had made over the Persian department, was far too timid to carry into effect any of my orders to him, to busy himself with the palms and sleeves of the Persian suite. He never even became acquainted with one of them. They lived many miles distant, but he must often have met them in the bazaar, to which the tether of my suite was restricted. My position at Khiva had quite paralysed the faculties of my followers; they were like men of weak heads, surrounded by precipices. Summud Khaun, indeed, with an immense assumption of importance, but infinite caution, raked about amongst the Afghauns, but this race could afford him little useful intelligence, being strangers and without influence, at Khiva. Ali Muhammud, the only one who understood the language of the country, had been fifteen years a slave at Khiva, and had there a wife and child. He was a new servant, and at a Court where a single false step of an inferior agent, may bring ruin upon the mission, where, to seek for intelligence, is a capital crime, I could not venture to employ him in matters of moment. Nizamm, whom I had found the dirtiest of Feraushs (or porters), and who had since become, by the usage of the country, the most slovenly of Nauzirs (or chamberlains), by a singular instance of good fortune, and by the very last means attributable to such a figure, procured me important intelligence, but it reached me late; and the rest of my people were mere grooms.

It appeared, however, that, at this primitive Court, the easy address, and command of language of the Persian ambassador, were thrown away, and that the Khaun Huzurut complained of his multiplicity of words, and, in speaking of him and of myself, to his Moollas, had given me the preference, as one who said little, and *that* the truth. It was the Khaun's custom, after dismissing me to send for the Persian, and cross-examine him upon the particulars which I had communicated; and, as this man had visited Europe, and was an intelligent fellow, and a detected lie might have cost him his life, but certainly the bastinado, his testimony generally corroborated mine, —a fact of the greatest consequence, because, at that moment, our Governments were at variance, and ourselves were regarded as rivals, at the Court of Khiva. The Persian ambassador, hearing one day, of two very beautiful women for sale in the bazaar, sent and purchased them. The Khaun Huzurut heard of it and was very angry, though on what plea, I know not. He sent, however, to the ambassador's house, and took from him his new purchase.

With the Persian ambassador, on his return to Tehraun, the Khaun Huzurut sent an agent of his own. I was suspicious of this, but was assured that it was only to play the game of words; that the message of the Khaun to the King of Kings was not very flattering,—" Your king offers to rescue my kingdom from a Russian invasion, and in return demands only 30,000 slaves as a gift. Tell Muhummud Shauh that he is yet a child; his beard is not yet grown. Why does he not first drive the Russians out of Persia?" I cannot answer for the truth, or even the probability, of this courteous speech; but, as it had been my care to explain to the Khaun Huzurut the subservience of Persia to Russian counsels, and make known to him the events which had lately marked the history of that kingdom,—its invasion by Russia; the kind offices of Great Britain; its rescue from absolute annihilation, only that, by the weakness of a monarch, who owed his sceptre to the British, it might dwindle into the condition of a province of our rival,—the substance of the message may possibly have been as above, however politely couched.

My private intelligence assured me that our supposed advance to Bulkh had occasioned great alarm; that the Khaun Huzurut vowed that he would put down slave-dealing throughout his dominions, a resolution easily taken, but practicable only as the result of long years of the most vigorous government.

In the evening of the 3rd March, I was summoned to my final audience. The Khaun asked when I should be ready to start. I replied in three days.

" And by which route?"

" The Khaun might ordain as he thought fit; but if allowed a choice, I should prefer that by Mungh Kishlauk. If any other route were determined on, I must positively have a guide, that should accompany me the entire journey to the Russian camp." I related what the Orenburgh guide had been heard to say in my presence.

"I will give you no order," said the Khaun, "but I recommend the Orenburgh route. You will, in attempting the other, be long impeded by the ice." He ran over the reasons already detailed, but they had been often answered; and I replied that, if his Majesty commanded, I would try the other road; but, after many inquiries, was assured that my mission, even should I reach the Russian camp, must be futile by that route; whereas, could I but reach any considerable Russian town, my Government would get intelligence of me, and I could no longer be put off by excuses and delays.

"I see," said the Khaun Huzurut, "that you do not believe my word."

"It is impossible for me to utter a falsehood, even in compliment; and if asked which route I consider best for your Majesty's interests, I must repeat, as before, the route which avoids Orenburgh."

"Why not then by Dahsh Gullah, Nuovo Alexandrofski?"

"I will try that, if your Majesty pleases. But it is a small fort; the commander cannot be a man of consequence. His Government may disown any act of his toward me; whereas the governor of any considerable town or district would fear to embroil his country by incivility to a British officer. Say but the word, and I will march direct thither."

I had brought matters to a crisis, which astonished all present. The Khaun Huzurut, for the first time in his life, had been resisted in a favourite project. When he accused me of distrusting his word, I had no answer. It was a position from which his own dignity should have saved me, the most embarassing in the world. I could not tell a black lie, and had no practice in making white lies.

The Khaun Huzurut sent for the guide, Hussun Mhatoor, chief of the Chowdhoor Toorcumuns, a tribe of 12,000 families, or about 60,000 souls, scattered over the tract between Khiva and Mungh Kishlauk, and all potent in the latter district. He entered; a tall, hale, handsome old man, who in his youth must have been very robust, and who, even now, betrayed no symptom of the enfeebling influence of years. His profile was noble, and a perfect model of manly beauty; his head, and long ample beard, were a study; but his deep-set eye was the very charnel light of avarice and treachery. The Khaun desired me to question him as I pleased. His answers fully corroborated my own opinion. "There was no snow on this route; the Caspian in a very few days would be free from ice. There were always plenty of Russian and Nogay boats at Mungh Kishlauk, of all sorts and sizes, waiting off shore for the Bokhara caravans. The present hostilities would in no wise banish them from the port, because there was an island not far off, where they could lie in perfect security until called to the port by signals from the caravans; that they carried cannon, and had therefore nothing to apprehend from the Toorcumuns by daylight: that he himself would give me the use of a boat, to visit, if necessary, the island or the Russian vessels lying off shore; that it was one or at most three days' sail from thence to Astrakhan; that at Mungh Kishlauk were no houses, but an abundance of Kuzzauk and Toorcumun tents, where I could procure everything."

This was for me a triumphant contradiction of all the arguments by which I had been assailed; but in fact it was no evidence; for my liberality to Birdler Beeg, my first guide, having got abroad, every guide was ready to swear his own route the best and most practicable, in the hope of some similar good fortune. The Khaun Huzurut then addressed Hussun Mhatoor.

"You will conduct Abbott Sahib in safety and comfort to Mungh Kishlank. You will procure him the means of embarking for Astrakhan."

Hussun replied that he had been so active an enemy

of the Russians, that he dared not himself approach any of their vessels, but that he had a boat at my service, and would put me in the way of speaking to the captains of vessels; that in this I need not apprehend the slightest difficulty.

"And if," said the Khaun to me, "you should not find a passage at Mungh Kishlauk?"

"In that case I must go on to Dahsh Gullah."

"Do so; and should you reach St. Petersburg, you will let the Queen of England know that I have not sent her Majesty any rare presents of arms or jewels, because you have represented that her Majesty is better pleased with the release from slavery of the daughters of the Afghauns."

"I will do so." At the same time I thought that it would have puzzled his Majesty to produce from the royal treasury anything that could be decently offered to a British queen. Emeralds and rubies of every ugly shape, uncut, and not worth the cutting, full of flaws, and set in the most paltry fashion, these may be said to form almost the only ornaments of the wealthy, bearing in these countries an inordinate value, but utterly worthless in the estimation of a London jeweller. A few rare exceptions are known amongst the royal treasures, but these are preserved with most jealous care, and nothing worth keeping is ever bestowed as a gift.

"You are sure," said the Khaun Huzurut, "that the Russians will neither murder nor imprison you?"

"Quite sure!"

"But they imprisoned my ambassador's brother."

"That was at a time, when your Majesty's dominions were far removed from the sight of Europe. The eyes of the whole world are now turned upon them, and upon my movements, watching both with intense interest."

"Wherefore?"

"Because your Majesty's dominions forming the

barrier between two of the mightiest powers of the earth, and being invaded by one of those powers attract the gaze of all mankind. Should the other, power awaken to a sense of her danger and true interests, the consequence may be, the convulsion of the world."

This sentence, I do not repeat in the explicit terms requisite to its comprehension by the monarch, to whom it was addressed. He replied with a smile, "It's very hard that they cannot find, in all the world, some other battle-field than just my dominions."

He again cautioned me to bear in mind his instructions respecting an exchange of captives; repeating and making me repeat his words. Of his sincerity, there could be no doubt. But as it was inspired by fear, I confess I was not very certain it would endure, after the failure of the Russian expedition, which, in the eyes of a nation so barbarous, would be magnified into a triumph. And I am still of opinion, that had any officer of less genius, prudence, and engaging manners than Captain Shakespear been sent after me to Khiva, the negotiation might have had a different result, from the brilliant conclusion to which his prompt and judicious mediation brought it.

The Khaun Huzurut now dismissed me, commending me to God. I assured him, and it was from my heart, that I would maintain his interests to the utmost of my abilities and my life. I had received from him more favour than he had perhaps ever bestowed upon another. I loved and respected his character; and even had not his interests been inseparable from those of my country, would have risked much in his service. His after-conduct annihilated every obligation I might have acknowledged to him, and brought me on the creditor's side; but I attribute to circumstances all that was to my disadvantage, and am willing, rather, to dwell upon the undoubted virtues of the sovereign and the man.

The remaining days were spent in the most painful negotiations for procuring funds for my journey. I must not weary the reader with more of these, than are requisite to exhibit the manners of the Court, and to shadow faintly one of my numerous difficulties.

Upon the strength of the Minister's repeated promises, I had not mentioned my pecuniary embarrassments to the Khaun Huzurut; for, as the custom of the country enjoined the Khaun to frank all my expenses through his dominions, and the Persian ambassador had actually received a large sum for this purpose; to have hinted at my necessity, would have been to ask the gift of so much gold; and I could not ask the king of Khaurism to be my banker. Since my last audience, the Mehtur had discovered that I should have applied personally to the Khaun Huzurut; and at the last day, after a variety of delays, he told me that he really dared not mention the subject to the Khaun, lest His Majesty should accuse him of having been bribed by me. This was pleasant: I was obliged, therefore, to write to the Khaun Huzurut, stating my extreme distress for money, without which I could not possibly proceed; that I had been cajoled with promises by the bankers at Khiva, and that his Minister, until the present moment, had promised to provide for me. That I begged His Majesty would order the bankers to honour my drafts, or allow me to cash them at the royal treasury. I sent this through the Minister; but getting no answer, and believing that he might have withheld it, I despatched Birdler Beeg to speak to the Khaun upon the subject. He came back in great confusion, saying, that the Khaun had given way to a burst of anger, on hearing that I wanted cash, and asked why I did not demand it at my last audience; that he would then have given me whatever I desired, but now would not hear of it.

I wrote another letter, stating the reasons that had made me reluctant to burthen the royal treasury, at this critical moment; the impossibility of a British representative's begging gifts, even of a king; that I asked no favour, but that which was requisite for the accomplishment of my mission, viz. that His Majesty would remove, by his furmaun, the fears of the bankers, and give them permission to serve themselves and me, by cashing my bills. That I was His Majesty's guest, proceeding on his business, burthened with the salvation of his empire, and staking my life and fame in his service. That to enter the wilderness with a journey of 2,500 miles before me, unprovided with funds, was certain destruction. That I had not mentioned this subject at my final audience, because his Minister had promised me the cash. That his Minister was well aware I could not proceed without it, etc., etc., etc.

This was conveyed by Hussun Mhatoor, to whom I explained, that should I start without cash, I should be unable to reward faithful service. No answer was returned. I was indignant at such unworthy and inhospitable conduct, which, if known, would shame the author in the eyes of even the savage nations of the world. To move without cash was madness, yet I had engaged myself to the Khaun to start on a certain day; that day was come, and the faith of my nation might suffer by delay. My people were in great consternation. All kinds of rumours were afloat. They entreated me to move; those who had saved gold, brought it to me, and pressed it upon me; but I would not hear of depriving any of that which must soon become as the breath of life to them. I consulted Hussun, the guide. Could I raise money, as my servants had been told I might, at old Oorgunj, or at Mung Kishlauk? "Oh! yes," he replied, "there should be no difficulty." I did not believe him, yet there was a faint chance, that he might be speaking the truth, and it was my only chance of accomplishing my mission; for Summud Khaun coming in at that moment, said, that my well-wishers at Khiva entreated me to begone, for that the Khaun was in a rage, at my having exceeded my time by a few hours, and had become more suspicious than ever of me; and that they feared he might, in his blind anger, yield to the advice of those who were urging him to destroy me and my suite. To have remained longer would have either produced this effect, or one that I dreaded even more, the renunciation of my services, at a crisis of such moment to my country. In answer, therefore, to a message from the Khaun, inquiring whether I intended to start, I replied that I would proceed instantly, since I had promised it: but that, unless I could raise cash, by the sale of my horses and appointments on the road, I should perish in the wilderness, his guest.

I left Khiva, therefore, under the most melancholy of auspices. I had just sufficient money to carry me to the shores of the Caspian, and there, with the sea on one side, and the desert on the other, unless I could, in the wilderness, find purchasers for my horses, arms, and garments, I must assuredly perish. Even should I escape destruction, my mission was in itself a sufficient load of anxiety and trouble. Success, which seemed improbable, *might* save me, but failure would be disgrace and ruin.

I have omitted a very material part of my final audience. The Khaun Huzurut insisted that on quitting his territories and entering Russia, I should write him a letter to that effect, and, upon the back of it, an English letter to the Envoy at Heraut, of similar purport. This obliged me to take my old Meerza, for I cannot write a decent Persian epistle; and, as he was helpless, I was obliged to take an attendant for his horse, etc., so that I thought it just as well to take my entire suite of seven people. Now that my prospects were so melancholy, I wished to send some of them back to Heraut; but fear had taken possession of them, and it could not be arranged; they dared not be separated from me. The Khaun had also, at my request, promised to send after me any messenger who might arrive within eight days.

Poor Ummeer Beeg, the released slave, came to bid me farewell. He wept again, as he kissed my hand, but this time it was for me, for the forlorn and hopeless circumstances under which I started on so wild a journey. I had intended to equip and provide him handsomely for his journey, that all might see how *he* is honoured and rewarded who faithfully serves my Government; but my funds were quite exhausted by what I had already given him. I bade him explain my melancholy prospects to the blind prince of H. M. Shah Shoojah's family, whom I had intended to send in honour to Heraut, and also to the unhappy female slaves of the royal family of Heraut, whom I found myself unable to enfranchise. I had begged they might be included in the number whose liberty was granted at my intercession, but my purpose was defeated, either by the Mehtur, or by some feeling of shame on the part of the Khaun, to return to Heraut princesses who had been exposed to such usage in his dominions; and now, for want of funds, I was obliged to leave them in captivity.

A large crowd had collected at my gate, to stare at me. I mounted my horse, and seeing Ummeer Beeg standing near, stretched out my hand to him, which however he would only raise to his lips and forehead, and then said aloud, and made my interpreter repeat it in Toorkish after me, "This is an honoured servant of the British Government. God preserve you, Ummeer Beeg, good and gallant and faithful follower!"

It was all I could now do to honour him in the eyes of those by whom he had been oppressed and despised.* Even in that desolate hour, my inability to reward the sufferings and faithful services of this gallant follower was felt as an additional woe.

* In all that I have written of Ummeer Beeg, the reader is begged to observe that I have written according to my knowledge of him. I am far from supposing that a man so educated should have been free from the almost universal faults of Asiatics. I vouch only for his high spirit, his courage, and his fidelity under trust, virtues found occasionally even amongst outlaws. My attention to him was so blended with sympathy for his sufferings endured in the cause of our Government, that it would have given me great pain to have detected in him any serious blemish; but my acquaintance with him was very slight, and I derived my high opinion of his fidelity and courage from Major Todd, whom he had served in Persia.

CHAPTER XV.

Departure from Khiva—Palace of the Toorruh—Priggery of the Toorcumuns—Umbarr, an ancient Site—Report of gigantic human Bones—Dahsh Howz—House of the Guide—His Obstinacy—Message from the Mehtur—The great Mare's Nest—Its Origin—Journey resumed—Inhospitality of the Guide—Capture of a Russian Interpreter—My Objection to see him—Journey resumed—Reception at the Den of Thieves.

OUR road traversed the richly cultivated and well-wooded valley of the Oxus, amongst the houses of the nobles and gentry of Khiva. The scene is not unpleasing; but the level character of the prospect deprives it of all pretensions to beauty, and, in my present mood of mind, nothing could be more melancholy. The prevalent trees are the poplar, plane, and elm, the latter a fine shadowy mass of tangled boughs and the densest foliage. All the trees at this season were leafless, and there was not a blade of grass, nor a wild flower upon any of the banks, a deficiency for which nothing can atone. Occasionally as we proceeded, the sandy desert, here utterly divested of its sprinkled shrub and herb, jutted into the tract of hard and fertile clay. Villages and small towns appeared at no long intervals; and on the road we occasionally met laden camels, one-horse carts, with their enormous wheels, each freighted with some fair Oozbeg, and driven by a male slave; and Toorcumun horsemen. Amongst the latter Hussun, the guide, had many acquaintance, on meeting whom he pulled up his horse, throwing his right arm, whip and all, across that portion of the body which mortals call the belly, but which, the sentiment originating the gesture, designates the seat of the affections, as undoubtedly it often is. These were picturesque groups, though somewhat monotonous. Hussun himself, well mounted on a white Tooreumun horse, his body bowed, and his head deep sunk upon his shoulders, was, nevertheless, the pre-eminent figure; his stature, his noble features, and flowing beard of snow were not to be matched amongst Tooreumuns.

Hussun Mhatoor, in addition to his office of guide, had charge of what was called a train of artillery, being in fact two bundles of fire-arms carried upon a camel; some of these were wall pieces, and the remainder matchlock rifles; they were destined for the defence of an important military post, were regarded with great complacency by him, and with much reverence by all the country.

At night we reached the residence of a Torruh, or prince of the blood royal. I was ushered into a guest-chamber, something worse than that I had occupied at Khiva, where dinner was provided, and I passed the night. This palace I found precisely similar to other buildings bearing the title in Toorkestaun, i. e. externally rather imposing for an Asiatic dwelling, internally a very indifferent kennel.

I had warned Hussun (whose title of Mhatoor, or the Hero, acquired by his prowess over the Russians, I shall generally drop) that I purposed starting at about two o'clock next morning, and that he must be ready at that hour. When, however, I rose, he was not forthcoming, and, on being summoned, sent to excuse himself. This was the first specimen of his insolence, but not the last. I started without him, and, of course, soon lost the road, which I recovered only by means of a Tooreumun, who was persuaded to accompany me. The country was precisely similar to that of the preceding day, excepting that the houses were generally smaller, and canals and sluices in abundance intersect the plain.

Summud Khaun, the steward, who had fallen into the rear, overtook me about midway, complaining that one of Hussun's relations, a Toorcumun, had stolen two of the cloaks of my suite. That he had discovered the fact, taxed him with it, and, upon his denial, had opened his bundle, and drawn out the missing articles in presence of many witnesses. This was an ominous commencement. The man was known, afterwards, by the name of Doozd, or the thief.

In passing over the abandoned site of the town Unbarr, walled around, as if to be re-occupied, I inquired of my interpreter, Ali Muhummud, the history. He said, it was supposed to have been the capital of Khaurism, under the Culmauks, whom we call Culmucks. That these were slain in an invasion by Russia. That the late Khaun purposed rebuilding this city, and had walled it accordingly; but that, in digging, some monstrous human bones were found, which proved it to have been a cemetery of giants. That the Khaun had, on this account, prohibited any profanation of the spot, by the erection of fresh buildings. That the Toorcumuns, nevertheless, resorted thither, to carry off the soil, which formed an excellent manure. That many of these gigantic bones, were turned up. That he had seen many. That they were decidedly human: he could not be mistaken, because he had seen the sculls and the teeth. That the former were of such size, as barely to admit of being embraced by his arms. That after a few days' exposure in the air, they fell to powder.

The last circumstance is the only one that gives an air of probability to the assertion, that these bones are human. Had they been fossil, they might have been confidently pronounced to belong to the brute creation; but it is difficult to imagine the preservation, in an osseous form, of animal remains from the remote period[*] when the Oxus could have been the resort of

[*] I have, however, since found large quantities of the bone of the

any of the larger varieties of mammalia; and, as few would be disposed to adopt Ali Muhummud's theory of a sepulchre of giants, his account is in some respect wanting in fidelity. The matter, however, seems worthy of investigation, and I much regretted that I could not stop for the purpose: but my mission was of far too great importance to be entangled with any of those suspicions, to which such investigations give rise in this barbarous land. I therefore recommend the subject to any who may succeed me.

At noon, we passed through Dahsh Howz (the stone cistern) a town, near which is a royal garden, and a mud fort of some size, of rectangular form, with curtains and round bastions, in a double row of defence. It is new, yet has already suffered from the weather. About three miles further, we reached the abode of Hussun Mhatoor, an ordinary farm house, standing unsheltered in the cultivated plain. Here there was much show of hospitality. A guest chamber was allotted me near the entrance, and my people were accommodated in another. Hussun soon informed me, that it would be necessary to halt here three days. I was now completely in this man's power, being cut off from all communication with Khiva. I argued, insisted, commanded, explained the extreme importance of my mission, the inevitable ruin to his country should it fail, as it must, if delayed, and the consequent ruin to himself, from the anger of the Khaun Huzurut; but my words were all thrown away upon this man, whose temper is as obdurate as his heart. He heard me with the greatest composure, and then quietly repeated his determination to remain. It is not easy to give the reader even a faint idea of my perplexity, and almost frenzy, at this senseless interruption of a journey fraught with such extreme importance to my country, and the land I would fain serve. I could argue and threaten, but could not

elephant, in an osseous form, in the soil immediately north of the village of Russool, on the left bank of the Jelum.

bribe; and the last was the only argument that could have had a chance of success. Hussun was aware of the state of my purse, and how little he had to expect from my liberality; and as to a note for cash upon Heraut, the idea was incomprehensible to this son of the wilderness, to whose speculations had never occurred the idea, that a shred of paper could be exchanged for gold, or that anything but fear could prevent the breach of a promise involving loss. My funds, indeed, were so low, that I could not even venture to promise him part of my property, horses, arms, or accoutrements; as they must soon form my sole means of purchasing my onward way.

Again, and again, I sent for Hussun, to expostulate with him, and at length solemnly assured him, that unless he obeyed the Khaun's orders, to conduct me with all speed to Mungh Kishlauk, I should quit his house, and return to Khiva, for another guide. This step I was extremely reluctant to adopt, because the news of my return would certainly reach the Khaun, through one of Hussun's emissaries, who would attribute it to my perverseness, and probably, in the present state of the Khaun's mind, induce some rash act, which would interrupt all harmony between the Governments; when, therefore, Hussun reduced his demand to a single day, I felt it prudent to consent, rather than resort to the alternative.

10th March, 1840. The arrival of a messenger from the Minister of Khiva was announced by my people, with many smiles. He produced a letter, and 100 ducats in silver; I had applied for 800. The letter stated, that these were all that could be collected in the capital of Khaurism, and that, being the property of a banker, interest was required by the owner for his risk. The excessive meanness of this transaction was a severe reflection upon me, for having treated this Court, as if either King or Minister could comprehend, far less appreciate, liberality and disinterestedness. In justice to myself, and the cause in which I was embarked, I should have wrung out of it every possible advantage, and have risked the least possible in return.

I sat down and wrote an order on Heraut for the sum, with interest, and in answer to the Minister's letter, represented that he had sent me just one-eighth of the sum I had required of him, and not sufficient to carry me out of the dominions of his master, whose guest, therefore, would most probably perish in the wilderness. That I hoped he would be able to procure and send me at least four or five hundred more ducats, upon the same terms. That I should, nevertheless, prosecute my journey so long as I had a ducat left, and did not grudge my life in the cause I had embraced; only I begged the Khaun Huzurut, for his own sake, to consider how utterly hopeless was my mission, under circumstances so straitened. I then gave the messenger five ducats, as a temptation to use his best endeavours to become the bearer of a fresh supply, adding my promise, that his reward should increase in the proportion of my ability.

My servants had been to me the night before, and had again pressed affectionately upon me their savings, amounting together, to a sum considerable enough, under my present circumstances. But I replied, that the cause in which I was embarked was that of my own, and not of *their* country; that my country could require, and was welcome to *my* life, but not to theirs; and that I begged they would never again mention the subject. By the most rigid economy, I might now, I thought, reach the Russian frontier, and it seemed probable, that some of the Russian sea-captains at Mungh Kishlauk might take my horses and arms in part payment of my passage to Astrakhan, and, at Astrakan, there was just a possibility that I might meet with some Afghaun or Jew merchant to cash my bills upon Heraut. This hope, faint as it was, supported me; more than once I had determined to write a positive refusal to proceed without funds, but the state of the Khaun's feelings towards me at that moment, would have closed all hope of being employed in a negotiation which every hour was rendering more delicate and more imperative. The enterprize before me, however discouraging, was not utterly impossible; and I remembered how often I had sought difficulty, and encountered peril, for the mere thrill of triumph.

Hussun, who had been all smiles, since the arrival of the silver, let me know that a fine horse was at the gate, awaiting my acceptance. I replied, that it was impossible for a British agent to accept gifts unless he could make a suitable return, which he well knew, was not my case; so, after much remonstrance, the horse was commuted for a sheep and a cloak, in acknowledgment of which I made his young son a handsome present of cash, and gave him a dress of honour.

The sleet had been falling all day, and, at night, lay upon the earth to the depth of ten inches. It still darkened the air, forming a gloomy and suitable preparation for the tale with which Ali Muhummud had alarmed my servants, and which, when night was well set in, the old Meerza brought for my edification and comfort.

"Salaam alikoom," said the old gentleman, entering.

"Alikoom salaam; take a seat."

He sat down, and spread his hands over the heap of ignited charcoal before me.

"Have you heard, Sir, anything regarding our guide, Hussun Mhatoor."

"Only that he is chief of the Chowdhoor Toorcumuns."

"He is a great villain, every one says so, and the greatest thief in the country, and all his people are thieves. You had a specimen this morning of a Chowdhoor's honesty."

"The greatest thief, in a country of thieves, is the only safe companion for a traveller."

"But Hussun is the most avaricious wretch in the world."

"I and my suite have not much to tempt avarice; he well knows how low my funds are."

"Ah! but your horses, Sir, your arms and clothes."

"Fear nothing. The Khaun knows the importance of my mission, and Hussun leaves his family as pledges of my safety."

"Have you heard, Sir, Ali Muhummud's tale?" in an indifferent tone of voice, and rubbing his hands over the fire, as if his whole attention were absorbed in them.

"No! what saith Ali?"

"Ali has a friend in the minister's service. This friend was bent upon accompanying Ali in your suite; but, the day we started, he came to tell Ali that he could not go."

"Well, what does his going or staying signify to me?"

"You have not heard his reason yet, Sir." Here the old gentleman rose, and, cautiously opening the door, peeped out, to assure himself there were no eaves-droppers. He then closed the door, resumed his seat, and proceeded.

"He not only excused himself from going, but urged Ali, in the strongest terms, not to think of it."

"Well! well! what is all this to the purpose. I suppose he had some silly tale of massacre to tell, and I have not the slightest doubt that Ali was ass enough to believe every word of it."

"He said," replied the Meerza, in a mysteriously low voice, "that he had overheard the minister say you had been discovered to be a Russian: that three fresh men had just identified you as such, on oath, before the Khaun Huzurut. That the Khaun feared to slay *you*, as he had slain the other Englishmen, in his capital, on account of the advance of your army to Bulkh, and had therefore sent you to be murdered in the wilderness.* That the Khaun was now fully satisfied that the interests of England and Russia were one and the same."

I laughed heartily at this tale, and sent for Ali, who repeated it.

" Do *you* yourself believe it?" I enquired.

" I do!"

" Then you are a great fool to accompany me. What did you reply to your friend?"

"I said, that my blood was not redder than my master's; that he had redeemed my child from slavery, and that I would not desert him at a pinch."

This child was redeemed at the Government expence, as Ali well knew; but he knew that I was a servant of Government, and that, in serving me, he served my country.

" Would you like," said my Meerza, "to see the young Afghaun Syud; he can tell you something more?"

" Another mare's nest (Ashiānch-i-Madiān). Yes! let him bring it in."

He entered, and asserted that the belief in Khiva was general, that the Khaun Huzurut, fearing to murder me in his capital, had sent me into the wilderness to be destroyed.

This report was so easily accounted for, that it gave me very little uneasiness, although it sharpened my attention to the most trifling incidents in the conduct of those around me. Let it be remembered, that the only persons known, or rather supposed, to be English, that had ever visited Khiva, had been put to the torture at night, by the reigning Khaun, murdered under the cloak of darkness, and buried in the desert, under the same circumstances of mystery. People spoke of the thing only in whispers, and with

---

* Strange as it may seem, Col. Arthur Conolly, who succeeded me at Khiva, gave full credit to this tale of treachery, and endeavoured to persuade his government of it. I, of course, fully refuted it.

extreme caution. These men, calling themselves English, and murdered as Russians, had, by their fate, confused together the two nations in the minds of the Khivians; and, as it was well known that many had identified me as a Russian, and as Russia was actually invading the country, and the British arms were supposed to have advanced to Bulkh, for the purpose, many believed, of concerting with Russia the extermination of Islaum; and, as the nature of my mission, and the explication of our policy, were strictly confined to the precincts of the Court, it was scarcely possible that the people of Khiva should form any other judgment of my destination than that which alarmed my followers. As for the man who had heard the minister say this, or that, he was probably a tool of Yar Muhummud Khaun, who had agents at Khiva, and was bent upon defeating, by every possible means, an alliance which would close against him this door of retreat, should his perfidy at length exhaust the patience of the British Government. To this arch-fiend I have little hesitation in attributing also the host of tidings tending to alarm the Khaun Huzurut, which at this moment poured in like a flood upon us; the messenger that had seen the Persian Gulf covered with our fleets; the other, who had seen our armies at Bulkh; and the third, who had been in the Rozeh Bagh (garden of fast), at Heraut, when a British force was encamped there. All these men were Afghauns. The endeavour to prevail upon Ali Muhummud to desert me, at this critical moment, was a master-piece of strategy, because, without him (the only one of the party who could speak Toorkish), my ruin was inevitable. That the Vuzeer kept up a constant intercourse with the minister of Khiva, I was aware; and, although I had trumped his best card, in dismissing his agent, Peer Muhummud Khaun, I knew the man well enough to be certain that his design would not be abandoned, whilst his personal enmity to myself would be inflamed.

On the other hand, my secret intelligence seemed quite worthy of dependence. It could not be a forgery of the Court of Khiva, because its tendency was to defeat the wishes of that Court. It could scarcely be attributed to Yar Muhummud Khaun, because the agent was the least likely person in the world to be applied to by me, or any one else, for information, and had not offered it voluntarily, but yielded it to the power of gold. Moreover, this intelligence tallied perfectly with my observation of the Court intrigues, and rendered the whole system intelligible; whereas the report just mentioned was at variance with a variety of important particulars, and tended only to confuse. None of my servants, excepting Ali and the old Meerza (who had the heart of a hare, nursed in a tea-field), thoroughly gave way to these base suspicions of the Khaun Huzurut. Ali Muhummud, unfortunately, owing to his long residence at Khiva, was a formidable authority against them; and being himself fully impressed with the sense of a peril which had paid him the compliment of addressing itself first to him, contrived, every now and then, to win the others to his views, and ended by himself abandoning them in toto.

I was aware that the Khaun's suspicions of me had lately gained great strength, and now perceived the cause. I knew, also, that the minister would do me as much mischief as he dared. I think it possible, that these reports may have encouraged the treachery afterwards practised, and that the perpetrators may have been assured of the minister's good offices to screen them from the consequences. But, be this as it may, no one will wonder, that the good people of Khiva, having at my departure the persuasion referred to, and seeing their anticipations fulfilled to the letter, should still attribute the villany to him from whom they had expected it. The reader, after what has been detailed of the meanness and inhospitality of my treatment, will scarcely suspect me of any undue bias in favour of the Khaun.

11th March.—Resumed the journey through deep snow, and a mist, hurried by the east wind back to its source, the Caspian; the vapour, in the process of congelation, had given out sufficient heat to temper the otherwise cutting wind. The road was well occupied by horsemen, amongst whom Hussun had many acquaintance. Two summits of inconsiderable height, rising from the right bank of the Oxus, were in view, but we did not approach within sight of that river. These hills are said to have yielded gold in former days. At about two o'clock, we halted at a Toorcumun village, where a tent was pitched for my reception.

Here Hussun again demanded three days' halt to procure camels, all of which might, under proper arrangements, have been waiting in readiness for me. My remonstrances were renewed, but with less effect than ever, for we had receded from Khiva, where alone could be found any counterpoise to the formidable power of this chief. He, moreover, insisted upon my laying in fifty days' supply of provisions for man and beast, and positively refused to stir with less, although there remained before us but fourteen days' journey. For this supply ten camels were requisite, which were to be hired of his relations. Exhausted as were my funds, I did not readily submit to this fresh imposition. The point was debated with much warmth through my interpreter. My principal objection to it was the plea it would furnish him for loitering on the road. Nothing, however, could move Hussun from his purpose. Accustomed from youth to an authority almost kingly, he seemed utterly ignorant of the art of obedience, and to expect that everything should yield to his simple *fiat*. Unfortunately, he had power to compel obedience, for to have parted with him had been inevitable destruction, and I was now too far advanced to recede. In the evening, my people came to say, that he refused to eat with them, and that they thought he might have taken offence at the warmth of my manner, when pointing out to him the consequences of his present conduct to himself and his Government. This was to be avoided on many accounts; and as he was an old man, and the head of his tribe, I did not scruple to enter the tent, and assure him, that if I had hurt his feelings by my earnestness, I much regretted it. That upon my movements depended the fate of Khaurism, and that I was acting, not for myself, but for his king. That I was his guest, and owed respect to his age, as well as to my relative position. He begged to assure me, that he had taken no offence, and that his present abstinence proceeded from his having just dined heartily at the funeral of a friend; and as I knew what one of Hussun's hearty meals amounted to, it was impossible for me to hope he should engulph any more aliment. He, however, ate several handsful of rice in proof of his good humour.

12th March.—I complete this day my 33rd year, and this day will long be remembered as one of the most miserable of my life. Here, after all my labours, my difficulties, and troubles, when nearly all that seemed arduous had been conquered, and hope had sprung from the ashes of despair; when my foot was forward, and my arm out-stretched to grasp the object of so many cares, I found myself fettered, cramped, and all but strangled under the burthen of this "old man of the sea." Loitering, to suit the ease of a subject of Khaurism, whilst speed alone could save that kingdom from destruction. Even the ruin which everywhere stared myself in the face was forgotten in consideration of the wide-sweeping mischief to others which this delay seemed to render inevitable. Five days were past, and we had advanced but one day's journey and a half on the road, and it was evident, from the supply of provisions demanded, that the guide intended to move very deliberately the remainder of the journey, instead of conveying me, as he had promised, to Mungh Kishlauk in sixteen days. The weather meanwhile was becoming milder. The army of invasion would soon be at liberty to advance, and should it reach Khiva ere I could reach St. Petersburg, all was lost. The anguish of that day beggars description.

13th March.—Still halting for the amusement of Hussun. News has arrived from the Russian frontier, that a fleet of seven boats, carrying supplies for the Russian fort, Dahsh Gullah, has been stranded on the ice, and burnt by the Toorcumuns, and Kuzzauks of Mungh Kishlauk. That a Russian officer also, who had visited the coast to purchase sheep, etc., of the Kuzzauks, had been seized, and was within a march of this spot, in custody of his captors, to be delivered to the Khaun Huzurut at Khiva. He is, it seems, an interpreter. Hussun offered to bring him to my presence, and it may be well believed, there were a thousand particulars which I wished to inquire of him, of extreme importance to my safety in the prosecution of this journey. I considered, however, that as our conversation would be conducted in a tongue, unintelligible to those around me, it would afford the Russian captive, or spy, whichever he might be, large opportunity of injuring my affairs with the Khaun, by misrepresentation; attributing to me speeches and arguments, utterly inconsistent with the good faith between Khiva and my own Government. He might even have declared me a Russian, and have sealed my fate without more ado. It will be seen, hereafter, what use was made of this man's supposed testimony against me. I therefore peremptorily declined the meeting, which Hussun and others pressed upon me. The destruction of the Russian fleet gave me serious uneasiness. It would probably deter other vessels from approaching the coast, and thus create fresh difficulty in the way of an enterprize, already sufficiently arduous.

The Toorcumuns of this village are rude and noisy. It is difficult to escape their constant intrusion, especially, as the customs of the country impute inhospitality to him, who closes his door. My followers are pestered by them, and we find it difficult to provide food sufficient for any meal, since we never can conjecture, how many guests there may not be. They laugh boisterously and constantly, a habit common to Toorcumuns, proceeding from a certain coarse good nature, high spirits, a sound constitution, and a superlative opinion of self.

14th March.—With the utmost difficulty, I have this day persuaded Hussun to resume the march. The road still skirts the clay valley of the Oxus, but the houses here are fewer, the tents in greater proportion, and the land newly cleared. The black tent is so much more comfortable, than any permanent habitation known in central Asia, that the Toorcumun abandons it with reluctance, and only when he has become, thoroughly and exclusively, an agriculturist. For many Toorcumuns, who have taken to the latter avocation, retain their love for the wilderness and its comparative freedom; and to continue to resort thither, yearly, to pasture their flocks and herds, which, at other seasons, are watched, there, by their children or retainers.

We approached, shortly after noon, a considerable Khail of Chowdhoor Toorcumuns, and our friend the Thief, handsomely mounted, rode forth to escort me to the tent of his elder brother, the Yuze Baushie, Kooch Muhummud. I was shown into a beautiful black tent, of the largest size and handsomest material, forming the most agreeable dwelling imaginable. The women of the house had collected to gaze. They are very fair, with high complexions, and irregular features; certainly not ill-looking; but seldom, I imagine, beautiful, when their blood is unmixed. As the Thief had here four brothers, the place has since been known amongst my people, as the Den of Robbers.

CHAPTER XVI.

Visits from Toorcumuns—Khail of Yahmoots—Dress of Toorcumun Women—Fierceness of the Watch-Dogs—Visit to the Ruins of Old Oorgunj, and to a Toorcumun Fair—Entertainment at a Khail—Cure of Jaundice—Toorcumun Dinner—Economy of a Toorcumun Tent—Dress of Children—Ruined Fort Shoomauki—Deserted Bed of Oxus—Distant View of Oxus and the Lake Londahn—Slaves—Cliffs of Chalk and Marl—Ruined Castle of Kohna Wuzeer—Of Barrasun Gelmus—Another Enchanted Castle—Ibrahim Aat'h—Entrance to Kuzzauk Land—Distant View of the Channel occupied by the Oxus when it fell into the Gulf of Balkaun—Anecdotes of the Bahrukzye Chiefs.

THE chief men of the Khail paid me a visit, and were treated to tea: and afterwards, the elder brother, Kooch Muhummud, a broad-shouldered, deep-chested, bull-necked, and bandy-legged Toorcumun, with coarse, good-natured features, rather an honest, trumpiform, red nose, and the voice of a bear, led in his young daughter, a child of some eight or nine years, and seated himself, at my invitation, near me. The little girl wore a scarlet hemispherical cap, with silver tassels and bells over her light brown hair, which was braided in four tails. Her introduction was regarded by my old Meerza with holy horror; and Summud Khann afterwards gave me a sermon, upon the same text, from which I learned, that a father should not see his daughter, after the age of eight or nine years. As for me, I was delighted at this symptom of escape, from the brutifying and hateful habits and prejudices of the Muhummedan world.

Four slaves afterwards entered, to pay their respects. One of them, a Tymunee of Herant, had sold *himself* to escape starvation. The number of captives in Khaurism is supposed to exceed the Oozbeg population of 700,000.

15th March.—Resumed my journey through a plain, less highly cultivated, and less densely inhabited, but cleared of jungle, and sprinkled with black tents. A march of twenty-four miles, in the teeth of a storm of sleet, which the loose dress of the country is ill calculated to resist, brought me to a small arm of the Oxus, having water about $2\frac{1}{2}$ feet deep. Konch (i. e. old) Oorgunj had been sometime visible, but was still five miles distant, and nothing could persuade the old sulky guide to advance a step further, until the arrival of the camels. We therefore sat an hour in the snow-storm, and then proceeded farther down the stream, to a Khail of Yahmoot Toorcumuns. Here the relations of my old guide, Birdler Beeg, welcomed me warmly—a couple of black tents were emptied for my accommodation, and speedily filled with heads and faces, in all moods and tenses of curiosity. A large wood fire was lighted in the centre of my tent, and half the covering of the sky-light was removed; and I found the change to these snug quarters, from the cutting wind outside, extremely grateful. Here I saw many Toorcumun women, engaged in various occupations about the camp; one of them appeared beautiful, the generality, comely, decidedly European; and often with features almost English. The eyes, indeed, though sparkling, are small, and the lids are ill cut, the arch above being precisely similar to that below. The complexion, even when the hair is light, cannot be termed blonde, because the white of the skin (so to speak), is a transparent sunny hue, such as we see upon a ripe nectarine, or an evening cloud. Their colour is rich. The hair is plaited in two tresses, which fall down either cheek. The head dress is a high caftan, nearly similar to that worn by male Ghubbres,* but of gaudy colours, usually crimson; a scarf, tied around this, falls behind, fluttering in the breeze. The dress is a pair of very ample-coloured drawers, and a chogah, or cloak, of striped chintz or silk. The dress of young maidens is a low, cylindric cap of coloured silk, and a chogah, or cloak, of the most gaudy and varied colours. They seem clad in the wings of butterflies. This dress is singularly becoming, and seems to confer upon them a fay-like kindred, with the wild creatures, and wilder fancies, proper to the desert. Many female faces came to peep through the crevices of the tent; and I hoped that some of the children, at least, would be permitted to enter. Our camels arrived at a late hour.

One of the inconveniences of lodging in these camps arises from the ferocity of the large watch-dogs. At our third stage, one of these lamed my Yahmootic horse by a bite on the haunch; and my Heraut horse narrowly escaped the same fate to-day. I left the camp to saunter toward the river; but, being warned by past experience, had my sabre under my arm. It was well that I had adopted this precaution;—almost before I could draw to defend myself, six fierce dogs were upon me. By the wildest capers and flourishes, which I cannot remember without mirth, I contrived to keep them at weapon's length; but had not a half-a-dozen Tooreumuns seen my predicament, and run to my assistance, should have been much torn, although I might have immolated two or three of the curs. This were a very unsatisfactory way of receiving inglorious and unpensioned wounds.

March 15th.—Although I am indebted to the people of these Khails for shelter alone, having a store of my own supplies, it is distressing to me to have no means of acknowledging their hospitality, especially as a surpassing notion of English wealth and liber-

---

* Fire worshippers.

ality prevails. Ere I quitted the tent, the youngest child, a little girl, was brought in to see me. She sat awhile upon my knee, but toddled off the instant I had given her a piece of sugar. I beckoned to four others, all little girls, and greatly delighted them with the loaf sugar, which is a rarity, although evidently not unknown. I now said, "Khoosh Ullah Yar" (farewell), and started, with two Toorcumuns, for the ruins of ancient Oorgunj; it is situated on the right bank of a river channel, said to have once held the main stream of the Oxus, and still communicating with it. The extent of this city was, perhaps, one mile by half a mile, with extensive suburbs on the north. At the east angle is the citadel, a brick fort of square figure, flanked by eight circular and projecting bastions. The site of this fort is artificially elevated about ten feet, and was girdled by a ditch; but the whole is now a ruin, as is the ancient city: the walls of the latter, which were probably of unbaked brick, having subsided into mere mounds. On the north of the site (I speak at hazard), stands a brick column, erected by Chengis Khaun; it is the frustrum of an extremely taper cone, surmounted by a cylinder, and is very sufficiently ugly; it has no base, and its sole ornaments have been zones of bricks, of alternating patterns. The frustrum continues erect, notwithstanding the mouldering of its base; but the summit is shattered, and has suffered a very obvious declension from perpendicularity by the violence of the north-east wind: close at hand, is the tomb of Huzurut Sheikh Shurreef, a very holy gentleman. It is a singular edifice, having a conical roof of coloured tiles, supported upon a prism of twenty-four sides, not inelegantly moulded into columns and recesses; the base is a square building, with door of pointed arch. It was far too holy for my unsaintly feet, as my people ascertained from the Toorcumuns, so I did not attempt to enter. Farther on I found another tomb, having the remains of a conical roof, which had surmounted and enclosed a vaulted dome. This building was once lined with glazed and coloured tiles, but only the roof retains them; it is elegantly constructed, but the tiles are coarse. It is said to have been built by a lady of the family of Chenghis Khaun, to the memory of her lover. These, love and death, are restricted to no clime, to no age of the world, and to no state of society; we find their record everywhere. They are the two great powers that influence the destiny of man, the one inspiring his thirst for, the other setting seal to, his immortality. The lady's tomb stands side by side with her lover's.

I had now seen all the curiosities of this deserted site, but, being still desirous to view a Toorkish market, rode on to the present inhabited site, which must not be confounded with new Oorgunj, a flourishing city on the banks of the Oxus. This is a mere village, about one and a half miles north of the ruins. I met here a party, headed by a venerable and well-dressed man, who saluted me. He begged me to accompany him to the governor's palace, which I did. There I received much civility, and a pressing invitation to put up at the palace, which I declined. The bazaar afforded but a poor spectacle, consisting of a few huts and a throng of Toorcumuns and Kuzzauks. Some Kuzzauk girls were of the number; they rode astraddle, unveiled, and without attendants: they are European in feature and complexion, but coarse and ugly specimens. Finally I found my tent pitched near a Khail, on the road to Mungh Kishlauk.

March 16th.—At 8 o'clock A.M. I started again, and the camels at noon being considerably in the rear, we halted at a Khail on the roadside, to allow them to join. Here I was consulted as a physician upon the remedies proper for the jaundice, with which the Khet Khoda was afflicted. After prescribing such attention to diet and exercise as I thought might benefit him in a country destitute of medicine, I found my advice fairly nonplussed by that of my Meerza, who knew a certain and very pleasant cure. "Jaundice," said he, with all the gravity of a father of the faculty, "proceeds from the heat of the blood. Now the fish is a cold-blooded, flabby animal, and lives in a cold element; therefore, it is an antidote to jaundice." I was rather angry with the old fellow, because as he wore a turban, a head-dress in these countries confined to learned and holy men, and I had but a Tartar cap of Cashmere shawl, his advice will certainly carry the day, and the poor yellow Khet Khoda will eat cold-blooded fish daily, without the slightest attention to necessary precautions. I was farther annoyed by hearing my interpreter Ali explaining to the roomful of Toorcumuns, in very good Toorkish, which he supposed unintelligible to me, the end, object, and nature of my mission.

Bread and trenchers of mutton-broth, having huge wooden ladles were now placed before us. The ladles were passed from mouth to mouth, the tongue being the only napkin ever found in Toorkestaun. The bread was plunged into the broth, and kneaded about by the filthy hands of the company in a truly horrible manner. Then a dripping handful was scooped up in the hand, and crammed into the mouth, which was held over the dish, that nothing might be lost, for there are no beards here to profit by the overflow. I had thought the Afghaun dinner sufficiently revolting, and the system of Khiva is some degrees worse; but the Toorcumun surpasses either, and I had yet to see the Kuzzauk.

We remounted, and proceeded on our journey, reaching at evening a Khail, of two or three tents, in a hollow; a tent was vacated for my use, and I was soon surrounded by a crowd of rude figures, who assailed me with numberless questions in Toorkish. I was not long in discovering the burthen of the chorus to be, "Give us some silver; give us some gold." But, as the state of my funds made it extremely inconvenient for me to understand so much Toorkish, I replied in long-winded stanzas of Persian, at which they all shook their heads, and exclaimed, "Wonderful!" One man, to back his request, produced his testimonials, not, as in England, a broken leg, an armless sleeve, or an extinct eye, but a rosary of large black beads, the symbol of a fuqueer. "Are they for me?" I asked innocently, making my meaning obvious by my gesture. The fellow could not help laughing, and there was as much mirth as disappointment at my stupidity. Two sweet little girls had long been peeping in at the door; one of them a pretty brunette, was encouraged to approach, and sit upon my knee. The other, a bona fide blonde, was more shy, and regarded me with wonder and fear.

To my surprise, the men now left the tent, and the mistress of the family, a woman of forty, entered and commenced preparations for the evening meal. An iron tripod was placed astraddle of the fire, which is always burning in the centre of the tent, and a huge hemispherical cauldron of cast iron, the work of Russia, was placed upon it. Then, with a clumsy wooden ladle, the good dame scooped from another cauldron, in which stood a high mass of snow, the subsided water, and transferred it to the cauldron on the fire. She then proceeded to knead some dough.

Four young kids were tied in a corner, listening and bleating by turns, for their dams. A sudden scuffle took place at the door, and in rushed two milch goats; and in spite of all opposition, forced their way to the spot where they were usually fed. One of my little play-fellows brought a dish of food for each of the goats; and whilst they were eating, I heard another scuffle, and in came a pretty little girl of twelve years, evidently in trepidation, at the step she had taken. She seized two of the kids, and carried them out in her arms, never lifting her eyes. All this while, I sat delighted. But my feeling can be appreciated only by those, who have been, like myself, seventeen years in a land, from which the companionship of woman is banished I played with the children, and took lessons in Toorkish from the dame; I soon found, however, that avarice, the universal demon of Asia, has dominion even in the female breast. Every time I caressed or noticed the children, the good dame enjoined me to make them a present, either of money or dress. I took care to answer all her demands in the unknown tongue, and we had much laughter, at our cross purposes. An unwelcome intruder now entered, my old Meerza. He came to say that my tent was ready. I had made up my mind to pass the night here, after the Toorcumun fashion, and objected to so many of my servants intruding upon the family, who had evidently no design of vacating this tent. It was far better, I thought, that they should occupy mine. But the old wretch had set his heart upon enjoying the blazing fire, and had a thousand arguments at hand. My tent was ready. All my goods and chattels had been arranged in it. Hussun Mhatoor had made the arrangement; and, in short, had I persisted, I might have been suspected of some ungenerous and inhospitable motive, so I yielded with a good grace. I had, however, the satisfaction to see the old Meerza served according to his deserts; for, no sooner had I left the tent, than the owner bundled him out without ceremony, and he passed the night under the freezing heavens. I was vexed at his officiousness, by which I lost a rare opportunity of studying the manners of Toorcumuns. But the fact is, that curiosity of this kind is so utterly incomprehensible to an Asiatic, that great caution is necessary in its indulgence.

Early next morning, I spied my two little playfellows half venturing towards my tent, then running back, laughing to their own, where their elder sister, the little maiden of twelve years, was encouraging them to persist, with many a nod and smile. She wore a close cloak or dress of chintz, of gay and fantastic, but becoming colours. On her head was a close cap of red cloth, fringed with black lambskin. Eight plaited tresses of brown, silky hair, fell from beneath this. Her face was too full for beauty: but she had a rich colour, sparkling black eyes, and pearly teeth. The two little things now peeped shyly into my tent; I caught them, and after inflicting sundry kisses, which they endured with all bashfulness, sent them back, each with a silver coin in her tiny hand. The elder sister was delighted, she ran in and brought the infant, whom she sat astraddle of the blonde's back, and sent in this cavalier fashion, to my tent.

I now took my position outside, but still perceived the little maiden peeping at me, from her tent door. The blonde, after much coaxing, took her seat at my side, and I was content. The cap, this little puss wore, was similar to those so often described, a close shell of red cloth, trimmed with black lamb's wool, worked with black silk braid, and tricked with small silver bells. From the borders of the cap, long tassels of black silk fell down on either side, mingling with her plaited tresses of light brown hair. This head-dress is so becoming to children, that one is often disappointed on nearer approach to features, that, at a little distance, had seemed so lovely beneath it.

March 17th. – Mounted and pursued my journey. To my extreme disgust, the obstinate old guide pulled up at the distance of twelve miles, and neither arguments nor threats could persuade him to progress. We, therefore, camped at a small Khail, close to the ruined fort Shoomaukie, deserted since the Oxus found its passage northward, and forsook the Caspian. Shoomankie is upon the high bank of one of the river channels; up to this spot, the whole plain, which is the valley of the Oxus, has been richly cultivated in former days, and is now much neglected.

18th.—Resumed march down the abandoned channel for about six miles, when, on climbing the high bank, or rather hills, left by the sinking of the river valley, a wide expanse of water burst upon my eye, which I concluded was the sea of Aral; my delight was very great. The Oxus was visible upon the horizon, pouring its waters into this lake, of which the N.W. Coast was formed of high cliffs and the southern portion of the river valley. To the east only, water was visible; I was, however, mistaken in my conjecture, for this is only the lake Lowdahn, which receives an arm of the Oxus.

Striking across the high ground, we after a mile, again descended some cliffs, which wall in another valley in a singular manner. The cliff is of alternate strata of chalk and marle. The latter preponderating. The high ground, over which we had passed, was stony. The bottom of this valley was clay or marle, covered with a jungle of bushes. Towards evening we put up at a Khail of three black tents.

On this march a little boy of Heraut, who is being carried by the Toorcumuns for sale to the Kuzzauks, attracted my attention. He is a beautiful child, of about seven years, with the regularly handsome features and large full eyes of the Herauties. He is full of spirit, and, in short, as fine a child as can be imagined. My people make much of him, I am deeply interested in his fate, and determined, that so soon as we reach Mungh Kishlauk, I will offer any horses and arms that cannot be sold for his freedom. A girl of about eleven years is another of the slaves. She is a Tymunnee.

March 19th.—Crossing this basin, in a direction nearly west, we reached, at the distance of ten miles, a cliff containing two artificial caverns, that have evidently been formed as habitations. Near them are some Kuzzauk tombs, formed of a circular palisade of thorny bushes, firmly fixed in the earth and bound around by withes. On the summit of this cliff, is the tomb of a man named Ibrahim, and the place is called Ibrahim Aat'h. We soon afterwards ascended from this basin, to the height of about three hundred feet, and camped at the summit of the cliffs walling in the valley. These cliffs are of strata of chalk and marle, surmounted by a stratum of shell limestone, containing very perfect petrifactions of the cockle, muscle, and spirorbis. The substance of this stone is hard and brittle. It rings like porcelain, and separates into broad laminae. It seems, generally, the uppermost stratum, but sometimes is covered with clay. It is almost entirely composed of the three shells above named, and I have never found any others in it, although I have examined a thousand specimens.

From this height, at the distance of twenty miles, on an Azimuth of 108° I saw the ruined castle Kohna Wuzeer, occupying an elevation in the midst of the wide valley, and isolated by steep and lofty precipices. It was built by demons in the reign of Adil Khaun; but more of its history I could not learn. Enchanted castles abound in these parts. About forty miles north of Shoomaukie, is one called in Toorkish, Burrasun Gelmus,* or "the castle from which there is no return." The ruins are girdled by a ditch full of quicksands, and exhaling vapour and flame. The gate is guarded by two mighty dragons, who have never been known to sleep; many have, in olden times, attempted to explore these ruins, in search of the rich treasure deposited in their vaults—many have entered its precincts, but none have ever returned. Its mysteries are as inviolate as the secrets of the tomb. Of late years, the attempt has been abandoned: men do not account themselves (at least not in eastern lands) wiser, or more valiant, or more holy than their fathers.

Another castle exists in these parts, but its name I could not learn, filled with treasure beyond price, and guarded by enchantment. Madreheem Khaun, the late king, sent, seventeen years ago, a party of

---

* The site of this enchanted castle appears to be the island in the midst of the sea of Aral. Ali could not give me any particular clue to the position of either of these ruins.

pioneers to explore the ruins. These had the courage to venture as far as the ditch of the fortress, when a venerable man, evidently a saint, from his snowy robes and flowing white beard, appeared upon the battlements, and exclaimed in a marrow-curdling voice, which, nevertheless, was mild and gentle, "Return, my children, return. This adventure is not for you; the season for it is not at hand. It is reserved for a man, Yclepd Muhummud, who is even now an infant, hanging from the breast. He shall come, in the year of the Hijjera, 1274, and shall prosper." The pioneers shouldered their shovels, and beat a retreat forthwith, placing the wheelbarrows on either flank; it was evidently not fear that inspired so masterly a retreat.

March 20th.—We pursued our route over high land, dappled with half-melted snow. The marle soil, saturated with snow water, yielded beneath our horses feet, giving them much toil. This is our first march in the Kuzzauk country, of which the boundary is at Ibrahim Aat'h; and Ibrahim Aat'h lies in a line, irregularly drawn from the south-western angle of the sea of Aral, west by south, to the Caspian. All, north of this line, is Kuzzauk land. Nevertheless, in the district of Mungh Kishlauk, and in some other parts, Chowdhoor Toorcumuns feed their flocks and herds; and upon the borders of the sea of Aral, are found some families of Kahra Kulpauk Oozbegs. At a shallow basin of snow water, at the summit of the ascent, I saw large flocks of the antelope or sheep (it is neither) of this steppe. We then descended, and encamped on lower ground, though still considerably elevated above the valley. Hence I perceived, gleaming in the distance, about twelve miles south by west, the wide, deep channel of the Oxus, filled with snow water, and tending in a direction nearly south-west, toward the gulf of the Balkaun Here then was a fact, fully established, of the accuracy of which so many have doubted, and which

I did not, until this moment, fully believe. The extent to which the country has been excavated, for a channel to the waters of this mighty river, admits of no doubt of the nature of the cause producing such effects—and having traced the river, thus far, there is no possibility of its finding any other termination than the Caspian, because the land northward of its channel, in this part, is elevated far above the river valley, and besides I have since traversed it in a line which must have crossed the river channel, had it returned toward the sea of Aral. The reader, if he has curiosity and patience sufficient, may find the subject detailed and discussed in the Appendix.

It is my custom, on long marches, occasionally to call my followers to my side, and make them relate some anecdote to beguile the way. Those of my Nazir, Nizaum, are very curious, but for want of timely notes, great part of them is lost. He was porter in the service of one of the Sirdars of Candahar, Ruheem dil Khaun, I think. This chief was married to a fierce Populzye of high family, who had been very beautiful, but was now somewhat passé, without having lost any of her pretensions. His brother's widow, however, a very lovely creature, won his heart, and she consented to marry him. He had kept the matter a profound secret from his wife, but he was obliged, at length, in decency, to inform her. They were sitting, at the time of the explanation, upon a carpet, a brazier of live charcoal before them, it being the winter season.

"And so," said the fair Populzye, in an indifferent tone of voice, shifting a little nearer to the fire, and stretching her hands over it, "so you are really bent upon marrying this lady?"

Delighted to find his wife take it so quietly, the chief put on an air of double consequence, as he replied, "We are!"

"Then take that with her," said the Amazon, emptying the brazier of live charcoal upon his face, and then marching out of the room with great dignity.

The retaliation was very severe. Not only was his face scorched and blistered, but nearly the whole of his fine beard, that *dulce decus meum* of a Muhummedan, was singed to the roots, leaving him in the most pitiable plight imaginable. Meanwhile, the approach of the English to the Kojuk mountains was announced, and he was summoned to aid his brother in council. He shut himself up in his Zenana, and pleaded illness. The moment was one of such urgency, that his reputation was at stake, as a man and a patriot, by his seclusion; whilst, to appear without a beard in public, and have it known that a woman was the destroyer, could not be thought of for a moment. The Populzye, however, would not suffer him to escape through his precaution. She spread the story abroad, and it soon became the theme of mirth throughout Candahar. This Amazon was a woman of great muscular strength, and used to beat her husband when it suited her purpose. He dared not put her away, on account of the power of her family, and she kept him in complete subjection. I enquired about the daughters of these chiefs, whether they were beautiful or not, but Nizaun replied—

"I have eaten their salt, and will not reveal their secrets."

"But surely it is no breach of trust to say that such a lady is pretty or ugly. Perhaps you have never seen them?"

"Yes! I have often seen them; but they would not like their secrets to be discussed."

I honoured Nizaun for this delicacy; and had never thought so highly of him as at that moment.

He described the chief, Kohun Dil Khaun, as the best of the brothers, in regard to abilities for government; but said that, disputes and jealousies between the three, prevented the adoption of any system of resistance. Had infantry pursued the chiefs, on our first reaching Candahar, he says, they would have overtaken them on this side the Helmund. Every one must regret that the vigorous policy urged by our Envoy and minister, on this occasion, was not pursued. He described the farewell of the chief, to those of his followers whom he had dismissed, as most affecting. Nizaum had offered his services, but they were declined, it being the object of the chiefs, to reduce the number of their suite, for the sake of celerity.

Unfortunately, my opportunities of committing to paper, any intelligence collected on this route, were so limited, that I have lost the greater part of Nizaum's anecdotes, many of which were highly interesting. We were often not settled until night, when, having neither chair, table, nor candle, writing was out of the question. At other times, we put up on the miry earth, in a storm of wind and rain, when it was just as much as we could do to defend ourselves from the weather. Writing, under such circumstances, is irksome, and often impracticable.

CHAPTER XVII.

Chase of the wild Ass—Miry State of the Steppe—Intense Cold on the higher Land—Antelope of the Steppe—Dry Basin of a Lake—Particulars of the Murder at Khiva of the two European Travellers and their five Servants—Manners of the Kara Kulpauks and other Oozbegs—Character of the Country—Chalk Cliffs, etc.

MARCH 21st and 22nd.—After traversing about fourteen miles of plain country, sprinkled with wormwood, we halted to refresh the horses, and suffer the camels to gain upon us. Observing here a herd of about a hundred wild asses, feeding at no great distance, I mounted, and went in pursuit. Two sportsmen, on foot, with matchlocks, were directed to circumvent them. Three mounted Toorcumuns rode in another direction, for the same purpose, and I, with two servants, filled up a fourth gap in the chain of this circle, our main party supplying the third. The herd took alarm, before our arrangements were completed, but, fortunately taking the direction of one of the footmen, the report of his matchlock checked, confused, and eventually drove them at full speed through the gap, between myself and the horses at graze. I spurred after them, but the state of the country was far too favourable to light weights. My enormous horse, encumbered by his body clothing, and his own and my weight, sunk, at the least infirm portions of the soil, over the fetlocks, and often above the knee. Nizaum, far better mounted, and less encumbered, shot ahead of me, but his horse's feet lighting upon an unusually deep slough, horse and man rolled head over heels. I could only approach near enough to give them a couple of long shots from my carabine, and they soon were far ahead of me, their hoofs leaving little impression upon the quaking soil.

We were returning in disgust, when we observed a straggler which we had cut off, endeavouring to rejoin the herd. So we spurred after him, and Summud Khaun, mounted upon a lighter horse, and having the start of me, soon gained upon him, to my great surprise. I was still more astonished to observe, that the wild ass, instead of increasing, slacked his pace, and eventually stood still, whilst Summud Khaun rode up to him with a pistol. The pistol burnt priming, and the ass attacked the horse with teeth and heels, not seeming to understand that the rider was in reality his enemy. Summud Khaun drew his sabre, and cut the animal over the crest, and one of the Toorcumuns coming up with a spear, despatched him.

I was disappointed in this game, which I had supposed infinitely more fleet and staunch. The fact is, that the wild ass which feeds in herds in the steppe, is very different from that which lives an almost solitary life, at the skirt of the mountains, in Persia, Heraut, and Syria. The difference is probably confined to their respective habits. The latter is chased with relays of dogs and horses; the former soon flags, becomes obstinate, and finally halts, to kick and bite the horse of his pursuer. Summud Khaun, who has chased many of these in the plains of Candahar, assures me, that a well-mounted horseman can always overtake them. The quarry just killed was a veritable donkey. The only observable difference, that the ears are not much larger than those of an ordinary horse. The back sinews are farther separated from the bone, and the hooves of wider spread. The black cross, also, over the shoulders was wanting, or I am mistaken. In size it did not exceed the ass of England. At the close of this march, we found ourselves on the skirt of a valley, formed probably by the

Oxus in very remote days. A coarse-featured old man rode out from the Kuzzauk Khail, to meet us, upon a double-humped camel, and having the usual bonnet of wolf's fur (hair inwards), which I and my people have been glad to adopt in this severe climate. His figure would have afforded an excellent subject for the pencil, and his double-humped camel was as strange an animal as himself. We could only learn from him, that some sugar would be very acceptable, and that we were welcome to his Khail. His language defied the ingenuity of my interpreter.

March 23rd.—A large bank of clouds had been visible all the preceding day, on the north-east, over the sea of Aral. In spite of a strong easterly wind, they appeared immoveable; but, being warned by previous experience, I anticipated rain and snow, nor was I deceived. The rain commenced during the night, and continued until the next evening, to our great discomfort. The country, already saturated with snow water, has become one wide marsh, and our perplexity is increased by the deceitfulness of appearances, the soil which the eye judges firmest generally proving the most treacherous. In other countries of such uneven surface, water runs off to the valleys, but this soil imbibes every drop; the earth probably having acquired porosity by the freezing of the water it contained, which would enlarge the pores; the subsequent thaw of this ice leaving them open. With infinite toil we accomplished ten miles, the rain falling all the while, and our horses sinking deep at every step. We then sat down upon some wet herbs, which we gathered, and disposed to prevent our sinking in the mud, and continued thus three hours in the rain, until the arrival of the camels. These luckless animals, heavily laden, sank at every step in the most hopeless manner. I pitched my tent over the mud, and took up my abode for the night, but not until I had seen my servants as well sheltered as circumstances would allow. The bags of grain, piled in walls, form some protection from the wind, and a large thick nummud or felt, stretched above, forms something of a roof; nevertheless, these, and their abundant supply of woollen and furs, would not have saved them from wet, had not the rain ceased early in the night.

March 24th.—We resumed our march through a country in the state I have just described, and proceeded fifteen miles with the utmost labour. No tent has been visible during the last two days. The sky was overcast, but the rain spared us. The surface, here, is furrowed by deep ravines, whose course is south by a point west. The soil was everywhere trampled by the hoofs of wild asses, and manured with their dung. We put up for the night beyond a trifling eminence, called Ulla Suckul, or the "piebald beard," in consequence of the snow melting from its ridges, and lying in the ravines.

March 25th.—The country to-day was somewhat firmer. The route, we have hitherto traveled, is practicable only in winter, when snow water is procurable. The summer route is farther north-east, but has no firewood. At the distance of fifteen miles we fell into this track, which is indeed bare. At twenty-five miles distance halted. No habitation in sight all day.

March 26th.—We entered, this day, upon a region much colder, from its elevation, than any we have passed, although we have made little north latitude, and the season has progressed sixteen days, since leaving Khiva. The snow was here lying in great abundance, and the spots from which it had melted were so miry, as greatly to distress the cattle. My best riding horse is spavined from his exertions. He was a present from Shauh Kaumraun, king of Heraut, to Major Todd, the British Envoy; a beautiful figure, and about sixteen hands high, but having no legs equal to his great weight. We struck south-west, to avoid a valley inundated with snow water, and encamped again in the wilderness. No human dwelling. The cold is now excessive. The cattle, though abundantly supplied with warm clothing, suffer from exposure to the wind all night, for it was not possible to secure their legs effectually, or to prevent breaches below, through which the wind penetrates to the belly and haunches. The intense chill of the north wind, in these parts, cannot be conjectured by any, who has not wintered on an extensive continent. The breath clings in icicles to the pillow and bed-clothes, within the tent. Towels, hung up to dry in a close room with a fire, or in the sun, are instantly stiffened into ice, and water freezes hard, within three feet of a charcoal fire. By dint of incessant manipulation, I contrived to preserve my nose in a liquid form (so to speak). All the rest of my head and face was snugly packed in fox's fur, but in spite of every precaution, my nose proved a projectile; every now and then, as I exerted the muscles of the nostril, I felt the process of congelation commencing, and although my fingers were of a violet colour, and stiff as sealing wax, yet my hand formed an arch, under which the heat of the breath collected and thawed the proboscis. My feet were however perfectly secure. Over cotton socks, I had drawn stockings of shawl-goat's wool, over these a pair of wolf's-fur stockings, (hair inwards), over these the huge riding boots of Persia, and over those a stocking of thick felt. The north wind was completely puzzled: but I was very helpless when dismounted, as all heavy dragoons are, the more especially, as these elephantine shanks were propped upon heels three inches high, and tapering downward to an acute point, so that a gardener might have followed me with young cabbages, and have dropped a plant into each heel print, as I moved.

March 27th.—Ascended some high land dappled with snow, and camped near a well called Ooroosse Kooia, because a Russian captive, halting here on his way to Khiva, assured his captors, that they would find water, by digging in this spot.

March 28th.—Ascended some high land covered with snow. Wind scarcely endurable. Thence descended into a valley, and camped at the distance of twenty miles. We every day see herds of wild asses[*] and flocks of antelopes (if so I may term them). One of the latter, a male was brought me to-day. the glare of the snow had blinded it. It is truly a singular animal. The body, legs, and tail, resemble those of the common, small antelope. The fur, however, is almost white, and the horns, shaped liked those of the antelope of Khorussaun, are white and pellucid. The ear resembles that of the camel. It is small, round, and hidden in the long hair of the neck. The head in profile is like the sheep's, the nose excessively arched, and formed of flesh and cartilage, not bone. It terminates like a double-barrelled gun, in two circular holes destitute of the fungus, common to that organ in the brute creation, and appears as if lopped of its natural termination by some sharp instrument. The nostrils are invisible in profile. These orifices however, have vertical muscles, by which the upper arch is brought down flat upon the lower, as in the camel's nose. The eye is small as the sheep's, but black like the antelopes. The head is singularly, ludicrously ugly. It has the action and habits of the antelope, but is much smaller than that of India. It seems to form a link between the sheep and antelope, and is essentially different from the wild sheep and goat of the mountains. The Toorcumuns call it Kaigh: they hunt it with their large coarse greyhounds.

March 29th and 30th.—The country continued as before, a high table land, deeply furrowed by parallel ravines, whose course is nearly south by a point or two west. The heights generally betraying the shell

---

[*] I counted 800 wild asses in a single herd.

limestone, upon which the soil rests; the whole sprinkled with wormwood, camel thorn, and a brown herb without scent, which is not eaten by cattle. When I call the whole of this country a steppe, it will be understood, that I have not seen the leaf of a tree, nor a permanent habitation, since quitting the valley of the Oxus; many of the Kuzzauks have never seen either. At the close of this stage, we descended nearly 1200 feet, into the basin of a quondam lake, and there encamped. The descent is by a ravine, scarped on either side by cliffs of crystallized carbonate of lime, of which large and beautiful masses had rolled to the foot of the precipice. The descent is very gradual. The bottom of this ravine is encrusted with saline exudations; and a crystalline spring, which tempts the eye, is strongly impregnated with salt.

In descending from the table land, I called Ali Muhummud to my side, and questioned him upon a variety of particulars.

"I was at Khiva," he said, "when the two English travellers were murdered."

"Why do you suppose they were English?"

"I know they were. They said so. It was not until they were tortured, that they confessed themselves Russians. One was a light-haired youth, the other was older and darker. They had five Persian servants, and had arrived from Meshed. Just then the Khiva ambassador had been insulted in Russia, his brother being imprisoned there. The king's Dewaun Beegie, an avaricious and ill-natured man, told the Khaun that they were Russians. He demanded their passports. They had none. He sent them to the house of the Dewaun Beegie, and soon after the Ghoosh Beegie was sent to them by night with a party of torturers. Red hot skewers were run through their flesh, and red hot iron trailed over their skin. The result is not known, but the Ghoosh Beegie, who had an eye to part of their plunder, said, they had confessed themselves Russian spies, and he gave this testimony to the Khaun Huzurut. The Khaun was still furious, at the repeated insults his ambassadors had received, and ordered their execution. They had on the first occasion been taken asleep, so could make no defence, and now they were unarmed. Their throats were cut in the dead of night, and their bodies and those of their five servants were carried out at night, and buried in the sand of the desert. People say they made no confession; but the Ghoosh Beegie and Dewaun Beegie had an interest in asserting the contrary. Their arms were lodged in the royal treasury. Their books were given to the Mehtur. No one dares to mention the circumstance at Khiva, especially since your arrival, for your case is exactly like theirs."

"And where was the late minister, Aga Yoosuph, who is so highly spoken of? Did he give no better counsel?"

"He, unfortunately, was on an expedition to the south, and did not hear of the matter until his return. It was then too late. He remonstrated strongly with the Khaun Huzurut upon the the cruelty of the procedure; and there is no doubt, that had he arrived in time, it would not have happened."

Such is the substance of Ali's answer to my queries. He had no proof to offer that these men were English; I had many circumstantial arguments against the supposition. Major Todd, the Envoy at Heraut, had resided many years, in an official capacity, at Tehraun, and had still correspondence with our functionaries in Persia. He had heard the circumstances of the case, and it was his firm belief, that the murdered men were *not* English, and that, in all probability, whatever their nation, they were spies of Russia. All the more intelligent natives to whom I had access were of the same opinion. The common people believed they *were* English, but had not even circumstantial evidence to support the supposition;

and as they had believed, until my arrival, that the Russians were the only European nation, so they now divided Europe between England and Russia; and in saying that such and such an European was English, meant no more than to assert that he was not Russian. Had these travellers been English, some of our authorities must, in time, have learnt the fact; but I could hear nothing of them from the Home Government; and my brother, who was in Persia when they were murdered, believes they were neither English nor Russian. The Russians explicitly deny them, and are very anxious that we should believe the travellers to have been English.

Ali had visited Ghoonghuraut, a town of the Kara Kulpauk Oozbegs, near the southern coast of the sea of Aral. He assures me, that the singular custom attributed to the inhabitants, is really observed by them. This I shall notice in the Appendix, lest it be stumbled upon at some unlucky moment. The picture he draws of the manners of the Kara Kulpauks, is sufficiently disagreeable. But we must be careful, in reprobating them, to avoid the injustice of condemning the people themselves; who must, of necessity, form their standard of morals from immemorial custom, and the example of their fathers.

The manners of the Oozbegs of Khiva are equally, if not more revolting. The wife, utterly neglected by her lord, is naturally careless of his and her own honour. Nay, it is asserted, that not a few wives divide with their husbands the wages of their humiliation. This is the more glaring, that the outward observances, in the intercourse of the sexes, are so extremely rigid in Central Asia; and the fallen angels of our European cities are here utterly unknown. Much of Ali's information will be found in the Appendix, mixed with that acquired from other sources; I shall, therefore, not here repeat more of the conversation of this day, from which I derived many interesting particulars. Ali is a sensible fellow, and has a good memory. But having been sixteen years a slave at Khiva, and being an extremely good-natured fellow, my Meerza and Summud Khaun have contrived to subject him to themselves, and from being my interpreter, he has fairly become their slave. I have several times interfered to prevent this, but to little purpose. Ali's easy nature renders the bondage light; and as soon as my back is turned, the others exert their authority, and Ali submits without a struggle. I mention this, because in the sequel it proved of the utmost consequence, confounding all my precautions against the treachery with which I was surrounded. Ali's good nature proceeded from no want of spirit. One of the Toorcumun camel drivers, after long provoking him, was laid flat on his back by a box on the ear from the quondam slave, who grinned his delight to see one of his old oppressors prostrate at his feet. Ali is a good-looking fellow, and has a handsome beard, which were probably the keys to his liberty, being irresistible arguments with the fair Oozbegs, who enrich their favourites at their lord's expense, being always keepers of the purse. He had accordingly purchased his discharge in sixteen years.

March 31st.—Everything here has the appearance of proximity to the sea. The basin of this large lake, scarped with precipices, and girt with land of considerable elevation, having a bottom still destitute of vegetation, dark and level, as if but a few years abandoned by its waters. The chalk cliffs visible in the distance, the whole form and character of the surface, lead one to anticipate a sight of the Caspian from every fresh height we ascend. Nevertheless, Hussun assures me, we have still some five or six marches before us; and as he always under-estimates the distance, it is reasonable to reckon it some eight or ten marches.

We crossed the bed of this quondam lake, which, notwithstanding the appearances I have mentioned, has not been occupied by water within memory of any of the Toorcumuns present, or of the traditions handed down to them. The portion visible at a coup d'œil is an area of about twelve by seven miles, but I suspect it winds on the south, until it reaches the Caspian. After passing this lake, we ascended chalk cliffs, which wall in the valleys here in a singular manner, speaking of a much higher level in the waters of the Caspian than they at present hold.

CHAPTER XVIII.

Rapacity of the Guide—Physiognomy of the Kuzzauks—Nizaum's extreme Amusement at the Sight of beardless Men—The Dragon of Heraut—The petrified Dragon of Candahar—Existence of a Species of Boa amongst the Mountains of Afghaunistaun—Anecdote of Shauh Kaumraun—Singular Fate of a Tent-mallet—Chalk Cliffs—Kuzzauks.

APRIL 1st.—We are now fairly in Kuzzauk land. The country is everywhere spotted with their black tents, their flocks and herds. Yesterday, whilst halting near a Khail to refresh the horses, half a dozen of the women came to me to beg. They were all so hideous, that my heart was not melted, so I gave the little children each a lump of sugar, and dismissed them. To-day, Hussun called at several Khails to plunder. At one of these a woman, with face like the sun in Cancer, and person half naked, was leading a young woman swathed in an old cloak. Never, surely, was there such a failure in the tailor's department. The effect was infinitely ludicrous, for the young camel did not half approve of the vestment, nor of the guidance of the fair Kuzzauk; whose fairest, by the way, was a hue more generally esteemed in beet root than in woman. The fair thing started when she saw us, and like the Irishman troubled with a short blanket, endeavoured, by a rapid counter-march of garment, to supply deficiencies. Indian women, on such occasions, are far more economical. They hide only the face; all the rest is a mere question in natural philosophy. The guide asked, if the master of the tent was at home, and received the invariable answer, "Yokh" (he is *not*). The Yuze Baushee entered the tent, and found him there. I pleaded hard for these poor creatures, but in vain. Avarice has no ears. The Yuze Baushee, as he remounted, was assisted by the fair Kuzzauk, who, whilst she held down the stirrup on the off-side, gave him her hand over the saddle, to the infinite horror and amazement of Summud Khaun, whose face lengthened pitiably, as he exclaimed three times, "La hola!" (avaunt). The Kuzzauk women have no bashfulness. It does not follow that they want modesty, as is generally believed.

We proceeded to another Khail. A girl of about thirteen years, dressed in a cloak, and having the head bound carelessly with a red scarf, was adjusting the tent. She had in her ears a pair of silver eardrops, set here and there with what seemed precious stones, and not less than half a foot in length. They were flat, and shaped like the head of a spear. Here the ceremony of plundering was renewed, but I would not sanction by my presence, that which my remonstrances failed to prevent. The Kuzzauks are the ugliest race I have yet seen. Their complexion is a dirty white, burnt here and there, as on the nose and cheek bones, to the colour of raw beef. The cheek bones are high. The face either circular or triangular. The lips are thin, eyes small, ill-formed, ill-coloured, and half opened. The nose is a hideous aquiline— with sprawling nostrils. The men have generally no symptoms of beard, which greatly amused Nizaum, who has six ill-conditioned bristles upon his own chin. He couldn't contain his mirth. This smoothness of lip and chin, and the similarity in the attire of the sexes, render it very difficult for a stranger to distinguish them. The head-dress is a bonnet of inverted lamb's or wolf's fur. The cloak is generally of skin. The feet are cased in hessians of brown leather. The average stature of those we have hitherto seen is about five feet three inches, but I am assured these are unfavourable specimens.

As we rode down the valley, I called Summud Khaun to my side, to enquire about a tradition I had heard at Heraut concerning the origin of the bridge there. He had not heard it, so I was obliged to relate it to him, in the hope that he might either add something to it, or give me another marvel in exchange.

In days that have left us but a few dim records of their existence, the city of Heraut was desolated by a monstrous dragon, which lived in a cavern at the foot of the mountains northward of the city, where his trail has left, to this day, a scattering of rubies. This monster, who had a predilection for human flesh, and who found, by trial, that young maidens were the choicest morsels, confined himself to this delicate dish. Now, as the Dragon was about three hundred feet in length, with great flapping wings in proportion, it may be supposed, that this nightly visit to the city, in search of his prey, greatly incommoded housekeepers, and other valuable and inoffensive servants of the state, inasmuch, as with his unconscionable tail and wings aforesaid, he sometimes squashed a dozen honest wives and husbands, in his search for the maiden of his choice, besides damage incalculable to furniture. The King, therefore, by means of his ambassador, Sheikh Robár-ool Islaum, compounded with the dragon for a scarcity of his presence, upon condition that he, the king, should send nightly to the monster's cavern, a young and tender virgin.

Now there lived at Heraut a brother and sister, whose hearts were knit together in the most devoted affection. The name of the youth is of no consequence to our tale, it was absorbed with his being, in the precious pearl of his affections, Murwarrie, the spirit of his spirit. They had early lost their parents, and their love it would be difficult to describe. The lines, which he addressed to his soul's companion, will but shadow an affection, so pure, so fervid, so absorbing. They were each the echo of the other's thoughts. When one spoke, the other sat as in a dream. The words had been before heard in the depth of the spirit, in the stillness of thought: the idea, fresh and new to others, was fresh to her, but not new: it had shaped itself into being before, but it waited to appear upon the lips she loved best. A cord no less real that it was invisible, knit those hearts together in a single sympathy. Often, the one paused and restrained his words, because he saw the thought that burthened his tongue in those mirrors of the soul—his sister's eyes. Mirrors of the soul I have called them. They were mirrors of his own soul, and when he would search out its hidden mysteries, he gazed into his sister's eyes. The lines he addressed to her, were feeble records of his love, and yet, the most tender language of which we are capable naturally moulds into verse. I cannot repeat them all, but here is a fragment:—

> We grew not, my Sister, as others have grown,
>   Twin buds, whom stern Nature's decree
> Hath combined, on one stem in appearance alone,
>   Whilst their hearts remain single and free.
>
> No! the blest bond of Nature was never so dear,
>   Nor the cord of accordance so sweet,
> As was proved, in contracting and closing the sphere,
>   Where our souls were to mingle and meet.
>
> For what was the life of my childish delight?
>   Oh! was it not centred in thee?
> And knew'st thou a bliss so engaging, so bright,
>   As *was* bliss till partaken with me?
>
> No! never was echo more true to the note,
>   Stealing lightly its slumber away,
> Nor the star in the lake to the planet remote,
>   Hanging o'er it in fondest delay;
>
> Than the soul of my sister was true to the love
>   Which reposed, like an infant at rest
> (When secure in the clasp that affection has wove),
>   On thine artless, thine innocent breast.

And again, when accidentally absent for a few days from the house, which was his country, since it encircled all that earth held for him of precious:—

> O doubly an exile, since sever'd from thee!
>   The wilderness blossoms no more;
> 'T is the fitting abode of the tameless and free,
>   But *my* heart loved the fetters it wore.
>
> The gentle gazelle, with her large, mournful eye,
>   Gleaming sad in the midst of delight,
> May love o'er its sands with the whirlwind to vie,
>   For her partner still lingers in sight.
>
> But had she a sister's affection e'er known,
>   The endearment of answering minds,
> How sad would she traverse that bleak waste alone,
>   'Mid the strife of the desolate winds.
>
> For 't is hard for two hearts that have grown up in love
>   Till their roots are inwoven and twined,
> To survive the stern wrench that would seek to remove,
>   Or the shock that would seek to unwind.
>
> Together they flourish'd, together they fed
>   At the same desert fountain, and all
> Their leaves to the same sunny radiance they spread:—
>   Together, together they fall.

Heaven is rich in blessing, to our thankless race, but has no blessing more pure, more precious, more lovely, than a sister's affection; neither is there aught, in the wide circle of the universe, which the Most Holy contemplates with greater complacency.

Now it happened, in the natural course of events, that the lot fell upon this maiden, to be devoured by the dragon. It was in vain that the brother, hearing of the sentence, implored the king to substitute him, in disguise, for his sister. The monarch, though touched by this instance of affection, dared not comply with a suggestion tending, if discovered, to incense the monster against his people; neither could the sister have survived her brother's loss. But, as it was equally impossible for him to live without *her*, he determined to accompany her to the dragon's den. It was then, when his resolution not to survive her had been taken, that his courage rose, and called upon his invention to save the being that was existence to him. He purchased the fattest sheep in the city, a Doombha, a sheep of mighty tail, a sheep goodly throughout, but increasing in goodness toward its latter end.

Ah ye Schoolmasters! Why! why was there no Doombha variety of school boy!

The Doombha, we have said, was purchased, and the youth proceeded to flay, to disembowel it, and to fill the cavity with quicklime. The fatal morning dawned, and found them at the mouth of the dragon's den.

Now, it was a peculiarity of this dragon's disposition, or anatomy, that he could not, or would not, commence with the head of his victim; certainly man is a wedge-formed animal, sharpest at the feet, and thickest toward the head. To have taken the head first, had been like driving a nail head-foremost; to which, as we know, there are some sensible objections. The brother and sister, aware of this, endeavoured each to protrude the feet beyond those of other, and the strife at length ended, by their lying, heads outward and feet together. They had not long lain thus, and the sun had already thrown his first gleam upon the snowy summits of the southern mountains, when a hiss resounded from the recesses of the cavern, and a volume of blue and yellow smoke, villainously rank of sulphur, issued from the den. Then was heard the rattling of scales, and that screeching, fiddle-related sound, which a blunt knife makes upon a tough windpipe. Two jets of fire spouted from the nostrils of the monster, shedding a lurid gleam upon the cold morning air. He approached, gliding in mighty and glittering folds of green and gold. The scales of his belly were transparent. The fire, rolling with the current of his blood, suffused them with a ruby hue. He lifted his head into the clouds, and, for a moment, the sun's light paled upon the distant mountains, in the glare of those terrific eyes.

But now he stooped his head slowly to the earth, and snuffed at his shuddering prey—for even love could not wholly quell the trembling of the flesh—he snuffed at the end nearest to him, and lifted his nose on high, to weigh and discriminate the exact nature of the aroma. "Ah!" he said with a sniff, inclining his head a little on one side, "brain—sniff—hair oil, decidedly—sniff—and—and sniff,—tortoise-shell combs."

He tried the other end:—the result was no more satisfactory.

The dragon was now thoroughly bewildered. His *disgust* may be conjectured by the gastronome, whose perverse cook hath reversed the order of dinner, commencing with apples, and winding up with soup. In fact, it was a pet whim of the dragon to end always with the head; for, when the body was down his throat, and his front teeth grinding on the skull, a dexterous movement of the jaw and tongue enabled him to get rid of the scalp, with its hair and all the accompaniments, of hair-oil, pomatum, and tortoise-shell combs, not to mention those long, sharp, double-pointed pins, the steel-traps of ladies' heads.

As he snuffed from end to end, in extreme perplexity, a something of that rosy, amberous, cinnamony hue, which mortals are familiar with on the surface of roast mutton, attracted his eye, and, at the same instant, a zephyr fluttering from the cage of Aurora, strewed upon his nostril an aroma so exquisite, that instantly he was bending over the carcass of the sheep.

He bowed his head caressingly toward it. He applied his nostril. He lifted his nose above six of the seven heavens, whilst with curling snout he drew in, to the very medulla of the brain, this new and delectable savour. He dipped his tongue, for a taste, into the marrow of the tail. He determined, henceforward to eschew raw maidens, and chew only roasted mutton. It was his first lesson in virtue. It proved his last. He laid himself, at full length, upon the earth, and sucked down, as a school-boy his last lolly-pop, the savory morsel.

The brother and sister, meanwhile, lay still as death, awaiting the result. Hour after hour passed, and the monster lay supine before them, groaning from excess of comfort, and lolling out his forked tongue. But, when the juices penetrated the mutton case, the irritation produced by the quicklime, occasioned an insufferable thirst, and the monster trailed his slow length toward the Hurrie Rood, where at present it is crossed by the Pool-i-Malan, or bridge of Malan. There, he plunged his head amid the waves, and drew the powerful current, from its immemorial channel, into the caverns of his own bowels. The tide, rushing through his parched jaws and gullet, and meeting the quicklime, burst forth into vapour, and then into flames. In vain the huge serpent wallowed in the cold and glittering waters of the river, they were but as fresh fuel to the consuming fire within. The men of the city, terrified with his groans, retired each to his inmost chamber, and secured the doors. The king issued a proclamation permitting his loyal subjects to funk. Even his Lord of the Kulleaun was not beheaded, although the tobacco burnt blue that night in the royal Kulleaun—an instance of mercy still quoted in honour of the better days of ages gone. But, at midnight, the groans and bellowing had ceased, and, when morning dawned, the lifeless carcase of the dragon was found extended across the river, and arresting the waves.

The brother and sister had risen from the earth, and embraced one another in a transport of emotion, which vented itself in thanksgiving and tears. These having subsided, they explored together the den of death. It wound for miles beneath the mountain, but the sulphurous trail of the serpent was a clue to the inmost recess. There they found his bed, a mighty heap of emeralds, rubies, and diamonds. They loaded themselves with treasure, and returned to report proceedings to the king. Being a singularly benevolent monarch, he graciously issued an edict, bequeathing to them and their heirs for ever all the husks and chippings of the jewels in the process of cutting, an edict which made them the richest subjects in the land. Their subsequent fate is not known, but the lady, in commemoration of this great deliverance, employed part of her wealth in building that wonder of the world (I speak as an Herautie) across the Hurrie Rood, in the very spot where the carcass of the monster was found.

I need not particularize how much of this tale I related to Summud Khaun, how much have since added. The tradition is a bona fide tradition of Heraut, and the embellishments, if such they be, will be easily detected.

Summud Khaun could tell me nothing additional to this tradition, which he had never heard, having been only fifteen or sixteen years at Heraut; but he related a similar tale, more generally known, and religiously believed, of a dragon which had almost depopulated Candahar.

"In the days," he said, "of his Highness Ali, whom his Highness Muhummud called the 'Sword of the Faith,' there dwelt, one short march from the city of Candahar, a terrible dragon, the very fac-simile of that you have just described; the same his size, his fiery breath, his propensity to human flesh, his unaccountable preference for young maidens. What is yet more remarkable, is the fact that the king of Candahar, who was an idolater, like all his people, made precisely the agreement you have narrated with the dragon, and every morning a young maiden was sent upon a camel to be devoured. But the Candahar dragon must have been very much larger than him of Heraut, for so soon as the camel and his burthen came within a certain distance, the dragon drew in his breath violently, thereby occasioning a whirlwind, which hurried both camel and rider down, through his jaws and gullet, into his meat-safe."

"Prodigious!" I ejaculated with due gravity, for, as these marvels form, it may be said, part of the religion of Afghauns, I would not, for worlds, insult their feelings by a symptom of incredulity.

"Now, when the lot fell upon the most beautiful of the virgins of Candahar, the whole city was plunged in the deepest affliction. She was placed upon a camel, and sent toward the dragon's abode, amongst the hills which you left to your right on the road to Girishk. By the mercy of God, his Highness Ali was riding toward Candahar, and met the maiden on the road. He was struck by her extreme beauty, and much more by her evident distress. He reined up his fiery steed, enquired the cause of her tears, and offered his services for her deliverance. She told her tale, hopeless of relief, for she knew not it was the Sword of the Faith that accosted her. But Ali bade her be of good cheer, and to believe that Heaven had sent her deliverance. He carried her to a shepherd's tent in the neighbourhood where he deposited her; and, himself mounting her camel, rode toward the monster's abode, on the summit of a ridge of heights. No sooner did the dragon behold the approach of the camel, laden, as he supposed, with his daily meal, than, sucking in his breath, he opened his huge jaws like the gates of hell, and the camel was hurried, like a shot, forward, as it seemed, to destruction. But, at the instant preceding contact, the hero rose high in his stirrups, and, giving full swing to his resistless sword, smote the dragon over the crest with such strength that he sank his head, writhing, to the earth, his neck half severed by the stroke.

"The rapture of the maiden may be imagined; the joy and jubilee of the inhabitants of Candahar cannot be described, but they soon found their triumph to be premature. The decay of a carcass so enormous produced a fearful pestilence, and the dragon in his death proved more mighty than in his life.

"In this extremity, the king sent a deputation to the ransomed virgin, entreating her to seek out Ali, and make known to him the state to which Candahar was reduced."

The particulars of the meeting were here related, but I have forgotten them; suffice it, that his Highness Ali consented to rescue them from this pestilence, upon condition that the king should issue an edict to all his subjects to believe in the true and holy God; and, as this condition was to cost the monarch only one sheet of foolscap, and the heads of about ten thousand of his subjects, who either could not, or at any rate would not, believe, his Majesty, of course, instantly complied.

His point gained, the saintly Ali caused proclamation to be made that no living thing should approach within a mile of the carcass of the dragon, an order obeyed by all, but an old woman and a goat, the two most wilful of animals; the latter because she liked to stay, the former because others wished her to be gone. Ali then bent his knee, and lifted up his eyes and hands to heaven, imploring Him who created all things to remove this scourge of his creatures. Instantly there fell from heaven, by the mercy of the Almighty, a petrifying influence, acting upon all substances within a limited circle. The trees, the shrubs, the fowls of the air, the insects, the mighty festering carcass, and the unclean birds and beasts that had approached to devour it, all were suddenly converted into stone. The old gentlewoman, who, with arms akimbo, was just beginning to laugh at Ali's prostrations, comparing him to a woodpecker tapping a hollow tree, and the old goat, who was just devouring a plant of assafœtida, because the cow had warned her that it would poison her milk, were alike changed into black rocks, and remain to this day as testimonies of the piety of Ali, the unsavoriness of dead dragons, and the perverseness of old women and goats.

"Have you ever seen them?" I enquired innocently.

"Seen them! of course I have; not only have I seen the old woman and goat petrifications, and the skeleton of the dragon, but have actually seen the gash made in the crest of the dragon by the mighty Ali. Did *you* never see them, Sir?"

"I can't say that I have actually seen them, but I have seen five or six people who have; I have, however, seen something almost as wonderful, a deep notch of some three hundred feet, in a ridge of mountains (on your left, after leaving Girishk for Furrah,) chipped by the sword of Ali, in a fit of idleness, as he sat upon another mountain, about five miles off; did you never see this?"

"No, Sir, but I have seen many people who have."

"The same thing, eyes are eyes, whosesoever head they may be lodged in. But what is the skeleton of the dragon like?"

"It has been so worn by the weather, that at present, it is no better than a chain of stones, each about three feet in height, stretched over the mountain ridge. They are now of a black colour, but no doubt were at first white, the colour of bones. The gash made by Ali's sword is very remarkable."

"And the old woman and goat?"

"They look just like rocks."

This tradition I had previously heard from several natives of Candahar, but was glad to allow Summud Khaun to tell it his own way, for the sake of comparing narration with others. There are, probably, few considerable cities of Central Asia, that have not their tales of dragons and young virgins. That a species of Boa-constrictor is found in the mountains, I can scarcely doubt, owing to numberless accounts, current, of their appearance. They are, I presume, similar to those found in the Himalaya range, seldom exceeding twelve or fourteen feet, but of disproportionate thickness, and great muscular power.

His Majesty Shauh Kaumrann Heraut, of Heraut, told me that he was one day resting his gun upon a rock in the mountains, to fire at an antelope, when a large serpent rose up beneath his gun. He coolly fired and killed the antelope, and then destroyed the snake. This account of the royal courage was confirmed by eye-witnesses.

At the termination of the valley we had been crossing, we ascended some cliffs, and encamped at the summit. Snow lay in great abundance under the brow of these cliffs, affording us a supply of excellent water.

Observing Summud Khaun driving tent-pins, with the back of his battle-axe, I inquired after the tent mallet.

"O!" replied Summud Khaun, "Nobody knows what has become of it."

Presently his horse, which he held by the bridle, stepped up to a small heap of firewood, collected for our use, and ate five or six sticks, of very decent dimensions, with evident relish.

"What can be hoped of a country," exclaimed Summud Khaun, "in which the horses steal our firewood and call it hay."

"O!" replied the old Meerza, rubbing his hands slowly over the fire, "that accounts for the loss of the tent mallet."

The entire want of grass, in a country famous for nothing but its horses, is a phenomenon. Our cattle, since leaving Khiva, have had nothing in the shape of fodder, excepting a little sapless brushwood.

April 2nd.—We continued our march over a country little altered in aspect, and encamped at night, in a high, bleak plain, where we were supplied from a puddle of snow water, clear and refreshing.

April 3rd.—At the distance of five miles, found ourselves at the brink of some chalk cliffs, and a difference of level of about seven hundred feet. Followed the brink about ten miles, and then struck over a table land on an azimuth of 385°, and encamped in a shallow valley. Five Kuzzauks, the most hideous I have seen of this ugly race, came and chatted with us. Hussun had plundered them of several articles of furniture, as tribute, alleging that he was in charge of two hundred horse, and half-a-dozen large cannon, besides an English ambassador.

April 4th.—After progressing twelve miles, we again reached the brink of the chalk cliffs, and descended into the deserted bed of some large river, that had once flowed into the Caspian, perhaps the Jaxartes. The bottom is hard sand, and extremely barren. Here we found a small Kawreeze (or chain of wells) called Sogun, but no fodder. At sunset we encamped near some Kuzzauk tents.

Here I, for the first time, missed our little companion, the Afghaun boy, belonging to the Tooreumun slave dealer. I inquired for him, and Summud Khaun replied with tears in his eyes, that the poor little fellow had been sold, the day before, to Kuzzauks of that neighbourhood, for a certain number of sheep. I was angry with my people, for not giving me timely intelligence. Some arrangement might have been effected for his freedom. I had set my heart upon it, and felt keenly the disappointment. The fate of this child hung heavy upon me for the rest of the journey. It had never occurred to me, that a purchaser might be found for him, ere we reached Mungh Kishlauk. His light-hearted prattle, his occasional moments of depression and of tears, when he remembered better days, all haunted me with sadness, which nothing could dispel.

April 5th.—During the process of loading the camels, I wandered towards the nearest Kuzzauk tents, which I found preparing for a removal; the tents and baggage being packed upon about sixteen camels, led by the women, in their high-peaked bonnets of wolf's fur, and coarse cloaks, girt at the waist with rope or leather thongs. The children were securely packed above the baggage, in a situation seemingly, on first view, sufficiently perilous. I saw a child of four years, wrestling with a young camel of four days, which had no notion of obeying such an urchin.

It was an absurd sight; the camel, although so young, towering far above the little bully, and twisting and writhing its long neck above his head to avoid the blows. Mind, however, at length mastered Matter. The women, at a short distance, resemble peonies. Their faces are furiously red. Their features extremely coarse. They have the figures of bears, and the dress of toad-stools, torn by the gale.

CHAPTER XIX.

Story of Hautim, the Arab—Face of the Country—Melancholy Prospects—Anecdote of the Ex-Ummeer Doost Muhummud Khaun—Some Account of the Descendants of Cyrus the Great—Herds of Galloways—Kuzzauks—The Snake—Ali's Dream—Origin of Tobacco—Lawfulness of Pigtail—Goat's Milk—Liberty of the Fair Sex *sometimes* abused.

WHEN we had mounted and ridden to some distance, I called upon the Meerza for a tale. The old fellow has a considerable store of anecdote which he relates with some humour.

"Did you ever hear the story of Hautim?" he inquired.

"Never! let me have it."

"Hautim was an Arab chief, in the days of Nowshirwaun. He possessed a horse, marvellous for its beauty and speed, the wonder and pride of Arabia. The king, who had heard of this horse, sent a nobleman of his Court to purchase it. This emissary arrived at Hautim's tent, when every item of household stores, his camels, sheep, goats, and even horses had been consumed in hospitality. The beautiful Arab horse alone remained. Hautim's heart bled for his steed, as, without hesitation, he slew him to feed his guest. The next day, the emissary opened his mission, by stating that he was sent by the king to purchase, at any price, Hautim's famous steed.

"I deeply regret," answered Hautim, "that you did not, at once intimate your purpose; you ate the flesh of my horse last night. It was the last animal left me, and my guest had a right to it."

The king, on learning his disappointment, instead

of admiring the munificence of Hautim, burst into a fit of fury, and sent another noble to bring him the head of Hautim, on pain of death to himself. This messenger, losing his road, was invited by a stranger to put up at his tent. There, he was entertained in a style of hospitality, so kind and magnificent, that he was struck with admiration, and penetrated with gratitude. After dinner, he related the purpose of his mission, and begged his host to put him in the way of discovering Hautim; to which the host readily consented. He retired to rest; at midnight he was awakened, and opening his eyes, beheld his host standing over him, with a drawn sword. He feared, at first, he had fallen into the hands of a robber, but his host quickly re-assured him.

"You seek Hautim," he said. "He stands before you. You require his head. Take it," (presenting the sabre, and baring his throat.) "You are his guest, and have a right to it. Fear nothing, but strike. My family are wrapt in slumber, your horse is saddled at the door. I did it with my own hand, that none might be disturbed. Why do you hesitate? Is it fear? You are perfectly safe; do you deem Hautim a niggard of his hospitality?"

The messenger fell at Hautim's feet, and with tears besought forgiveness. Death awaited him on his return to his master; but it seemed a light penalty, in comparison of the crime of murdering Hautim. He returned to the monarch, and related his tale, expecting instant execution. But the king's heart was at length touched. He repented of his cruelty, and wishing to make some poor amends, and farther to put to the proof the generosity of Hautim, sent to beg of him a hundred beautiful camels. Hautim instantly despatched messengers throughout the land, to purchase the choicest, and soon sent the king a hundred camels, without blemish, and of the best blood. The king ordered them to be laden, from the royal treasury, with all that was beautiful and rare, and returned to Hautim with their burthens, as an offering of admiration and esteem. Hautim most gratefully acknowledged the king's liberality; but it was not in the nature of this high-minded Arab to profit by it. He sent the camels, each to its original owner, begging his acceptance of it, and its burthen of merchandize; reserving for himself only the gratification of such munificence, and the praise of being superior to the bounty of a king.

Such was Hautim, until the angel of death removed him from a world unworthy of him. His brother, fired with emulation, determined to imitate his princely generosity. But his mother rebuked him, saying, "My son, this is not for thee. Thy brother, when an infant, would not take my breast until I had given the other to thee: but thou, whilst thou wert taking thy food, didst hold my other breast with thy little hand, that none might participate thine enjoyment. Meddle not with things too high for thee. The world had but one Hautim, and it hath pleased heaven to bereave the world."

April 6th.—The country to-day was undulating, the soil remarkably smooth, being sand, tempered with clay and vegetable matter, and resting upon shell limestone, beneath which is chalk and marl. It is sprinkled with very low herbage. Hussun Mhatoor sent, last night, to beg I would give myself no anxiety, for that in five marches more, we should reach our journey's end. It is just six days, since he assured me we had but five marches to make. He now adds, that as we are in a fat land, where he makes money at every step, he hopes I will not be in a hurry, but allow him to glean it down. I have replied, that he will have to reckon with the Khaun Huzurut for this delay. That the Khaun, when he knows that the object of my mission has been defeated by his (Hussun's) avarice, will, in all probability, put him to death.

Indeed, although I have forborne to weary the

reader with a daily detail of my melancholy feelings; my prospect is overcast with misery. I have, already, been as long upon this trifling portion of my journey, as might have sufficed to carry me to the Russian capital. Should I fail of finding a passage to Astrakhaun, ruin stares me in the face; my supplies are almost consumed, my purse is at a low ebb, and I am thousands of miles from aid that could avail me; my name will suffer with my Government; as success alone could have reconciled them to such an undertaking, and success no longer appears possible.

I called Summud Khaun to my side, and asked him if he had no tale to divert my melancholy mood.

"A merchant of my acquaintance," he said, "came from Cashmere to Cabul, with some handsome shawls; and being a stranger at Cabul, deposited them with a merchant of that city, whose honesty was highly extolled, and who had made him an offer for them. Upon demanding his shawls of the Cabul merchant, the latter denied having ever received them; and the Cashmere merchant could not identify the persons, who had been present during the transaction. He related the circumstance to some people of the Court, who recommended him to appeal to the Ummeer, Doost Muhummud Khaun. He did so, and the Ummeer directed him to repair, at a certain hour, to the shop of the Cabul merchant, and not to be astonished at any thing he should see or hear, but to answer all questions, as if he had anticipated them. Next day, the Ummeer in great state was proceeding through the bazaar, when opposite the Cabul merchant's shop, he perceived the Cashmere merchant, who immediately dismounted, in deference to the Ummeer. 'Ah!' exclaimed the Ummeer, 'is that you? Whence are you, and how long have you been in Cabul? It is an age since I had the pleasure of seeing you. I trust you have not presumed to fix your abode anywhere, but at my palace?'

"Then, causing one of his train to dismount from

the handsomest of his horses, he made the Cashmere merchant take his place, and ride by his side to the palace, where he appointed him quarters. A few hours afterwards, the Cashmere merchant was informed, that a person wished to see him on particular business. He ordered that he should be admitted, and was not astonished to behold the Cabul merchant, who threw himself at his feet and implored pardon, having brought back all the stolen merchandize, and a handsome present with it.

I have no reason to doubt this tale, although I should be sorry to vouch for its truth.

I enquired of Summud Khaun, particulars of the descendants of Cyrus the Great (Ky Khoosro), who are just now living at Heraut, having been driven out of the last of their hereditary possessions, in Seistaun. The names of the brothers are Humzur Khaun and Jellalooddeen Khaun, and there is a third, son to the first. They retain, in a remarkable degree, the personal beauty which distinguished their fathers. Jellalooddeen Khaun is said to be without a rival in this respect, and the family resemblance is very strong. When Captain Pottinger was presenting shawl robes to some of the nobles of Heraut, none could be found of sufficient length for Humzur Khaun and Jellalooddeen Khaun, and it was necessary to make up a set, expressly, for the sons of Cyrus.

"When Jellalooddeen Khaun appeared at any public festival," added Summud Khaun, "he walked like the peacock amongst lesser birds. His majestic stature, graceful person, and perfect features, attracted universal admiration, and every thing was forgotten, to gaze upon the son of Cyrus. His eyes, in particular, are the largest and most beautiful in the world. Humzur Khaun was the seventh in descent of his family, since it has been driven into a small principality of Seistaun. Of this he was dispossessed five years ago by Muhummud Rezza

Khaun, one of his own family, who still retains possession."

At the distance of about thirteen miles, we found five or six wells in a valley, and near them a small cemetery, in which rude attempts had been made, to rear and carve monuments, of the coarse shell limestone of the hills. One of these graves, had, at the head, an upright piece of wood or stone, around which was wound the hat of the deceased, a female. It appeared to be of coloured silk. I could not regard it without emotion. Ali, my interpreter, gave this explanation of the symbol; but I have never seen any silk stuffs amongst the Kuzzauks, whose bonnet is lamb-skin or wolf's fur, inverted. Another upright headstone was carved into figures, resembling somewhat the fleur de lis. Others had enclosures of limestone flags, built up like boxes, and having but one small aperture. All were more or less mutilated. Perhaps by cattle, perhaps by the rapacity of man.

We now entered a tract of shallow valley, absolutely devastated by the vast herds of Kuzzauk galloways; so that we could find no spot capable of yielding our horses even the miserable browse of wormwood, their sole fodder, since leaving Khiva. At night, we pitched near two or three Kuzzauk tents. A young woman, from one of these, brought out a mattock, and commenced digging the dry stems of the wormwood, as firing for us. Nizaum, supposing she was working for herself, very gallantly hastened to her assistance, and worked away furiously. The lady, accustomed to the selfish neglect of her own people, did not understand his devotion, and left the wormwood untouched, for his use; but Nizaum was far too high-spirited to appropriate it. At an intermediate halt, he asked my permission to take a lesson in carpet weaving, of the inhabitants of a neighbouring tent. I saw him there, between two fair instructresses, laughing and learning and making love in a breath.

April 7th.—We marched, this day, about twenty miles in a drizzling rain. Hussun entered a black tent, midway, leaving me very politely, without a guide, to sit in the rain during his absence. We crossed again the deep, wide river channel already mentioned, and which we had been following at a short distance. Its course is to the Caspian, a little north of ours, and it is here about one and a half miles in breadth. On the left bank, we found three children, seated in a circle, playing with pebbles. The eldest, a little girl, was beautiful, although a Kuzzauk. Our guide, a Kuzzauk deputed by Hussun, could not forbear remarking upon the security of a country, where children can amuse themselves, without protectors, at a distance from home. Half a mile farther, we reached a Kuzzauk Khail, and our guide chatted with the inmates, who came out to see him. The Kuzzauk salutation is made, by interjoining the four hands. Women and men thus salute. The Toorcumun women salute men, by laying their two hands on the men's shoulders. My Afghauns are scandalized by this profane intermixture of sexes; but it is welcome to me, as a symptom of our approach to lands, where woman holds her just position in society. The women appeared at the tent doors, laughing at my strange attire, and that of my horse, the latter being a particolored body clothing, of red and green worsted, beautifully woven by the Toorcumuns, but quite unknown to Kuzzauks. These women have a hideous disguise. A posteen, or cloak of sheep's hide inverted; the yellow, and usually greasy, leather appearing outward. This envelopes the whole body, and renders it impossible to conjecture what is beneath; unless indeed we happen to be aware of the great scarcity of water in this country, and that the fur is never washed, from the day it leaves the sheep, to the day its last tatter falls from the owner's back. We may then congratulate ourselves, on the intervention of this leathern case, between our senses and the person of the wearer. The greasy and clumsy boots of buff leather appear below this, and above, is a fiery red, round face, pierced with two small holes and a large one, and having a broad tumulus between; the whole swaddled in linen, intended to be white, (which passes in a ragged turban round the head, and in a filthy bundle under the chin) and looking very like a red-hot warming pan, singeing its way through a dirty dishclout.

A few steps farther, we came upon a small snake. Summud Khaun had lifted his sword to kill it, when the Meerza shouted aloud. "Stop, stop, let the Sahib catch it."

I had been telling him of the ease and security with which the most venomous serpents may be caught by the hand, and although not overpleased with the old man's officiousness, thought it of less consequence to resent the disrespect, than to prevent my people supposing me a romancer. I therefore dismounted, seized the reptile by the throat, opened his mouth, and finding therein a pair of fangs, which no harmless snakes possess, perceived that he was worthy of death, threw him on the earth, and killed him with my horse-whip, to the great horror of Yakoob, the Meera-Khor, who declared that the whip would now poison my horse. I remounted, and proceeded. After riding a short distance, it suddenly occurred to the Meerza, that I had just fulfilled in part a dream, which Ali Muhummud had told us, two days ago. Ali in his sleep had seen a venomous snake approach our party, at sight of which my people took to flight: I killed this snake. From its blood sprang a bird, which I knocked down with a stone, ordering him, Ali, to pick up its feathers. This dream had been much discussed, for all my followers are firm believers in such supposed revelations, and various enquiries were drawn from it, relative to my mission, most of them flattering me with success. The serpent was Russia, my people the Toorcumuns, who had fled the serpent. But what the bird or bird's feathers could possibly signify, no one could conjecture.

"This," said the Meerza, "is, unless I mistake, the very viper that his Highness Muhummud restored to life. Did you ever hear the story?"

"Never; let me hear it."

"His Highness, peace be to him, was passing in winter over the desert, when he found a small frozen viper. He was touched with compassion, and placed it in his sleeve, where after a while the heat of his blessed body restored it to life. The viper, upon feeling itself perfectly recovered, poked its head from out of the sleeve, and said, 'O prophet, I am about to bite you.'

"'Wherefore,' enquired the prophet, 'have I done you injury?'

"'On the contrary, you have done me good; nevertheless, I'll bite you.'

"'Wherefore? give me a sound reason, and I will be content.'

"'Your people kill my people constantly.'

"'Your people bite my people constantly. The balance between our kindred is even; between you and me it is in my favour, I have done you good.'

"'And, that you may not do me harm, I will bite you.'

"'Do not be so ungrateful.'

"'I will; I have sworn by the most high God that I will.'

"At that name, the prophet no longer opposed the viper, but bade him bite on, in the name of God. The viper fixed his fangs in the blessed wrist, and the prophet, shaking him off, would not destroy him; but put his lips to the wound, and sucking out the venom, spat it on the earth. From these drops, say those Muhummedans who chew tobacco, sprang that wondrous weed, which has the bitterness of the serpent's tooth, quelled by the sweet saliva of the prophet. Therefore, it is allowable to chew pigtail."

"There is but one little objection to this tale," I replied, "which is, that tobacco was first discovered about 900 years after the demise of his Highness Muhummud, in a country which he had never heard of, i. e. Yungee Doonia (the new world). The same fact is proof that tobacco is not forbidden by the Koraun, since it was quite unknown to the author of that book. Therefore the Faithful may chew pigtail, Q E D."

As all my people are more or less votaries of the weed, either in a solid or a gaseous form, they were well contented with this settlement of a question which still troubles the weak conscience of many a devout, tobacco-loving Moslim. Let us look at home, and see if *we* have not scruples as absurd, and infinitely more mischievous, which take the place of that true religion of the heart, which owns neither form nor ceremony, nor any excuse for uncharitableness, rancour or discord; but which scruples not to mingle its spirit with whatever is pure and beautiful in the religion of a brother, though prevented, by the fear of misconstruction, from conforming to any outward ceremonies excepting those of his own people and faith.

Finally, I reached the spot destined for our halt, and, spreading my carpet, and drawing round me my cloak, sat two more hours in the rain, until the camels were announced. A few black tents were at hand, and from these, in spite of the weather, I enticed several children around me, by means of loaf-sugar. With them came two women, and sat themselves upon the skirt of my carpet, delighted with the sugar. When the camels had arrived, and my tent was pitched, one of them brought me dried horse-dung for fuel, and then a skinful of fresh sheep's milk, villanously flavoured with the aroma of mutton, a common defect, proceeding, perhaps, from some want of care and cleanliness in milking; camel's milk is far preferable; but for tea, commend me to fresh, frothing goat's milk; mare and camel's milk are preferred by the Toorenmuns. Of the former a fermented liquor is made, which I afterwards tasted in Russia, and to which the Oozbegs are very partial. I, who dislike the effect of fermentation upon liquids, am no judge of its merits.

I had, yesterday, vindicated the liberty of the fair sex, and, in upholding that enjoyed by the Kuzzauks, had appealed to the virtue of the daughters of my people as an example. The evening did not pass; ere I found reason to regret the comparison; for the two fair Kuzzauks made a somewhat overfree use of theirs.

CHAPTER XX.

Ferocity of Tooreumun Horses—Cliffs of crystallised Lime—Account of the Death of Futteh Khaun, Vuzeer of Heraut—Resistless Power of Destiny—The Falcon and the Crow—Perverseness of Guide—Tent of Dana Bae, the Kuzzauk—The Napkin of Khaurism—The Desert Bird.

APRIL 8th.—Hussun Mhatoor, coming to me this morning, as we were preparing to start, proposed leaving the Yuze Baushie and his party to follow at leisure, whilst he himself rode on with me. To the first proposition I agreed, but objected to the second; for he had the day before left me outside a Kuzzauk tent, exposed for two hours to the rain, whilst he entered to plunder it. I insisted, therefore, upon having a guide to ride on with me on such occasions, as I could not sanction, by my presence, his depredations.

Meanwhile, a most unpleasant commotion had arisen amongst the horses of my suite. The presence of a gelding, ridden by the Kuzzauk guide, had made them all furious. They broke from their pickets, and attacked one another with teeth and hoofs, so violently that we had the utmost difficulty in separating them, and not until they had several times rolled together upon the earth, and Ali Muhummud's horse had been lamed and otherwise wounded. Yet these animals, when neither mare nor gelding is brought near them, are the most quiet and tractable of creatures, travelling in very compact bodies, without either kicking or biting.

We descended into a wide valley, scarped with lofty

cliffs of shell limestone, marle, and crystallised lime. Nizaum here discovered that he had dropped my silver drinking-cup, and rode back with Summud Khaun to find it. We sat at the foot of a cliff. Large masses of crystallized carbonate of lime had rolled down from above. The weather, acting upon these, moulded them into figures of great beauty, and a surface yielding all the prismatic colours. The masses were often cubes of a foot. I selected a few of the smaller specimens.

My servants now joined me, having found the silver goblet in the road. Summud Khaun, who had been much about the person of Shauh Kaumraun, gave me the following particulars of the death of the Vuzeer, Futteh Khaun. It is a characteristic page of Eastern history.

Futteh Khaun, Vuzeer of Shah Maimood of Cabul, was sent to the aid of the king's brother, Hajji Feeroozooddeen, viceroy of Heraut, who was threatened with invasion by Persia. He was kindly treated by the viceroy; and, on the third day, getting possession of the gates of Heraut, seized upon the government in the name of Maimood's son, the prince Kaumraun. Hajji Feerooz fled to the hills, where, during five days, he had nothing to eat but grass and the roots of wild herbs. He then descended to the valley, and sought refuge in the cottage of a husbandman, who at once recognised him and treated him kindly. From this cottage he rode upon a bullock to a neighbouring place of pilgrimage, where he thought he should be more secure.

The prince Kaumraun, hearing that Heraut had been seized in his name, hastened to take possession, announcing his arrival in the neighbourhood to the Vuzeer Futteh Khaun: but the latter, perceiving the sweets of supreme authority, seemed in no hurry to vacate the throne.

From the hour of Kaumraun's arrival, jealousy and distrust were visible. An impression prevailed amongst the followers of either, that each had designs upon the liberty of the other. Three days had elapsed, and Futteh Khaun had not called to pay his respects to his prince. Shah Pussund Khaun (at present chief of Laush) determined to call upon Futteh Khaun, and sound his disposition. The prince Kaumraun consented, with reluctance, to this step, fearing that his friend might be seized. Shah Pussund Khaun, with a handsome suite, waited upon Futteh Khaun, and was received with all appearance of cordiality. Their attendants were dismissed, whilst they held secret consultation. A copy of the Koraun was produced, and each swore solemnly upon it. Futteh Khaun, that he would warn Shah Pussund Khaun of any intention, on his own part, to seize the prince; and Shah Pussund Khaun, that he would warn Futteh Khaun of any intention of the prince to seize him. Futteh Khaun then gave very handsome presents and dresses of honour to Shah Pussund Khaun, and all his suite; and so they parted.

Next day, Futteh Khaun waited upon prince Kaumraun. The prince treated him with the utmost affection and distinction, and lavished rich presents upon him. A few days afterwards he called again, and received still greater marks of favour. Futteh Khaun, himself the most treacherous of mortals, might have been warned by such a profusion of cordiality of his impending fate. The prince, taking from his own side a remarkably costly dagger, placed it in the girdle of Futteh Khaun, and bad him take command of an expedition against Meshed; Futteh Khaun prepared himself accordingly, pitching his camp upon the spot since occupied by the Persian army of investment.

He then waited upon the prince to take leave. Those who have visited the dwellings of kings and nobles in Asia, are acquainted with the variety of contrivances by which a visitor is separated from any effectual aid of his followers, in approaching the lion's den. The narrow, dark passages, often lined on either side by armed men, through whom he has to squeeze his way. The narrow, precipitous staircases, terminating above in a pigeon hole, which is crept through almost on all-fours, so that an old woman may master the visitor ere he can stand upright,—all these approaches place *him*, who is obliged to pay his homage at Court, completely in the power of the monarch; and the failure of such homage leaves no doubt as to the nature of the subject's views. Futteh Khaun, throughout the whole of these manœuvres, betrayed the grossest inattention to the signs of the times, and the most deplorable obliviousness of the nature of the game he was playing.

On this occasion, instead of finding the prince in open Durbar, to which he could bring his followers, he was admitted, as a particular mark of confidence, to the prince's inner apartment, which was to be attained by ascending a narrow flight of stairs; as he was stooping to pass through the door above, he was seized from both sides at the same instant, pinioned, and thrown upon his back. Red-hot irons were instantly brought, and his eye balls were seared. It is probable, that Kaumraun, having no longer cause to fear him, would have been content with this punishment, or rather precaution. But Futteh Khaun had been a reckless character, guilty of much violence, and his blood was demanded on all sides, by the relatives of those he had wronged. Kaumraun, not yet established in his government, dared not disgust so many, and yielded to their demands. Futteh Khaun was, therefore, brought into a tent, pitched between Heraut and the river, in which sat a circle of his mortal foes.

They commenced, by each in turn accusing him of the injuries received at his hand, and heaping upon him the most opprobrious epithets. Uttah Muhummud Khaun then stepped up to him, and seizing one of his ears, cut it off with his knife, saying, this is for such and such an injury, done to such an one of my relatives. Shahaghaussie Nuwaub cut off the other ear. Each, as he wreaked this unmanly vengeance upon the victim, whom he would have crouched to the day before, named the wrong of which it was the recompense; thus depriving him of the highest consolation the mind of man can possess under torment, —the conscience void of offence. Another of the barbarians cut off his nose: Khana Moolla Khaun severed his right hand; Khalook Dâd Khaun his left hand. The blood gushing copiously from each fresh wound. Summundur Khaun cut off his beard, saying, this is for dishonouring my wife. Hitherto, the high-spirited chief had borne his suffering without either weakness or any ebullition of his excitable temper. He had only once condescended, in a calm voice, to beg them to hasten his death. The mutilation of ears and nose, a punishment reserved for the meanest offences of slaves, had not been able to shake his fortitude; but the beard of a Muhummedan is a member so sacred, that honour itself becomes confounded with it; and he, who had borne with the constancy of a hero, the taunts and tortures heaped upon him, seemed to lose his manhood with his beard, and burst into a passion of tears. His torments were now drawing to a close. Gool Muhummud Khaun, with a blow of his sabre, cut off his right foot, and a man of the Populzye tribe severed the left. Uttah Muhummud Khaun finished his torments by cutting his throat.

Such was the end of one of the most talented and extraordinary characters of Eastern history. I have inserted in the Appendix Elphinstone's sketch of his history, which is the more curious, that he may be considered a type of his countrymen, exhibiting traits, more strongly developed, indeed, in his own instance, yet common to all Afghauns. The courage, the talent, the fickleness and inconstancy, the occasional generosity, the unscrupulous treachery, the genius to conceive, the promptitude to perform; disconcerted by a want of system, by an inability to resist tempting opportunities, diverting him from the end of his enterprise. If we consider his moral character, it is not perhaps much fairer than that of other Afghauns who have enjoyed power, or rather been cursed with opportunity to do evil. But his foes, by their barbarous and cowardly revenge, have blotted from our memory all that was damning in the page; and left us only his brilliant and versatile talents and powers, sealed in his last moments by the courage and constancy of a hero.

I inquired, whether, at his seizure, he had not made resistance, as might be expected from so energetic a character.

"No, Sir; when a man's death is decreed, he is powerless to struggle against destiny. Futteh Khaun had in his girdle a brace of detonating pistols and a dagger. Yet he made no attempt to use either."

"It is surprising that one so conversant with peril, so prompt, and courageous, should not have struck one blow."

"It was not the will of fate. I remember when Hajji Feeroozooddeen endeavoured to cut down three unarmed prisoners who were brought before him. His weapon was a Damascus blade of great price, keen as a razor, and capable of severing iron; but it was not the will of heaven that it should harm those men; and, after several vain efforts, he threw away his beautiful blade in anger, and desired that it might never again be brought into his sight.

The Meerza soon after related a fable, which is probably not very new. A falcon soaring over a tree in which a crow was cawing, was struck with the music of the notes, and immediately desired to cement an alliance. This continued for some time, until the falcon, returning one night from an unsuccessful foray, sat down hungry and out of humour near the crow. "Vuzeer," he at length exclaimed, in a voice of thunder, "how is it that you presume to sit at your ease in the pleasant sunshine, whilst I am standing here in the dark?"

"Oh! king," replied the poor crow, "your gracious Majesty mistakes; it is night, and darkness is around us both."

"What! you miserable reptile, do you presume to make *me* a liar?" And falling upon the poor crow, he ate him up with much relish.

We now emerged from the valley upon a high plain, and saw on our right, in the distance, the double summit of a dark hill, or Kara Daugh, at which, so far as we can understand, lies Dahsh Gullah (the stone fort), the Russian settlement on the coast of the Caspian. A long, low, black line of clouds on the North traced out the course of the sea, of which we are entering one of the promontories. We encamped near some Kuzzauk tents.

April 9th, 1840.—Starting as usual, we soon reached a valley, in which we found several copious wells, surrounded by flocks of Kuzzauk sheep. Two Kuzzauks were watering them. A third good-naturedly watered our horses in a trough of Russian manufacture. The valley was scarred by innumerable impressions of wells which have fallen in. We afterwards descended into a wide and deep valley, scarped with cliffs of very rotten sandstone; and passing up one of its narrow tributary ravines, watered our horses at the highest of a long chain of wells. The water was very pure. Snow was lying in the shadow of the cliffs. Emerging from the valley, we encamped for the night upon a high unsheltered plain, ill supplied with the coarse herbage of the steppe. This appears like a manœuvre of Hussun to distress my people and cattle. He and his followers are secure from the weather in the black tent which, I believe, was sent by the Khaun Huzurut for my accommodation. The wind all day had been excessively bleak, attended with drizzling rain from the inlet of the Caspian on our North, and we have had no night so comfortless as the last.

April 10th.—The morning was bleak and foggy.

We lost our road, perhaps intentionally on Hussun's part, as he wished to breakfast at the expense of the Kuzzauks. Accordingly, he inquired of some men tending a large herd of galloways, the way to the nearest tent. At this we were hospitably received by Dana Bae (pronounced Boy), the master. On entering the black tent, I found four or five women still within it, the men having vacated it for me. The eldest woman took both my hands between her own. I went forward, and met rather a pretty girl of fifteen years, who seemed half shy of the salute, but returned it when I put out my hands. We were soon seated, the women still remaining. I felt quite in my element in this rustic household. A screen of reeds on one side hid a flock of young kids and lambs, some of which, however, contrived to extricate their heads or noses, and see what was going on.

Hussun Mhatoor asked, whether he should allow them to kill us a sheep. I objected. He said they were pressing it upon me, and that he should like to taste it. I thought it better to give my consent, determining to remunerate the good people. All the matrons wore the dirty white cloth, elsewhere described as their head dress; but the two maidens had the Kuzzauk bonnet of inverted fur, which, like all small bonnets, is becoming to the face. Their hair was braided in rich and heavy tresses, partly concealed by the bonnet. I gazed upon them with much interest. Observing a tall and rather handsome young man standing behind the master of the tent, I was struck with their mutual resemblance, and asked, if they were not father and son. The old man was evidently gratified by the discovery, and with some reason, for he is himself an ugly little fellow. The family have better features than the generality of Kuzzauks, and no Tartar peculiarities. The second daughter is decidedly a pretty girl, and the elder is not ill-looking. The bonnet of black lambskin, shadowing the wild and prominent features and restless eyes of the young man, gave him a romantic air. Nevertheless, his was not a prepossessing countenance, and the old man's expression was that of one of the meaner of the Jewish race. These men were destined to exercise over my fortunes an influence which I could not foresee.

A large, hemispherical, cast-iron cauldron, was now placed over the fire, and a sheep was led to the door to shew its face: a ceremony that quite unfitted me for the banquet. Summud Khaun objected to the food being dressed before me, and Nizaum was called to dress it after my own fashion; but I replied, that the friends who had provided the entertainment must complete their kindness by preparing it. Whilst it was in preparation, the old man asked for some tobacco, a weed with which travellers in these parts should be provided. Hussun gave him a piece, and our Kuzzauk guide volunteered to pound it into snuff. Seizing a wooden goblet, and the handle of a spade, as pestle and mortar, he commenced accordingly. The root of some wild plant was reduced to ashes and cast amongst the tobacco leaves, probably to assist granulation. The pounder filled his mouth with water, which, from time to time he spurted in. Whether the product was Prince's mixture, or Blackguard, I will not take upon me to say. I observed that all articles of furniture were Russian, either of cast iron or of wood turned upon a lathe.

The food was now brought in, upon a dozen wooden bowls, or platters, and placed before us. It consisted of boiled mutton, soused in its own soup. Bread and vegetables are things quite unknown in these parts. Kuzzauks are exclusively carnivorous. The whole party fell on, like a pack of wolves; my own stomach, weakened by sight of the victim's face, was quite turned by the scene before me. Never did I see so much flesh devoured in so brief a space. Yet I have witnessed the feasts of tigers and wolves. The father and son would not partake until the guests had concluded, although I entreated them to do so. The women did not appear until chins had done wagging; but two of the senoras entered, afterwards, to serve out curdled milk (mahss) in large bowls. The broth of the mutton, also, was brought in and distributed, being swigged as if it had been beer. The bowls were handed to the women, who scraped them clean with their thumbs, then plunged those members into their mouths, and again into the bowls, with a rapidity truly admirable. The thumb and tongue are the only napkins in Khaurism—water is never thrown away upon either bowl or person. The Tartars are right not to eat with their women. Imagine a pretty girl, with a sheep's head in both her lily hands, tearing off the scalp, picking out the eyes by the insertion of her fore-finger, cracking them between her teeth, like gooseberries, thrusting the same pretty finger in after the brain, and sucking away at the apertures. All which I saw executed by one of the men, in a most natural and edifying manner.

Summud Khaun, who, being steward, and knowing what is good, has generally several pounds of sugar and other sweetmeats in his breeches pockets, greatly delighted the party by distributing them. I singled out the prettier of the maidens, and made her blush, as I presented her a lump of loaf sugar. We rose and took leave. I met a grandson of Dana Bae, carrying an empty bowl. Into this I slipped four rupees, rather more than the ordinary price of a sheep. The old man followed me to my horse, and shook hands cordially with me. He seemed to have expected some gift; but I felt delicacy in paying him, in person, for his hospitality. We proceeded, but could not find our camels; we therefore made across the country for a Khail, where we obtained direction, and overtaking them, encamped in a valley, near a wall of loose stones, of semicircular form, piled up by travellers as a screen from the north-east wind. While I was sitting waiting for the complete preparation of my tent, one of the camel-drivers brought me a little bird, resembling the water-wagtail, one of the rare inhabitants of the steppe which, by a homeless, friendless wanderer like myself, had ever been regarded with peculiar tenderness. He had injured the poor little thing in catching it, and grinned as he gave it wounded, and half dead from fear, into my hand. I rebuked him harshly for his inhospitality, and placed the little bird in a hollow in the loose wall, where it was tolerably secure; at night, when my candle was lighted, it hopped in, and took its seat near the foot of my bed. I was touched with the incident, and disposed my baggage so as to shelter it from accidental injury. None but he who has been similarly circumstanced, can conjecture the hold which the little thing had taken upon my heart. In the morning, my first care was to attend to my wounded guest. I found it lying dead in the spot where it had slept. I dug it a little grave, and buried it there. My servants tried in vain to make this incident into a fulfilment of part the second of Ali's dream. The bird had indeed risen, as it were, from the dead serpent, and had been destroyed, but not by my hand, which would gladly have saved it. Incidents, trifling as this may seem, affect the tone of our feelings, and I was melancholy on the death of the little desert bird.

CHAPTER XXI.

Cliffs of Shell Sandstone—Burial Ground—First Glimpse of the Caspian—Difficulties suggested by the Guide—Entire Absence of Boats—Desperate Posture of my Affairs—Expedient suggested by the Guide—His Refusal to accompany me farther—Prospect of utter Ruin—Alternatives—Basin and Cliffs of the Caspian—False Report of Sails in sight—Signals—Resolution to proceed to Dahsh Gullah—Repetition of Signals—Their Fruitlessness—Appearance of Dana Bae, the Kuzzauk—His Agreement to conduct me—Announcement and Departure—Letter to the Khaun Huzurut—Suspicious Circumstance—Ruinous Habits of my Interpreter.

APRIL 10th.—The reports I received, from time to time, from Kuzzauks, made me very anxious. One declared, that no vessels had, this season, appeared off the port, and that none ever came, without express licence, from Astrakhan. Another man assured me he had seen a large fleet, about twelve days ago; that they sailed close to the promontory, as if in search of caravans from Bokhara, and, after lingering for some space, returned to the neighbouring island; but, since the destruction of the Russian fleet by the Toorcumuns, I fear that all boats will be excessively wary in approaching this coast.

After marching about ten miles, I reached a cliff of shell sandstone, resting on chalk. This, in past days, has been rudely fortified, and, so far as I can learn, was occupied by a very extensive camp of Calmauks. Some miles farther, in a sheltered nook, where the furious and bleak north wind, that has met us all day in the teeth, is scarcely heard, I found a considerable cemetery of the Salars, Chowdhoors, and Kuzzauks. The headstones are of chalk, and of soft sandstone.

The former carved with some elegance, and inscribed in Persian characters. I read one or two of the inscriptions, which proved to be genealogical rolls, sometimes running up seven or eight descents. There was some resemblance between these tombstones and those of Europe. A building, which had once been rudely domed, enclosed the circle of rest of some chieftain; but the monumental portion was gone. Another Goombuz, or domed building, stood on the height, at hand. Such objects are curious only to the wanderer of the steppe. A few miserable mulberry trees, out of leaf, had contrived to spring here, the first trees we had seen for thirty days. The spot was sheltered, and well chosen. We, who had just emerged from the cutting and blustering wind, felt it to be a place of rest.

Emerging from this valley, we traversed a high plain, covered, like the rest of the steppe, with a low growth of wormwood, amongst which some scattered blades of grass appeared. From Shawl to Orenburgh, a distance of some 2000 miles, the country is a wormwood-covered waste, broken only by an occasional chain of mountains. The plain we had entered was well sprinkled with black tents and large flocks of sheep; near one of these tents we halted for the night. Once I caught a glimpse of the blue Caspian, about twenty miles away on the south.

April 12th.—I was now close to that Caspian, so long and earnestly desired, which had seemed to recede from me in proportion as I advanced. The rich Kuzzauk, whose tent was at hand, sold me a sheep, which was a welcome addition to our almost exhausted supplies. I sent for Hussun Mhatoor, and desired him to find for me some camping ground upon the brink of the sea. He said that the Russians frequently land there, and massacre all whom they meet; that he dared not encamp there, and that if I was determined upon it, he must separate from me, and could afford me no protection; that he would choose for me the nearest safe neighbourhood to the landing-place, and that I could ride thence as often as I pleased to visit the coast. To separate from Hussun, I knew to be destruction, so I was obliged to comply with a measure to which I was extremely averse. At the distance, therefore, of three miles from the Caspian, I occupied a spot selected by Hussun, and, leaving there my baggage, rode with him and a few of my suite to the landing-place. We proceeded over a high, irregular plain, and at length came in sight of the wide expanse of blue waters, from the edge of a cliff of some 700 feet.

I cast my eye over the waste of waters, and perused most anxiously the line of coast, but not a vessel was in sight. Again and again I explored the long-desired Caspian, and again my eye, wearied and worn out, rested in despair from its wandering.* That gaze was one of the most disheartening, the most appalling, my eye had ever known. I enquired of Hussun what method merchants adopted to advertise the Russian vessels of their arrival. He replied that in general there was no want of boats lying off shore, but that the burning of the Russian fleet at present deterred them from approaching, and might prevent their visiting the coast at all. I reminded him of the assurance he had made me, in presence of the Khaun Huzurut, that I should find abundance of vessels, and no difficulty whatever in embarking, and of his offer to supply me with the use of his own boat. He denied having made this offer with the utmost effrontery: said that there was an island about five hours sail from shore, at which there were always vessels. He recommended me to sell my horses, and purchase a boat and two Russian slaves to man it; to embark in this boat for the island, and there procure a vessel for the conveyance of my suite and baggage to Astrakhan.

* The loss of my telescope, which I had been obliged to present to the Khaun Huzurut for want of proper gifts, was now keenly felt, the distances being far too remote for the naked eye.

This was truly a promising expedient. The sale of my horses would have rendered it impossible for me to return to Khiva, or to proceed to Dahsh Gullah, the Russian fort, should I fail to procure a vessel. Nor was this all; for I was so ill provided with cash, that I depended upon the sale of my horses for the means of prosecuting my journey, and could not afford to part with them for the mere use of a boat for a single day. Neither could I venture to quit the coast without my servants, as any plausible report of my departure would have been seized by Hussun as a plea for plundering my goods, and selling my people as slaves, or the governor of the island might detain me, when *their* destruction would be certain. I therefore declined this offer, and told him that, if next day no vessel should arrive, I must proceed, as the Khaun Huzurut had desired, to Dahsh Gullah.

"And who will conduct you?" he replied.

"You of course will, according to the Khaun Huzurut's instructions."

"The Khaun gave me no such instructions; he ordered me to conduct you hither, and I have done so. If you like to wait here for a vessel, I will remain with you; or, if you prefer returning to Khiva, I will be your guide, but I will not go a step *farther* with you."

"Then you must find me a guide."

"No; I have no orders to do so."

"Then I will go alone; and if any evil befall the Khaun Huzurut's ambassador, he will visit it upon you and your family."

"What do *I* care for the Khaun Huzurut?" was his reply.

I begged all present to mark the words he was uttering. Three or four Kuzzauks and Toorcumuns, for whom my speech was translated, grinned at the appeal. Hussun was alarmed, for had it reached the Khaun's ears, the whole of his family had been instantly extirpated. He qualified his words, therefore, by adding, " I have done the Khaun Huzurut too good service, to have anything to fear from him."

I then appealed to the Tooreumuns and Kuzzauks present, Ali Muhummud interpreting after me. " I take you all to witness, that I have required Hussun Mhatoor's guidance to Dahsh Gullah, according to the desire of the Khaun Huzurut, signified to me in the presence of Summud Khaun and Hussun Mhatoor himself. Summud Khaun, what were the Khaun Huzurut's instructions?"

" The Khaun Huzurut asked you what you would do, in case no boat were procurable at Mungh Kishlauk. You replied that you would go on to Dahsh Gullah. The Khaun Huzurut said, Do so. All this I heard. The Khaun Huzurut added, Hussun Mhatoor cannot accompany you into the fort, but will bring you within sight of it."

" You all hear this. Now I take you to witness, that Hussun Mhatoor refuses to guide me himself or to furnish me a proper guide, although he knows that the Khaun Huzurut's interests are at stake."

Hussun Mhatoor gave me a surly look in reply, and rode off, leaving me to my reflections.

These were sufficiently appalling. Before me was the sea, without a vessel; behind and around me was the desert, inhabited by Andun Khors, as they are called, men-eaters. My food and forage were reduced to ten days' supply; neither grain nor forage was procurable at a nearer distance than four hundred and fifty miles. My guide and sole protector was the greatest robber in Khaurism, who was on the watch for some plausible pretext to plunder and destroy me. For this, a single unwary step of mine would be sufficient; or, failing that, it was easy for the chief of 60,000 cannibals, whose power in this district rendered him almost independent of his sovereign, to procure false evidence, that I had quitted his guidance, under circumstances that freed him from all responsibility. To separate from him, promised destruction. To remain, even a few days here, would render advance and retreat, alike impossible. To return to Khiva, was worse than death; it was dishonour. The alternatives therefore, were either to wait here, hoping for the appearance of a boat, or proceed, at all hazards, towards Dahsh Gullah. Now, even should boats arrive, I was not certain they would receive me. The Government of Russia is so jealous, that I was inclined to believe the assertion of one of the Kuzzauks, that no captain would venture to receive me, without express permission from the governor of Astrakhaun. Had I money, indeed, I might bribe them to the risk: but my purse was nearly exhausted. The chances, then, should I remain, were that I should be disappointed of a passage; and, my supplies being exhausted, should be obliged to make over my horses and property, item by item, to Hussun Mhatoor, in exchange for the merest necessaries of life. Already, he had contrived to quadruple, around me, the price of such articles of food as the Kuzzauks would sell. The price would, of course, rise with our necessities, until a draught of curds would be exchanged for a horse or a sabre. I believed, that in order to ensure such a result, he would not hesitate to warn off Russian vessels from the coast, and place me under suspicion with the captains. The end of this seemed to be, that we must sell ourselves as slaves, and pass the rest of our days as Kuzzauk shepherds. To this, with the chance of escape, I had not so strong an objection as my servants evinced. It would be a new page of life, a new lesson in philosophy. Superior as I should be to all around me, I might, upon acquiring the language, become the chief of a tribe, or the king of a state of my own founding. I had, from the first, foreseen the probability of my thraldom; and ere I left Heraut, had chalked out the scheme, by which I might turn it to the confusion of my enemies, and to shaping for myself a career, that should not soon be forgotten.

I had often marvelled, that the energetic character

of a captive, had not contrived to overturn the throne of Bokhara: but there was an objection to such a fate, which nothing could balance. My mission must be lost, and with it the kingdom of Khaurism, to be gained by a nation, whose nearer approach in that quarter, my country was so much concerned to prevent.

The alternative was to proceed, at once, towards Dahsh Gullah; and as Hussun was determined not to accompany me, to procure, if possible, another guide. I called Ali Muhummud, the only counsellor I had in this emergency, being the only one possessed of any information regarding the habits of the people of Khaurism. He would try to procure a Kuzzauk guide, he said, and thought that the Kuzzauks of those parts were too strong to be in awe of the Toorcumuns, and that they could protect us. He considered them a better and more honourable race, than either Oozbeg or Toorcumun. I objected to the first part of his proposition, inasmuch as we had seen Hussun plunder the Kuzzauks at his pleasure. He replied, that those were poor and weak individuals. That, if we could procure the guidance of a man of wealth or consequence, he thought we should be secure. I did not feel convinced by his arguments; but this alternative was cheered with a ray of hope, which the others wanted; so I bade him use his utmost endeavours to procure such a guide.

Meanwhile, the sea was before me—an object longed for, during an exile of seventeen years. An object of affection, almost of reverence, to the children of the Isles. The storm was gathering blacker and blacker over my head. Thought was torture, and reflection was care of the least welcome kind. I perceived that the future had few sunny hours for me, and I determined to enjoy the moment; and as, in my light European attire, (which I had put on, in the prospect of meeting Russians,) I bounded down the cliff, I felt my spirits rise, and determined to submit my soul as little as possible to the dominion of desolating care. I first, however, despatched Ali on horseback, to a spit of sand, projecting about a mile into the sea, with instructions to load his horse with grass and dry weeds on the road, and light a fire at the extreme point. Such, he had heard, was the usual signal made by the Bokhara caravans.

The cliff I was descending, could not be less than seven hundred feet high, it was of chalk, marle, and shell limestone. The basin of the Caspian, I found here, to be a clean wave-worn vase of the same shell limestone, precisely similar in texture and contents, to the limestone I had found throughout the steppe. I examined, all along the shore, the shells thrown up by the waves. They were of three kinds only. The cockle, the muscle, and the spirorbis. Precisely the same shells, and no others, are found in the shell limestone from the neighbourhood of Khiva to the shores of the Caspian, sometimes elevated, by my estimate, about two thousand feet above the level of this sea. Here, then, is a proof, that this table land has once formed the basin of the Caspian; though how elevated, or why deserted, remains a mystery. All other seas produce a greater variety of shells; and therefore, when the shell limestone in question was formed, the Caspian must have been, as now, a lake dissevered from the ocean, although, possibly, connected with the Euxine sea.*

I found the water very salt, but not bitter. It was clear as crystal. Its colour, in the distance, is a very delicate and liquid blue. Gazing from the cliff, toward the island of Koulali, I had perceived the white line of ice, which girdled it on the 12th of April. But I was now at the foot of the cliff, amongst huge masses of shell limestone, watching the crystal waves, as they dashed themselves against this iron binding of the shore. I stripped off my clothes, and leaped

* See Appendix.

from a rock into the sea. But the chill of waves, scarcely restored from a solid to a liquid form, almost paralysed me, and I was glad to scramble back to land, and bask for a while in the sun. I spent here an hour, thankful for this respite from my troubles, and then proceeded to reascend the cliff. I was scarcely half way to the summit, when my servants shouted to me in a joyful tone of voice. So soon as I could catch their words, I found they were warning me of the appearance of several vessels, close at hand. I turned to the sea; but it was just as before, an unbroken expanse of blue. I therefore hastened to the summit, and inquired of my people the cause of their shouts. "Oh," they replied, "the ships have arrived. Maimood was the first to see them. There, Sir, there," pointing down to the spit of sand, where Ali and his fire were barely distinguishable, and where the breakers, curled by a fresh breeze from the west, were hurling themselves in foam upon the sand. "Now don't you see them, Sir?"

I looked over the waters in vain, now to the coast, now to the horizon: at length, after much interrogation, I discovered that the breakers were mistaken by my people for the white sails I had bade them search for. As they now saw the sea for the first time in their lives, they had begged me to explain to them what a ship was like. I told them, they would see a dark speck upon the waters, surmounted by a little pyramid of snow. And, as snow had suddenly appeared, where none had previously been, and the natives of the inland countries of Asia have a shrewd suspicion that our vessels travel under water, like fish; it was not very surprising, that honest Maimood, the groom, should have fallen into the error. I was less disappointed, at discovering the nature of the new arrivals, than in perceiving how poor a figure Ali and his fire cut, even at this small distance. The strong wind from the sea prevented the smoke from rising in a column, whilst the flame must be buried in the convexity of the earth's surface. That, at twenty miles distance, such a signal should be visible, seemed quite out of the question.

We spent the rest of the day upon the most conspicuous point of the promontory, and erected a flag, viz., Ali's spear, surmounted by a white muslin turban, spread out to the winds. There was just a possibility, that ourselves, the horses, and the flag might be discoverable, by aid of telescopes, from the island. Toward evening, I recalled Ali from his watch-fire, and we rode back slowly to our bivouac. I endeavoured, on the road, to organize means of securing some Kuzzauk guide in my interests, and the rest of the evening was spent at my tent in discussing the probable result of any measure I might decide upon. The case was sufficiently grave; but we helped it out with a little merriment, as each selected the part he was to play in Kuzzauk land, should we sink to the condition of slaves. We endeavoured to flatter ourselves with the hope, that Kojeh Muhummud, the eldest son of Hussun, a young man of the highest character, and one who openly expressed abhorrence of his father's villany, might join us here. Could we have ascertained the exact position of his tent, I should have made for it at once; but the Toorcumuns in our company could, or would, give us no information upon the subject. Indeed, it is probable, that they were ignorant of the present locality of a tent, which had been wandering whilst they were absent.

Two short marches back I had learned, that Dahsh Gullah was distant two short marches for a horseman. It, therefore, could scarcely be farther from Mungh Kishlauk than three days' journey for a horseman, or five for laden camels. Several persons on the spot confirmed this calculation; and I fancied the hill had been pointed out to me, beneath which the fort lies. Excepting Summud Khaun, all my followers were sanguine that we could make this distance without much hazard, could we secure the guidance of some trustworthy Kuzzauk. Ali Muhummud was especially confident. When I objected, that Hussun Mhatoor could raise thousands of horsemen to follow and attack us, he replied, "Openly he dare not attack us, for fear of the Khaun Huzurut; and during the three or four days of our march we will never be out of the saddle, nor off our guard for a moment."

As this was my sole resource, I was glad to see even one of my people in such good heart, and would not damp his confidence, but I confess I regarded the enterprise in a far more desperate light; for I knew, that Hussun's influence in those parts was sufficient to enable him to dog our steps with thousands of Toorcumuns, or, if he feared employing his own tribe, with Kuzzauks of the country; and I had but four fighting men including myself, if, indeed, I could venture to calculate as fighting men mere domestics, who had never seen the gleam of more deadly steel than the metal of a carving knife.

The next morning, 13th, I again rode to the cliffs of the Caspian. My principal object in desiring to camp on the shore, was the facility it would afford of kindling beacons at night. I could not do this at present, because Hussun refused to attend, or to send me any of his people; and had I attempted it alone, he would probably have organized some attack upon me, which could plausibly be laid at the door of Russia. Nevertheless, had I intended to remain another day, I should have made the attempt. To do so, with the prospect of departing next day, was quite useless, as the signal, if observed, could not be answered in time. I renewed the fire at the spit of sand, and again spread my flag upon the most conspicuous summit. The wind blew the smoke violently along the surface of the shore, and I felt that there was no hope of its attracting notice. About the island of Koulali, I could just perceive some sails, or rather vessels, apparently anchored off this island.

One or two others seemed sailing to and from the east, in the direction of Dahsh Gullah. I watched them with an intentness which my desperate position begot.

Once or twice I fancied a vessel was making in the direction of this port; but hours passed, and my hopes were for ever dispelled. Nevertheless, I continued anxiously to watch them until evening, when I rode back to camp, more disheartened than ever, and more than ever convinced of the necessity of hurrying on to Dahsh Gullah, whilst any provisions remained.

On dismounting from my horse, I was greeted by a little Kuzzauk, who seized my hand between his own. His face was familiar, but I did not instantly recognise Dana Bae, my late entertainer, who had been profuse of offers of service, and whose name I had written in my pocket-book. On entering my tent, Ali Muhummud came and informed me, that he had spoken to Dana Bae, and found him ready and willing to guide me to Dahsh Gullah. After dinner, I sent for Dana Bae, who repeated this assurance, saying, that five days would suffice for the journey, and that he would himself furnish me with camels. That he knew the route well, and could ensure my safe passage, but must stop short of Dahsh Gullah, lest the Russians should molest him. I promised to indemnify him for all loss sustained in my service, and to reward him handsomely. "But," I said, "what will Hussun Mhatoor say to this arrangement; have you nothing to apprehend from him?"

"What has Hussun Mhatoor to do with me;" he replied, "is he my lord?"

"Hussun Mhatoor has great authority in this district; could he not attack you?"

"He dares not. The Kuzzauks here are too strong for him. It will be necessary that you proceed first to my tent, that I may make arrangements, procure camels, etc."

I fixed upon the following day for this movement.

I then sent for Hussun Mhatoor, from whom I anticipated some opposition. But he at once proposed it himself; a circumstance that gave me some uneasiness, especially as I afterwards heard that Hussun was in some way connected with Dana Bae's family. I lay down that night relieved of the most anxious part of a dangerous undertaking—the decison. The plan adopted was full of peril, but it afforded also a glimmer of hope, which I could not view in any other.

The next morning, April 14th, Hussun Mhatoor was sent for, and entered my tent, where, after the ceremony of tea, I thanked him for his escort thus far; regretted that it was here to cease; mentioned how ill provided I was with the means of rewarding service, but begged him, in token of kindness, to accept the tent in which I was sitting (and which I knew he coveted), and gave him a dress of honour. I then had the camels laden, and proceeded on my journey, accompanied by the old rogue, who hoped still to get something from me. My servants begged me to satisfy him ere we parted. I asked them whether they had observed the basin of the Caspian. "Yes." "Then fill up that, and I will satisfy Hussun Mhatoor." I would, indeed, have purchased his forbearance at any price, incensed as I was against him. But my circumstances were no secret to him, and I reflected that avarice such as his would only be inflamed by possession. That the more of my property I should bestow upon him, the more he would covet the remainder; and upon the sale of this property, at an immense loss, I depended for defraying my journey to Astrakhaun.

The reader has seen, that I had pledged myself to the Khaun Huzurut, to write His Majesty, and the British Envoy at Heraut, an intimation of my departure from the territories of Khaurism. Hussun Mhatoor had no right to demand this, because my journey still lay through the Khaun's territories.

But he would not suffer me to depart without some certificate of his having quitted me, and I had no means of bringing him to reason. I had now no tent, and was dependent upon a cloak of felt for shelter from the weather. I was sitting on my wet carpet, wrapped in this cloak, whilst the heavens were pouring their surplus waters upon me, when Hussun had the insolence to beg I would give him this sole defence left me from rain and storm. I considered the demand so wanting in respect, that I refused it in toto. We were at this time near a Kuzzauk tent, which the owner was cleaning for my accommodation. It was about seven miles from our late camp. I entered it, and wrote to Major Todd, the British Envoy at Heraut, dictating a letter for the Khaun Huzurut, which my Meerza wrote upon the back of the other, according to the Khaun's particular instructions. In the latter epistle, I stated, that owing to the great delay experienced on the road, the Russian vessels had visited, and again quitted, Mungh Kishlauk. That, through the same delay, the fifty days provisions I had taken, for a march of sixteen days, were nearly exhausted; so that I could not linger at Mungh Kishlauk, on the chance of getting a vessel, but was hastening, according to His Majesty's orders, toward Dahsh Gullah. That Hussun Mhatoor would conduct me no farther, but had furnished me with a Kuzzauk guide, etc. etc. etc. The old Meerza was so nervous at the presence of Hussun Mhatoor, that he but imperfectly expressed what I dictated. I, of course, did not venture to state, the extent of Hussun's misconduct, in a letter which he was to carry. I afterwards regretted having written this letter at all, because it served as a certificate that I had quitted Hussun's guidance. But I am not certain that it would have been possible to refuse it. I am to this day ignorant whether it ever reached the Khaun Huzurut. I sealed and delivered this letter to Hussun; and as evening was fast falling, walked forth to look at the flocks, assembling for the night around the tents. All the young lambs and kids, of which there were about one hundred, were tied neck by neck, in a spot apart from their dams. Each, in turn, was allowed a swig at its mother's teat, and afterwards withdrawn. The quantity seemed to me insufficient for the nourishment of the young. In the day time, the stronger and older of these kids form a separate flock, attended by one of the children of the family; and being of every pretty colour, look very beautiful, browsing upon the sides of the ravines. The sheep of Tartary is as tall, perhaps taller, than the common English breed. It is the Doombha, or large-tailed sheep, common throughout Central Asia. The tail is a huge sack of fat, in two lobes, growing at times to an enormous bulk. All the fat of the kidneys seems to be absorbed in the tail of the Doombha. And this fat is a delicious marrow. When the army of the Indus entered Candahar, the Europeans, unaccustomed to any thing so delicate, ate too freely of it, and many lives were in consequence lost. The fat was found congested in their bowels. The natives of the country, accustomed to it, eat it without restraining their appetite. Being the only oil possessed by the Kuzzauks, it is very valuable to them.

It may be believed, that with so many causes of anxiety, surrounded by men, plunderers from habit, whose language I did not understand, my eyes were sharpened to scrutinize keenly the countenances and gestures of those with whom I had to deal. Some of Hussun Mhatoor's Toorcumuns, who, heretofore, had seldom ventured to approach me, were now thrusting their heads into the tent, pointing at articles of my property, and gazing upon them as if already in their clutches. All this added nothing to my sense of security. I pointed it out to my people, wishing them to use all their faculties of observation, in order to get timely warning of any treacherous attempt. But there was a supineness about them all which nothing could awaken. Ali Muhummud was their oracle. They feared and hoped, exactly as they observed these passions in him. Ali again, had submitted himself so long to the Meerza and Summud Khaun, that he was now helpless. He really had no time to attend to my injunctions. Being fond of the Kullean himself, and dependent upon Summud Khaun's pipe and tobacco, which the latter worthy was much too great a man to prepare with his own hand, his whole life was taken up in preparing, and afterwards smoking this instrument of enjoyment. Commands and expostulations availed only for a few brief hours. A tobacco smoker, like a drunkard, has not the power to follow the suggestions of his reason, and Ali's slavish obedience to bullies, had been fostered during sixteen years of the severest bondage, at Khiva. I was, therefore, thrown upon my own resources, and could I have spoken the language of the country, these might have been sufficient. As it was, though I watched whilst my people slept, and endeavoured by day to multiply my presence and my observation; this incessant anxiety and wakefulness, and care, served but to defer the evil for awhile, and to add a few more grey hairs to the record of untimely suffering. I passed that night in the Kuzzauk tent, and the ensuing morning took leave of Hussun Mhatoor, who blessed me very devoutly, even as the jolly priest, in Hogarth's Gate of Calais, blesseth the English sirloin of beef. I then started, in company with Dana Bae, the Kuzzauk, for Dahsh Gullah.

CHAPTER XXII.

The treacherous Messenger—Perplexities—Resolution to return—How altered—Farther Symptoms of Treachery—Appearance of a Clump of Tooremmun Horse—Bivouac in the Rain—Symptoms of Treachery in the Guide—Fresh Perplexities and Difficulties—Reach a Kuzzauk Tent—The Kuzzauk Bride—The Hyæna—Reach Dana Bae's Tent—Interchange of Spoons—Arrangements for the Journey—Greed of Dana Bae—His formidable Oath—Dismissal of the Hyæna—Night in a Kuzzauk Tent—Journey resumed—Incessant Anxiety and Watchfulness—Arrive at a Chain of Mountains—The Black Russian Ambassador—Singular weather-worn Rocks—Fresh Causes of Suspicion—Reach the Caspian.

APRIL 15th.—We had proceeded upon our journey about nine miles, hoping that evening to reach Dana Bae's tent, when we heard loud shouts in our rear, and soon after a hideous Kuzzauk, clad in the skin of a bay horse, hair outward, and having a bonnet of black inverted sheepskin, rode up, vociferating loudly his injunction to us, to turn; for that a fleet of ten Russian vessels had just arrived, and anchored off shore.—" Did you not hear their guns?" he said; "you must be deaf not to have heard them." The air and aspect of this man were singularly suspicious. His tale was in the highest degree improbable; and yet, far too important to be neglected. I called him to my bridle, and enquired who sent him.

"No one sent me; I was wandering along the shore, when I saw ten ships approach and anchor close to the beach."

"What is Hussun Mhatoor's advice?"

"I have not see Hussun Mhatoor. I know nothing

of him. You must come back, or you will miss the ships. They saw your signal from the island."

He spoke with a great deal too much vehemence to be speaking truth, and his mission was exactly what might be expected of Hussun Mhatoor; who, having my letter of dismissal, would now be doubly anxious to detain me, at Mungh Kishlauk, where I should gradually melt into his jaws, without his incurring responsibility. I interrogated Dana Bae. He at first urged me to press on, but after considerable parley with the new comer, who appeared to be pressing upon him certain arguments of self-interest, which he was evidently anxious should be heard by no one else, he appeared to hesitate. I asked who this Kuzzauk was, whether he, Dana Bae, knew him.

"Oh! yes," he replied, "he is a near relation of my own."

"Do you believe his assertions?"

"I do."

"But you did not, just now."

"But he has given me fresh reasons."

I had now to balance difficulties. If Dana Bae was to be trusted as my guide, he was to be trusted in his opinion of this man's honesty, of which he must be a good judge. My first idea was, to send back one or two of my people, to ascertain the truth of the Kuzzauk's intelligence, and to remain in my present position, with Dana Bae and the baggage. But when I considered the extreme hazard to my people, of separation from me: that only Ali Muhummud knew the language; that I should be helpless without him, and my people equally so; that, during their absence I should be fettered to the spot, in the most painful anxiety on their account, I determined to leave my people and baggage with Dana Bae, at a neighbouring Khail, and myself ride back, to the port of Mungh Kishlauk. For this purpose I halted the camels, and, taking out my military uniform, proceeded to cast off my Asiatic attire. During this operation, I perceived the Kuzzauk engaged in a secret, but very interesting discussion, with the Toorcumun camel drivers, who had, hitherto, dissuaded me from attending to his advice. This awakened fresh suspicion. My change of attire being effected, I looked around in vain for the messenger. I enquired after him. He had gone to the Khail, at which I purposed leaving my servants and baggage. I did not like this. What was his object? He had declared it to be the purchase, for Hussun Mhatoor, of some tobacco. Therefore, he was either lying, and had some sinister design in this visit, or else he had lied in his solemn assertion that he had not seen Hussun. In either case, there was little doubt, that he was an emisary of Hussun, and that Hussun wished to entice me back, without himself appearing in the transaction. But this was not all, for Ali, whom I had instructed to watch him, had seen him take from his bonnet a folded note and shew it to the Toorcumun, as a preconcerted signal, that he was sent by Hussun Mhatoor.

My resolution was at once formed,—I perceived the imminence of the peril. I would *not* go back with this man, but hurry on to Dahsh Gullah. To my fresh discomfort, I found, on expressing this resolution to Dana Bae, that he was dissatisfied with it, although by the other plan he would have lost a job, for which I knew him to be most anxious; viz., the carriage of my baggage, and guidance of myself to Dahsh Gullah, for which he was to be handsomely paid. I had, therefore, little doubt, that Hussun had promised him a reasonable share in the plunder. I perceived that matters had become desperate. To return, was certain destruction; to advance seemed to offer this much of hope, that when Dana Bae was separated from Hussun and his agents, I might make it better worth his while to serve, than to betray me. I pressed on, accordingly, but was soon overtaken by the Kuzzauk, who vehemently insisted upon my return. I replied, that I would decide upon reaching

Dana Bae's tent. At present, I could give no answer. The reader must not suppose that the reasoning I have detailed, has been deduced from subsequent experience. It is a faithful transcript of part of what occupied my mind at the moment. To give any idea of the perplexity occasioned by my ignorance of the language at such a crisis, would be utterly impossible; it was to walk blindfold over heated plough-shares.

We proceeded in a drizzling rain, beating upon us under a violent and piercing wind, and adding nothing to the cheerfulness within. On the road, the Kuzzauk entered into many secret and earnest conferences with Dana Bae; and Ali Muhummud, with his usual inattention, suffered much to escape him, being indeed driven to the task of attending to their conversation, only by repeated threats. On the road, we passed many Kuzzauks, feeding their flocks of sheep and herds of galloways. With all these, the Kuzzauk had a great deal to say. He took each, in turn, aside, and spoke earnestly to him. I fancied he was urging them to ride back and inform Hussun Mhatoor of my movements. My position was so desperate, and I was so certain that this man was betraying me, that more than once my hand was upon my pistol with intent to shoot him.

Proceeding thus, it was close upon the evening hour, when I spied a party of horse, whom I knew, by the compact order of their march, to be Toorcumuns. They were ten in number, bearing down, from the right, direct upon our course. I supposed them, of course, to be sent by Hussun Mhatoor, in pursuit of me, and made arrangements for their reception. They kept us in suspense for some time, but when they approached within gun shot, turned off to the north, and were lost in the shades of darkness. This was the first time we had ever met a body of horse since leaving Khiva.

We continued to advance, and night set in, with continued wind and rain. Dana Bae had promised that we should reach his tent by sunset, but now he talked of midnight; and, at midnight, we found ourselves upon what he called the ground of his late encampment. It was now but a portion of the desert. I urged the necessity of obtaining shelter for the night. It was not so much on account of the weather (for that we had often braved) as that I fancied the rude honour of a Kuzzauk would be guarantee for our safety, whilst under his roof. Dana Bae, accordingly, went over the ground, upon pretence of searching for the mark which is usually set up to denote the direction taken by the late residents. After half an hour, he returned unsuccessful, and said, that we must put up for the night in the open air. We had no alternative; so, covering our goods with felts, and picquetting the horses, and turning loose the camels to graze, I sat down in the mire, back to the wind, and drew over me my cloak as a defence from the rain, which beat upon us all night; my servants, in spite of injunctions to vigilance, were soon asleep under nummuds, and, as I conceived, that such moments were their only intervals of peace, I could not find the heart to disturb them.

I therefore took up my own position sufficiently near theirs for speedy communication, but, at the same time, so as to command the motions of Dana Bae, the Kuzzauk messenger, and the camel drivers. The determination of Dana Bae,, that we should not enjoy the protection of his roof, just after the appearance of a body of Toorcumun horse, was suspicious. We had not the slightest reason for believing this to have been his late encampment, but, as I watched his motions throughout the night, I was convinced that his fidelity could not be relied on. Instead of sleeping, he was in close and earnest converse, now with the Kuzzauk, now with the camel drivers, speaking always in the lowest and most cautious voice, and endeavouring to elude my glance.

April 16th.—Morning at length broke, under the

same miserable skies. The earth was ancle deep in mud, and the rain still poured unceasingly upon us. Dana Bae would have left me to look for his tent; this I would not suffer, his presence being our sole protection, whatever that might amount to. The messenger was therefore sent, and in an hour returned with tidings. I ordered my people to lade the camels, and proceed to Dana Bae's tent. The camel-drivers objected. The Kuzzauk messenger had been in close converse with them all night, and had persuaded them not to risk Hussun Mhatoor's anger, by forwarding my views. They would take me back to Mungh Kishlauk, if I pleased, but not a step the other way. On referring to Dana Bae, he declared, that if I used these camels, even to reach his tent, he would instantly quit me. I made Ali reason with the camel drivers, and offer them rewards, and endeavour to learn from them the real state of my position; but all was vain. After many secret conferences, and stormy debates, they were leading off their camels, when I placed myself, armed, in their path, and effectually checked them. As for my servants, throughout the whole of this march, they were utterly useless. They had neither eyes, nor ears, nor minds, nor limbs, for my service. The most reasonable answer I could extort from any of them was, " A man cannot struggle with destiny. Whatever is to be, will be." Had we been left in the desert without camels, Dana Bae might have kept us there as long as he pleased, and until it was convenient to my enemies to fall upon and massacre us. He had only to say he could procure us no camels, and, not being in his tent, we should not have been his guests.

After another interval of about two hours, the Kuzzauk returned with Dana Bae's camels. We laded them, and proceeded toward the latter's tent, the camels and our horses sinking deep in the mire, at every step. Two hours' ride brought us in sight of a Kuzzauk tent, from which sallied a scarlet faced woman, with a wooden bowl of curdled milk, which she offered me to drink. A little further on, we were received hospitably at some tents, the inhabitants killing and boiling for us a sheep. The rain having somewhat subsided, the natives crowded to the door, and to an opening in the tent, to gaze upon me. One of these was a young bride, having a round red face, grey eyes, and on her head a high obelisk-formed hat, around which was wound the dirty-white cloth, that afterwards, passing under the chin, conceals the throat. The bride seemed to have no objection to admiration, and readily accepted our invitation to enter and take place in the circle, with her husband. The latter did not appear in the least to care for the freedom his wife took. I begged her to allow me to see her head-dress, which is peculiar to brides, and she readily removed the cloth and displayed it. I can remember only that it was covered with cornelians of all colours, set in silver.

The sheep was now brought, and we sat in a circle to discuss it. It had been boiled as usual, without any accompaniment of vegetable, meal, or bread; my stomach was not yet accustomed to eat flesh from which the warmth of life had not departed; but the others made a hearty meal, especially the Kuzzauk messenger, who, with his two monstrous claws, crammed huge masses of meat into his mouth, and then, taking the solid thigh bones of the sheep in his hand, twisted off the balls and sockets with his back teeth, and chewed them to powder, which, after sucking, he threw into the fire before us, then, with a strong knife hanging at his girdle, he scooped out the fibrous lining of the bone, which he treated in the same fashion, and, having devoured everything he could lay hands on, began to scrape, with the point of his knife, the tartar from his strong, short teeth, wiping the knife upon the upper leather of his boot. He looked so like a hyæna, whilst chewing the large mutton bones, that I pointed out the resemblance to my people, and he has since been known by the title of the Hyæna (Kuftarr).

Having remunerated these good people, I bade them farewell, mounted, and in the evening reached Dana Bae's tents. The old woman and her two daughters were in the tent when I entered. They saluted me by presenting both hands, which I clasped in mine; my baggage was carried into the tent, my horses were picquetted outside. This tent was a circular area, of about twenty-four feet diameter; one side was occupied by me and by Nizaum, who attended me. On my right was a screen of reeds, enclosing about twenty young lambs and kids, which thrust out their little heads, and bleated from time to time. On my left sat Dana Bae, his wife, and daughters. The door was opposite, and, in the centre, a fire, over which stood the hemispherical, cast-iron cauldron, so often alluded to, in which alone is cooked the flesh eaten by Kuzzauks. A sheep was killed; my stores supplied flour and rice, the use of which was evidently known, being occasionally obtained from the Russians. The meal was served up, and I insisted upon all the family attending. Their name was legion, and the scene to me was extremely gratifying, from the number of little faces that thronged in, until the tent seemed bursting with its contents. Just before the dinner came in, Dana Bae's eldest daughter, a girl perhaps eighteen years, took down a wooden spoon having a circular bowl, and presented it to me. It was neatly finished, polished, and varnished, the workmanship of Russia, and doubtless a valuable treasure in her eyes. I supposed she had merely intended me to use it at dinner, but her father, who was sitting by, said, "She makes you a present of it, you must keep it for her sake." I pressed the spoon to my lips, and, taking up one of my silver spoons, begged her acceptance of it, in exchange; then, seeing her younger sister, a far prettier girl, looking hurt, I made Nizaum get out another of my spoons, and presented it to her. All this was sufficiently absurd, and cuts a bad figure translated into English, but, amongst Kuzzauks one must be a Kuzzauk, and had I asked for a lock of the fair Kuzzauk's hair, in lieu of the spoon, not only should I have been esteemed a necromancer, who had some design upon the girl's life; but it would have been a day's labour, for the whole family, to have placed *me* in *exclusive* possession of the ringlet. It was scarcely possible to persuade them that the spoons were really silver. They bear my crest and initials, and may perhaps puzzle some future traveller. My drinking goblet was of silver also, and excited great admiration. The Hyæna seizing it, thrust it into his bosom, saying, "This is mine." But it was taken from him, for I was in no mood to gratify one who was plotting my destruction. It had been my purpose to dismiss this man with a dubious message to Hussun Mhatoor, previous to entering with Dana Bae into any arrangements for my further progress, but nothing could persuade him to leave me.

Dinner having been discussed, and all the bowls, platters, and spoons rendered as clean as the tongues and thumbs of the fair Kuzzauks could make them, I proceeded to arrange with Dana Bae for the journey; reminding him of his promise, to convey me to Dahsh Gullah in three days from that spot. This he now declared impossible, and demanded eight days. I remonstrated, and argued; but was eventually obliged to agree to make the journey in five days, it being about 150 miles. Then came the terms, in which we found we had to deal with a thorough-bred rogue; for he charged me, for the use of his camels for five days, a sum equivalent to their full value if purchased, besides remuneration to himself and son, for escorting us. In these terms he was inflexible; and although I had no money to spare, I was obliged to acquiesce, upon condition that he would swear solemnly, on the Koraun, to be faithful to me, and convey myself, my people, and goods safely to Dahsh Gullah in five days.

The Meerza's Koraun was accordingly produced from a variety of wrappings and boxes enclosing it. It was treated with infinite reverence, and handled as if it had been the apple of an eye. Each, ere he passed it from his hands, touched his forehead upon it. and stroking his beard, said, "God is great!" Dana Bae took it into his hands; and whilst we sat amongst his children and grand-children, beneath the roof of his tent, denounced upon himself and all his relatives the most fearful curses, if he should ever prove false to his solemn oath to be true to us, and to conduct us in safety. He then smeared the Koraun over his forehead, eyes, face, and beard; and my servants seemed to think his fidelity, from that moment, rivetted. I was glad to see them in good heart. But I am one of those who think good faith is not to be bound by words or forms of any kind, and that he who would prove traitor to the promise of a glance would not hesitate to infringe the most solemn covenant.

On commencing these discussions, the Hyæna said, "I will not suffer you to go towards Dahsh Gullah. I will arrest you."

"Will you?" I replied, touching significantly the small pistol which I wore in my belt, and looking him in the eyes. He immediately altered his bullying tone, and said, "If I do not, you must give me a present."

I replied, that it was not the English custom to give presents to those who threatened. That if he opposed me in the execution of the Khaun Huzurut's wishes, I should shoot him without remorse.

"But I have rendered you important service; I brought you news of the arrival of the Russian vessels."

"Very well; for that I thank you, and you shall have a dress of honour. But another time, do not threaten."

I sent for the dress accordingly, and he was apparelled in it. I then bade him ride back to Hussun Mhatoor, and say that I could not return to Mungh Kishlauk upon the representation of a stranger, who denied having seen him, Hussun; but that if he would send any one whom I knew, with the letter I had given him on parting, I should then be assured that the messenger had come from him.

I hoped to have got rid of the Kuzzauk at once, that he might return to Hussun, under the impression that I was waiting at Dana Bac's tent for an answer; but he still lingered about the camp, and did not quit it until the following day, when, of course, all my arrangements were known.

We lay down to rest, Dana Bac close on my left, succeeded by his wife and some of his children. His eldest daughter would have taken her place at my other side, had not Nizaum already fallen fast asleep there. She and her father were long in consultation about it, and seemed inclined to awaken Nizaum; but it ended by her leaving the tent, I thought reluctantly; and I was relieved from the most embarrassing of positions, the result of which it was impossible to foresee.

I was so little satisfied of Dana Bac's good faith, and so uneasy at what I had observed of his conduct, when he supposed me asleep or inattentive, that I would not now close my eyes, but assumed a half-recumbent posture, my hand ever upon the hilt of my dagger. A thousand trifling circumstances, which can scarcely be detailed, had led me to this distrust, and confirmed my resolution to be night and day upon my guard, to watch his slightest movements, and wake whilst my servants slept. My property, of inestimable value in his eyes, was now under his roof: a dagger stroke would have made it his, or, at least, have given him a very considerable share. His avarice I knew to be unbounded, his word unworthy of trust. He had vehemently opposed my journey to Mungh

Kishlauk, until the Hyæna whispered something in his ear. He then suddenly changed his mind, and recommended as strongly as he had opposed it. He had once unwarily designated my property — *his* property.

The night passed without incident; but being myself awake, I perceived that Dana Bae slept little, and was constantly stirring. The ensuing day, 17th April, at about twelve o'clock, all Dana Bae's arrangements were complete; and bidding the family farewell, we started, Dana Bae and his eldest son serving as guides, and my baggage being carried upon his three miserable camels, one of which was a female, followed by her young one. I observed, by my compass, that we made East by a point North, marching upon a dark mountain, which, from its position, I supposed to be that pointed out by a Kuzzauk as the locality of Dahsh Gullah. It proved, however, to be only the first of a chain of similar summits, whose course, nearly East and West, severs from the main land a considerable peninsula, of which I know not the correct designation.* At night we reached the verge of some chalk cliffs, and encamped upon the summit; that is, lay down in our cloaks upon the earth, whilst the horses were picquetted, and the camels set free to browse the wormwood.

April 18th.—Two hours before daylight resumed the march, descending the chalk cliffs into a narrow valley, up which we pursued our course for five or six hours, when we reached a Kawreeze† of pure water, where also appeared a few cultivated fields, the first we had seen since quitting the borders of the Oxus. Having here refreshed ourselves and cattle, we continued ascending several valleys, generally scarped by chalk cliffs, and encamped at night in one of them. According to my resolution, I never slept at night; at least, if my eyes were closed, 'twas but for a few

---

* In one of Arrowsmith's maps it is called Bacadzi.
† Chain of wells.

minutes at a time, and I looked out constantly to observe the motions of the guides. These were this night suspicious. They were awake, great part of the night, whispering together, and often looking toward me. I reclined always dressed and armed, ready to act upon a moment's notice; and I am convinced that this circumstance, and my wakefulness, saved my throat this night at least. How long I could sustain this system I knew not, and feared I must sink under it. It was, however, absolutely necessary, for my people were all heavy and determined sleepers, whom nothing could arouse.

April 19th.—Resuming the journey, under a drizzling rain, which had been treasured for us in the black mantle of clouds, that swathed the mountain chain in front; we continued ascending a steep path until noon; when after eight hours of toil, under a continual shower, we reached the summit of a range of heights, parallel to the dark mountain ridge on the left. Here we found some Kuzzauks feeding their flocks of sheep, and here we sat down for a couple of hours, to let our cattle graze, whilst the wind beat the rain in torrents upon us. We had attained a considerable elevation, having ascended during eighteen hours, and latterly, by a steep acclivity. Yet the dark peaks of the chain on my left were, still, very much elevated above me; I conjectured, that they must be two or three thousand feet higher than the level of the Caspian. They stretch nearly East and West, in line regular as a wall. The summits are bare, ragged, isolated, and I could count a triple range, of nearly similar height, in the same parallel rows. Their surface is singularly rugged, dark and barren. They are amongst the most antique-looking and weather-beaten mountains, that I have ever met with; and I have seen not a few. So far as I could guess, from the debris at their feet, and their general aspect, I should judge them to be of old sandstone formation.

To the foot of this mountain chain we descended, and put up for the night. Again, my vigilance was tested, and again the conduct of the guides confirmed my suspicions. Ali Muhummud had stopped at a black tent, to ask particulars of the route. The master of the tent said, "We hear that a black Russian ambassador is on a mission to the white Russians, at Dahsh Gullah. Is that he?" Ali Muhummud answered in the affirmative; and then came laughing, to report to me. I, however, considered it no joke. Some messenger must have preceded us, to have given this intelligence; and there was no safety in being mistaken for any Russian whatever, whether black, white, or grey. I commanded Ali, on all future occasions to disclaim for me such kindred, and to declare me to be an English ambassador, from Hindostaun, bearing the despatches of the Khaun Huzurut to the white king (Auk paudshauh), i. e. the Emperor of all the Russias. This, however it might bewilder them, being the truth, was, I thought, the safest and most advisable title. My guides had taken up a position for the night, where they could watch me without being seen. I made them quit this, and place themselves, so that without turning I could watch them. Long acquaintance with peril had taught me to sleep with one eye open. The slightest sound awoke me to full possession of my faculties; and I was always the person, to rouse up my servants for the march. The rain poured down upon us all night without mercy, and rendered our flight, for such I had ever considered it, very forlorn; for being encumbered by baggage, from which our pursuers were free, we could not hope to keep the advantage with which we had started, very long, over a country in so miry a condition.

April 20th.—We arose, under the rain, which had soaked us throughout the night, and followed the course of the mountain ridge on our left, always descending. We made little progress, owing to the depth of the mud in some places, and the slipperiness of the harder soil. The exposure was far from agreeable, but neither myself nor my people ever knew what it was to catch cold; and I believe, with Franklin, that it is a disorder unknown to dwellers in the open air. At noon, we reached a spot deserving notice: viz. a portion of the valley strewn with gigantic spheres of sandstone, many of them eight or ten feet high. It might have been the bowling green of the Cyclops. Indeed it was difficult to look at these mighty spheres, and consider their position, without fancying figures, of bulk sufficient to handle them. They appear to have been originally square blocks of sandstone, the angles of which, being worn off by the weather, had left them, short, round-headed cylinders. The base and upper angles of these, again, absorbing moisture, had given way at the edges, as we constantly see in ruinous brick-buildings, and thus an almost perfect sphere had been formed, of the original cube. This process was still incomplete in some of the cubes. What a subject for fable would not this have been, in the Highlands of Scotland! The anxieties and perils that beset me, prevented the enquiries I longed to make, for the legend attached to so singular a phenomenon.

Remounting, we pursued our course, still parallel with the mountain chain, which sentinelled our left flank in gigantic rank and file. I was not at all gratified by the appearance, about a mile on our right, of a clump of Kuzzauk horsemen, riding in close file, a thing extremely unusual. They did not approach nearer than a quarter of a mile; but bore off West by North. At night we searched for pasture; but the earth was too barren to bear any decent crop of wormwood, and the poor camels and horses, wearied as they were with their exertions in the muddy soil of the two preceding days, were picquetted in the rain, with almost no fodder.

April 21st.— Morning dawned upon us, through a

dripping mantle; but the earth was becoming rather firmer. At about noon we passed the last mountain of the range, and found that its successive and parallel ridges are here cut, at right angles, by the high and undulating steppe. Here we met some Kuzzauk camps on the move. The children packed securely in baskets upon the baggage, the women leading the strings of camels, excepting the more venerable dames, who were accommodated with seats on the camels. Some Kuzzauk horsemen appeared, one of whom, Yar Muhummud by name, wore the sheep-skin bonnet covered with broad cloth, which generally denotes wealth or dignity; he rode up to Dana Bae and his son, and entered into close conversation with them. Watching their movements, and seeing how anxious they were to conceal their conversation, I felt all my distrust revive, and desired Ali Muhummud to listen to what they said; but he very imperfectly obeyed.

Dana Bae's pony, which had always been a wretched animal, was now dead lame, and I insisted upon his changing it. This, after much demur, he consented to, but under some circumstances, the exact nature of which has escaped my memory, but which left no doubt upon my mind, of his treachery. I was careful to point out such facts to my people, and in particular to Ali, that it might incite them to vigilance; but Ali, about this time, began to take up a notion of Dana Bae's good faith, from which the most open demonstrations of treachery could not shake him: the consequences will be seen.

We proceeded over highly undulating ground, whose valleys and ridges bore North and South. Toward evening, we surmounted the last of the ridges, and saw in front, and perhaps a thousand feet below, a bay of the Caspian, which appeared both narrow and shallow, and which must have been, I imagine, the South-west corner of the inlet Kara Soo. Not a sail was visible upon it, and the guide declared, that vessels do not frequent this coast. He stated, that Dahsh Gullah was still about eighty or ninety miles from us. The sight of the Caspian was cheering. It was a point long looked for, and knowing that the Russian fort lay upon its borders, I felt less helplessly dependent upon our treacherous guides. In descending, some flints appeared on the hill side, which my people saw, for the first time, in their natural state, and eagerly searched for fragments, fitted for the purpose of striking fire. My servants, like myself, were a little cheered at the sight of the sea, but after all, said the Meerza, we ought never to have ventured upon this journey.

"Why not?"

"Because we tried a *fahl**⁎* the day previous to leaving Khiva. The question proposed was,—Whether this journey should be to our advantage; and the answer came, 'Thou shalt not go.'"

"What book did you use?"

"The word of God."

"I could have told you as much as that it would be most dangerous and difficult: I believe I did not conceal that from you. But it was *my* duty; and in such cases a servant of Government has no right to think of either danger or trouble."

We selected for our bivouac the least barren spot. I was ill pleased that the younger guide went, on pretence of discovering water, to a Kuzzauk Khail in the neighbourhood. It was, indeed, extremely difficult to prevent him from intercourse with people of the country, for at one spot he would profess ignorance of the position of water; at another he would lose the road; at another it was necessary to inquire for spots, affording the least scanty growth of wormwood for the

---

⁎ A process for attempting to penetrate the secrets of fate, not unknown in Europe. A question is proposed, and after prayer, the book, either Koraun or Poem, is suddenly opened. The line upon which the eye first falls is received as an answer.

camels and horses. Ali had orders to follow him about, but he frequently eluded these, being confident in the Kuzzauk's good faith. The camels, imperfectly fed, and suffering from toil in the mire of the country, were fast failing; and the horses were nearly exhausted, upon their reduced rations of hard rice, the only food we had for them.

CHAPTER XXIII.

A Rencontre—Its Result—Hasten our March—Toilsome Ascent of the Cliffs of the Caspian—Suspicious Conduct of the younger Guide—Bivouac at the Summit—Absence of the younger Guide—Meditations—Carelessness of my People threatening us with Ruin—Lighten the Camel Loads—Farther Preparations—Resumption of Journey—Ahris Mhatoor—Descent—Treacherous Conduct of the younger Guide—Attempt to secure the Elder in my Interests—The Monk—Bivouac—Suspicious Action of Dana Bae—The Alarm—The Night Attack—Result—Reflections—The Interposition—Fate of three of my Suite.

APRIL 22nd.—Last night I was more than ever vigilant, believing we should have been attacked. In the morning we proceeded to the shores of the Caspian, the ground here shelving much toward the water from the heights, whilst a few miles further on steep chalk cliffs, 700 feet high, rise abruptly from the waves. I was riding ahead, with Dana Bae, my servants following at some distance with the younger guide and the camels. On reaching the shore, six Kuzzauk horsemen, armed in various ways with long spears, swords, &c., rode up, and parleyed with Dana Bae. I called Ali, to interpret, and found that they desired me to turn back with them to their Khail, as they expected an order for my recall from the Khaun Huzurut; that the black Russian interpreter, whom they had sent prisoner to Khiva, had informed the Khaun that I was a spy, and that they were in daily expectation of the order aforesaid.

I enquired how they knew all this.

They said that the Hyaena had been sent by Hussun Mhatoor, to order them to arrest me, and that a Toorcumun had given the same instructions.

I replied that, if they would produce any order from the Khaun forbidding my advance, I would obey; but that, having his *order* to proceed in my pocket, I could not attend to their *expectations*. They replied, with many menacing gestures, that they would stop me by force. My people stood at some distance with the camels; Ali was near, but evidently not disposed for fighting. I rode up to them without more ado, and drew my pistols from the holsters. At sight of these little implements, they retreated some forty paces in great dismay, but, finding they were not pursued, turned, and sent one of their party, a young man of some two and twenty years, on foot, to parley. He drew near with some caution, and finding no hostile demonstrations, sat down upon the ground to argue the point with Dana Bae. His arguments have been detailed; he repeated them, thumping the earth every now and then in a decisive manner with his thick whip. Ali stood by to listen. Dana Bae upon this strongly urged me to go back, and wait for the Khaun's order. I had in my pocket the only order the Khaun would ever issue on the subject, and was well aware that it was a trap of the arch-fiend Hussun Mhatoor, whose prey I, my servants, and all my property must inevitably become, should I listen to the suggestion. I replied, as before, that I bore in my pocket the Khaun's commission, was his ambassador, proceeding upon business of the most vital importance; that if any one checked me, Khiva would be lost, and the wrath of the Khaun Huzurut wreaked upon the intermeddler; that, having such commission, I should treat as the Khaun Huzurut's foe any one who attempted to obstruct my path, and shoot him without hesitation. As for Dana Bae, I insisted upon his immediately proceeding toward Dahsh Gullah. He complied very reluctantly, lingering and looking often behind him, I asked him why he did not make haste. He said he feared the horsemen. I desired him to give himself no trouble about them, to be faithful, and to obey my orders, and to leave the horsemen to me. The younger guide seemed still more reluctant. We lost sight of the horsemen as we gained the hollow of the sea-shore; but this was little satisfaction, for our camels, half dead with fatigue, and our horses in bad condition from short commons, it were easy for them at any time to overtake us. By daylight, and in any but overwhelming numbers, I cared little for the idea of an attack; but, as our guides were evidently acting in concert, we might be surprised at night, and cut off by a handful.

I called Ali to my side, and questioned him upon the Kuzzauk resources. He said that hundreds of horsemen could be mustered at a few hours' notice, but that, at the sound of fire-arms, all would take to their heels. This determined me to commence hostilities with a discharge of fire-arms. I then called my other followers around me. The old Meerza had one of my best Persian sabres; but, although I knew he would faint at the sight of it unscabbarded, I could not dishonour him by depriving him of that necessary appendage to the gentleman. I therefore bade him and the others remember that they were the triumphant defenders of Heraut (one of them had actually been there during the siege), that they had there found 5000 Herauties equal to 40,000 Persians, i. e. one Herautie to eight Persians; that each Persian was well known to be equal to two Toorcumuns, and one Toorcumun to ten Kuzzauks; therefore one Herautie was equal to 320 Kuzzauks; that now was the time to prove the correctness of this estimate, for that if we came to blows, it would be for life and liberty. Summud Khaun had my double carabine and a sabre, not to mention a defensive armour of about three pair of slops, filled full of sugar, biscuits, tea, tobacco, flints, and steel knives of all classes and sizes, tea-cups, spoons, handkerchiefs, etc. etc. etc. and as many tough cloaks as might have puzzled a six-pounder shot. Ali Muhummud carried a long Kuzzauk spear, a formidable weapon in a true hand; and at his side was my regulation sword, a piece of excellent stuff, if he but knew how to use it. Hajji had a sabre, but Yakoob and Maimood were without arms, my poverty on leaving Khiva having prevented the purchase. Nizaum had a sabre, and was mounted upon my best horse, a Toorcumun. I told Yakoob to remember that I had found him a groom, and promoted him to the dignity of my Meer-a-Khor (lord of the manger); that I expected him to signalize his new title, and let the Kuzzauks know the weight of arm of a Knight of the Manger. I promised to give him a sabre the instant we should stop. I made them talk over our predicament lightly, and help it out with a little laughter. Yakoob swore a tremendous oath, that he would not be wanting in the melée; and even Maimood readily agreed to charge the Kuzzauk array, hatchet in hand.

We pushed on, following the borders of the sea, until we came to the cliffs, under which we found a rocky path, that, soon turning to the right, scaled the heights by a very steep ascent. At a third of the ascent, the female camel fell under her burthen, and when half an hour had been lost in endeavouring to get her up, another half hour was expended in shifting her burthen to the other camels, overloaded as they already were. Whilst thus busied, Nizaum's and Ali Muhummud's horses commenced a furious combat upon the steep side of the cliff, falling and rolling repeatedly, and again renewing the fight. The ferocity of Toorcumun horses, on such occasions, is to be conceived only by those who have viewed it. I feared that both would have been precipitated down the cliff, just at the moment their services were most required: but we at length secured them, and struggled on, leaving the female camel on the road. At about 200 feet from the summit, we found ourselves opposed by a sheer precipice, without footpath. The younger guide had slipped away in the confusion, upon pretence of driving on the female camel. I did not like his absence, but it was extremely difficult to prevent such a casualty, owing to my own ignorance of Toorkish, and the pleas our position continually afforded, for one of them getting away.

We turned back, the descent proving almost as harassing as the ascent, to the overtasked camels. Dana Bae's son met us, and immediately pointed out the right path; but, not content with this, he clambered up, and, taking off his large bonnet, began waving it at the full sweep of his arm, in pretence of signal to us, who were near enough to see a motion of his finger, but in reality, to the horsemen below; to whom, the whole time, his eyes were turned. I called him to me, and drawing a pistol, assured him I would blow out his brains, if I saw him make any more signals. This stopped him for a while, but his vigilance was unceasing, and he had a thousand ways of signalling, upon pretence of shewing the road, or scratching his head, or helping on the camels. I felt assured that there was no safety in company of this villain. I therefore pointed out to my people the signals of the younger guide, ordering them to cut off all communication between the guides and the Kuzzauks of the country; and begged Ali, in particular, to throw off his lethargy, and put his whole soul into the task of watching the guides, in which lay our sole hope of safety. Ali replied, "I will answer for it with my life's blood, that these guides are true men."

I was excessively disgusted: for any one possessing eyes must have observed the conduct of the younger. But Ali was infatuated; and my commands, though assented to, were never half fulfilled. I perceived, therefore, that all depended upon myself, and determined to renew my vigilance. Could I have conjectured what motive the miscreants had for their treachery, I should have adopted another precaution: but I did not even suspect, until the catastrophe, that Summud Khaun, who, as steward, had charge of the silver for current expenses, fearing, in case of treachery, that this circumstance might point him out as a particular mark for violence; had made over a bag containing 700 tungas (small silver pieces, each worth five pence), to the younger guide. This sum, constantly before his eyes, and an unheard-of treasure in his estimation, was an irresistible incentive to treachery: for the whole became his, unknown to any one, and in addition to any claim he might have upon the plunder, if he could only get rid of me. Had Summud Khaun given me a hint of this characteristic act of his, I should at once have solemnly conferred the money upon our guides, in addition to the reward promised them on our safe arrival.

On reaching the summit of this lone and toilsome ascent, I found the camels quite incapable of moving without rest and food, and although speed was our only chance of safety, was obliged to consent to a halt of two hours. No water was procurable. The younger guide rode with a skin in search. I had seen half melted snow under the cliff, so that he ought to have been able to fill the water-skin immediately. I, meanwhile, was busied in changing my dress for one better suited for active exertion, and my heavy boot for half-boots of English fashion, so that I might be able to relieve my horse by walking. I braced on the sabre which I carried as a present from the Khaun, and made over my own more beautiful blade to Nizaum, who bequeathed his, in turn, to Yakoob. Summud Kaun was directed to carry on his person, i. e., in his breeches, the jewelled harness; stowed away there with some ten pounds avoirdupois of grocery and hardwares; the jewelled dagger I wrapped up carefully, and bound in my girdle, wearing my own dagger beside it. I then ordered the goods to be overhauled, and every article that could be spared to be left behind, in order to relieve the camels. I made them distribute to each horseman about 15 lbs. of rice, the only grain left, both as a relief to the camels, and in order to render us independent of them, in case of absolute flight. But, in selecting property to be sacrificed, the avarice of my people constantly interfered. Although death was close upon our traces, every thing depended upon speed; yet each article excited their cupidity, and many they had not heart to part with. For instance, two large gaudy tea-trays were seized by Ali, who entreated permission to carry them upon his own back. There were also some articles of bulk and value, which I reserved to be bartered for food or passage at Dahsh Gullah. About half a camel's burthen was all that I got rid of; these we could not leave upon the road, or they would have incited to pursuit the whole country. We made them over to Dana Bae, who lodged them in a Kuzzauk tent, at hand.

Meanwhile, the absence of the younger guide excited my suspicions. I armed myself, and proceeded alone on foot to the cliffs, in search of him. I found here water, not a quarter of a mile from our bivouac, yet he had been absent a full hour. I met him returning up the cliff. For want of the Toorkish language, I could not interrogate him; but I had little doubt how he had been employed.

I descended a portion of these gigantic cliffs, and took up a position from which I could command both the Caspian and the plain we had quitted. I gazed intently over the latter, but could observe nothing stirring, which only made me apprehend that our pursuers were screened at the base of the cliffs. I listened attentively. Not a sound was stirring, excepting the faint murmur of the waves of the Caspian, as they fell amongst the rocks below. The Caspian itself lay smiling before me, blue and serene as the unclouded heavens, but without a sail, without an ark of refuge, cold and pitiless as the grave. Yet an Englishman is never thoroughly at home when remote from the sea—the bulwark of his liberty, the field of his renown; and the aspect of these waters recalled to me many sad and sweet memories of the past, and many an unrealised dream of the time to come. My present situation of peril and anxiety was not forgotten, but ceased to burthen my mind; and I enjoyed a luxury long foreign to me, but indulged in too freely in former days.

When I aroused myself from this dreamy mood, I found my hopes brighter and my heart lighter. I was in the most imminent peril, it is true; but all was not yet lost, and provided that by vigilance I could guard against surprise, I thought that superior courage, the weight of our horses, and the despair with which we ought to be animated, might carry the day against great odds. Peril, with all its disagreeables, has for its accompaniment a chord of the sublime; and had my men been of the fighting breed, or myself acquainted with the Toorkish language, I would not willingly have exchanged my position for one of greater safety.

I walked back to the bivouac, where arrangements were still in progress for the march. Here, in spite of my repeated orders, I found a Kuzzauk of the country, who had arrived on a camel, in close conference with the guides. The supineness of my followers was baffling all my precautions. The camels were now very lightly laden, and though exhausted by an ascent which had occupied several hours, contrived to crawl forward under their loads. My Yamoot horse was, however, quite gone, and could with difficulty be led forward, and the horse I rode was fast failing, so that I was obliged to trust much to my feet. We pressed on over a high plain, by a course nearly parallel with the shore, but not in sight of the sea. At about three o'clock we passed near a Kuzzauk Khail. Several of the inhabitants came forth to gaze at our cavalcade; and the guides pleaded the necessity of inquiring about fodder and water. Ali was ordered to listen to every word, but being quite confident of the honesty of our guides, was much more occupied in smoking the Kulliaun. One of these

Kuzzauks, whom I afterwards knew as Ahris Mhatoor (i.e. Ahris, the hero), was a tall raw-boned fellow, of the most hideous aspect. He wore a scanty and peculiar cap of tawny lambskin fur, scarcely covering the upper part of the head. With him the younger guide contrived, in spite of my exertions, to exchange many private words and significant glances. We rode on over a high steppe scantily supplied with wormwood, and occasionally marked by Kuzzauk cemeteries. Evening was closing when we found ourselves descending the cliffs into a deep and wide ravine, with the prospect of immediately re-ascending. All this was sad work for our exhausted cattle. My horse was almost past work, and I was obliged to walk, refusing all the proffers of my people; for in cases of life and death, all are on a level: and as we had only now sixty miles before us, I did not fear on my own account.

On this descent, the younger guide contrived to lag behind, when not actually driven forward by my orders; and from time to time, I observed him turn and wave his arms wildly. I rode up to him, and sternly commanded him to keep his face in the direction of our march. On myself looking round, I perceived several human figures amongst the rocks in the distance; but these might be shepherds, of whom there were many tending their flocks in the neighbourhood. When the young miscreant perceived that I would not quit him, he stopped on pretence of saying his prayers, a ceremony he had never before performed, and turning his person round, went through the usual prostrations, signalling to the people amongst the rocks, whenever he thought my eye removed from him. I waited patiently the conclusion of his prayers, and then made him precede me.

I had at our late halt called Dana Bae to me, had taken out and displayed to him one of the Khaun Huzurut's letters, bearing the royal seal, and explained to him the nature and importance of my office, and how much the Khaun's heart was set upon the success of my mission. Should it be interrupted by any one, I assured him the Khaun would root out him and his whole family from the earth. I told him all the anxiety of the Khaun for my safety, and the strict orders he had given Hussun Mhatoor respecting it. Finally, I assured him of rich and ample reward, beyond his highest expectations, if he proved faithful to me. He was lavish of his professions; and as I could make it, I thought, worth his while to be faithful to me, I did not altogether discredit them. I did not know that Summud Khaun had made him my purse-bearer.

The country we were now entering is broken by wild crags and chasms. On the pointed summit of one of the heights stood a dark figure, far too gigantic to be human, yet resembling a monk in a cloak and cowl, with hand outstretched as if warning or threatening. Being on foot, I could not get near the guide to inquire what it was.

On reaching the valley, a barren clay soil appeared, producing scarcely a blade of vegetation. Evening had fallen, our cattle were exhausted. The high cliffs were to be ascended; the moon would not rise for some hours. Anxious as I was to push on, and much as I disliked such a position of bivouac, there seemed no possibility of surmounting those cliffs without refreshment to the cattle. Our guides insisted upon the necessity of this; and I reluctantly complied. We chose the only spot presenting a few stunted plants of wormwood. The guides had, of course, brought no food for the camels, in a country where grain is unknown. They were dependent upon this miserable browse. A deep water-course was on the south, occasionally fringed with shrubs. Around us was the shadow of the cliffs. The sky was overcast, and it was a spot of gloom. I ordered my people not to lay aside their arms, nor unsaddle their horses, but to be vigilant, and ready to mount at a moment's notice. I calculated that we were beyond pursuit of any but cavalry. Indeed, in a country so abounding in galloways, it is contrary to the genius of the people to attack on foot; and as the earth was very hard, I reckoned upon hearing the approach of horses in time to mount and form a front.

I had finished a hasty repast, and was awaiting the rising of the moon to renew the journey. Having the prospect of a walk of sixty miles before me, I found it necessary to husband my strength, and was reclining on my carpet, listening to every sound, armed and on my feet at the slightest stir. I laid my ear along the earth from time to time, the better to catch the sound of hoofs. My people had finished their dinner, and were variously disposed of. I had no means of posting sentinels, for each servant found ample occupation in attending to his horse, etc. Nevertheless, we kept a decent look-out. Suddenly, Dana Bae rushed forward to the spot where I reclined, having Summud Khaun's battle-axe raised above his head, and almost stumbling over me. Thinking he was about to strike, I caught up and presented a pistol. He paused, shaded his eyes with his left hand, made some apology, and left me. The gesture was suspicious; but amid so many causes of suspicion, I was sometimes inclined to believe my fancy was exaggerating. He immediately proposed that we should extinguish the fires, as tending to point out our position to an enemy. This precaution, constantly adopted in warfare, rather re-assured me, and I ordered that it should be carried into effect. I afterwards learned that it was a preconcerted signal. It saved a few lives, for the light of the fires would have enabled me to strike without fear of killing my own people. Hitherto there had not been the slightest noise. I was aware, indeed, that the younger guide had slipped away in the darkness to a neighbouring Khail, under pretence of getting water; but this was a daily occurrence, and I rather expected the attack would be deferred, until we should be entangled in the passes of the cliffs ahead, where resistance was extremely difficult, and our superior mounting of no avail.

Suddenly cries were heard in the direction of the water-course. My impression was, that our enemies were endeavouring to cripple our march, by stealing a horse or two; I therefore snatched up my pistols, and rushed toward the horses. Here I found Nizaum and Hajji with their sabres drawn. Yakoob assured me the horses were safe, and as the sounds now came from another spot, I hastened thither, followed, as I supposed, by Nizaum and Hajji. Here all was confusion, but the darkness was so great, that I could distinguish nothing but moving figures; whether servants or robbers I knew not. My finger was upon the trigger of my pistol, but I dared not fire, lest I should kill my own people. Suddenly, I was struck from the rear by three clubs, falling together. I staggered, but, the clubs being of willow, I did not fall, until the blows were, the next instant, repeated, and I was prostrated, though without losing my pistol. I sprang to my feet; but the Kuzzauks, who were standing over me, instantly struck me to the earth, and one of their clubs falling upon my arm, struck the pistol out of my hand. I believe I was stunned for the moment. When I recovered, having still my sabre at my side, I laid hand upon it, and had reached my knee and right foot, when several clubs took effect, and stretched me upon my back, and two Kuzzauks threw themselves upon me, the one seizing my sabre, and endeavouring to wrench it, belt and all, from my body; the other trying to tear away the Emperor's jewelled dagger, bound in my girdle. A third, with a light club, showered blows from behind upon my head and shoulders. The struggles of the plunderers recalled me to consciousness, which previously was almost lost. Their tugs at my girdle assisted the strength still left me; I suddenly sat up, and drawing my own dagger, stabbed at the junction of the throat and thorax the Kuzzauk in front of me. The mad exultation of that moment is indescribable. He fell, and I was turning upon the other, when I saw the arm of a fourth raised to strike me with some weapon. I raised my dagger to guard my head. The sabre fell upon my hand, severing two fingers, disjointing the thumb, and shattering the solid ivory handle of the dagger. Other blows of clubs, from the rear, stretched me again upon my back, no longer able to move. I know not whether I lost my senses; but if so, when they returned, they were clear as the noon day. My right hand was numbed, but I knew not the extent of damage, and tried to rise. The slightest motion of the head produced vertigo, and my limbs were quite powerless, the flesh being, in fact, beaten to a jelly; but whenever I lay still, the clearness of all my faculties returned upon a mind, as calm as ever I had known it.

I collected my scattered thoughts. I reasoned, as often I had reasoned in extremity. I summed up the full bitterness of my present condition, wounded, helpless, in the hands of robbers, in a desert far remote from my people, on a shore scarcely known by name to the civilized world; death threatening me at every moment, escape utterly hopeless, and worst of all, my mission lost; all my anxieties, toils, and sufferings, endured in vain; and I asked myself, whether I had ever been worse: and I referred to sufferings, compared with which, the present seemed a jest. The hand of God had, unhoped, delivered me from those, and now I inly prayed, not for deliverance, but for constancy and strength to encounter the worst, without faltering, or disgracing my country, or my name. The moment was sufficiently gloomy, but there flashed upon my mind the remembrance of hearts, precious in the sight of the most High, whose daily prayers were for a son, a brother: and whilst this beacon burned for me, I could not utterly despair.

The exact succession of thought I cannot remember; but having often afterwards recalled those moments, whilst the impression was recent, I recollect all that passed through my mind. Every now and then a Kuzzauk spied me out, and cut at me, in passing, with sabre, hatchet, or club. Thinking it would be something to save my eyesight, I laid my left hand over my eyes, as I lay helpless on my back. A sabre fell upon it, inflicting a deep gash, and laying open my right eyebrow. The hand would probably have been severed, but for a ring which a sister had drawn upon it many many years previously, and which had never since been removed. If ever she read this record, she will have pleasure in the thought, that her gift has saved me from being utterly crippled. As at each fresh blow I felt my senses reel, I fondly hoped it was death. I held my breath sometimes, to assist the escape of my spirit: I would not rise a hand to break the blow I saw aimed at me. But the swoon was only momentary: my senses and my reason returned, clear and calm as ever: and the difficulty of finding death, re-awakened that instinct by which we cling to existence.

Just then a Kuzzauk bent over me, and thrust his hand into my bosom. I supposed he was seeking plunder, but soon found that he laid his hand upon my bare breast, as if to ascertain whether I still lived. If, thought I, he finds me still alive, he will mangle me a little more, and leave me just as much alive as ever. I instinctively held my breath, and he left me uncertain of my condition. He, however, soon returned, and again thrust his hand into my bosom; and finding me still warm, and probably detecting the pulses of my heart, stood over me, and with his matchlock warded off the blows made by others as they passed me. Nizaum, at that moment, reeled up to the spot, under the blows of several of the brigands, crying aloud for quarter. He fell at my head, and seeing me to all appearance lifeless, forgot his own condition to weep over me, saying, "Aye, Sahib, Sahib!" Summud Khaun I had long heard on my left, groaning and uttering aloud the profession of the orthodox, under the apprehension, perhaps, of being mistaken for his Feringee master; the black Russian necromancer, idolater.

Perceiving that this Kuzzauk (Cherkush Bae,*) had friendly intentions, I touched his foot. He bent his head to mine, and I whispered, "Tillah," gold, a word common to both Persian and Toorkish. He answered eagerly, have you gold? I endeavoured to draw out my purse with my right hand, and then discovered, for the first time, the extent of the damage. I, therefore, with the left hand, which was less injured, gave him my purse. Then pointing to Nizaum and Summud Khaun, who lay on each side of me, and afterwards to heaven, I said, "For the love of God;" an Arabic phrase also current in Tartary. He pressed my hand, and signed me to lie still, which I afterwards did, being indeed unequal to any exertion. Cherkush Bae stood over us, protecting us from the other brigands.

I again rolled my eyes around, endeavouring to get some hint of the fate of my other followers, and to impress upon my mind a scene which, should I get out of my present predicament, would be worth remembering. The night was still sufficiently dark. Uncouth forms were rushing here and there, in their horse-skin dresses and sheep-skin bonnets, brandishing clubs and hatchets. Shouts and sounds, as of strife, were still heard, but they were fast subsiding. Indeed, we were taken at such disadvantage by the assailants, between forty and fifty in number, who, being in correspondence with the guides, had arranged everything as they pleased; that only two of the people had even drawn a weapon, and not a blow was struck on our side, excepting the dagger stroke above mentioned. The two swords were instantly beaten down,

* Cherkush, a corruption of Sirkush, the Rebellious.

and blows fell so thick, that there was no time to answer them, even could we have seen at what to strike. The Kuzzauks who had been watching our motions for some time, had never lost sight of one of us, and accordingly struck with confidence and effect.

One of my pistols, which had fallen from my hand, was now picked up by a Kuzzauk, and discharged, either intentionally or by accident. I saw two or three of them take to their heels at the report, in the wildest terror. I was good-natured enough to hope it had astonished them, in more ways than one. I could nowhere distinguish Ali Muhummud, Yakoob, the Meerza, Hajji, or Maimood. It seemed scarcely possible that they should have escaped a snare so artfully set. I feared they had been killed; and yet death was the best fate I could possibly hope, for myself, and those at my side. One or two of my horses were standing near, the rest seemed to have escaped. Several times Kuzzauks approached to rifle me, but were driven off by Cherkush Bae; once, when he left me for an instant, a fellow seized my half-boot and endeavoured to drag it off; and another time a Kuzzauk, catching my mangled hand in his, dragged me like a sack along the earth, and cast me down near one of our fires, which had been rekindled, that he might see the better to plunder. I made no motion, and he thought me dead. Cherkush Bae came back in time to save me. He led Nizaum to the same spot, and thither Summud Khaun was dragged, groaning like fifty, and uttering his articles of belief. Here, also, several of the assailants collected, to examine the spoils they had taken, and talk over their exploits. They pointed often at me, and several times weapons were lifted to finish me; but so far as I could guess, Cherkush Bae told them I was already dead. Again a Kuzzauk seized me by the foot, and endeavoured to draw off my boot. The leg recoiled, perhaps, with too much elasticity, and he declared that I was still alive. This Cherkush Bae seemed to deny. He stood over and effectually protected me.

At length one of them, the youth, I think, who had parleyed with us in the morning, drew his sword, and aimed a blow at my head. I was taken by surprise, and flinched, which set my existence beyond doubt; I therefore prepared for death. What prevented this I know not, or rather, I know not what arguments were used by Cherkush, in the stormy debate that ensued, to save my life; perhaps the general order of the Khaun Huzurut, to save the lives of all Russian prisoners. He now placed a folded cloak under my head, and, whilst he was doing this, I contrived to slip cautiously into his hand all my despatches, excepting one, a letter from the Khaun Huzurut, which I kept as a testimonial of my office, as the Khaun's ambassador; I also gave him my gold seals and keys.

Yakoob, Knight of the Manger, was now led up under the blows of several Kuzzauks, and forced to sit near me. Many melancholy greetings passed between him and Nizaum, and I exerted myself to mutter a few kind words to him. It appeared that he was not much hurt; his weapon had been struck out of his hand ere he could draw it. Nizaum's right arm was numbed by a blow from the back of a hatchet, but whether broken or not he could not say. He had been armed with my beautiful Damascus blade; but the blows of the assailants fell so suddenly, and so thick, that he could only raise it above his head to ward them. Two or three of the clubs of soft wood were divided upon the edge of this weapon, as if they had been deal shavings. Ahris Mhatoor, however, rushing forward, beat down the sabre with his hatchet, and then felled poor Nizaum with a blow of the back of that instrument; it being the object of the Kuzzauks to save the lives of all but myself, in order to sell them as slaves.

Summud Khaun, who, since entering Kuzzauk

land, had volunteered to carry my carabine (knowing the fear of Kuzzauks for fire-arms), had just carefully drawn the leathern case over the gun to shield it from dew, when the Kuzzauks rushed upon him, smashed the carabine with a blow, and compressed, grievously, with sundry others, the half-dozen cloaks upon his shoulders, breaking whole pounds of biscuit and loaf-sugar in his breeches pockets, and finally rolling him over and over, like a large ball of worsted, now head, now heels to the zenith. As soon as his extreme astonishment had somewhat subsided, his wit returned, and perceiving the great inconvenience of being mistaken for a Russian, necromancer, and idolater, he set up his pipes, as we have seen.

At this moment, the poor old Meerza was led up to the fire; his hands bound together; his shaven head covered with bruises, and streaming with blood; his face bloody, and one of his eyes forced almost out of the socket, as I supposed, by the pressure of the brain from within. He staggered forward, saying to each of the brigands in turn "Have the goodness to untie my hands," as if it were a request which could not be refused. They answered him with blows and kicks. He then appealed to his fellow-servants. They begged him to be quiet, for that the hand of God was upon us, and we must submit. He again turned to the robbers, his wits evidently were deranged; "Baba Jan," he said, "Baba Jan, dust-i-mauh Kullass-koon." A brutal Kuzzauk bestowed upon him two violent kicks upon the back. He fell upon his face, and did not afterwards move; I hoped he was dead. But the brutality of this act so roused my blood, that I could not lie still; I endeavoured to lift my head from the folded cloak, and fell back swooning, I hoped dying, but my time was not yet come.

CHAPTER XXIV.

Hilarity of the young Guide—The Letter—Scene—Consultations and Reports of the Kuzzauk Assailants—Night on the Field of Strife—Meditations—Desperate Posture of my Affairs—Triumph of the Coward Yar Muhummud—State of my Party—Symptoms of a Move—Ahris, the Hero—Retrograde Movement—Helpless Condition of my Meerza—Our shattered and melancholy Cavalcade—Halt at Soosun Uttah—Summud Khaun's Sagacious Arrangement for our Safety—Spite of the younger Guide—The Curse of the Koraun—Arrival of Tents—Arrangements for our Disposal—Yar Muhummud and the Tempter—First Repast as Captives—Soft Flattery in an unknown Tongue—Character of Ahris Mhatoor—The Covenant—Night Alarms—Varieties of Death—Second Night of our Captivity.

THE Kuzzauks continued to collect at the spot where I lay, until about twenty were assembled; amongst these were the two guides, the younger, laughing and enjoying the joke exceedingly. As most words used in Toorkish to denote the products of civilised life are borrowed from the Persian tongue, I had little difficulty in comprehending the topics of discourse, although unable to follow the speakers. The young miscreant told them, as a great joke, that I had a letter as long as his arm.

This letter, I now made Nizaum spread before Cherkush Bae; and as he could speak a few words of Toorkish, I made him point out the royal seal, and explain, that I was the Khaun's ambassador, and no Russian as they supposed. The letter was handed round the circle, but none present could read it. All therefore gravely shook their heads, and it was returned to me. I fancied, however, that it had occasioned some doubt. I kept this letter always upon my person, that I might desplay it on emergency. I could not move my head without swooning, but so long as I lay still, I had the fullest possession of my faculties. They were mercifully spared me, for none of my people made the slightest use of theirs, excepting, indeed, Summud Khaun, whose groans and creed were so characteristic of the man, that, despite my exhausted condition and forlorn predicament, they struck me with a sense of the ludicrous.

There was indeed a dash of comedy mixed up in this melancholy scene. A young Kuzzauk had already apparelled himself in my embroidered uniform, and was strutting before me in evident content; others were half dressed in their own uncouth attire, half in mine, or in my servants, and looked as might look a detachment of hogs and bears, rigged out for a masquerade; several rudely endeavoured to tear my furred cloak from my back: but this was prevented by my protector. He could not, however, prevent them from wrenching from my side the silver-mounted scabbard of the Khaun's sabre. The blade had been carried off when I was cut down. In endeavouring to loosen for them the clasp of the belt, the shattered condition of my right hand became manifest, and excited much discussion, the nature of which I could only faintly conjecture, from the expression of their rude countenances, dimly lighted by the glare of the fire. Cherkush Bae expressed much sympathy for the injury, which he proceeded to examine, handling the limb with great tenderness. "Well, Nizaum," I said, "I suppose all the fingers are lost?" Such, indeed, was my impression, for I felt them dangling in every direction.

"Not all, Sir," replied Nizaum. "One is safe, praised be God; nay! two."

"Which are they; the little finger, I know, is dangling?"

"No, sir, that's the forefinger that dangles past the little finger."

Such proved to be the case. The forefinger hung

only by the sinew. The middle finger was cut through the bone, close to the knuckle. The thumb was disjointed, but the mischief had ended at the third finger, in which was a deep gash. Cherkush Bae gave me to understand that the forefinger must come off. I put my hand into his, and signed to him to cut away. He laid the sinew upon the handle of his hatchet, and drew from his belt an ugly lump of iron, passing current in those rude countries as a knife. This proved to be so blunt, that he was obliged to sharpen it upon the back of the hatchet; even then, it was long in cranching its way through the tough sinew. He then bound up, in coarse rag, the shattered hand, without attempting to adjust the fingers, and twined some scraps of linen round the wounded fingers of the left hand, carefully concealing the ring, which (as it was impossible to draw it off otherwise) might, if seen, cost me another finger.

Several hideous Kuzzauk women had for some time appeared. The Meerza, it would seem, had been bound by these, after being struck down by the clubs of the men. They lighted a second fire, and prepared a pilau of rice and mutton. Around this a group soon collected, curiously composed, of the wild, scarcely human costume of the Kuzzauks; horses' skins with fur outward, bonnets of wolf's and lamb's skin, and our garments hanging upon unaccustomed backs. I perceived, by their glances, that much of their conversation related to me, and as it was conducted in whispers, augured from it no good to myself. One of them, upon being questioned, glanced at me, and then drew his finger significantly across his throat. I determined not to struggle.* I perceived that only three of my horses were present, and hoped that my three missing servants might effect their escape upon the remainder, if indeed they had not been slain.

After supper, the Kuzzauks lay down to sleep; one

---

* I have since supposed that he was alluding to the wound in the throat which I had given one of my assailants.

or two only keeping watch. The night was very cold, which added to my suffering, although perhaps it saved some effusion of blood. The quantity I had lost, no doubt prevented the worst consequences to be apprehended, from the violence my brain and whole frame had suffered.

My mind was very desolate. My mission was unfulfilled: a mission which success alone could redeem from the charge of rashness. All my foresight, toil, and watching had been rendered futile by the blind obstinacy of my people, and for myself there remained the alternative of slavery or death. But the last had then fallen to me, and it was now my wisdom and duty to submit. I calmed my mind accordingly. I hardened myself to fulfill my allotment of suffering. To enter upon death. To read that mystery, which none can violate. To penetrate that secret, which has occupied the speculations of every noble mind; which it has been the end and object of my life to fathom.

It may be believed, that in the course of that long and cheerless night, other thoughts, however resisted, *would* occasionally intrude;—my unprotected home, my widowed mother, the sisters, who had yearly looked for my return from exile. The torture of such thoughts was scarcely endurable, and I clung to any of the bitter alternatives in preference.

April 23rd.—At daybreak, several of the Kuzzauks, after consultation, mounted my horses and rode in pursuit of my missing servants. Three others took hatchets and a spade, and retired to the adjoining water-course. In the gloomy tone of my feelings, with so many reasons to expect death, I fancied they had gone to dig my grave. The shores, I thought, of the Caspian, will form a melancholy circle in the map of the world, to the few lonely hearts who love me.

Yar Muhummud drew near, and took a seat by my side. Nizaum contrived, very imperfectly, to interpret for me. Pointing to my hand, he said, "You stabbed one of us in the throat, and I cut off your hand. We are now even: your wounds have saved your life. Were you not wounded, I would kill you." This is the leader of the party of horsemen, who, six in number, had shrunk away from the face of a single armed man. He now alluded to the circumstance, with rather ill-placed triumph. "You were very fierce and lofty with me, this morning. You drew your pistols, and had I not retired would have shot me. Will you fight now?" drawing out his sabre.

I pointed to my shattered hand.

"What! you have had enough of it? you will never draw trigger again with that hand. Why did you not turn, as I desired you, in the morning."

I produced the Khaun Huzurut's letter, and endeavoured to explain, that I was the Khaun's guest and ambassador. He and his companions sat long in consultation, and then returned me the letter, saying, "You should have produced this yesterday morning. But you defied us, and we have wounded you We will now return you your property, and let you proceed."

I replied that my property was of little consequence. That I would freely bestow it upon them, if they would suffer me to proceed with my people, in safety, to Dahsh Gullah. Cherkush Bae, who was near, and had been paying me many little attentions; supporting my head, which I still could not raise without swooning, and speaking what seemed words of comfort, now looked in my eyes and said, "Fear nothing, I myself will carry you upon my camels to Dahsh Gullah." I give these sayings as we interpreted them at the time. I felt very helpless in the loss of Ali Muhummud; but would not, for the world, have involved him in our difficulties. He, Maimood, and Hajji were still missing; and toward noon, the Kuzzauks, who had pursued them returned unsuccessful, and three others mounted and started in the search. Hajji, who was concealed amongst the rocks close by, watched his opportunity, and delivered himself up. The wisest step, perhaps, under his circumstances, as he was still sixty miles from Dahsh Gullah, in a country without food, of the language of which, as well as of that spoken at Dahsh Gullah, he was utterly ignorant.

The Kuzzauks, left upon the ground, now prepared to move. Cherkush Bae, saddling one of his camels, desired me to mount. I gazed around, but saw no preparation for my servants. I made signs to Cherkush Bae, that I could not move without them. Just then, the traitor, Dana Bae, approached, and begged for his dismissal. I asked him, as well as I could, what they were about to do with us, and why they wished to separate us. Whether it was only to carry me a little farther on the road, and then cut my throat.

He replied in the affirmative.

I returned to take leave of my servants. Nizaum exclaimed, "Do not let them separate us from you, Sir; let *me*, at least, accompany you."

"It is better;" I said, "that we should be separated; for, me they intend to murder, and he who accompanies me, will share my fate."

I supposed, all this while, that they were about to carry me on the road to Dahsh Gullah, as Cherkush Bae had promised.

Just then, Yar Muhummud approached, and pointing at a tall, raw-boned, ruffian one of the assailants, who was flourishing the hatchet he had wielded in the late affray, said "Ahris Mhatoor (i. e. Ahris, the hero) is a terrible fellow." This man, younger brother, of Cherkush Bae, became one of the principal actors in the drama. His great strength and courage, made him a man of consequence in those parts; and I afterwards found, that but for him, the others would never have had courage to attack me. Had, therefore, his tent, which is moved every three days, not been, at the moment I passed, in that precise spot, I should probably have reached the Russian frontier in safety. Upon such slight threads hang the destinies of man. I did not, at the time, know the relationship of Ahris to my preserver; but the hideous and ominous expression of the features, and whole person, of the former, prepossesed me against him.

I earnestly enquired of Cherkush Bae, whether he purposed carrying me to Dahsh Gullah. He replied, "Not now. We go back at present; but I will carry you to the fort, from the spot to which we go. Thus, I perceived that the word of the one solitary being, whom heaven had sent to my rescue, was unworthy of credit. By dint of much entreaty, I persuaded Cherkush Bae, to let my people mount the other camels and ponies; and myself mounting a camel, for I could not, with both hands disabled, sit a horse, proceeded, in much pain from the wounds and bruises with which I was covered. My own sufferings, however, were quite lost, in sympathy for those of my poor Meerza, who, fearfully disfigured by the blows he had received, his reason lost, his strength exhausted, every joint of his body crippled by bruises, was with much difficulty held upon a camel. Ere half the journey was completed, he was obliged to dismount, and falling heavily upon his face, remained long insensible to every attempt to arouse him. In fact, his case seemed so hopeless, that Summud Khaun chid the person who endeavoured to shake him from his lethargy, saying, "Why disturb his last moments. Let him lie here and die in peace." I was secretly of his mind: but at length the poor creature was lifted up, and reseated on a pony, a person holding him on either side.

We retraversed part of the road of the day preceding in the most gloomy mood of thought. I turned over and over our position in my mind; but I could see no chance, how remote soever, of escape. An Englishman is far too remarkable a person to be kept secretly a slave in those lands; and the knowledge of my fate had been certain ruin to all concerned in it. The approach of death was no bugbear to one who had so often confronted it, but the fate of my people was a source of constant anxiety. They had become, as it were, my children; and never were a parent's sympathies more powerfully excited.

At a high plain bordering the Caspian, called Soosun Uttah, we were stopped, made to dismount, and allowed to seat ourselves. Some show of respect was still maintained toward me; but men, who would have crouched in presence of the meanest of my retinue, now seated themselves at my feet. Yar Muhummud was one of these. I observed that his cowardly, hyæna eye shrunk always, like a guilty thing, from mine. Dana Bae and the young miscreant, his son, came again to ask for their dismissal, and for a letter to the Khaun Huzurut in their favour. This I, of course, refused; and they were departing in a sullen mood, when Summud Khaun called the younger back, and said, "Where are the 700 Tungas (silver coins of the value of 6*d.* each) that I lodged in your hand?"

This was the first hint I had ever received of such an insane and selfish act. It was in vain that the young man denied the charge *in toto*, then declared that they were the price of the camels; the other brigands were delighted at the prospect of fresh booty, and rose to examine his camel furniture. Upon this he brought the bag of silver, which was counted out, and delivered to me. I made it over to Yar Muhummud at once, knowing that such must be its eventual fate; but he returned it to me, for the present, with a thousand protestations.

The younger guide was enraged beyond measure at losing the reward of his treachery. He glared upon me like some ill-omened bird. He exhausted himself in invectives; and taking Yar Muhummud apart, whispered in his ear. Yar Muhummud immediately came up to me, and said, "You call yourself an ambassador of the Feringees. All the chiefs of the Feringees wear epaulettes. Let me see yours." I replied, that he would find mine in a tin case amongst my property. Dana Bae's son had seen me at Mungh Kishlauk, dressed in an English surtout without epaulettes, when I expected to meet the Russians. He thought, doubtless, that I had none, and was now disconcerted.

"Ask him," he exclaimed, "whether ambassadors suffer common people, like us, to sit near them?"

"Ambassadors," I replied, "as well as kings, have no choice of their company, when prisoners."

Again he took Yar Muhummud aside, and whispered. Yar Muhummud immediately came and demanded of me the sling which supported my shattered hand, and which, being a crimson silk scarf, was valuable in the eyes of those savages. I had no substitute for it; but (as the Arabian nights have it) just then "To hear was to obey," and I begged Nizaum to take it from my neck and give it up. Here, however, the other brigands interfered, thinking probably that this was a partial method of dividing the booty. Summud Khaun called to Dana Bae, as the latter prepared to quit us, and said, "Take with you the curse of the Koraun, which shall smite and wither you, and your offspring. These men have injured us under misapprehension, supposing us Russians and enemies. But you knew us to be the guests of your Khaun. You, when we were guests under your own roof, and lying side by side with your children, swore upon the Word of God the most solemn oaths of fidelity, and then sold us into the hands of these men. Be assured that the curse of the Word of God will smite you." Dana Bae slunk away, amid the curses and execrations of all: even the other Kuzzauks joined in cursing such a foul traitor. His son still lingered, bent upon mischief, shooting the most malignant glances upon me; unfortunately, his power of mischief was still considerable over prisoners ignorant of the language of the country, the objects, alike, of the avarice and fear of all.

Whilst sitting thus, awaiting the next turn in the tide of our destiny, I took opportunity to sound Cherkush Bae, and to represent, as well as our miserable Toorkish vocabulary would allow, the nature of my office as an ambassador, and a guest of his sovereign. Cherkush Bae heard me with a smile; and one of the Kuzzauks, grasping the forefinger of his left in his right hand, said, "So much we care for an Eelchie, and so much," changing the fore for the little finger, "for the Khaun Huzurut." This was rather comforting, for I knew they cared the thickness of a thigh for our betrayer, Hussun Mhatoor.

Two Kuzzauk detachments of laden camels now arrived, bearing the tents, women, and children of Cherkush Bae and Ahris Mhatoor. The tents were pitched, and half the wall of another tent was erected, to screen us from the piercing wind. The baggage being piled at the entrance of this semi-circular wall, formed a kind of enclosure, into which I beckoned my servants. We were now brothers in misfortune. The Meerza was still utterly insensible. Summud Khaun groaned enough for five, but no one believed him to be much damaged.

The women lighted a fire, and boiled my rice and meat for their dinner. Several Kuzzauks sat always at the entrance of my little enclosure. The younger guide, watching his opportunity, when only Yar Muhummud was present, and when I was reclining on my left elbow, my throat quite exposed in the most tempting of attitudes for a headsman, began whispering in Yar Muhummud's ear; both looked fixedly at me. It was not difficult for me to comprehend what the young miscreant was saying. Yar Muhummud was the man who wounded me, and could scarcely hope for life should I survive. As the fiend insinuated, the Kuzzauk seemed more and more tempted. The act, indeed, would be deemed good service by all, although none dared execute it. He hesitated, he drew the blade half out, he felt the edge with his thumb, then glanced at my throat, then at the blade, whilst the tempter, seeing his advantage, pressed keener and keener his arguments and encouragements, until his eyes seemed absolutely on fire with malice. I would not stir. It was a clean death, and a worse might be the substitute; but I fixed my eyes firmly upon Yar Muhummud's, and saw *his* quail beneath the stare. He shuffled, looked up, looked down, returned the sword to its scabbard, and evidently had lost the resolution. Just then Cherkush Bae arrived. The fiend, with countenance fallen and malice disappointed, upbraided Yar Muhummud for his infirmity. The moment of weakness was past. The opportunity had escaped him.

When the food was ready, Cherkush Bae brought some to me. We had no stomach it may be supposed; I least of all, for my wounds and bruises had left little life in me; but I exhorted my people to eat, and set them the example. I told them they must husband their strength for any emergency; that opportunity of escape might be lost, if their vigour were impaired. It was a sad and solemn meal; it was probably to be my last. When night fell, Ahris Mhatoor piled up the baggage, so as more completely to enclose us; then placed outside armed sentinels, himself still wielding the hatchet he had used in his attack on our party, and stalking about with his usual hideous grimace. The whole aspect of this man was ominous and dreadful. He seemed made by nature for the perpetration of enormities, and yet I do not believe this was his character, although certainly he was reckless, selfish, and faithless. But he was introduced to me under circumstances peculiarly unfavourable, and it was not astonishing that I should receive an exaggerated impression. With the most violent and threatening gesticulations, he gave us to understand that we should be murdered, if we stepped beyond the limits of our shelter. He was then retiring, when Nizaum called him back, to whiffle in his ears soft promises and dulcet flattery, in a jargon of which the sole intelligible words were "yes, no, good, bad," all the verbs, substantives, pronouns, etc. being formed by gesture and grimace. Love, however, had formerly taught Nizaum to make the most of such scanty elements; and fear, and I verily believe attachment to me, now rendered him eloquent after a fashion.

"Yar Muhummud," said Ahris Mhatoor, "is a bad man (Yummun, Yummun). He wishes to murder your master; it was he who wounded him, and he dares not now suffer him to live." For my part, I did not think that Yar Muhummud had courage to attack even an unarmed man in broad daylight and face to face; whereas, there was about Ahris Mhatoor a boldness, a promptitude, a restlessness, that caused him ever to take the lead; and should there be any bloody work to transact, he would inevitably be chief performer. Although far from being the richest or most considerable man of the gang, every one yielded to him; even over his elder and richer brother Cherkush Bae, he maintained the ascendancy due to extreme energy. The other was calm, courageous, immoveable in his determinations; by nature a noble and a beautiful character. At present, I knew of him little more than his whisper of extreme eagerness, "Have you gold?" had informed me, as I lay wounded on the earth. Upon this I desired Nizaum and Summud to work; to surrender whatever money they could not conceal to him, with promises of abundant increase, should he render us service. We had not yet been regularly stripped and examined, and part of the gold had escaped their search. I now made Summud Khaun and Nizaum divide this gold into shares, and distribute it amongst all the servants, as a means of escape, rendering each independent of the others. As for myself, I was not in a condition to attempt escape, and therefore had use for none. I desired each to look after himself, and not think of me, whom it was impossible either to carry with them or to aid by remaining. I had made up my mind, I said, if my life were spared, to see a little of Kuzzauk life, and feed sheep and camels upon the steppe. I should at least acquire an useful language, and read a new page in life.

When night had fallen, and I found opportunity of speaking quietly to Nizaum, I extorted from him a solemn promise that, in case of my death and his escape, he would bear my mother the assurance that my last thoughts had been of her and of my home.

Nizaum readily promised to execute my orders; and I found my mind calmer after this last preparation.

In the first edition of this work, I had unwarily published, word for word as found in my private journal, all the feelings and events of this night; but they are scarcely subjects of interest to the public. Suffice that, from the circumstances of our position, and the bearing and words of our captors, I did not think it would have passed without violence. While, therefore, my servants slept, I watched as before; for I felt assured I could offer such arguments for saving their lives and restoring them to their country as must be unanswerable, could I but get opportunity of speech with those who might offer them insolence or carry them into slavery. The night, however, passed without incident, excepting that twice the sounds of approaching footsteps were heard, and that shouts came from the tent of Ahris Mhatoor. It was, upon the whole, a more weary night than the preceding. Yet it had its own sense of sublimity, baffling all expression: for I stood on the brink of eternity, and a few minutes might make me wiser than the wisest of the children of men.

CHAPTER XXV.

Capture of Maimood and Ali Muhummud—Consultations of our Captors Third Night of Captivity—Further Consultation—Harassing Demands—Division of Booty—The Blandishments of Beauty out of her Teens—Sentiment of Sheep's Tails—Delicacy and Sympathy of Kuzzauk Women—Misery of our Position this Day—The Poor Meerza's View of the Case—Further Partition of Spoils—Recovery of the Royal Presents—Rape of the Cloak and the Kerchief—Three of my Suite taken off as Slaves—Rescue of Nizaum—Survey of Summud Khaun—State of my Wounds—New Guide to Mecca—Lamentable Want of Religious Fury amongst the Kuzzauks.

AT daylight, many Kuzzauks from neighbouring Khails, collected to stare at us, and afterwards consult as to our disposal. Great anxiety was expressed, for the return of my interpreter, Ali Muhummud. But, although very helpless without him, I earnestly trusted that he and Maimood, the groom, had escaped. At noon this hope was frustrated. Maimood was brought back by a party of Kuzzauks; and soon afterwards, Ali Muhummud himself appeared, bound, and slightly wounded. They stated, that being struck down in the first assault, they had crept into a thicket, whence they had witnessed the conclusion of the affray. They heard a pistol fired, which inspired them with some hope; but, soon after, a Kuzzauk had passed, dressed in my garments, which persuaded them that I was slain. At daybreak they pursued the route toward Dahsh Gullah, and had already travelled more than half the distance, when they were pursued, fired at, taken, mercilessly beaten and wounded. Poor fellows, our greeting was mournful indeed.

The assembled Kuzzauks now made a hearty meal

of my mutton, rice, and sugar, the two latter articles being great luxuries in their eyes; and then, forming a circle, consulted how they should dispose of us. All we could learn, was an imperfect report, that there being a general order in force, that Russian prisoners should be sent alive to Khiva, their goods being the property of the captors, they proposed so to dispose of us.

The consultations lasted until night. We were then secured as before. I had been conversing with my people, upon the extreme improbability of the Kussauks committing such a blunder as to spare me; and endeavouring to prepare them for my death, and for their own condition as slaves, when I should be gone; authorising them to offer, in the name of the Envoy at Heraut, any sum as their ransom. They resisted the notion, and I was in the very act of giving my reasons, when six of the brigands approached slowly, entered our little circle in silence, and deliberately arming themselves, half drew their swords, and felt the edges with their fingers. It was a moment of strange suspense. I perceived in the eyes of all my people, that a single impression was common to all, as they sat breathless around me. The Kuzzauks lingered some time, eyeing us without uttering a word, and then departed to Ahris Mhatoor's tent, as slowly as they had come. Again I sat up all night, to watch over the safety of my people. Once or twice, I was startled by wild halloos, but they proved to be no more than the efforts of Kuzzauks to awaken the dogs that guard their sheep. The baying and swift footfalls of these guardians of the night might be heard in full chase of a wolf or a fox. But even this night had its morning, the morning of the most trying day it was our lot to witness.

The Kuzzauks early assembled, and again sat in consultation. They betrayed less respect than ever for my person. One of them had the effrontery to put on my uniform close in front of me. I appealed to Cherkush Bae; for I felt the extreme importance of preserving what remained of my dignity. He chased away the intruder. A violent fellow, who had been in close conference with our younger guide, commenced a violent dispute with the youth who had assumed my garments: and at length became so furious, that making at the young man, he boxed his ears, and tore the clothes from his back. This, I well understood, was from no love to me. The denuded Kuzzauk mounted one of my horses, and galloped off.

One of our greatest torments had been the constant demand, made by Kuzzauks, for some article of our equipment, whether of dress or horses. This, my people were obliged to find for them every five minutes, and to receive back when their caprice was satisfied. These demands were now made with increased assiduity. Sometimes, I had to rise, whilst a Kuzzauk examined the carpet upon which I sat, and again threw it down in a heap before me. Sometimes, I was desired to surrender my furred cloak, which was an object much coveted by all; having, indeed, cost, at Khiva, about twenty guineas. In the last case, I always appealed to Cherkush Bae or Ahris Mhatoor, for I was aware that even " Majesty " will not bear the loss of externals. They readily interfered, to prevent my being stripped.

My property was now collected in a heap. The bags were opened, and the Kuzzauks seated themselves around them. Ahris Mhatoor, hatchet in hand, cried in a loud voice to each of our assailants in turn, to come and choose. After a pause, and some consultation, Ali Muhummud was called and directed to select and set apart his own horse, arms, and clothes. I feared that they were about to form lots, for the distribution of each individual with his arms and goods: but it proved, that Ali had declared himself to be a servant of the Ghoosh Beegie of Khiva, and that they feared to molest him. The selection went on rapidly. First, were chosen the cloth cloaks, then those of silk, then the pieces of broad cloth, afterwards coverlets, swords, and inferior articles; and last, my Cashmere shawl, of which none knew the use or value.

Whilst this business proceeded rapidly, an old woman of ninety years, mother of Cherkush and Ahris, toddled up to my little forlorn circle. I made her take a seat. She smiled upon me lovingly, calling me her Chiraug, literally, "lamp," and it must be remembered, that Kuzzauk lamps are fed with the fat of Doombha tails, a circumstance that somewhat perplexes the sentiment. Nevertheless, as the Chiraug is their only light, it has become their fondest term of endearment.

"Ah, my Chiraug," said the ancient dame, with a smile of blandishment; "are all these goods yours?"

"They were mine just now."

"And all these servants?"

"Yes!"

"How rich you are. Pray give me a gift, a cloak, or a shirt, or a silk kerchief."

I assured her I had no longer power over the goods; but she replied, "Ah, my lamp, I *must* have something. Some little gift."

I pointed to the Kuzzauks, and recommended her to ask them, and off she stumped on the errand. I soon perceived that her eloquence had been rewarded with a cloak, which one of the Kuzzauks threw over her shoulders. Several other women came to condole with us, and to beg of me gifts. There was something ludicrous, yet infinitely chilling, in all this. It was the triumph of avarice over feelings naturally tender. It was, as if one of our delicate European females should approach the live ox, from which a Tartar had just cut his beefsteak, saying, "Ah! my poor pet, my heart bleeds for you; just stand, whilst I cut a leetle slice from your shoulder." The Kuzzauk women shed tears over our melancholy condition, and ere they were dry, plundered us of the few miserable articles, which their sons and husbands had left us.

Our condition throughout this day was truly wretched. A state of torturous suspense which no certainty can equal. Despair, like those acids which destroy the nerves, arms the heart with an insensible panoply, proof against further suffering. Suspense is a demon, that lacerates without deadening the nerves, and wreaks its spite upon the most sensitive and least vital portions of the soul. Some of my horses had been at once carried off. Two or three had been left, but in a condition so wretched, that it was misery to behold them. Two or three days' hard work, without food, had reduced them to skeletons. The poor Meerza, whenever for a moment wakened from his lethargy, enquired after his horse. "Aye, Ali Muhummud, where is my horse? Has he been fed? Is he surely fastened? And aye, Ali Muhummud, what are we doing here? It is much better to be moving. I feel as if bruised all over. Look at my hands! What can be the matter with them? and my head is so heavy, that I can scarcely hold it up. Aye, Ali Muhummud, where is the Word of God? Are you sure it is safe? Let us get on quickly to Dahsh Gullah. It is useless to loiter here. Aye Ali Muhummud, some one has taken my whip: I don't see it. What can have become of it?"

To all this Ali Muhummud, whose extreme good nature had made him, as we have seen, the servant of several of my suite, could only reply, "Aye, Meerza, we are as it has pleased God to ordain. Ask no questions, but go to sleep again." The Meerza, after two or three more ejaculations, obeyed an injunction, which the injury his brain had sustained rendered imperative. We found the poor Meerza's whip, and gave it him. He stuck it in his girdle, and for a fortnight afterwards it served to abate his anxiety to be moving: for when his hand fell upon it, he was persuaded that preparations for the journey were in progress. Poor fellow! the first four days he lay motionless, in a dead sleep, from which it was scarcely possible to arouse him. When wakened, he would eat nothing, and resisted all our efforts and persuasions. After some days this lethargy abated; but his wits were gone. It appeared that he had been asleep the night of the attack, and had awakened only in time to be felled by repeated blows upon his bald head, as he attempted to rise. He never, therefore, could understand what had occurred; and as he lost thereby much of the anxiety and suffering *we* endured, we were not over anxious to inform him. At times, however, a sense of his position dawned upon him, and then much keen cunning was displayed.

When the goods had been distributed, and some fifty rude Kuzzauks made gay with our spoils, two or three of them came and demanded the bag of silver, which the guide had been made to restore. I ordered Summud Khaun to surrender it. It happened, that he had added to the bag ten or fifteen small silver coins, which he now withdrew. Ahris Mhatoor, thinking there were a part of the original sum, drew a sword, and was with difficulty prevented from murdering him. The coins were equally distributed: but Yar Muhummud had contrived to appropriate ten golden pieces belonging to the Meerza.

When Ali Muhummud first returned, after explaining more fully the nature of my mission, I had begged the Kuzzauks be careful of the sabre and jewelled dagger and harness, entrusted to me by the Khaun Huzurut; as well as all the papers in my possession. I made them welcome to everything else, upon condition of their immediately conveying me and my people to Dahsh Gullah; search was made for the articles. The sabre and dagger were soon found. The former was openly worn, in utter ignorance of its value, by the young fellow who had paraded in my uniform. A side-blow from a club had, however, ruined its symmetry. The dagger was also discovered, without much difficulty; the brigand who had torn it from my side, not conjecturing that its rich jewels were anything more precious than glass; but the harness was long in appearing, not that the gold and jewels with which it was studded were recognised as such, but because it was a piece of finery of extreme value in the eyes of a nation of horsemen. The dagger, in spite of my remonstrances, was returned to me, for as I had now no longer the means of guarding it, I did not like to be burthened with the responsibility. Fifty times a day, it was in the hands of some rude Kuzzauk, who would draw the handle, examine, and afterwards return it.

As soon as the division of spoils was complete, and whilst I and my people awaited our sentence, with no enviable feelings, the violent fellow who had despoiled his companion of my garments, stepped up to me, and insisted upon having my furred cloak. I remonstrated. He drew his sword, and gave me the choice of death or surrender of the garment. I accordingly stripped it, or rather caused my servants to strip it from my shoulders, and he carried it off in triumph. Yar Muhummud followed, and took from me the sling which supported my shattered hand; and as the remainder of my garments were sufficiently costly in their eyes, I expected to have been left naked.

Just then a boy of thirteen years, son of Ahris Mhatoor, approached me. He had previously visited me several times, and by his smile of encouragement, led me sometimes to hope that mercy would be shewn us. He now took me by the hand, and led me into his father's tent. The old Meerza followed, but some of my people were arrested in the attempt, and forced to remain without. Summud Khaun and Ali Muhummud were taken to Cherkush Bae's tent. The women and children shewed me many little attentions. They consisted of the ancient dame already mentioned, Ahris Mahtoor's wife, a woman of forty, who must have been handsome, the boy of thirteen, a girl of eleven, and four other children, of whom the youngest was an infant. Maimood, the groom, soon followed me, bathed in tears. "They are carrying me off to slavery," he said. I remonstrated earnestly, but to no purpose. He knelt down and covered my hands with tears. I laid my hand upon his head, and commended him to God's keeping. He was then dragged away. Hajji and Yakoob shared a similar fate. Yakoob and Maimood were bosom friends, and their separation from one another was a most mournful sight. Even the rude Kuzzauks were moved. But when they would have led away Nizaum also, he escaped into the tent, and throwing himself at my feet, exclaimed, "Aye, Sahib, Sahib, all my hope is with you. I have left my widowed mother to follow your steps. Do not suffer them to separate me from you." I made a last effort, and laying my hand upon the shoulder of Ahris Mhatoor, besought him, in the most earnest manner to spare Nizaum. He hesitated. I renewed my pleading. At length he yielded, saying, "If you have any money, give it to satisfy those to whose lot Nizaum has fallen." I consulted Nizaum, and found, to my great joy, that a bag of Russian silver had escaped their search. I made him surrender it to Ahris, who divided it amongst the claimants. These, however, were not yet satisfied. They took a survey of the rest of my suite. The poor old Meerza was mere carrion; and Ali Muhummud, under his assumed character of servant of the Ghoosh Beegie, they dared not touch. Summud Khaun was keenly scrutinized. His grey beard, which had been dyed a jetty black on leaving Khiva, was now shewing sundry autumnal tints of bright red, where the indigo had given place to the henna. He was a seedy-looking fellow, full of groans, and wealthy in old cloaks and measureless inexpressibles. They didn't half fancy him. One of them, however, after a long examination of his beard, and perplexed comparison of it with his physiognomy (for dyes are unknown to the Kuzzauks), enquired his age; and as he is not much past fifty, he coolly answered five and twenty; vanity, for the moment, mastering his habitual caution. This produced a shout of merriment, which made the tent ring. Fortunately, he was not believed; and his utter apparent helplessness disinclined any one to the burthen of feeding one, whose jaw appeared his most active member, and who was so fundamentally objectionable. I afterwards asked Summud, what *could* induce him to tell so barefaced and impolitic a lie. He declared it was no lie. That when asked his age, he considered that the age of his manhood was intended, and dated accordingly from the full growth of his beard. The parting was very mournful. So long as we were together, all seemed not lost. We were a mutual support and solace. Yet I confess, I thought the condition of those led away to a certain fate, although that fate was slavery, preferable to ours, who were destined to linger on from day to day, with no hope of rescue, but continual expectation of some sentence, of which the most lenient we could look to was an easy death.

This business discussed, Cherkush Bae came to examine and dress my hand. The first day and two nights it had been tied up with no attention to the position of fingers, or the bringing together of the lips of wounds. The second day I had made Nizaum renew the bandages, and place the members in some shape. Cherkush now handled it with great tenderness; but I foresaw, that for want of proper ligaments, the middle finger, which was hanging on, would be lost. I begged him to glue strips of paper from the finger to the hand, to keep it in position, and prevent the ends of the bone from chafing one another. My ignorance of the language rendered it impossible for me to convince him of the necessity of this, and the finger was eventually lost. To the wound he applied burnt alum, which gave much pain, and I think did no good. Over the alum he spread a tent of scraped leather, and he supported the disjointed thumb upon a splint of wood. My other sabre cuts, of which I had three, were mere scratches. I never knew how I received them, for the blow of a sabre and that of a club produced nearly the same sensation, and the night was too dark for the eye to distinguish one weapon from another. A rag, that had once flourished in the coarse petticoat of my hostess, profoundly ignorant of the watery element, from an unknown number of years, was now, after a soaking in melted snow, adjusted as a sling to my arm. Even this miserable wreck of an ancient petticoat was almost daily captured from me, and recovered with difficulty, so destitute is this primitive race of what we consider the coarsest articles of comfort.

My pocket sextant was brought to me, and its use demanded. I declined answering, for necromancy was one of the charges against me; and a solar observation would have been the very grandfather of the forbidden art. Ali Muhummud replied for me, that it was a Kibla Noomah, or compass pointing out Mecca. This greatly delighted them; and if their prayers have not made, through means of it, successful voyages, it is neither my fault nor Ali Muhummud's. My ignorance of the language sometimes saved me great embarrassment; for, as Ali's safety was dependent upon mine, he was careful never to interpret for me any part of a question which might have elicited from me a dangerous reply; at least, from observation of gestures and countenances, I was inclined sometimes to suspect such to be the case; and it is probable that he occasionally took liberties with my replies. Not many searching questions, however, were put. For these simple shepherds are quite ignorant of those nice distinctions of faith upon which more civilised nations damn and murder one another. They take it for granted, that every one who worships one only God must be a good Moosulmaun, and that all others are Kawfurs or infidels; of whom they naturally enough conclude the Koozulbaush (an epithet embracing the whole Persian nation) to be the most venomous, because nearest themselves in faith, and within reach of their forays.

CHAPTER XXVI.

Inmates of Ahris Mhatoor's Tent—The buxom old Girl of Ninety-five—Her Relish of Bon-bons—Ahris' Wife, Children, Dogs, Lice, and other Quadrupeds—Kuzzauk Diet—Voracity—Contempt of Medicines—Rescue of the Cloak—First Night as Prisoners in a Kuzzauk Household—Hopeless Prospect around me—Melancholy induced thereby—Cherkush Bae—His Wife's Pity for me, and Love of my Apparel—Humanity of Kuzzauk Maidens, how evinced—How by civilised Ladies—Persons of my People searched—Meerza's Astuteness—Summud Khaun's Wit—False Alarm—Change Camp—Intrigue for our Liberation—Resolution of the Grey Beards—Negotiations for our Release—Again shift Camp.

I HAVE already enumerated the inmates of Ahris Mhatoor's tent. The old lady lay at my head. She was prodigal of her personal charms; and we had difficulty in convincing her, that garments were either useful or ornamental. She made Ali, in front of us all, about the coolest proposition I ever heard from a lady of ninety-five. She had a little pet whim, which sometimes rather disgusted me. When on any grand occasion a sheep was slain, the head was her morsel. She gnawed it well over night, and then popped it under her pillow, as children dispose of sugar-plums, to be the subject of her dreams all night, and her first waking care. The gnawing of this sheep's head, with all its horrible appurtenances, eyes, ears, tongue, and brain, would at any other time have sickened as well horrified me. But hardship is a good tutor, and the simple milk diet of the Kuzzauk leaves no irritability to the nerves of the stomach. The sight was very hideous. I sometimes fancied I had fallen from my grade in the creation, and become the mate of wolves and hyænas.

At other times, I speculated upon mutton-eating in general. I figured to myself the most lovely of our English ladies, in a state of nature, and in a land possessing, like this, neither fruit nor vegetable, but an abundance of fat-tailed sheep. I imagined a call from the larder. How would it be answered? She goes forth into the steppe, she climbs the most elevated point. She throws her wild keen eye around the horizon. She sinks suddenly on the earth. She has spied her fleecy prey. She creeps cautiously, on all fours, along the steppe, her dishevelled locks droop to the earth. Her eye, so blue of late, is suffused with blood, it shoots through those long locks, tongues of fire. It is a comet, consuming the azure of heaven. See how she winds and crouches, for the shelter of the smallest bush, or tuft, or hollow. The sentinel of the muttons is beginning to stare. He smells something very like a rat. He twinkles his yellow eye. He wrinkles his forehead. He doesn't half like it; would not take upon his conscience to declare, etc., etc. He swings his tail like the great bell of Moscow. He is just about to feather it, has actually collected wind into his lungs to utter that redoubtable Baa-a, and lifted his foot for that decisive stamp, at which the whole army will take flight; when he feels a something tickling in his ear, and stealing into the fattest cockle of his heart. What *can* it be? The very voice of his own little son and heir. His Benjamin, the child of his old age, the picture, the living image of himself. His heart is melted. He looks affectionately toward the sound. A keen red gleam of fire shoots through him, like a red-hot spit, curdling his very tallow. What can it be? His doubt lends a dash of the sublime to his parental emotions: he puts back his head just to scratch his back bone with the tip of the right horn. In an instant, the wild creature is upon them. Scarcely has he time to utter the first letter of his Baa, or wish his huge tail at Jericho; so imminent is the peril, so headlong the flight. One, two, aerial bounds! Beautiful, graceful, mischievous creature, where learned ye that pas de zephyr? A third. She is upon him, even him, the genius and the hope of the flock. Her snow-white feet are on his woolly back, her lily hands are busy with his throat. He speeds, he lashes his tail, he roars with a roar that would addle the wits of the bravest mutton. It dies into a gurgle. It ceases. He falls heavily to the earth. Those beauteous arms around his throat, those taper fingers on his windpipe. He kicks,—once, twice, thrice. He was no common mutton. She purrs over him with delight. She gnaws one leetle hole just under his ear. *There* are pressed her ruby lips. Her warm sweet breath will surely fan him to life. Has she let blood for this purpose? Is it remorse, soft pity that moves her? Look at her eye, and consider: for I can follow her no farther. Is this woman, lovely woman? No! Thanks to him who invented butchers, it is *not*.

My hostess, Ahris' wife, was a thoroughly good woman. She had protested against the attack upon me, and now did her utmost to alleviate our sufferings, lavishing upon me a thousand trifling attentions, which my situation rendered very acceptable. I shared with her children, equally, the food she possessed; and if by accident, any Kuzzauk from the Russian frontier brought a handful of coarse meal into the tent, a Benjamin's portion of the little cake, cooked from it, was ever mine.

Two dogs completed the circle of this tent, in which the Meerza, Nizaum, and myself were prisoners. But we seldom lay down to rest with less than one or two guests. The beds consisted of Nummuds, or thick felts, full of lice, upon which the person of a female was deposited, en chemise, that of a man in a state of innocence. The cloak of sheepskin was drawn over the person, and if more covering were necessary, it was, in like manner, found, in the clothes worn by day. Darkness served as a dressing room to all parties.

The sheep, to the number of five hundred, about seven female camels, and a pony; all the property of the two brothers, were collected at night near the tent, and slept there, under the protection of four or five large dogs. The milk of the sheep and camels formed the sole sustenance of the two families. When brought home, it was poured into the large caldron so often mentioned, and heated by a fire of brushwood. As soon as the scum was formed, the children collected around it, brandishing each a wooden spoon, which passed from mouth to milk, and from milk to mouth with the utmost celerity, until the scum formed upon the milk was quite consumed. It was then poured warm into the skin which had contained the curds of the preceding day; the acid of which curdled the fresh supply. It is in this form alone that milk is consumed by the Kuzzauks. It was at first very disagreeable to my palate; but habit and hunger soon taught me to deem it delicious. An addition of five open mouths to the household, induced our hostess to add a moiety of snow-water to the aliment, by way of eking out the quantity. This, of course, was no improvement. Cheese and butter I have never seen in Kuzzauk tents, although the former is made by Toorcumuns: and cream was too expensive an article for any but the wealthy: for the miserable pasture of the steppe can yield but a poor return in milk.

At long intervals, a sheep is slain, cut up with wondrous celerity, and tossed warm and almost alive into the caldron. It is then eaten without any accompaniment of bread, rice, and vegetable; things, which the country does not produce, and which are purchased, at a heavy expense, in very small quantities, on the Russian frontier. Two hours or so after the death of the sheep, not a vestige of it remains.

The very bones are chewed, and pieces of the skin are fried in the embers and eaten. No provision is left for the unfortunate dogs; and the steppe produces none. I never could understand how they subsisted. During winter, when the supply of milk fails, the Kuzzauks live greatly upon the flesh of their flocks and herds, which they salt and dry for the purpose. But I confess, it is an enigma to me, how this supply can ever suffice, without aid of grain or vegetables; for I have been present, many times, at the discussion of an entire sheep, when milk was abundant, and have never known a particle of the flesh left for a second meal: so that, during three or four months of the year, a sheep would be requisite every day, for the subsistance of a household; undoubtedly, large numbers *are* consumed during the winter, which renders strict economy necessary during the spring and summer months.

The milk diet is so conducive to health, that disease is a thing unknown to the Kuzzauks; and when, upon opening a packet of my medicines, I endeavoured to explain the use of them, they had great difficulty in even comprehending my meaning, and cast the drugs away as useless. They have, nevertheless, great faith in all vulnerary applications; several of which, as isinglass, alum, vitriol, they procure from Russia. The effect of the milk diet upon myself was peculiar. A draught of curds produced the exhilaration of nerves which is experienced from a cup of tea or coffee; and heaviness never followed the most copious potation. Indeed, my hunger was seldom appeased, so great was the extra demand occasioned by myself and people.

When Ahris Mhatoor perceived that I had been robbed of my cloak, and understood the circumstances, he sallied forth with a Kuzzauk whip in his hand, of the thickness of three ordinary fingers, and, overtaking the spoiler, belaboured him until he surrendered it. I begged him to accept it for his pains, but he was ashamed to do so, although evidently under strong temptation; and I, knowing the importance of preserving a decent exterior, did not press him beyond a certain point. He, however, had no scruple in making Summud Khaun surrender a handsome cloak, which *he* wore, and which Ahris immediately appropriated.

In the tent with me was the old Meerza; in the other tent lay Summud Khaun, Ali Muhummud, Cherkush Bae, his old wife and grown-up daughter, the latter a raw-boned, square, and crimson-faced damsel, of some two and twenty years. Night fell, and we lay down to rest. Sleep in my case was impossible, owing to the pain of my shattered hand, and my dread lest the dogs occupying the tent should touch it in passing; for more than a month I could not rest it upon my body or the earth, but at night propped it an upright posture upon the elbow. The poor Meerza had forgotten, not only that I was his master, but that I was endowed with sensation: he rolled and tumbled about whenever he awoke, to the great peril of my wounded limb. I had already *enjoyed* abundant leisure for the consideration of my position, in all its hopelessness. It was evident that the Kuzzauks, having added robbery to violence, could feel secure only in my destruction, especially as it was impossible to persuade them that the Russians were not my friends or kindred. Hussun Mhatoor had a still deeper interest in my death, and was all-powerful in those parts. The instant, therefore, he should get tidings of my position, my death-warrant would probably be issued. My servants would then become slaves for life. As for flight, even for them it was impracticable, through a desert without food for man or beast, the wells of which are known only to guides, the language of which they could not speak, every inhabitant of which is by profession a dealer in human flesh. In the sufferings and hardships I had undergone during the past year, I had become almost utterly callous as to myself; I scarcely cared whether I lived or died, was what men call happy, or what they term wretched; my mind was worn out and exhausted; the trouble of being happy had been a pain. Things that we suppose without thought or sensation, the rock, the stock, the motionless and joyless clay, these were the objects I was disposed to regard with envy; the gaiety of the bird was an impertinence, and the very life of the breeze a weariness to thought. Even death, as a door to future and more exalted powers, often sickened my heart, and I thought of it, excepting in moments of excitement, rather as a state of rest, with a longing to resign a worn-out being, and cease for ever and for ever.

But when the case of others came before me, it was power enhanced by the loss of all the rival claims of self; it awakened me to a new existence; it aroused me to thought, to feeling, to hope and fear. I felt that I had a sacred trust still reposed in me by Him who gave me my being; my mission on earth was not ended, whilst my unhappy followers were undelivered; the darkest of fates was impending over them, and with *my* life their hope must become extinct. It was this which aroused the strife, and kept alive the vulture of the heart.

Night passed, and morning dawned. I went forth, and sat upon a fragment of earth upon the desolate plain, whilst the women lighted the fire, and milked the sheep and camels. A drizzling rain was falling. The weather was in keeping with my thoughts. Presently, Cherkush Bae approached, bearing a wooden bowl filled with mahss (curdled milk). He offered it with a smile of encouragement that went to my heart. I lived upon this man's smiles during the remainder of my captivity. I divided the bowl with my servants, and, that they might never be neglected, as inferior in importance to myself, I made it an invariable custom to share with them all, even to the most trifling article of comfort, that at any time fell to my lot. I found every member of the two families anxious that we should want for nothing with which they could supply us.

Many Kuzzauks visited the tent this day, some of them men of rank amongst that wild race. One of them, a very handsome man, of very unprepossessing countenance, protested in strong terms against the sin and shame of attacking an ambassador. "Yes," replied I, when Ali Muhammad had interpreted his words, " he has not shared in the plunder. I was amused with the conduct of the women with whom we dwelt. Whilst shedding tears of sympathy over our misfortunes and my sufferings, they were cutting up our clothes into dresses for themselves, and stealing from us every trifling article which their husbands had spared. Cherkush Bae's wife would come and kneel at my feet, and weep over me; but in the midst of her tears, her hands stole involuntarily to my cloak, which she fingered with equal tenderness and affection. I fancied I could hear her say, " Poor thing! what a very soft skin it has. What a pity that it must die! What a pity that it should die out of *our* tent! One day, when I was disgusted to an unusual degree by those crocodile tears, I made Ali translate to the lady her own sentiment. She was dreadfully shocked; yet the fingers could not leave off fingering the furred cloak. Her daughter's sympathy betrayed itself in a more amiable and less questionable manner. If she saw me fairly nonplussed, through my crippled condition, in the endeavour to free myself from those intruders, whose name was " Legion," she would fly across the tent to my rescue, dodge the intruder into a corner, seize him by the nape of the neck, and send his indignant spirit full trot to the shades below. A civilized maiden would shew her humanity by cracking a heart. The fair Kuzzauk evinced her's by cracking a l———. I leave it to philosophers and divines to judge between them.

Many Kuzzauks this day crowded the tent to stare at us. Nizaum had yielded up cash after having been searched. It struck them that there might be more. Nizaum was examined, but nothing was found upon him. The Meerza was next stripped, and we sat in breathless suspense, awaiting the result, for he had thirty ducats of his own and thirty gold coins of mine in a belt around his loins, and, as he was quite deranged, it seemed improbable that this money should escape the spoilers. But an Asiatic's wits must be far gone, indeed, to desert him when money is at stake. Although he had hitherto lain quite helpless, and almost insensible, recovering only from time to time, sufficiently to betray the complete derangement of his intellect, yet now he acted his part with the most consummate skill. There were at least a dozen pair of eyes searching him keenly, and hands were passing over his body and garments from head to foot. He fought his way peevishly, step by step. Not a garment was yielded without a battle, and the multiplicity of wrappers being each in turn examined without effect, the searchers began to despair. Still there remained the nethermost garment, but this the old gentleman would not suffer to be removed; and at length, even the Kuzzauks were ashamed to insist upon his open exposure. They passed their hands carefully over his body, but decency prevented them from hitting the golden vein; and, to our great relief, almost amusement, we saw them retreat, completely baffled, and the old man resume his garments, and reseat himself at my side. This, however, was the utmost effort his reason was capable of. The instant he found himself dressed, he began to whisper in my ear, in a voice that rung through the tent, "I've got your thirty tillas round my waist, and my own thirty ducats. I tell you, but won't tell any one else." I touched him, and signed to him with my eyes to be silent, but all was lost upon him. "Tilla and bh'joglie,"* names well known to the Kuzzauks, rang

---

* Tilla, literally "gold," is the name of the gold coins of Khiva and Bokhara. Bh'joghe is applied to the ducat on account of the figure of Mercury which it bears.

loudly, attracting the attention of all the women; the very whisper at that moment was sufficient to excite suspicion. Fortunately the men were at this time utterly bewildered in the numberless unmentionables, cloaks, etc. of Summud Khaun. He too had money; where, I know not, for every garment he possessed was in itself a labyrinth: the search of one would have occupied a week, and their number seemed infinite. He, too, was more than a match at this work for a dozen Kuzzauks. He growled and snarled at them, right and left, and fairly bullied them into the belief that he had nothing. It was evident that the work was new to the Kuzzauks, for they did not prosecute it in a masterly manner. The old Meerza continued during the remainder of the day to doze and wake alternately, losing no opportunity of whispering to me the secret of his possession. I perceived that there was no safety in leaving the gold upon him, the more especially as it seemed improbable that he should long survive the violence he had suffered, when the money would be seized by the Kuzzauks. I therefore determined to relieve him of the charge of my thirty gold pieces by the earliest opportunity, still leaving him the richest of the party.

Another day wore away, and another night. Another morning dawned upon us, and again I was seated upon the rock, looking over that dark, desolate plain, wrapped in a sense of utter helplessness, and vainly endeavouring to shape some means of deliverance. Ahris Mhatoor passed me, matchlock in hand: I perceived that the match was lighted. He set up a horse's skull upon a stick, as a sign-post to warn any who should seek the family, after their departure, of the direction they had pursued on breaking up camp. Ahris, soon after, mounted a horse and rode off, and the women pulled down the tents, and packed them and their goods upon the camels. The sheep and lambs were entrusted to the children. One of my horses was found for me. The Meerza was placed upon a camel; but the rest of my people were obliged to walk.

"This is sad work for you, Nizaum," I said, as he led my horse, which my bandaged hands prevented me from guiding; "your horse, too, will scarcely like a change of masters."

Nizaum had one answer for every occasion. "It is my destiny, Sahib; and whatever is a man's destiny comes to pass."

This is a piece of rare philosophy very comforting to some minds. It is, as if one should say to *him*, whose head is just broken by a hammer, "Iron is iron, and bone is bone, therefore be content." A spot being found near the brink of the cliffs, where the snow was still retained in certain hollows, and where the young grass was springing, the women pitched the two tents, whilst the children drove the sheep and lambs, in separate flocks, to pasture. Whilst the women were thus engaged, I seized the opportunity, and taking my people to some little distance, demanded of the Meerza the money he had in charge. The forlorn state of his intellect placed us in some jeopardy, for he did not like relinquishing his charge, and spoke loudly in answer to my enquiries. It was, however, at length accomplished, and I divided the thirty gold pieces amongst my people, so as to make nearly an equal distribution of funds to all.

Our life in these rude tents was too monotonous to form subject for a diary, unless, indeed, I had detailed daily, whilst fresh in my remembrance, the conversations of the Kuzzauks who visited us, and the hopes and fears to which they gave rise. My own thoughts and feelings, too, under these circumstances, might be curious, for, from my infancy, I have been prone to philosophise, and draw results from the present aspect of circumstances, very different from those which content mankind. But, although I endeavoured at the time to impress such particulars upon my memory, that memory has subsequently been over-tasked, and it is only in particular instances that either the scenes or the thoughts of those days of heaviness are to be recovered.

The mystery of Cherkush Bae's services to me, were now explained. He had an only son, a prisoner at Dahsh Gullah, having been betrayed to the Russians, by the treachery of a comrade. When he heard of the proposition to attack the Russian ambassador, and seize his property, he consented readily to become a party, determining to save the Russian's life, and exchange him for his only son, for whom he had long been pining. Hence his anxiety about me, as I lay wounded on the field of strife, which I had often, but vainly, endeavoured to account for. Hence his emotion, when I spoke of gold, which might purchase the ransom of his child; hence, too, the fact, that whilst the other assailants in the division of booty were handsomely provided for, he and his brother had charged themselves with little more than the burthen of five months.

We were not altogether idle. By means of Ali Muhummud, I endeavoured to place before the eyes of the brothers such hopes as should induce them to take up my cause with zeal, and do something more than give me vague promises of rescue. My desire was to push on to Dahsh Gullah. There lay my duty, my mission was still unfulfilled; and when I calmly weighed together the difficulties of either route, it seemed to me that Khiva was out of the question. I found, however, that this proposition was always most coldly received, and the cause I soon learned.

One night, Ahris Mhatoor (who was generally absent great part of the day), returned late, and had a secret conference with his wife, which Nizaum overheard. She urged him to set us free, and re-conduct us to Khiva, assuring him that he might rely upon my gratitude: that it was evident, from my affection for my servants, that I never forgot a kindness, and that all my people declared this was the character of the English nation.

He replied, that he had just returned from consulting the elders of the tribe, who agreed that the injury I had received was not to be forgiven, and that there was but one way of disposing of him, whom they had so deeply injured.

I lay down to rest this night in the supposition that I should never again rise. I even lay in such a position that the death-stroke might not awaken me. It had always seemed to me, that the pain of death was a mere want of resolution to die—the last despairing struggle. As, in the case of one whom an infant could disable by a touch upon the mangled and inflamed hand, any such strife must be utterly hopeless, I had, from the first, resolved to suffer without a struggle. Day and night I kept jealously before my eyes the image of death, and made myself familiar with his every form, and endeavoured to harden the imagination to all those particulars from which it naturally shrinks. I endeavoured to sleep, but my mind was excited, and the pain of my wound was ever unfavourable to repose. Twice in the night I saw the naked gigantic form of Ahris Mhatoor stride across the crowded tent. I lay perfectly still, controlling my excited fancy. He passed me, and returned to his bed. The night, with all its accompaniments of sublimity and gloom, at length rolled away, and again I blessed the All-merciful for the light of an added day.

I must not omit a melancholy concomitant of my captivity. One of the female camels of Cherkush had lost its young; and the skin, according to the custom of the country, had been stuffed, and was shewn to the camel whenever they wished to milk her. I could not distinctly ascertain the motive of this; but the effect of the contrivance was a constant renewal of the sorrows of the unfortunate mother, which were expressed in a tone so human, so like those of a woman wailing over her only child, that it was impossible to witness them without the most mournful of sensations. The poor thing stood over the image of the lost one, her large, dark, languishing eye suffused with tears. Her head drooped towards the object of her grief, and then lifted, to utter that heart-piercing wail. That expression of a grief which *will not be comforted*—of a heart utterly desolate, and beyond cure. Often, as I lay awake from the pain of my wound, those notes of anguish filled the silence of the night. To me, a captive, in hourly expectation of death, they seemed prophetic of sorrows I dared not contemplate, that soon must arise in a distant land.

The day following, I again pressed Ahris Mhatoor to carry us, either to Dahsh Gullah or to Khiva, urging the necessity of despatch in whatever he might resolve upon. He replied, "We should have carried you on, the first day, to Dahsh Gullah, had you not been wounded. But now, we are at a loss what to do with you; for if *you* forgive us, the Russians will not. A Tooreumun came from Mungh Kishlauk, to tell us that you were a black Russian, a necromancer, and an infidel; and that the Khaun Huzurut had ordered us to kill you, lest you should join your companions, the Yellow Russians, at Dahsh Gullah. We are utterly without blame in this matter."

I replied, that I fully acquitted the Kuzzauks of all blame. That I knew they had acted under false impressions. That if I had received injury from the villain Dana Bae, yet I had received life, and kindness, and protection from himself and his brother. That as for my wounds, they were received face to face with the enemy, and were not, therefore, dishonest, nor fit subjects of malice toward the inflicter. "If, indeed." I said, laying my hand delicately upon the shrine of honour, "you had touched me up here, I had never forgiven it."

There was a loud shout of laughter at this; but although I believe all were, for the moment, convinced of my sincerity, they still objected, that the Russians would send to ravage their possessions, on learning the violence I had suffered.

I replied, that the Russians were not my people, that I was neither their subject nor ambassador. That they had interests distinct and opposite from those of my nation, that they had neither motive nor inclination to avenge my wrongs. That, if he would conduct me and my people to Dahsh Gullah, I would do my utmost toward the liberation of Cherkush Bae's only son. If to Khiva, I would not only obtain there pardon for the Kuzzauks (excepting always the guides), but reward him liberally, and give him all the plundered articles he could recover. He listened eagerly to this, and readily promised to conduct me to Khiva upon his own camels.

"Is this a bargain?" he demanded, stretching out one of his huge hands, and making one of his usual very horrible grimaces. I put my bandaged left hand into his, and assured him it *was* a bargain. I had not, however, the slightest faith in his sincerity.

Three days we remained in this spot. On the fourth the women struck the tents, and packed them upon the camels for a move. The old woman and younger children were lashed upon the furniture, the wives led the camels by a string, and the elder children drove the flocks. We descended the cliffs by a steep and rugged path, and encamped in the valley, on the brink of the dry water-course, in which the fatal ambush had been laid; but higher up. Here the valley was narrower. The approach of spring had called forth a scanty and miserable sprinkling of grass upon the sides of the acclivities.

The daughter of Cherkush Bae, already mentioned, took the camels daily beneath the brow of the cliffs, and there loaded them with snow, which being piled in a heap in the iron cauldrons, afforded water, as it melted, for all culinary purposes. Notwithstanding that melted snow is almost the only water drunk by Kuzzauks (the springs being chiefly supplied from this source), I have never yet known an instance of goitre amongst them; whereas, that disorder is extremely common in the northern part of the Bareilly district, in Hindoostan, where snow has never been seen, and the rivers take their rise in the plain. A small rocky hill separated our tents from some others; and we learned that Ahris Mhatoor had come hither, to be within reach of support from his own tribe. Here we continued about six days, Ahris Mhatoor daily saddling one of my horses and riding forth, apparently to consult upon his next movement.

CHAPTER XXVII.

Embarrassment of Ahris Mhatoor—Considerations—The scotched Snake—Fidelity of Cherkush—The Bond—The Negotiator—The Shippish—Sensation he produces in London—Whether he acknowledges the Emperor of all the Russias—Liking of a Kuzzauk for Nizaum—Messenger from Hussun Mhatoor—News from Dahsh Gullah—Valuation of plundered Property—The Golden Banquet—Shift Camp—Virtue of Patience—Golden Colic.

THE position of Ahris Mhatoor was embarrassing. He had been the principal leader in the attack upon me, for which his courage and great strength well qualified him. He now perceived that the story of the Tooreumun, by which he had been led to attack me, was utterly false, and that I was in fact the ambassador of his king. But, his brother had saved my life, and he had recovered the Khaun Huzurut's property. He might therefore hope for pardon, through my mediation, if he could only transport me to Khiva. Between that city, however, and his own tent, there lay a waste of nearly 500 miles, producing neither grain for cattle, nor food for man; and our horses having been turned loose, without food, amongst the mares, were become mere anatomies, scarcely able to support the weight of their own bones. In this waste, almost to the very walls of Khiva, the influence of my old guide, Hussun Mhatoor, chief of 60,000 Chowdhoor Tooreumuns, was supreme; and, as my arrival at Khiva would be the death warrant of this chief, it was not to be supposed that he would ever suffer me to reach Khiva, or forgive any attempt to carry me thither. Ahris might, indeed, collect Kuzzauks of his own tribe, sufficient to guard me from other Kuzzauks; and his own name was a safeguard, owing to general dread of his prowess. But, no number of Kuzzauks would venture to oppose a band of Toorcumuns of this powerful tribe, by whom they have been robbed and oppressed, time out of mind.

Again, should Ahris await the arrival of Hussun Mhatoor, it was clear that his own ruin, as my preserver, must ensue; unless he could personally conciliate that formidable chief; who could, at any time, make the violence which the Khaun Huzurut's ambassador had received, an excuse for plundering and murdering the Kuzzauks engaged in it; ingratiating himself with the Khaun Huzurut, by their ill-treatment.

To Dahsh Gullah he dared not carry us, because I could from thence afford him no protection, from either king or chief; and it was certain, that without my protection, one or both, would fall upon the Kuzzauks, the instant I should be free. There was but one solution of the Gordian knot, viz. to cut it, i. e. my throat, and to sell my servants. The matter might then be hushed up. The Khaun Huzurut would hear that I had proceeded to the Russian frontier. The Toorcumuns would perhaps be appeased by the plunder, and would scarcely venture upon any outrage upon the Kuzzauks, lest it should lead to discovery of facts, by way of retaliation. Even this solution of the difficulty could not be attempted, without some understanding with Hussun Mhatoor; and it seemed to me, that my life was prolonged, only that his concurrence in my death might be previously obtained.

One night, when Ahris Mhatoor, after a long absence, (avowedly to visit the Yuze Baushee Mooraub Ali,) returned to his brother's tent; Ali Muhummud overheard the conversation which ensued, between the brothers. Ahris said, he had farther consulted the Auk Sukkul (white beards) of the tribe. That they adhered to their former verdict of death, as the sole means of their own security. That, as to their suffering the two brothers to set us free, they saw in that safety for the brothers, but none for themselves. They would not, therefore, hear of it. Ahris Mhatoor confessed that he saw no way but to yield to the general voice, and to murder me; and he urged his brother to concur with him in the design.

Cherkush Bae replied, "Never!" I saved his life, the night of the assault; from that moment, I regarded him as my son. Heaven has taken my only son from me, and given me this in exchange. I swore to him, when the tear was in the eye of either, never to forsake him, and I will be true to my word."

Ahris Mhatoor, who had repeatedly sworn to the same effect, was ashamed of himself, and without reply. With him were the presents entrusted to my charge. He often drew them out, and examined them. It seemed to me at times, to use an eastern expression, that his eyes grew red upon them. He often asked whether the jewels were genuine or counterfeit, and demanded the price. The price, I could not say: but as they were presents from monarch to monarch, it must be considerable.

Daily, we urged upon Ahris the subject of our liberation, daily with less hope on our part, and stronger protestations on his. A letter, making him master of all recoverable property on my arrival at Khiva, and ensuring him protection against the Yuze Baushee Moorand Ali, was insisted upon and granted I made Ali Muhummud translate it into Toorkish, and put my seal to it. He declined receiving it, however, until his arrangements were complete. That night, he was unusually eloquent, swearing solemn oaths of fidelity, and stretching across the tent, to seize my hand, in attestation of mutual good faith;

and repeating the ceremony with each of my servants, especially Summud Khaun, who was always forward in these debates. My people were greatly edified; but even had I been ignorant of his late acquiescence in the project for my assassination, my distrust would have increased in exact proportion to the strength of his forced efforts to win my confidence: for never did he appear so hideous, and revolting, as at such moments.

He had scarcely ceased, when there entered the tent, a chieftain of the Kuzzauks, attended by two servants. After embracing the men and women of the family, he seated himself opposite me, and entered upon business. He was a short, square, bustling figure, with florid complexion, a small restless well-opened eye, and a nose disdainfully elevated. A man of talent in his own line, and evidently one, who placed himself forward in all discussions. He spoke in a tone of decision, as if his word were law, using no ceremony, but addressing me as a prisoner, wholly in his power. "We'll send you to Dahsh Gullah," he said.

"Indeed! My arrangements are made with these brothers to return to Khiva."

"But you shan't go: we'll exchange you with the Russians, for our captives at Dahsh Gullah."

"I am the Khaun Huzurut's ambassador, and claim to be taken before him."

"Ah! we care nothing for the Ullah Kooli (meaning the Khaun Huzurut). We know nothing of ambassadors."

"The Russians are not my countrymen; they will not thank you for releasing me. They will give you nothing in exchange."

"Yet you have offered your interest at Dahsh Gullah for the release of Cherkush Bae's son."

"Because, if I reach that country as an ambassador, and a guest, I shall have claims upon them. At present, I am not their guest: and if sent to them as a captive, shall be neither guest nor ambassador."

"Never mind! we'll try the experiment, at any rate. We'll keep your people here, and send you for trial."

"Not with my consent; I am the guest of Cherkush Bae and Ahris Mhatoor, and claim their protection."

The fact is, that I had no confidence in this man's sincerity; otherwise, the expedient, much as I disliked it, might have offered a better hope of escape, than the attempt to return to Khiva. But the separation from my people was always a sufficient objection to any project, and I made it such to many. I was their sole earthly safeguard. Could I be got out of the way, they would immediately be sold as slaves.

The new comer slept in a neighbouring tent, refusing Ahris Mhatoor's invitation, because the latter had rejected his formal application, for my delivery into his hands. It appeared, that he had two connections, prisoners at Dahsh Gullah.

I lay down, that night, with increased doubt, how long the firmness of our protectors might withstand the threats and cajolery of this hard-hearted and self-sufficient negotiator. I reflected, however, that every act of my preservation, in extremity had been contrary to all reasonable hope. It seemed, that I had got entangled in one of those strong currents of destiny, in which the struggles of the swimmer produce only disappointment; whilst the waves, that oft-times seem most dangerous, become the instruments of deliverance.

The next day, the Kuzzauk chief, assisted by some others, renewed the attack from morning until night, and at length left the camp, on terms of defiance with our protectors.

The day following, I was sitting as usual in Cherkush Bae's tent, wrapped in my cloak, whilst Nizaum endeavoured to free my only silk shirt from the

Shippish who daily entered upon possession, and the finest of which, all the Kuzzauk women declared, were a colony from the old Meerza. Nizaum observing my body to be but one mass of bites, lamented had that I had no previous training.

"Training," I replied, "I never had seen a Shippish before; I knew not his shape nor physiognomy. He had appeared to me, indeed, in my dreams, a thing of mystery, an element of the sublime, but that was all. I had the utmost respect for him."

"Doesn't he grow in London, Sir?"

"Grow! if it were known or suspected, that he had entered the city, the drums would beat to arms, and the guards turn out, and the Lord Mayor and Aldermen (Reish Sofaid) would muster to the attack, and they would hunt him with fire and sword, until he were exterminated. The English are a clean race."

"Does he grow in Russia, Sir?"

I really could not tell; and now, having been their guest, *will* not tell. Russia must answer for herself, whether amongst the diversity of peoples who call her emperor "Father," there be or be not such a race as the Shippish.

"Ah! Nizaum," I said, "if you could but see an English bed, white as the snow, softer than the summer breeze. You would know what a change it is from that to the filthy felt of a Kuzzauk tent. My poor mother, could she dream that the bed I occupy were even damp, would never close her eyes. Heaven be praised, that she knows not, and cannot guess, of my present condition." Little did I dream at the time, that it was reserved for me to taste again the luxury of an English bed, smoothed by the hand of a mother.

The subject took Nizaum in flank, for he had, the evening before, found a wooden goblet which his mother had brought him, as he quitted her at Candahar; and it had been in his hand and pressed to his lips the whole night, and prevented him from closing his eyes. She was the sole being, for whom he seemed to have any strong affection; for he is dissocial, and no favourite of his fellow-servants.

Whilst thus engaged, there entered the tent two Kuzzauks, who sat down in front of me. The one a young man, with large dark eyes and fine features, but an air of recklessness and insolence. He was evidently urging his companion to some act, of which the other was either ashamed or afraid. At length, he himself laid his hand upon my furred cloak. I shook him off, and drew myself up, to shew that I resented his insolence; and when he again took a similar liberty, I sent for Cherkush Bae, and claimed his protection. He rebuked the fellow sharply, but did not expel him; and both visitors continued to haunt the tent. At length, when Cherkush Bae was absent, the dark-eyed gentleman said, "Would you like to go to Mooraud Ali?"

I replied that Mooraud Ali, being greatly inferior to me in rank, might more properly wait upon me.

"But he won't come. You had better go to his tent. Will you go?"

This was said, with a wink at his companion, and a smile that made me sufficiently uneasy. I, of course, declined the journey, understanding the proposition as an attempt to decoy me from the protection of the brothers. The spokesman left the tent in the course of the day, but his companion continued lying at full length, on his belly, with his head raised, and his eyes fixed upon Nizaum. He was the man, to whom Nizaum had been allotted, and from whom I had redeemed that unlucky worthy. Poor Nizaum was as comfortable, under his glance, as a chicken under that of a serpent. He looked, first at the Kuzzauk, then at me, and then heaved profound sighs. I really feared, that the gaze of the Kuzzauk, which lasted the remainder of that, and the whole of the ensuing day, would produce some mischevious effect upon him.

He had, however, in his captivity, acquired a habit which relieved the monotony of existence. This was the manufacture and consumption of snuff. He begged tobacco leaves from the women, and pounded them up with ashes in a wooden bowl, with the handle of a spade. He and Cherkush Bae's wife became inseparable gossips, from a similarity of tastes. Being a soft-hearted fellow, he had parted with all his rings of turquois set in silver that had escaped the spoilers. He never could resist a female tongue. He was a queer compound of selfishness, obstinacy, and fidelity. I believe, that he was the most sincerely attached to me of all my people; and yet he was the only one that ever thought of quitting me.

It was about this time, that a Toorcumun arrived at the tents, nominally from Hussun Mhatoor's son, and certainly from the father. He stated, that he was sent by the former to express his deep regret and sympathy, and to beg me, for the sake of despatch, to come with him to a camp on the road to Mungh Kishlauk, whither both father and son were hastening; and where the chiefs of the Kuzzauks were already assembled, to consult upon means for the recovery of my property. I saw through the snare, and replied, " Tell Hussun Mhatoor, that I deem it an unlucky day, that separated me from his company. Up to the day of this separation, I had been perfectly secure; the instant it took place, I was beset and plundered. Had he continued my guide, this had not happened. He still has the power to rescue me, and if he will now be true to me, I will be true to him. At present, I am protected by Cherkush and Ahris, and cannot prudently quit their shelter. If Hussun would wish to make a bargain with me, let him send his son, Khojeh Muhummud, who bears so high a character, that I can implicitly trust him!"

I knew that a suspicion of my acquaintance with the treachery of Hussun would have been the death-warrant of myself, and ruin of my people, whom I had cautioned to avoid all hints that could lead to such an impression. The Toorcumun departed, and three Kuzzauk chiefs called. These pretended not to have heard my story, and inquired who and what I was. Upon hearing the tale, they expressed the deepest sympathy, and recommended me in the strongest terms to accept Hussun Mhatoor's proposition, promising to secure my safety with their own lives. The scoundrel who made these protestations had too much of the devil in his face to deceive me. I returned him a thousand thanks, but declared that I would adhere to my league with Cherkush Bae and his brother. Cherkush Bae kissed my hand, and when the Kuzzauks had left the tent, recommended me to beware of all such offers, for that, if once separated from him and his brother, their power to protect me would be forfeited.

The next day was marked with the usual claims upon my anxiety. In the evening, there arrived a Kuzzauk, who had been despatched to Dahsh Gullah to collect intelligence, and purchase sundry articles. He said, that the Russians had heard of the attack made upon me, and were anxious to learn my fate. That he, fearing they might send a foraying party hither, were the truth known, had assured them that my property had been restored to me, and that I had returned to Khiva. He produced a few pounds of extremely coarse rye-flour, some very black tobacco, and some isinglass for my hand. How the latter was to be applied, I never understood, for it was not used. I wished Cherkush to glue with it strips of paper to the severed finger, to support it in position. The arrival of so much bread occasioned a jubilee in the rude tents; and even myself and servants knew once more the taste of that luxury, though in the most sparing quantities.

Previous to the mission of this messenger, and after agreement with Ahris to make him master of all the plundered property upon condition that he conducted me in safety to Khiva, I had explained to him the value of my Cashmere shawl, worth perhaps thirty guineas or more at the Russian frontier; and had recommended him to purchase it from the present owner, and exchange it at Dahsh Gullah for Cherkush' son. He listened with long ears to the advice, sought out the present possessor, and persuaded him to part with it for about seven shillings. Fortunately it had not yet become a pair of breeches, a fate to which it had been destined. Ahris was, however, still afraid to dispose of the shawl, lest Hussun Mhatoor, on his arrival, should demand it of him.

My beautiful Damascus blade, which I had purchased for thirty-five guineas, and which was worth perhaps a hundred, was sold by another Kuzzauk for eighteen shillings. I had taken the precaution at Khiva to conceal its workmanship with a coating of tar, lest it should become an object of plunder to my guide, or the people through whom my journey lay. Being obliged, the night of the attack, to carry the sabre entrusted me by the Khaun Huzurut, Nizaum had worn this sword. After shredding the Kuzzauk clubs like straws, it had been beaten down by the oblique blow of Ahris Mhatoor's hatchet. Whenever I recalled that night, I regretted that I had not trusted to the sword instead of the pistol; I could at least have warded blows with the former, which might have given me an opportunity to return them. But I believed I had to deal with cowards, who would not come within reach of a sword; and I calculated that the report of fire-arms would in itself be worth a dozen sabres. After all, it was as well that no more mischief was done; for my long life hung upon the recovery of the wounded Kuzzauk. Had he died, as was at first expected, nothing could have saved me from the vengeance of his family.

Here, I was one day inquiring of Nizaum how he had disposed of the gold I had given him. "O!" he replied, "I have eaten it."

I supposed, of course, he was speaking figuratively: for it is a common phrase, "I eat so much a month," that is, such is my expenditure: but I could not imagine how he could have spent even one gold piece in a Kuzzauk tent. I found, however, that he was expressing himself literally. That the night after the distribution, he and the other servants had deliberately swallowed all their gold ducats. Summud Khaun twenty-six, and Nizaum fifteen. Now these ducats were quite as sharp-edged as the knife with which my finger had been amputated; and the milk diet, upon which we had been suddenly placed, seemed to render their extrication quite hopeless. Summud Khaun, not content with bolting twenty-six ducats, had commenced upon the tillahs, which are nearly twice as large, and have a rough saw edge. Most fortunately, the very first he tried stuck fast in his throat, like a Russian proper name, and the noise he made in coughing it up, nearly led to the discovery of his diet; the consequence of which would have been, the instant opening of his bread-basket by insertion of a Kuzzauk knife. He was, therefore, deterred from any farther attempts upon the tillahs; indeed, he he might just as safely have bolted a gross of circular saws.

I was horrified when I discovered the truth; for it seemed scarcely possible that any of them should recover. I searched for some pills which had escaped the plunderers, and administered them forthwith, but they had not the slightest effect upon persons confined exclusively to a milk diet. I would have given something to have seen my people gravely and deliberately bolting ducats, like cranes drinking at a plate. The best of it was, that Yakoob, the Meer-a-Khor, not relishing the operation, had got Hajji to swallow *his* for him; an arrangement which led subsequently to a curious dispute, quite worthy of the Court of Chancery.

After about six days spent in this spot, I saw preparations for departure. I was mounted upon Summud Khaun's horse. Ali Muhummud rode his own. We started, but the poor beast could scarcely carry me ten paces; so that I was obliged to exchange him for Ali Muhummud's horse, which was in a condition almost as miserable. "Such," I said to Summud Khaun, "are the horses upon which we are to traverse a desert of five hundred miles in sixteen days. These are the sole hope left us."

"Our only hope," replied Summud Khaun, "is in God."

"You are right. We are in his hand, and have little or no power to help ourselves. Yet what little we have, we must exert." I accordingly began to turn over the chances and hopes afforded us by each several mode of procedure. But Summud Khaun had settled into the habitual indifference of a Fatalist. "What is the use," he said, "of thinking. Wait, Sir, wait and exercise yourself in patience. It is a good thing to wait."

I was a little disgusted, and gave him a sharp reply; for it was by *waiting* that we had fallen into the ambush laid for us, which the slightest alertness on the part of my people would have disconcerted. Summud Khaun was shocked at my want of patience, and hurt by the sharpness of my reply. But really, it was a little too bad to be betrayed by this *patience* of my followers into a predicament the most hopeless possible, and then to have the virtue of patience preached to me by the very person who had had the greatest share in my betrayal.

We rode down the valley, and then struck up a narrow ravine, in which the tents, when pitched, were quite concealed. Nizaum arrived here, about half an hour after me. I found that he was suffering torture from the state of his bowels, and became seriously alarmed for him. Summud Khaun was also suffering from his twenty-six ducats, but not in the same degree. I enquired of the Kuzzauks, whether they knew of no cathartic; but they had never heard of such a thing. I then endeavoured to procure some oil or fat. But the former is unknown, and the latter so precious, that I had the utmost difficulty in obtaining even the smallest quantity. Poor Nizaum continued writhing and groaning all day, upon the floor of the tent. I could not relieve him, but I sat down beside him to offer him all I could, the assurance of my deepest sympathy.

CHAPTER XXVIII.

Hopelessness of our Predicament—Ali Muhummud's Project—The Afghaun Horsemen—Congratulations of a Bear—Apparition of Saleh Muhummud—Greetings—Recapitulation—The Search—Confabulations—Happy Disposition and bright Mind of Saleh Muhummud—Consultations—Joy of my Party—Confusion of Enemies—Ummeer Beeg—Delicacies unknown to Heliogabalus—The Tit-bit.

EVERY attempt I had made to bring Ahris Mhatoor to some speedy decision, had been answered by a profusion of promises. He would, next day, go to liberate the three servants from their bondage; the day after, the camels should be ready, and we would start for Khiva. One day, in pledge of the solemn covenant between us, he had led a sheep, first to me, then to each of my servants, then around the interior, and afterwards the exterior of his own tent, and then, with much ceremony, had slain it, and poured out the blood at his door. But latterly, he had evidently cooled in his purpose; and it was easy to account for this, by the influence Hussun Mhatoor would exercise over my fate, the instant he should hear that I still lived. He had, several days, been fully advertised of all; and, I confess, my hope was utterly abandoned, when I found time given by our protectors, to admit of this. Had we started when Hussun was ignorant of my existence, we might have got beyond pursuit; and, as we approached Khiva, he would not have ventured to attack me. I was satisfied that all must now depend upon Hussun, whose power, here, was without rival, unless, indeed (as Ali Muhummud supposed), Mooraud Ali, in virtue of his relationship to the royal clan, might have the power and the will to interfere. Ali Muhummud, one day, came to sound me respecting himself. "If," he said, "you, Sir, were out of difficulty, I should mount my horse and escape to Khiva."

I replied, that as for myself, it signified very little what became of me, and, were I alone, I should insist upon his (Ali's) doing as he hinted. As it was, I should give him no commands; only, I thought, that if he left us without any one to interpret our meaning, all our people would inevitably be made slaves, whilst his own escape upon a horse, in such miserable plight, would be extremely uncertain. I thought his idea of escaping to Mooraud Ali's tent less extravagant; at the same time we were utterly ignorant of this chief's disposition. Had it been friendly, he had most probably interfered long ago, as our condition must long have been known to him; and as Ali was utterly ignorant of the position of his tent, and of the landmarks of the intervening desert, I knew not how he was to reach the tent, and feared that his death would be the consequence of failure. He said that, for himself, he had rather run the risk of death than that of slavery, of which he had had sixteen years' experience; but, that it would be a base thing to desert me. He accordingly gave up the design. Remembering how greatly my disaster was attributable to this man's unaccountable blindness to the conduct of the guides, that he had run away and nearly escaped on the night of the assault, and was now treated with more consideration than any other of my people, I was sometimes inclined to suspect him of treachery. But a calm and deliberate comparison of facts past, and of those which ensued, entirely annihilated this idea. Even now my case was so desperate, and his own so involved in it, that only fidelity could have induced him to stand by me when he had means of escape; for I had supplied him with gold, and he had a horse, sword, and spear.

Ahris continued his protestations, that we should immediately start. But the failure of these no longer disappointed me. I perceived that with all his boasted influence, he really dared not stir a hand or a foot in our deliverance, and every day rendered our case more desperate, by bringing around us more of the meshes of Hussun Mhatoor's treachery.

In this helpless state we were now left, with nothing to hope and abundant cause for apprehension.

Even should the Khaun Huzurut learn, in time, of the outrage committed upon me, I could not certainly foresee the consequence. The suspicions under which I quitted Khiva, might have been confirmed by fresh artifices of Yar Muhummud Khaun; or fear that Great Britain might attribute the act to him, might lead him to hush it up; or, he might feel gratified that I had fallen into trouble, in pursuing a route which he dissuaded me from attempting, although the treachery of a guide might equally have been met with, whatever the direction of my route; or, the Russians might (as I greatly feared), have advanced upon his capital, and left him no room for thought of me and my mission. In short, the chances against me there seemed two to one of those in my favour, even should timely intelligence reach Khiva.

It was the second or third day of our abode in this spot, the sixteenth or seventeenth of our captivity. A huge bear of a Kuzzauk chief, in a cloak of a bay horse's skin, and bonnet of black sheep's skin, had just left the tent, after fruitless efforts, of some hours' duration, to make the brothers give me up, and to persuade me to quit the brothers. I was sitting beside poor Nizaun, who still rolled in agony on the ground, affording him such miserable consolation as an assurance of sympathy might amount to. Summud Khaun and the old Meerza sat in the shadow of Cherkush Bae's tent, outside. Ali Muhummud was good-naturedly swallowing all Summud Khaun's superfluous kostch-zuns,* and making ready his Kulliaun. The old Meerza was wondering what *could* be the matter with his broken head, that it should feel so heavy, and holding up his hand to the light, as had been his wont every hour of every day since the attack, and calling upon each in turn for his opinion whether it was not swollen, and then wondering what could have happened to him, and what could have become of the two back teeth, one on each side of the mouth, which he had boasted when he left Khiva, and which had been fairly shaken down his throat by the blows he had received on his head. Summud Khaun was turning over the leaves of the Koraun, and in the midst of the sacred Arabic inserting a "kostchzun" parenthesis, of *pure* Persian, for the benefit of Ali. Suddenly there appeared, upon the heights overhanging the tents, a young man in Afghaun costume, handsomely dressed, and well mounted upon a dark grey horse with silver bridle. He was approaching the tents, followed by some Kuzzauk horsemen. Such an apparition, at such a moment, in such a desert, was rather startling, for the gracefulness of the Afghaun attire is in strange contrast with the rude, and scarcely human costume of the Kuzzauk, and the young man who wore them, was as different, in elegance of feature and figure, from the coarse, clumsy race around us, as a blood racer from the cattle of a country farm.

"Ah," grumbled Summud Khaun, "Here comes Yar Muhummud, dressed out in our finery. He's got the Meerza's turban, and one of our cloaks, and the Sahib's shawl, but whose horse is he riding?"

"Our spoils," observed Ali Muhummud, "have rigged out some thirty of these cannibals."

They altered their note when the stranger approached them more nearly.

I was inside the tent, as I have already noticed. I

* Literally : "Your wife's no better than she should be."

heard a bustle at the door, and in rushed the old bear of a Kuzzauk who had just quitted us. He seized me by the left hand, which was scarcely cicatrized, and almost wrung it off, with the grasp of a steam vice, wishing me joy of, I knew not what, unless it were, that *one* of my fingers survived the mangling. He then rapidly enumerated the benefits he had conferred upon me. These formed a respectable catalogue, but may, for brevity's sake, be summed up in the single item of an endeavour to deliver me over to my enemies. "From all this it appears," concluded he, "that I am your active and zealous friend, and I expect you to be mine, with the Khaun Huzurut."

I bowed, and assured him that any one who should do me service, should not be forgotten; but observed, that I must, in the first place, be re-conducted to Khiva.

"Oh!" he replied, "the Khaun Huruzut has sent a messenger, and a party of horse, to deliver you."

I thought, at first, I had heard amiss, and I made him repeat his words; Nizaum interpreting for me, between the paroxysms of his pain.

"The Khaun Huzurut," I observed, "cannot yet be aware of my captivity."

"Oh! yes he is!"

He was interrupted by a young man in Afghaun attire, who, throwing aside the curtain of the door, rushed past him, and, casting himself upon my neck, exclaimed in Persian, with many tears, "Thank heaven, I have found you at last! I have come to deliver you. I have a letter from the Khaun Huzurut for you. Lift up your head, Sir. Your sufferings are at an end."

I returned his embrace, and gave him tear for tear. But my head was giddy; I could not believe my senses. I was persuaded I was in a trance.

"Whence are you?" I said. "Who are you? How came you here?"

I pushed him back, that I might regard him more

attentively. The features were familiar, but I was too confused to remember where I had before seen them.

"Don't you know me?" he cried; "don't you remember Saleh Muhummud, to whom you shewed kindness at Merv?"

I remembered him well, and again embraced him. Yet I could not conjecture how he came hither. Poor Nizaum leaped up from the earth, forgetting awhile his torture, to throw his arms around Saleh's neck. Summud Khaun and Ali Muhummud succeeded; and the old Meerza, after a brief salutation, shewed Saleh his broken head and swollen hand, and asked if he could tell him what had happened, or what *could* have become of the last of his teeth? I looked around and saw Abris and Cherkush sitting disconsolate. The arrival of Saleh had thunderstruck both. I bade them draw near, and told Saleh to embrace them, as our preservers. We then went outside the tent, to converse at greater liberty, whilst the brothers slew a sheep, in honour of the new guest. All was still a profound mystery. Saleh seemed to have dropped from the clouds. We had a thousand questions to ask and answer; a thousand explanations to receive.

On reference to the early part of this Journal, it will be seen, that, I met, at Merv, this young man, son of the principal Cauzie (or Judge) of Heraut. That I was struck with his intelligence, frankness, and gentlemanly manners; and wrote Major Todd, the British envoy at Heraut, that I should like to have him near me at Khiva; as I foresaw that I should need such an assistant, to give me hints as to the exact measure of attention due to each individual: to intrigue for me abroad, and perfect my Persian, by conversation at home; offices for which my old Meerza was quite unfit. I thought also, that as bills could not be cashed at Khiva, Saleh Muhummud might be the bearer of money for my expenses there. On reaching Khiva, and finding that his father, in a moment of pique and disappointment, had denounced me as a spy; I had written to Major Todd, begging him, that whomsoever he might send me, it might not be one of that family.

Providentially, this letter did not reach Herant, until Saleh had reached Merv, in progress to join me, with a sum of money in gold, and a packet of letters. I had left Khiva ere he quitted Herant; so that, by the time he reached the former place, I ought, by calculation, to have been near St. Petersburgh. The Khaun Huzurut had promised to send after me any messenger arriving within eight days of my departure. But, as Saleh did not arrive until the twentieth day, the Khaun found excuses for his detention for twenty days more. Meanwhile he contrived, by means of a secret agent, to abstract from Saleh's girdle during the night, the packet of letters he bore for me. Having opened these, and (probably by means of an interpreter from Persia) translated their contents, and having found therein nothing at variance with the good faith professed by our Government, he had at length yielded to Saleh Muhummud's earnest entreaty, and suffered him to depart, giving him an escort of six Toorcumun horse, of the Chowdhoor tribe.

When Saleh found himself at liberty, I had been from Khiva forty days; the period I had calculated for my journey to St. Petersburgh: and any other in the world, but Saleh Muhummud, would have relinquished pursuit of me, as hopeless. But he burned to distinguish himself in the eyes of the British, and declared, that should I have embarked, he would follow me to St. Petersburg. He accordingly started in pursuit, urging his escort to their best speed, in spite of their grumbling. At length, when within about 100 miles of my present position, he learned that I had changed my course, and proceeded towards Dahsh Gullah, a piece of intelligence of the most vital consequence to me, because it saved him about 350 miles of route, and brought him to me ere

Hussun Mhatoor's plans for my destruction were completed. At the next stage, he heard that I was murdered. This, instead of deterring, only inflamed his zeal to advance: but his Toorcumuns, who were at once guard and guides, learning that their own chief, Hussun Mhatoor, had instigated the deed, feared to enter the lists against him, by bringing Saleh Muhummud upon my track, and refused to advance upon the plea that the horses were exhausted. It was in vain that he promised, expostulated, threatened, even drew his sword upon them. They feared their chief even more than the Khaun Huzurut, and would not stir. He wandered from tent to tent, ignorant of all but a few words of their language. By means of these, his winning manners, and the promise of reward, he procured a Toorcumun guide, and continued his course. Intelligence, however, could scarcely be procured in a country so thinly peopled, and from Kuzzauks who had their own reasons for misleading. At length, he learned that I was still alive, although wounded and a prisoner. This caused him to redouble his speed, so that his guide could not, or would not, keep up with him; and he was traversing alone a wild desolate steppe, without path, almost without inhabitant, and with no clue to guide him but the ever-shifting position of the sun. For hours, he had thus wandered, without meeting an inhabitant. He then reached the shore of the Caspian, at the southern extremity of the inlet called Kara Soo (or the black water). He looked around him in despair. No symptoms of a habitation were visible. The sea was without a sail. He saw it for the first time in his life. He strained his eye as he searched the horizon around. At length, he distinguished a moving speck upon the distant cliff. He made towards it: it grew as he approached to the size of a small insect, and he knew it, by its figure, to be a camel. This assured him that some human habitation was near. He urged on his horse, and found the camel to be the property of Cherkush Bae.

"Now," he said, "Sir, all will go well; my arrival will put all right; I have a letter for you from the Khaun Huzurut. The very sight of it will confound your enemies; I have a guard, too, not far off, of six Toorcumun horse. Those who have most injured, will now be most zealous to serve you."

I did not feel so confident of my security; for my escape to Khiva would be the death-warrant of Hussun Mhatoor and his whole family, as he well knew; and the six Toorcumun horse were of Hussun's tribe, and (as they had proved themselves) mere creatures of that arch villain. The Kuzzauks, too, were deeply concerned in preventing my return to Khiva; and there were a thousand ways of effecting this, without any overt act of violence. I could not, however, discourage one who was so happy in his enthusiasm; and, insensibly, I found his young and fearless, and sanguine spirit, inspiring me with a hope which reason disallowed. I proceeded to question him of my friend Major Todd, and of the affairs of Heraut. "Todd Sahib," he replied, "is well, and thinks only of you. I have letters from him for you. If you will come apart, I will tell you more."

We went some paces down the glen, and sat upon a rock. There, touching his girdle significantly, he said, I have a belt full of gold for you here, and the shroffs at Khiva are prepared to cash your bills for as much more; shall I give you the money now?

"No," I replied; "I am stripped every day to the skin, and the belt would certainly be seen; you must continue to wear it for awhile. How are matters at Khiva? What news of the Russian force?"

"All is well at Khiva. The Khaun Huzurut became more suspicious of you than ever after your departure. He stole my packet of despatches from my girdle whilst I slept, and had them opened and read. He saw that you were true to him, and then he suffered me to follow you, and gave me six Toorcumuns, and told them to carry me in their hands to Abbott Sahib, wherever he might be. That he had instructed you to proceed to Dahsh Gullah, if boats were not waiting at Mungh Kishlauk, and that they must, in that case, carry me within sight of the fort, and watch until I should enter."

"And what of the Russians?"

"They are still detained by the snow, and by want of camels."

"Heaven be praised. Yet you have been sixteen days on the road, and they may, by this time, be close upon Khiva. Indeed, what is to hinder them? The snow is quite dissipated, and the steppe open."

He strove to soothe me. He assured me the Russians would not, should not advance. That I should return in triumph to Khiva, and there be honoured, and made much of for my services, and sent again, with better provision, to the Court of St. Petersburg. "Heaven be praised," he said, "that I have found you. I thought I never should have got over the ground. But all my care and anxiety are repaid, and all will now go well. The Khaun Huzurut will be delighted to honour one who has done and suffered so much for him."

He rattled on incessantly. There seemed cruelty in the very thought of interrupting the bright current of his happy fancy; and there is luxury in listening even to promises, of the delusiveness of which we are aware. This was just the spirit which my own needed in that hour, dark, abandoned as it long had been by hope, and finding a species of gratification in pondering the black and gloomy prospect that hemmed it in on all sides.

It would not, however, answer to lose time in reflection, when the moment for action was at hand. I consulted with Saleh Muhummud. Separated as he was from his guard, any attempt of ours to reach Dahsh Gullah, would be met by an ambush from Hussun Mhatoor, to cut us off at a spot where the blame would fall upon Russia. It was necessary, in the first place, to recover his guard, which must be done by a retrograde movement toward Khiva. He had brought a camel, laden with barley and rice, to within two marches of our abode; the Toorcumun guard must, he thought, have come up with this camel, as they were to follow, leisurely, his steps. Now, as far as could be learned, the tent of the Yuze Baushee, Mooraud Ali, was not far from the spot where he had left the grain; and, as some protection from the artifices of Hussun Mhatoor was necessary, I deemed it wise to hasten at once to Mooraud Ali's tent, and throw myself upon his protection. This would, at any rate, prevent the hushing up of the fact of my existence, and render it more difficult for Hussun to make away with me. I sent for the brothers, Ahris and Cherkush, and told them I should depart the following morning for Mooraud Ali's tent, and begged them to procure camels and ponies for the purpose. They made a thousand objections, but I overruled all with Saleh's assistance. The most formidable was the continued detention in bondage of my three servants. But, as Ahris had daily promised me their freedom, and daily disappointed me, I thought it wiser to negotiate that object from Mooraud Ali's tent, than to give Hussun Mhatoor time to counterplot. The move, therefore, was fixed for the following morning.

It is possible only to him who has been rescued from a bondage so hopeless, by a sudden and unexpected interposition of Providence, to conjecture the state of our feelings at this moment. The gloomy mood of mind, that had become habitual, was insensibly broken through; the stagnation of the faculties was no more; an impulse had been given, that vibrated throughout the whole frame of my being; and without anything to hope for in this world, the call to action inspired me with vigour, with confidence in my own resources, and in the guardianship of Heavenly care. All was so wonderful, so unlooked-for, so impossible, that I felt shame in distrusting the continuance of a sunshine so graciously sent in upon our souls. As for my servants the tent resounded with "Ool humm'd Ool illah! Shookha! Ool humm'd!"* Poor fellows, they had trusted God in their adversity, and he had not forgotten them.

The appearance of Saleh Muhummud was like the fall of a live thunderbolt amongst my enemies. He was elegantly clad and handsomely mounted, and known to be son of the principal judge at Heraut, and he paid me more respect than I had received from the meanest of my followers, who, to say the truth, had been a little spoiled in this respect by the equalising influence of misfortune. He therefore added consequence to the little dignity I had contrived to maintain, and proved to them that I had assumed less than was my due. He was also armed with a letter from the sovereign to me, an honour rarely conferred, and had a guard from the Khaun Huzurut, who were to be added to my retinue.

I called Saleh constantly to my side, to repeat my questions; and during the remainder of our sojourn together, whenever I felt inclined to the gloomy view of the future, which care, long suffering, and defeated hope naturally induced, I would summon him to while away the clouds of my fancy by his gay light-hearted prattle. "What news have you, I said, "of Ummeer Beeg?"

"I met him, Sir, at Merv, journeying with Birdler Beeg to Heraut. The Khaun Huzurut had opened and read your despatches which he carried."

Whilst talking together, answering and asking a thousand questions, Saleh's Toorcumun guide arrived.

---

* Praised be to God! Thanks to Him, and praise!

and brought a bag of barley for Saleh's horse. I regarded it with a covetous eye. "Are you," I said, "really about to give all that delicious food at once to a horse? Let me have a handful, if you love me."

He filled my hand, and I filled my mouth, enjoying the raw barley, as might a lotus-eater his favourite aliment after long banishment from the Nile. It seemed a species of insane extravagance to give such delicious food to a horse. Unfortunately, our poor horses had little enough of this, their sole aliment. Saleh begged me not to eat raw barley; and, running to his saddle-bags, brought me some biscuit, hard, indeed, as flint, but welcome as concreted nectar. I divided it amongst my people, and gave some to the children of Ahris Mhatoor. I was now an epicure in full glory, with my barley and my biscuit.

Our enjoyment, however, was sadly damped by the condition of poor Nizaum, who lay writhing in torture upon the floor of the tent. The arrival of Saleh Muhummud had given force to my earnest prayer for a morsel of fat, to administer internally in a melted form. After much tumbling of tent furniture, a lump of yellow horse's fat was produced, which was not much above seven months old, and had probably been put by the old woman under her pillow at night, to be devoured the first thing in the morning. Thence it had made its way by some accident into a sack, from which it was now produced, amid a variety of items, the inventory of which would set aghast the civilized world. We melted the tough and venerable morsel from the blood-red flesh adhering to it, and poured it hot down the sufferer's throat. The sheep just killed lent us a corner of its tail for a second dose, and in some hours poor Nizaum's sufferings were abated.

END OF VOLUME FIRST.

www.ingramcontent.com/pod-product-compliance
Lightning Source LLC
Chambersburg PA
CBHW050850300426
44111CB00010B/1207